AMERICA
LAND OF BEAUTY
AND SPLENDOR

READER'S DIGEST

AMERICA
LAND OF BEAUTY AND SPLENDOR

THE READER'S DIGEST ASSOCIATION, INC.   PLEASANTVILLE, NEW YORK / MONTREAL

America: Land of Beauty and Splendor

STAFF

Project Editor
Inge N. Dobelis

Project Art Editor
Joel Musler

Editors
Fred DuBose
David Palmer

Associate Editor
David Diefendorf

Art Associate
Susan Desser

Project Research Editor
Eileen Einfrank

Research Editors
Kathryn Bonomi
Sandra Streepy Burgheim

Associate Librarian
Nettie Seaberry

Editorial Assistant
Vita Gardner

**With special assistance from
Senior Staff Editor**
Richard L. Scheffel

CONTRIBUTORS

General Consultant
Robert H. Mohlenbrock, Ph.D.
Senior Scientist, Biotic Consultants, Carbondale, Illinois

Art Production Associate
Bruce R. McKillip

Research Associate
Mary Hart

Researchers
Tim Guzley
Mary Lyn Maiscott
Eleanor Schwartz

Writers
Craig Canine
Jared Carter
Ben Cate
Rita Christopher
Cort Conley
Richard Comerford
Jack Connor
David A. DeVoss
Sharon Fitzgerald
Jean Freeman
Jill Goetz
Alice Gordon
Lea Gordon
Martha Hailey
Kenn Kaufman
B. Cory Kilvert, Jr.
Scott M. Kraft
Mary Lyn Maiscott
Howard Millard
Frazier Moore
Richard Nelson
Karla Powell
Ronn Ronck
Rollene Saal
Kathy Sagan
Mitchell J. Shields
Susan Spano Wells
Henry Wiencek
Suzanne Winckler
Mel White

Map Artist
Laszlo Kubinyi

Flower Artist
Susan Desser

Bird Artists
John Dawson 56, 68
Walter Ferguson 44, 76, 93, 100, 120, 128, 136, 144, 152, 159, 198, 214, 222, 232, 241, 248, 264, 285, 293, 298, 306, 322, 359, 368, 395, 404, 410, 416
Albert Earl Gilbert 11, 16, 181
Pedro Julio Gonzalez 82, 113, 336
Cynthia J. House 256
Lawrence B. McQueen 166, 378
Hans Peeters 206, 274
Douglas Pratt 27, 36, 313, 342
Chuck Ripper 174, 191, 330, 350
John Cameron Yrizarry 386

Picture Researchers
Romy Charlesworth
Penne Franklin
Paula Gillen

Copy Editor
Marianne Emmet

Indexer
Sydney Wolfe Cohen

The editors thank the following organizations for their assistance
Adobe Systems Incorporated
Hammond Incorporated
The Flag Research Center

READER'S DIGEST GENERAL BOOKS

Editor in Chief John A. Pope, Jr.

Managing Editor Jane Polley

Executive Editor Susan J. Wernert

Art Director David Trooper

Group Editors Will Bradbury, Norman B. Mack, Kaari Ward

Group Art Editors Evelyn Bauer, Robert M. Grant, Joel Musler

Chief of Research Laurel A. Gilbride

Copy Chief Edward W. Atkinson

Picture Editor Richard Pasqual

Rights and Permissions Pat Colomban

Head Librarian Jo Manning

Opening photographs
Page 1: Wheat fields, Washington
Pages 2-3: New River, Virginia
Pages 4-5: Ontario State Park, Oregon
Pages 6-7: Bald eagles, Montana
Pages 8-9: Grande Ronde Canyon, Washington

Contents

Preface

America is a feast for the eyes. Travelers from near and far flock here to savor scenery as magnificent as any on earth. But who could see it all firsthand?

Now you can take a visual tour of this vast country — simply by opening the covers of AMERICA: LAND OF BEAUTY AND SPLENDOR. The awe-inspiring sights that make our land a traveler's treasure have been recorded by many of America's finest and most imaginative photographers and collected in one volume.

The photographs are as varied as the great land they depict. Consider, after all, that the United States covers 3½ million square miles. The alpine splendors of the Rocky Mountains stretch from Alaska to Mexico, encompassing icy peaks and glacial lakes in Montana, glistening streams in the San Juan Mountains of Colorado, and flower-filled meadows in New Mexico's Sangre de Cristo range. Hawaii's blue waters and green-ridged volcanic slopes lie a full 5,200 miles from the languid lagoons and coconut palms of Florida's southern tip.

Each state possesses its own kind of beauty, often surprisingly diverse. Tennesseans claim theirs could better be called three states: East Tennessee, where the Great Smoky Mountains predominate; pastoral Middle Tennessee, with its elegant horse farms; and, on the bluffs of the mighty Mississippi, West Tennessee and its fertile farmland. Idaho, for another example, changes abruptly from lofty mountains to prairie, from woodland to desert. And in addition to the broad panoramas of mountain and plain there is hidden beauty everywhere: shaded lanes and old millponds, mysterious bayous and sunlit gardens, natural bridges and secluded glades.

Arranged alphabetically, AMERICA: LAND OF BEAUTY AND SPLENDOR contains 50 unique and revealing portraits — one for each state. Complementing the breathtaking photographs is an essay that conveys the flavors and textures of the state, touching on its history, people, culture, and terrain. Special features highlight the outstanding and the unusual — Florida's unlikely "mermaids," for example, or Frank Lloyd Wright's architectural embodiment of the Illinois prairie, Connecticut's Charter Oak that symbolized liberty, Vermont's swift, strong Morgan horse, and the remarkable pottery art of the ancient New Mexican pueblos.

Rounding out these portraits is an illustrated fact-filled two-page almanac that captures the essence of each state at a glance. Here are the state's vital statistics, its flag and motto, historical highlights, notable people, oddities and specialties, places to visit, and things to do. The centerpiece of this collection of information-in-a-nutshell is a specially commissioned pictorial map showing major cities and rivers, with colorful drawings of places, products, natural wonders, and other regional attractions.

Every corner of America is filled with beautiful places both familiar and little known, and all of us would like to get to know them better. This gallery of portraits shows you those beautiful places — and evokes the singular qualities of each of our 50 states in a way that readers will find both fascinating and informative.

— THE EDITORS

WASHINGTON

Columbia River

OREGON

MONTANA

Missouri River

NORTH DAKOTA

MINNESOTA

IDAHO

WYOMING

SOUTH DAKOTA

Mississippi

Great
Salt
Lake

NEVADA

NEBRASKA

IOWA

Missouri

UTAH

River

CALIFORNIA

Colorado River

COLORADO

KANSAS

MISSO

Arkansas River

Pacific
Ocean

ARIZONA

Rio Grande

NEW MEXICO

Arkansas River

ARKA

OKLAHOMA

TEXAS

HAWAII

ALASKA

Rio Grande

Yukon River

LO

Rio Grande

COAST RANGES

The United States

Lake Superior
Lake Huron
Lake Ontario
Lake Michigan
Lake Erie

WISCONSIN
MICHIGAN
MAINE
VERMONT
NEW HAMPSHIRE
MASSACHUSETTS
RHODE ISLAND
CONNECTICUT
NEW YORK
PENNSYLVANIA
OHIO
INDIANA
ILLINOIS
NEW JERSEY
DELAWARE
MARYLAND
WEST VIRGINIA
VIRGINIA
KENTUCKY
NORTH CAROLINA
TENNESSEE
SOUTH CAROLINA
ALABAMA
GEORGIA
MISSISSIPPI
FLORIDA
LOUISIANA
URI
SAS

Hudson River
Ohio River
Mississippi River

APPALACHIAN MOUNTAIN

Atlantic Ocean

Gulf of Mexico

National flower: Rose

National bird: Bald eagle

National flag

Five broad regions, all generally running from north to south, define the landscape of the United States. In the east, the gently rolling terrain of the *Atlantic coastal plain* starts as a narrow band in New England and gradually widens to encompass the Gulf Coast.

Plunging southward from Maine, the *Appalachian Mountains* rise along the western edge of the coastal plain in the north and jut into the interior of the plain farther south. Once a lofty range, the pine-forested mountains are so old — more than 600 million years — that in most places they have been worn down to little more than 3,500 feet.

The *interior plain* stretches from the eastern Great Lakes westward to the Rocky Mountains. It narrows to the south, eventually merging with the Atlantic coastal plain near the Rio Grande. The vast interior plain has two major subregions. One is the central lowlands, where fertile fields of corn and cotton stretch to the horizon. The second major subregion is called the Great Plains and, as it moves west and becomes drier and higher, the High Plains. It is a major producer of wheat.

The *western mountain system* dominates the area west of the plains. The Rocky Mountains, with elevations of more than 14,000 feet, run from Alaska to Mexico. To the west rise the Cascades, the Sierra Nevada, and the Coast Ranges.

Between the Rockies and the far western ranges is the arid *intermountain plateau*, dominated by the Great Basin. This desert-like basin is an interior drainage system where rivers either dry up or empty into evaporating lakes, rather than running to the sea.

Beyond the continent, more than 2,000 miles to the southwest, lie the Hawaiian Islands, formed almost entirely by volcanic action.

Alabama

Water and woods in the heart of the South

Rushing brooks and streams slice through Alabama's dark forests, then join to form rivers and mighty waterways. Here, in the Heart of Dixie, is more navigable water than in any other state — a 1,350-mile system so much a part of Alabama's history that rivers form the dominant element in the state's Great Seal.

Here, too, are vast reaches of sweet gum, yellow poplar, and pine. After years of reforestation, the amount of land covered by trees remains the same — about 65 percent — as when Spanish explorers first arrived in 1519.

The north of Alabama is dominated by the green mountains and valleys of the Appalachian Highland. The once-wild Tennessee River loops through this part of the state, its fury tamed by a system of Tennessee Valley Authority dams. Farther south, the mountains soften into wooded hills, the hills into a gentle coastal plain. From this plain much of the continent's fresh water drains into the Gulf of Mexico, carried there by the Alabama and Tombigbee rivers. Along these rivers, stevedores once loaded cotton onto steamboats for shipment to the port of Mobile.

ALABAMA FEVER

In the early 1800's cotton lured hordes of settlers, mostly southerners who made their way to the state in a migration so fast and furious that "Alabama fever" was said to sweep Georgia, Virginia, and the Carolinas. Most of the new arrivals tilled the thin soil of the northern hills and southern plains. The center of the state, named the Black Belt for its

An ancient river sculpted sandstone into a natural bridge that still stands in northwest Alabama.

The deepest gorge east of the Mississippi was cut by the Little River in Alabama's northeast corner. Now called Little River Canyon, the craggy-walled chasm was inhabited by Cherokees when Hernando de Soto and his band of explorers came upon it in 1540.

AMERICA: LAND OF BEAUTY AND SPLENDOR

dark clay soil, became the domain of the legendary southern planter. There the still-potent myths of plantation life were born — of elegant homes, wealthy landowners, and southern belles who had little more to do than stroll among the azaleas — even though planters actually made up less than 1 percent of the state's white population by 1860.

Cotton ruled the Black Belt until boll weevils ravaged the fields and compelled farmers to diversify. Yet the land bestowed more than favorable soil for farming. Still more rivers snaked underground — not of water but of veins of coal that converged with deposits of iron in the north-central part of the state to provide the key ingredients for steelmaking. Only a few tiny villages stood in these ore-rich hills as late as 1871; then sharp-witted speculators bought up land and sold it off, lot by lot, to prospectors — and gave birth to Birmingham. Huge steel mills and foundries sprang up to turn the city into an industrial giant. Today the mills stand silent; but Birmingham, its industry now as diversified as the state's agriculture, remains a vibrant city.

South of Montgomery, closer to the coast, is the area that locals affectionately call L.A.: Lower Alabama, with its rolling hills thick with shortleaf and loblolly pines. To the southeast is the Wiregrass, named for the tall, stiff grasses that once covered the land and now a prime producer of peanuts. And still farther south, between Mobile Bay and the Florida border, lie the marshes, swamps, bayous, and white sand beaches of the coastal lowlands.

WHERE RIVERS MERGE

On the Gulf Coast stands Alabama's oldest city, Mobile. This is where the rivers merge, and where ships have set sail for foreign ports for almost three centuries. It remains an active seaport as barges ply the new Tennessee-Tombigbee Waterway that connects Mobile with the Ohio and Mississippi river systems farther north. Most of the state's other rivers, with names like Black Warrior, Cahaba, and Tallapoosa, carry no commerce today but still draw people to their peaceful banks — quiet and perfect places from which to savor this land of water and trees.

The marsh grasses of Mon Louis Island, on Mobile Bay, are home to alligators and great blue herons. Offshore, the waters teem with shrimps and blue crabs.

The sultry climate of the coastal lowlands feeds the Spanish moss that symbolizes the romantic South. An epiphyte, or air plant, the moss actually belongs to the pineapple family. After several years it grows long enough to brush the ground from the branches of its host trees, as it does from this venerable oak near Mobile.

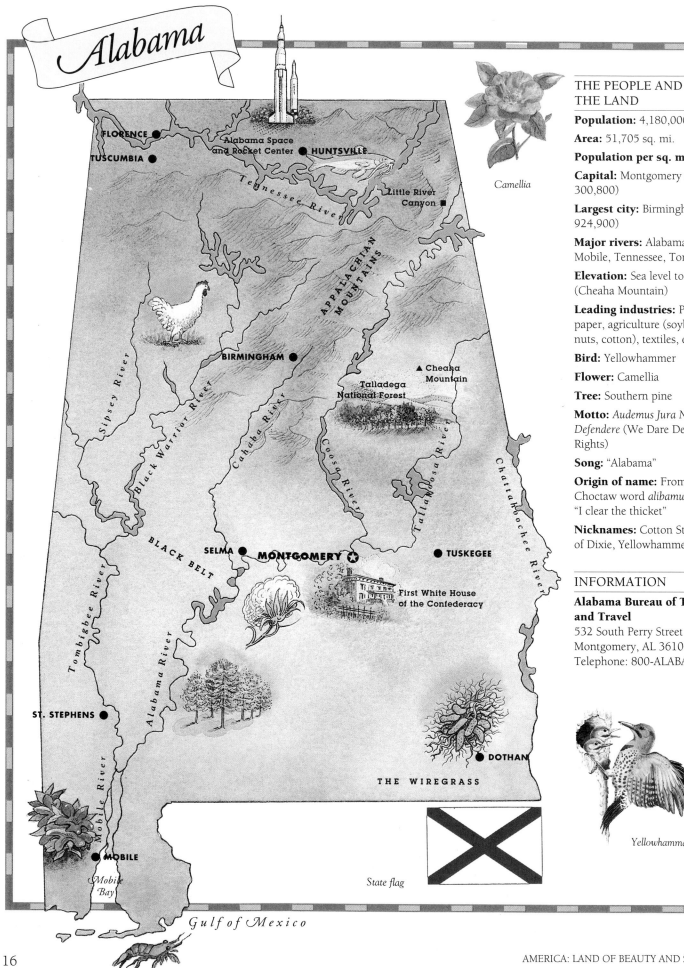

Alabama

Camellia

Yellowhammer

FLORENCE
TUSCUMBIA
Alabama Space
and Rocket Center · HUNTSVILLE

Tennessee River

Little River
Canyon

Sipsey River

APPALACHIAN MOUNTAINS

BIRMINGHAM

Black Warrior River

Cahaba River

▲ Cheaha
Mountain

Talladega
National Forest

Coosa River

Tallapoosa River

Chattahoochee River

Tombigbee River

BLACK BELT

SELMA · MONTGOMERY ☆

TUSKEGEE

First White House
of the Confederacy

Alabama River

ST. STEPHENS

DOTHAN

THE WIREGRASS

Mobile River

State flag

MOBILE

Mobile
Bay

Gulf of Mexico

THE PEOPLE AND THE LAND

Population: 4,180,000

Area: 51,705 sq. mi.

Population per sq. mi.: 81

Capital: Montgomery (pop. 300,800)

Largest city: Birmingham (pop. 924,900)

Major rivers: Alabama, Coosa, Mobile, Tennessee, Tombigbee

Elevation: Sea level to 2,407 ft. (Cheaha Mountain)

Leading industries: Pulp and paper, agriculture (soybeans, peanuts, cotton), textiles, electronics

Bird: Yellowhammer

Flower: Camellia

Tree: Southern pine

Motto: *Audemus Jura Nostra Defendere* (We Dare Defend Our Rights)

Song: "Alabama"

Origin of name: From the Choctaw word *alibamu*, meaning "I clear the thicket"

Nicknames: Cotton State, Heart of Dixie, Yellowhammer State

INFORMATION

Alabama Bureau of Tourism and Travel
532 South Perry Street
Montgomery, AL 36104
Telephone: 800-ALABAMA

HISTORICAL HIGHLIGHTS

1519 Spanish explorer Alonso de Piñeda sails into Mobile Bay.

1540 After Hernando de Soto's explorations, Spain claims lands west and north of Florida.

1629 England claims the region when Charles I deeds Carolinas to Sir Robert Heath.

1682 Sieur de La Salle reaches the mouth of the Mississippi, and France establishes its claim.

1763 France cedes possessions east of the Mississippi River to Great Britain.

1783 Britain cedes to the U.S. all lands east of Mississippi except Florida.

1814 Defeated by Andrew Jackson at the Battle of Horseshoe Bend, Creek Indians are forced to cede to U.S. 20 million acres, the heartland of Alabama.

1817 U.S. Congress creates Alabama Territory, with St. Stephens as temporary capital.

1819 Alabama joins Union as the 22nd state.

1861 Alabama secedes from Union. Delegates from seven states meet in Montgomery to write a constitution for Confederate States of America.

1864 When the Union's lead ship is sunk at Mobile Bay, Union Adm. David Farragut orders his own ship into the lead, shouting, "Damn the torpedoes. Full speed ahead!" The Confederate fleet is defeated.

1881 Tuskegee Institute opens in eastern Alabama, with the purpose of providing a practical education for blacks.

1888 First steel from Alabama pig iron is manufactured at Bessemer, near Birmingham.

1915 The boll weevil begins its devastating attack on Alabama's cotton crop.

1933 The Tennessee Valley Authority, authorized by Congress, undertakes conservation and flood control work in northern Alabama.

1955 After the arrest of Rosa Parks for refusing to give up her seat in a Montgomery bus to a white man, blacks under leadership of Rev. Martin Luther King, Jr., boycott city buses.

1965 The Reverend Dr. King leads marchers, eventually 25,000 strong, from Selma to Montgomery in support of black voter registration.

1972 Gov. George C. Wallace is shot in Maryland while campaigning for the Democratic presidential nomination.

1989 The nation's first civil rights monument is dedicated in Montgomery.

FAMOUS SONS AND DAUGHTERS

W.C. Handy (1873 – 1958). Often called the Father of the Blues, Handy brought this traditional black musical form into the mainstream by writing it down and performing it with his band. His most famous composition is "St. Louis Blues."

Helen Keller (1880 – 1968). Left blind and deaf by an illness in infancy, Keller learned to read, write, and speak. Later she was graduated from Radcliffe College and earned a living by lecturing and writing.

Joe Louis (1914 – 81). The Brown Bomber, world heavyweight boxing champion from 1937 to 1949, lost only 3 of 71 professional bouts.

Willie Mays (1931 –). Superior center fielder and daring base-stealer, Mays slammed 41 homers, batted .345, and led the N.Y. Giants to a world championship in 1954. He was named

the National League's Most Valuable Player that year, and again in 1965.

Jesse Owens (1913 – 80). His prowess in track and field won this legendary black athlete four gold medals and two new records at the 1936 Olympics, held in Nazi Germany.

Hank Williams (1923 – 53).

Through his success as a singer and composer — he wrote more than 400 songs, including "Your Cheatin' Heart" — Williams helped to popularize country music outside the South.

ODDITIES AND SPECIALTIES

On Nov. 13, 1833, "stars fell on Alabama" in the heaviest meteor shower ever recorded.

In the 1850's farmers in northern Alabama considered forming a new state, "Nickajack," which would be loyal to the Union.

In 1919 the town of Enterprise erected the Boll Weevil Monument to honor the tiny insect that by persistently destroying the region's cotton crop had forced farmers to diversify — and prosper.

Alabama produces one of every 8 broiler chickens eaten in the U.S. In Birmingham, medical schools and hospitals now employ more people than the steel industry.

PLACES TO VISIT, THINGS TO DO

Alabama Space and Rocket Center (Huntsville). The world's largest space museum, open daily, offers a simulated space shuttle ride and the chance to fire a real rocket engine.

Azalea Trail and Festival (Mobile). Azaleas bloom throughout the city from February through March, when a festival is held and a number of historic homes are open for tours.

Bellingrath Gardens (near Mobile). From azaleas to camellias to chrysanthemums, the flowers bloom year-round. The gardens' bird sanctuary shelters some 200 species.

First White House of the Confederacy (Montgomery). Built in 1835, this frame house was President Jefferson Davis's home during the first months of the Confederacy, when Montgomery was the capital.

Helen Keller's Birthplace (Tuscumbia). In the garden of her home stands the pump where young Keller first grasped the meaning of the word *water*.

Oakleigh (Mobile). This magnificent antebellum mansion, built in 1833, is an outstanding example of America's Greek revival architecture.

U.S.S. *Alabama* **Battleship Memorial Park** (Mobile Bay). The World War II battleship and a submarine are open for tours. War planes are also on display.

Alaska

*A wilderness of glaciers and mountains
at the edge of the Arctic*

Alaska, wild and immense, is one of the planet's treasures — a vast landscape of cloud-swept peaks, deep blue lakes, and mammoth glaciers. Between its mountain ranges stretch endless forests and tundra plains, where wolves howl from their lookouts and herds of migrating caribou flow like dark waves across the countryside.

The size of this state is legendary: twice as big as Texas, its area is almost one-fifth that of the other 49 states combined. Yet Alaska is home to fewer than 600,000 people, more than half of whom are concentrated in two urban centers, Anchorage and Fairbanks. The rest live in isolated towns whose populations range from a few dozen to a few thousand. In the outlands and offshore roam Alaska's more numerous inhabitants — an estimated 600,000 caribou, 250,000 walruses, 150,000 moose, 150,000 sea otters, 25,000 beluga whales, and 3,000 polar bears.

"CLOSED DUE TO SUNSHINE"

For travelers who approach Alaska from the part of the U.S. the locals call the lower 48, the state begins with the protected waterways and forested mountains of the southeastern panhandle. Carved from the western edge of Canada, this rugged strip contains more than 1,000 islands of every size, including 2 larger than the state of Delaware. Winding through broad straits and steep-sided fjords is the Inside Passage, the maritime highway for freighters and passenger ships.

This part of the state is rain country. Saturated winds from the Pacific bring constant

Wreathed in mist, gargantuan Mount St. Elias looms over trekkers in southeast Alaska.

Grizzly Lake is named for the bears that roam its woods. In the distance stand the Wrangell mountain range and snow-covered Mount Sanford.

clouds and a yearly rainfall that often exceeds 200 inches. Accustomed to the perpetual wetness, residents seldom bother with rain gear, although most wear the knee-high rubber boots they call Alaska sneakers. On the rare occasions that the weather turns clear, coastal towns take an unofficial holiday. Signs reading "Closed Due to Sunshine" may appear in shop windows as townspeople set off to enjoy the suddenly brilliant scenery while they can — emerald mountains towering against blue sky, silvery streams threading toward the sea, and massive glaciers looming like mirages amid the rough peaks.

The mountains here are clothed in a dense, temperate rainforest of hemlock, cedar, and spruce. Many of the trees are destined for pulp mills in Ketchikan and Sitka, but those that are left uncut in the deep valleys reach heights of 200 feet and live a thousand years or more. The forest provides a sheltered home for bears, mountain goats, and black-tailed deer. Bald eagles nest in ancient snags overlooking bays prowled by seals and humpback whales. And each summer millions of salmon swarm into the streams to spawn.

Far to the west, across the Gulf of Alaska, the barren Aleutian Islands stretch more than a thousand miles across the northern Pacific, remnants of the land bridge that once connected North America to Asia. The western-

most of these volcanic outposts lies only 50 miles from Siberia. Scattered among the islands are villages of the Aleut people, whose culture is related to that of the Eskimos but includes an overlay of traditions adopted from Alaska's early Russian settlers.

On the eastern side of the gulf stand the St. Elias Mountains, a maze of serrated peaks

Valleys sloping down from the Brooks Range turn lush and green for nine weeks in summer, even though they lie inside the Arctic Circle.

ARCTIC WANDERERS

Hundreds of thousands of caribou still wander free over the vast northern wilds of Alaska. Stately and imposing, these migrating animals are actually a type of deer. Males wear a magnificent arch of antlers measuring up to four feet; female caribou, unique among the world's deer, have antlers too — but theirs are small and graceful.

Caribou are well adapted to their environment. Every hair in their dense coat is hollow, making it one of the best natural insulators in the world. Their broad hooves spread wide for support on boggy tundra. And a penchant for wandering keeps them from overgrazing the lichens, grasses, and succulent plants that make up their diet.

Thirteen herds wander across Alaska, separated from each other by the state's great distances. In the summertime some herds favor the arctic tundra and mountains above the timberline, where steady wind brings relief from tormenting mosquitoes. One herd, the Porcupine (named for the river that joins the Yukon in northeastern Alaska), gathers 170,000 strong on the North Slope for a mass calving, the sheer size of which helps to protect the young from predatory wolves and grizzly bears.

With the early snows, most of Alaska's caribou migrate to lower elevations or make long treks south to more temperate wintering grounds — a trip of up to 800 miles.

Dwarf fireweed, a species of evening primrose, blankets a slope in Katmai National Park.

Dangerous and beautiful, ice caves are sculpted inside glaciers by warm meltwater. The density of the crystalline ice makes the walls glow an eerie blue, as they do in this cave in Muir Glacier at Glacier Bay National Park. A sudden warm spell can flood a cave in a flash.

stretching into Canada and dominated by 18,000-foot Mount St. Elias. Rivers of ice twist down the valleys and coalesce into Malaspina Glacier, which covers an area larger than Rhode Island. Farther along the gulf, near busy Prince William Sound, is Cook Inlet, its shores a wilderness until civilization looms up near the inlet's northernmost point in the form of bustling Anchorage. Some 43 percent of Alaskans live in this fast-growing city and its suburbs, speeding along highways and shopping in malls that, for a few square miles at least, give the lie to Alaska's popular image as an untamed frontier.

JACK LONDON COUNTRY

Inland from Anchorage is yet another great mountain wall, the Alaska Range, with Mount McKinley and Denali National Park as its centerpiece. Alaska's immense interior stretches off to the north, extending to the icebound Brooks Range.

The interior climate is marked by extraordinary extremes. In midwinter, when the sun appears for only a few hours a day, temperatures seldom rise above zero. In midsummer, the days last more than 20 hours, temperatures often reach the 70's, and residents cool off by waterskiing on the lakes and rivers.

This is a land of clear skies and vast horizons, of rambling mountains, wide valleys, and sinuous rivers. Mightiest of the rivers is the Yukon, which flows nearly 2,000 miles from northern Canada to the Bering Sea.

Jack London described the Yukon in *The Call of the Wild*, when it was peopled with hermitlike hunters, trappers, and prospectors. Even today you can find the same rugged types living in remote cabins and riverbank villages. But the days are gone when hordes of gold seekers followed the Yukon northward — an odyssey that left some men rich, some poor, and some buried under the snow.

Like a cloud catching the sun, Mount McKinley floats over the landscape. Called Denali ("the great one") by Athabaskan Indians, the mountain was renamed in 1896. Its south summit, the highest point in North America, was first reached by climbers in 1913.

Gambier Bay on Admiralty Island, 60 miles south of Juneau, harbors a rich assortment of sea life in its temperate waters. The forested island, made a national monument in 1978, shelters a large population of brown bears and the highest known concentration of bald eagles in North America.

Most of today's adventurers come looking for wilderness rather than gold. Even residents of Fairbanks, the interior's largest city, get a taste of frontier life — when the thermometer reads –50° F and the brilliant curtains of the aurora borealis dance across the night sky; when downtown streets are closed for dogsled races; and when moose drop in to browse the shrubbery in suburban backyards.

Beyond Fairbanks lie limitless tracts of forest, swampy peat bogs, and a good number of Alaska's 3 million lakes. For millennia, Athabaskan Indians have inhabited this wild land, trapping game for subsistence. Nowadays they hunt with rifles, ride snowmobiles, and travel in motorboats. Times may have changed, but not all of the older ways are forgotten. In isolated trapline cabins along the timberline, elders can be found telling children how to catch a fish by snaring its tail or how to transport a fresh-killed moose in a boat made from its own hide.

THE NORTH SLOPE

Beyond the northern edge of Athabaskan country, the craggy peaks of the Brooks Range ease down to the North Slope. There are few places on earth where the wind has such freedom to blow — from the unbounded expanses of the Arctic Ocean across a terrain so featureless that winter travelers may have difficulty telling where the land ends and the ice-covered sea begins. In some areas, permanently frozen soil, called permafrost, extends 2,000 feet below the surface. But not all of this arctic terrain is rocky and barren. During the nine-week growing season, tundra plants burst into a glory of green, caribou gather in great herds on calving grounds, and throngs of sandhill cranes and tundra swans nest and raise their young.

Few people outside Alaska had heard of the North Slope until 1968, when oil was discovered there. Today drilling rigs are strewn across the flatlands, and a huge industrial complex stands on the shore of Prudhoe Bay. Life here is hard. Equipment is sheltered to protect workers from windchills of –100° F and colder. The sun sets in mid-November and does not reappear until late January, while

GLACIERS ON THE MOVE

Alaska's glaciers form when winter snowfalls accumulate over hundreds of years to tremendous depths and crystallize under great pressure into glacial ice — a substance so dense that it is more like metamorphic rock than ice. The resultant glacier is heavy enough to be driven downhill by its own weight, usually at a rate of no more than three feet a day. But for reasons unknown, the ice may abruptly surge ahead 10 to 100 times faster than normal.

In May 1986 surging Hubbard Glacier formed an ice dam hundreds of feet high across the mouth of Russell Fjord. Freshwater runoff raised the new lake to 80 feet above sea level, flooding forests, trapping marine life, and threatening salmon streams. In October the dam broke, releasing a torrent of water into Disenchantment Bay.

Glaciers can also "retreat." Retreating glaciers terminate at the sea, their ice walls rising hundreds of feet. The warmer seawater causes huge chunks of ice to break away, or "calve" (thus are born icebergs); and if calving exceeds snow accumulation, the terminus of the glacier will gradually fall back.

The most dramatic retreat in modern times took place in southeastern Alaska. When Capt. George Vancouver sailed there in 1794, he passed a wall of ice 300 feet high. Were he to visit the same spot today, he would see an entirely different scene. Over the last two centuries the climate has warmed and the ice has retreated more than 60 miles, opening a spectacular world of mountains and fjords now called Glacier Bay National Park — much of which had been entombed in ice for eons.

gales pound the snow into pavement-hard drifts and the sea becomes a continent of ice.

Yet, from this lonely northern outpost to the populated bays in the south, Alaska offers vivid testament to America's breathtaking beauty: polar seas, tundra flatlands, dense north woods, glacial mountains, and coniferous rain forest — all within the borders of one vast and magnificent wilderness.

HISTORICAL HIGHLIGHTS

1741 Vitus Bering, a Dane in the service of Russia, becomes the first European to reach Alaska.

1745 – 59 Russians, looking for sea otter furs, arrive in the Aleutian Islands chain.

1784 Russians establish a base on Kodiak Island.

1804 Sitka becomes the capital of Russian Alaska.

1867 Amid public protests over the purchase of an "icebox," U.S. pays $7.2 million for Alaska — about 2 cents an acre.

1899 Thousands of prospectors stampede into Nome after gold is discovered on the beach.

1900 Juneau is made the new capital. The move from Sitka involves three government employees and seven filing cabinets in one boat.

1912 Congress makes Alaska a U.S. territory.

1957 Oil is discovered near Swanson River on the Kenai Peninsula in southeastern Alaska.

1959 Alaska joins the Union as the 49th state.

1964 The most severe earthquake in North American history shakes Alaska, destroys most of Valdez, and kills 115 people.

1968 More oil is discovered near Prudhoe Bay in the Arctic Circle.

1971 The federal government grants 40 million acres and $962,500,000 in cash to Alaska's Eskimos, Indians, and Aleuts.

1977 An 800-mile Alaska oil pipeline from Prudhoe Bay to Valdez is completed.

1989 A tanker runs aground in Prince William Sound, causing largest oil spill in U.S. history.

FAMOUS SONS AND DAUGHTERS

Alexander Baranov (1747 – 1819). Trained as a merchant in Siberia, this administrator of Russian Alaska's early fur trading company ruled Sitka like a provincial czar from 1799 to 1818. During that time he brought law and order to the rowdy colony.

Susan Butcher (1954 –). A sled dog trainer from the bush community of Manley, Butcher became Alaska's best-known "musher" by winning the 1,150-mile Iditarod Sled Dog Race four times in five years.

Ernest Gruening (1887 – 1974). Territorial governor from 1939 to 1953, Gruening was the force behind the drive for statehood. He then served as a U.S. senator for two terms.

Howard Rock (1911 – 76).

This Eskimo painter and scrimshaw artist spurred the battle for native rights and lands when he established an activist intertribal newspaper, *The Tundra Times*, in Fairbanks in 1964.

Don Sheldon (1912 – 75). The legendary "glacier pilot" flew his small plane some 800 hours every year for 27 years, transporting mountaineers, skiers, and scientists to remote mountain ranges and using glaciers for airstrips. He went through 45 airplanes but never injured himself or a passenger.

ODDITIES AND SPECIALTIES

Seventeen of the 20 highest peaks in the U.S. are in Alaska.

In 1942 the Japanese occupied the Aleutian islands of Attu and Kiska, the only North American soil held by enemy forces in World War II.

Eskimos, who carve household utensils and everyday objects from walrus tusk ivory, are the only Alaskans allowed to own the scarce commodity.

Eighty percent of Alaska's terrain is permanently frozen.

Barrow, the state's northernmost town, is only 800 air miles from the North Pole.

The Yupik and Inupiaq Eskimos, who live on the coasts of the Bering Sea and Arctic Ocean, have almost 100 words for sea ice.

Alaskan Eskimos make their traditional "ice cream" by mixing snow with seal oil and berries.

If it were not for a westward jog in the international date line, the far islands of the Aleutian chain would share a time zone with Russia and Japan.

PLACES TO VISIT, THINGS TO DO

Denali National Park and Preserve (125 miles northwest of Anchorage). This is the best place to view grizzlies, caribou, moose, and Dall sheep. Towering Mt. McKinley dominates the background.

Glacier Bay National Park and Preserve (Gustavus). Small planes or boats from Juneau take visitors to this meeting place of 16 glaciers, some of which tower 200 feet above the water.

Iditarod Sled Dog Race The famous dogsled race is held each March. Mushers and their teams of huskies travel from Anchorage to Nome in about 11 days.

Kenai Fjords National Park (Seward). Some of the world's most spectacular coastline can be viewed on day-long boat trips along the temperate Kenai Peninsula, called Alaska's Riviera.

Sitka The early capital of Alaska retains some of the flavor of its Russian origins. St. Michael's Russian Orthodox cathedral houses antique icons; Indian and Russian relics are on view at the Centennial Building.

Skagway Once the tumultuous gateway to the Klondike, this small town houses relics of the gold rush in its museums and restored buildings.

Tongass Historical Society Museum and Totem Heritage Center (Ketchikan). Unique totems, tools, baskets, and ceremonial objects of the Haida, Tlingit, and Tsimshian Indians are on display.

ALEUTIAN ISLANDS

Wrangell – St. Elias National Park (Glennallen). The largest national park in the U.S. is notable for its towering peaks and massive glaciers.

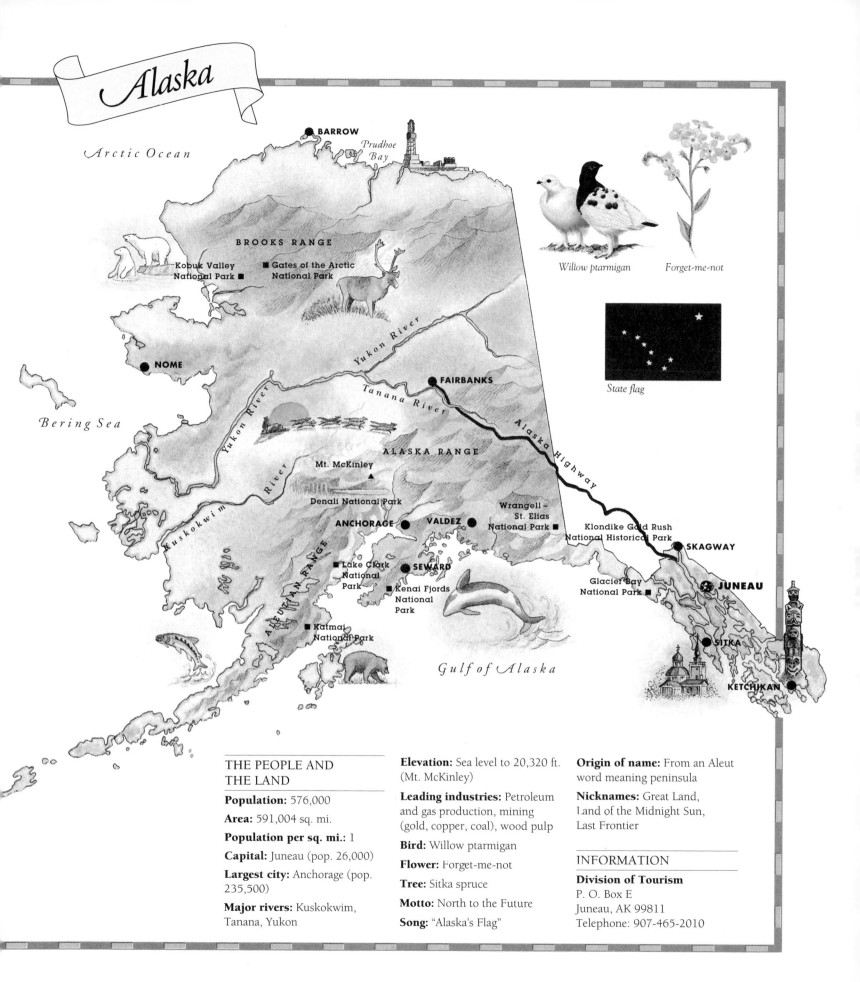

Alaska

Arctic Ocean

● BARROW

Prudhoe Bay

Bering Sea

BROOKS RANGE

■ Kobuk Valley National Park

■ Gates of the Arctic National Park

● NOME

Yukon River

Tanana River

● FAIRBANKS

Yukon River

Kuskokwim River

ALASKA RANGE

Mt. McKinley ▲

Denali National Park

Alaska Highway

● ANCHORAGE ● VALDEZ

Wrangell – St. Elias National Park ■

Klondike Gold Rush National Historical Park

● SKAGWAY

■ Lake Clark National Park

● SEWARD

■ Kenai Fjords National Park

Glacier Bay National Park ■

⊛ JUNEAU

ALEUTIAN RANGE

■ Katmai National Park

Gulf of Alaska

● SITKA

● KETCHIKAN

Willow ptarmigan

Forget-me-not

State flag

THE PEOPLE AND THE LAND

Population: 576,000

Area: 591,004 sq. mi.

Population per sq. mi.: 1

Capital: Juneau (pop. 26,000)

Largest city: Anchorage (pop. 235,500)

Major rivers: Kuskokwim, Tanana, Yukon

Elevation: Sea level to 20,320 ft. (Mt. McKinley)

Leading industries: Petroleum and gas production, mining (gold, copper, coal), wood pulp

Bird: Willow ptarmigan

Flower: Forget-me-not

Tree: Sitka spruce

Motto: North to the Future

Song: "Alaska's Flag"

Origin of name: From an Aleut word meaning peninsula

Nicknames: Great Land, Land of the Midnight Sun, Last Frontier

INFORMATION

Division of Tourism
P. O. Box E
Juneau, AK 99811
Telephone: 907-465-2010

Arizona

Harsh beauty
carved by water and time

Although home to the ruins of an age-old culture, Arizona is one of the youngest states: the nation's lawmakers held off granting statehood until 1912, making it the last of the contiguous 48 to be admitted to the Union. And that is only one of Arizona's paradoxes. Though much of it appears barren, the state is rich in wildlife, vegetation, and minerals. Though dry, it was formed by ancient seas, and rushing rivers carved its breathtaking canyons. Though harsh and arid, it harbors a fragile beauty, with solitary juniper trees springing from its cracked soil and fledglings nesting among its cacti.

HOME OF THE NAVAJO AND HOPI

In the northern part of the state, the Colorado Plateau is flat and sparsely vegetated, even though most of it is elevated above 5,000 feet. Scorching heat, violent thunderstorms, stinging dust storms, and the occasional blizzard blast the landscape from season to season. Nevertheless, man has survived and even thrived here for centuries.

At Canyon de Chelly, on the lonesome lands of the Navajo Indian reservation, are ruins left by the çliff-dwelling Anasazi people who lived there until some 700 years ago. Ancient paintings and carvings adorn the red sandstone cliffs that plunge down to crumbling pueblo houses, groves of golden cottonwoods, and flocks of sheep. Today Navajos occupy the canyon, with many of their tribal traditions intact. Women in velvet blouses bedecked with silver and turquoise jewelry

Giant saguaro cacti, some as tall as 50 feet and weighing up to 6 tons, rise from the floor of the Sonora Desert in southwestern Arizona.

Like a divine afterthought, a rainbow arches over Cathedral Rock in the wake of a summer shower. This and other sandstone formations stand in Oak Creek Canyon near the Mogollon Rim, the southern edge of the Colorado Plateau.

still weave rugs, while men on horseback herd sheep and cattle.

Nearby, on the southern edge of Black Mesa, stand Hopi Indian villages. One of them, Oraibi, is believed to be the oldest continuously occupied spot in the United States. Dry, sparse, and windy, this is a forbidding place, but to the Hopis it is one of the most sacred spots in the universe.

CHASMS AND COOL MOUNTAINS

For all the mesas thrust upward from the Colorado Plateau, there are also chasms gouged deep — most notably, the fabled Grand Canyon. The rock of its inner gorge is 2 billion years old — some of the oldest exposed rock

on earth — but the huge abyss is relatively young, since the Colorado River began chiseling it out only about 5 million years ago.

Today up to 4 million people a year flock to see this unparalleled treasure, perhaps the most famous natural wonder on earth. Yet it was not so long ago, in a time when man thought of nature as existing only for his own benefit, that the Grand Canyon was seen as less than inspiring. The first Spanish explorers to lay eyes on the yawning chasm cursed it as a nuisance that impeded their westward march. One of the early trappers in the region described the "horrid mountains" of the canyon in his journal, and Lt. Joseph Ives, leading an exploration party in 1857, found the

The falls and pools of Havasu Canyon gave a name to the Indians who have inhabited the area for hundreds of years — the Havasupai, or "people of the blue-green water."

"Slot canyons" are deep slashes that may measure less than a yard across at the top but extend hundreds of feet into sandstone bedrock. As they descend, the canyons can curl and arch into fantastic shapes, the legacy of the swirling water that formed them. One of the largest of these geological curiosities is in Antelope Canyon in northwestern Arizona.

canyon "altogether valueless. Ours has been the first, and will doubtless be the last, party of whites to visit this profitless locale."

Curving southeastward from the canyon for more than 200 miles is the southern border of the Colorado Plateau, an escarpment known as the Mogollon Rim. From its heights one sees a green swath of rugged peaks and narrow valleys to the south — an oasis in the midst of a barren land. This is the central mountain country, with stands of timber and spring-fed streams. Early settlers found relief from the harshness of the desert in these pine-shaded mountains, which also offered the promise of rich veins of gold. One of the pioneers' earliest towns, Prescott, became the

A winter storm clears over Mojave Point at the Grand Canyon. The upper reaches of the canyon area are usually blanketed with snow for much of the winter.

second capital of the Arizona territory in 1864, its capitol building constructed from ponderosa pine logs cut from the surrounding forest.

CACTUS COUNTRY

South of the central mountains, the desert again claims most of the land. But not all. The city of Phoenix sprawls across one of the region's saucer-shaped valleys, radiating outward from the same life-giving Salt River that the Hohokam people lived on as early as 300 B.C. Clean, dry air was among the drawing cards that lured people to Phoenix and turned it into a capital of high-tech industry in the 1980's. Ironically, the smog generated by

thousands of new automobiles deprived the city of the very quality that first made it thrive. But Phoenicians have enacted strong antipollution measures, determined to regain their treasured desert air.

Phoenix, surrounded by irrigated fields and picturesque mountains, is not the only oasis in the desert terrain of southern Arizona. In the southeastern corner of the state, the Chiricahua region, with pinnacles and spires that eerily resemble standing crowds of people, has miles of forested slopes, shady glens, and twisting trails. This part of the country was home to the Apaches (today their reservation is some 150 miles to the north), and here their chief Cochise eluded the U.S. Army from 1861 to 1871. Gun-toting outlaws also found a haven here.

To the southwest, beyond the booming city of Tucson, spreads the Sonoran Desert. Titan of this rust-colored land is the saguaro cactus. Towering in the air, arms reaching toward the sun, these plants probably more than any other are etched into the popular imagination as a symbol of the desert Southwest. Their accordion pleats expand and contract to maximize storage of precious water. Holes pecked out of the fleshy trunks provide many birds — elf owls, gilded flickers, Gila woodpeckers — with protected nesting sites. Atop the saguaro's trunk and arms (which appear only after the plant is about 75 years old), creamy white blossoms lasting only a day unfold in May and June.

Other cacti — prickly pear, fishhook, barrel, organ pipe, jumping cholla, pincushion — stand sheathed in needlelike bristles and, in some seasons, sprout brilliant, delicate flowers as if on cue. Wild gardens of purple owl clover, gold Mexican poppies, and blue lupine further paint the scene. Coveys of Gambel's quail and lone roadrunners dart among the varied vegetation. Wild pigs, coyotes, bighorn sheep, mule deer, and even mountain lions live in the desert, as do eight-eyed wolf spiders, tarantulas, scorpions, Gila monsters, and rattlesnakes.

Like the flower of the saguaro cactus, nothing seems to last long in the Arizona desert. A thin veil of snow descends overnight; by early the next morning, the slush has been swallowed up by the thirsty soil. Some black thunderclouds hover ominously over the land, only to dissipate without fanfare. Others cause flash floods, transforming dry, sandy washes into torrents of silt and roots and releasing the powerful fragrance of wet creosote bush. An hour later the washes run dry and the sweet smell is gone.

This is a place where nature is conspicuously in flux. And yet the varied and brilliantly colored desert landscape seems eternal. Twelve thousand years of human habitation notwithstanding, Arizona's beauty — stark, rugged, and mysterious — endures.

Bent by heavy snowdrifts, some stands of aspen saplings on the north rim of the Grand Canyon grow into crooked forests.

NATURE'S HEIRLOOMS

Two hundred million years ago, northeastern Arizona was a subtropical swampland studded with inland seas and active volcanoes. Giant salamanders inhabited a terrain forested with towering pine trees called *Araucarioxylon arizonicum*, long since extinct.

Most of the pines rotted away after they died. But some did not. Rivers flooding down from the mountains picked up the dead trees, tumbled them end over end, and stripped them of branches and roots. The trunks piled up in tremendous logjams on the lowlands, where they were gradually buried under layers of mud, sand, and volcanic ash.

Because this dense mixture contained little oxygen, the tree trunks decomposed extremely slowly. Water filtering down through the layers of sediment left a silica residue that leached into the cell tissues of the logs, where it turned into quartz crystals. Other minerals tinted the quartz in striking hues of red, yellow, orange, purple, and blue-green.

Over millions of years, the climate changed, the waters receded, and the soil that had entombed the trees eroded away, exposing the jewel-like fossilized trunks that lie strewn over more than 147 square miles — an area known today as the Petrified Forest.

THE ANCIENT ARCHITECTS

Nearly 2,000 years ago a mysterious people came to live on the Colorado Plateau. Called the Anasazi, or "Ancient Ones," today, the earliest of them were basket weavers who lived in homes of poles and brush in low-lying caves. But by the time they left the plateau 1,300 years later, they had progressed to the building of houses that remain the most intriguing feats of ancient North American architecture — the famous pueblo cliff dwellings.

The ruins of Anasazi villages are found from Arizona to Colorado. But none are more dramatic than those of Canyon de Chelly, positioned as they are within a labyrinth of sheer-walled sandstone passages. Built on ledges, within shallow caves, or nestled at the bottom of towering cliffs, the shadowy adobe houses grow so organically from their surroundings that they appear to be part of the earth itself. Three-story towers with stone walls rise above the round subterranean chambers (kivas) that were used for religious rituals. Other structures, some of them plastered with stucco, form intricate geometric shapes along the faces of the cliffs. Once occupied by several families, these multilevel buildings could be called early apartment houses.

Named *pueblos* ("villages") by the first Spanish explorers, the crowded settlements lent their name to a number of tribes that are now generically known as Pueblo Indians — tribes that include the Anasazi-descended Hopis but, surprisingly, not the Navajos who occupy Canyon de Chelly today.

With the Ajo Mountains as their backdrop, golden poppies spring to life in March and April in the southwestern Arizona desert. Fully adapted to a harsh environment, the flowers go to seed in a matter of days instead of the two weeks it takes for most poppies — in a rush to reproduce before the scorching summer heat can kill them off.

After 5 million years of wearing away at bedrock, the Colorado River winds through 277 miles of the chasm it carved. Although peaceful in this part of the Grand Canyon, called the Grand Cathedral, the river abruptly changes character and becomes a torrent of whitewater in more than 150 stretches.

Arizona

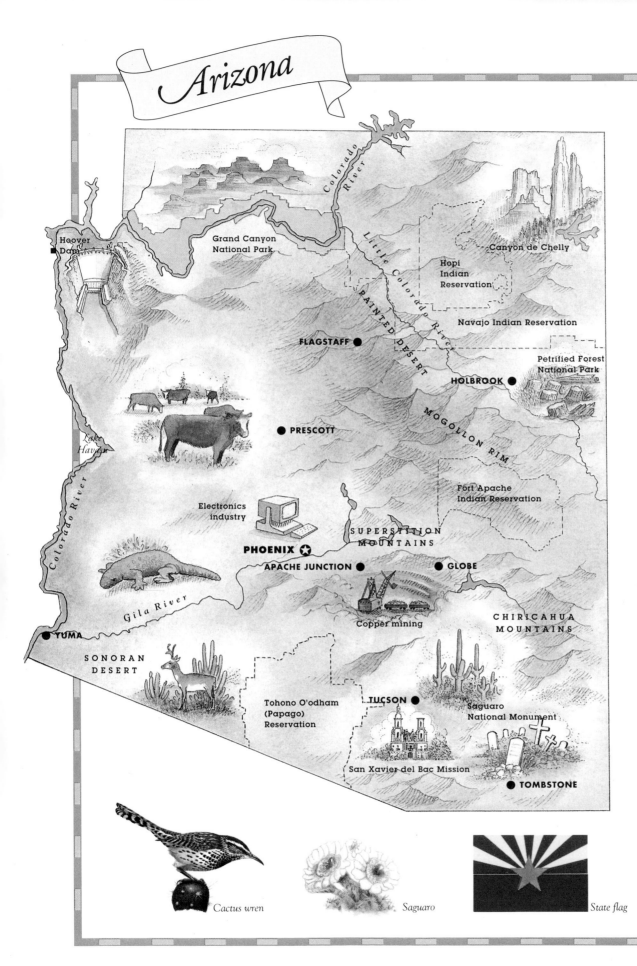

Hoover Dam

Grand Canyon National Park

Colorado River

Canyon de Chelly

Hopi Indian Reservation

Little Colorado River

PAINTED DESERT

Navajo Indian Reservation

FLAGSTAFF ●

Petrified Forest National Park

HOLBROOK ●

Lake Havasu

PRESCOTT ●

MOGOLLON RIM

Electronics industry

Fort Apache Indian Reservation

Colorado River

SUPERSTITION MOUNTAINS

PHOENIX ★

APACHE JUNCTION ●

GLOBE ●

Copper mining

CHIRICAHUA MOUNTAINS

Gila River

YUMA ●

SONORAN DESERT

Tohono O'odham (Papago) Reservation

TUCSON ●

Saguaro National Monument

San Xavier del Bac Mission

TOMBSTONE ●

Cactus wren

Saguaro

State flag

THE PEOPLE AND THE LAND

Population: 3,752,000

Population per sq. mi.: 33

Area: 114,000 sq. mi.

Capital and largest city: Phoenix (pop. 2,073,600)

Major rivers: Colorado, Gila, Little Colorado

Elevation: 70 ft. (Yuma) to 12,633 ft. (Humphreys Peak)

Leading industries: Copper mining, agriculture (beef, cotton, citrus fruit, lettuce), electronics

Bird: Cactus wren

Flower: Saguaro

Tree: Paloverde

Motto: *Ditat Deus* (God Enriches)

Song: "Arizona: The March"

Origin of name: From a Papago word meaning small springs

Nickname: Grand Canyon State

INFORMATION

Arizona Office of Tourism
1100 West Washington
Phoenix, AZ 85007
Telephone: 602-542-8687

Owls call a saguaro cactus home.

HISTORICAL HIGHLIGHTS

1540 Spanish expedition under Coronado enters Arizona and discovers Grand Canyon.

1691 Jesuit Eusebio Francisco Kino begins missionary work in southern Arizona.

1752 First permanent Spanish settlement, a military post at Tubac, is established.

1821 When Mexico wins independence, Arizona passes from Spanish to Mexican rule.

1848 Mexico cedes Arizona north of the Gila River to U.S.

1853 With the Gadsden Purchase, rest of present-day Arizona is acquired by U.S.

1854 First Arizona copper ore is mined at Ajo.

1858 Gold is discovered at Gila City on the Colorado River.

1862 First Confederate, then Union troops occupy Tucson during Civil War.

1864 Some 9,000 Navajos surrender to U.S. troops after attack on Canyon de Chelly.

1881 In gunfight at O.K. Corral in silver-mining town of Tombstone, Wyatt Earp and two brothers gun down three men.

1886 Geronimo, leader of the Apache raiders, is exiled to Florida, and Indian raids on Arizona territory end.

1888 Copper production passes gold and silver in value.

1889 Capital of Arizona territory is moved from Prescott to 19-year-old city of Phoenix.

1912 Arizona enters the Union as the 48th state.

1919 Congress establishes Grand Canyon National Park.

1936 Hoover Dam starts supplying water for electricity and irrigation to Arizona, Nevada, and Southern California.

1950 – 60 Arizona's population increases 73.7 percent, faster than any other state.

1985 Central Arizona Project begins operation, directing water from Colorado River to arid rural areas and the cities of Phoenix and Tucson.

FAMOUS SONS AND DAUGHTERS

Geronimo (1829 – 1909). In the 1870's this skillful guerrilla fighter encouraged his fellow Chiricahua Apaches to desert their newly established reservation and resume their war against white settlers. In 1886 he gave himself up.

Barry M. Goldwater (1909 –). This U.S. senator (1952 – 64, 1968 – 87), known as Mr. Conservative, aroused national controversy as Republican presidential candidate in 1964 when he declared, "Extremism in defense of liberty is no vice."

Carl T. Hayden (1877 – 1972). This politician set a record for length of service in the U.S. Congress, as representative from 1912 to 1927 and senator from 1927 to 1969.

George W. P. Hunt (1859 – 1934). Hunt came to the territory as a gold prospector and later pioneered the development of irrigation systems during his four terms as governor.

Percival Lowell (1855 – 1916). Founder of the Lowell Observatory (1894), this astronomer predicted the existence and position of "Planet X." It was discovered 14 years after his death and named Pluto.

Sandra Day O'Connor (1930 –). A lawyer, O'Connor was appointed to the U.S. Supreme Court by President Ronald Reagan in 1981, making her the first woman justice.

ODDITIES AND SPECIALTIES

More telescopes (some 30 in all) are located near Tucson than anywhere else.

Blue corn, grown by Arizona's Hopi Indians for centuries, proved a boon to Indian farmers in the 1980's when it became a sought-after gourmet item.

In 1962 an enterprising American bought the London Bridge that since 1831 had spanned the Thames, and transported it to Lake Havasu in western Arizona, where it now stands.

Arizona has 37 kinds of lizards.

Hopi and Navajo Indians are among the best silversmiths in the U.S. Each tribe makes its own distinctive style of jewelry.

The continent's largest known meteor crater — almost a mile across — was formed some 30,000 years ago when a meteor weighing thousands of tons smashed into the Arizona desert.

True desert covers less than 1 percent of Arizona, but more than 40 percent is desert scrub.

PLACES TO VISIT, THINGS TO DO

Apache Trail (Apache Junction to Globe). This 78-mile road, once the route of raiding Apaches, affords good views of the Superstition Mountains.

Canyon de Chelly National Monument (Navajo Indian Reservation). This magnificent canyon of steep red cliffs contains Indian cliff dwellings dating back to A.D. 350.

Grand Canyon National Park The visitor standing on a rim of the breathtaking Grand Canyon is looking at 2 billion years of geologic history.

Monument Valley Navajo Tribal Park (Navajo Indian Reservation). Huge monoliths and spires of red sandstone loom high above the desert floor.

Painted Desert (northeastern Arizona). Intricately patterned by erosion, these badlands extend 300 miles from the Grand Canyon to the Petrified Forest.

Petrified Forest National Park (near Holbrook). The world's largest display of petrified wood lies at the southeastern edge of the Painted Desert.

Saguaro National Monument (nine miles east of Tucson). Thousands of saguaro cacti grow in this stark desert forest.

San Xavier del Bac Mission (nine miles southwest of Tucson). This mission serves the Papago Indians today. Completed in 1797, it is a fine example of early mission architecture.

Tombstone This town in southeastern Arizona, once the symbol of the lawless Old West, has been preserved so that tourists can still see the O.K. Corral, Bird Cage Theatre, and other sites in their original state.

Arkansas

Quiet hills and rivers preserved in timeless beauty

Drifting along the Buffalo River past towering limestone bluffs, negotiating the winding streets of Eureka Springs in the Ozark Mountains, following the Great River Road across the flat and verdant Delta, or standing in the evening darkness amid the pines of the Timberlands — throughout Arkansas one finds tranquillity and remoteness that seem inherent in the land.

Even native Arkansawyers are often unfamiliar with large stretches of the 53,000 square miles that make up their home, though they would argue that they are far from isolated. The state is, after all, bordered on the east by the Mississippi River, the nation's busiest waterway, and two interstates cross at the state capital of Little Rock.

When Arkansas was admitted to the Union in 1836, however, it barely had the 50,000 residents required for statehood. Most pioneers found its vast swamps along the Mississippi River too daunting a barrier and moved west by other routes. But as the swamps were drained and dammed the state grew, and by 1860 its population had increased tenfold.

BACK-COUNTRY ORIGINS

To most Americans, Arkansas means the Ozarks in the state's northwestern quarter, a peaceful land with steep hills and deep hollows. The Arkansas Ozarks were pioneered by small, independent farmers, who tended to keep to themselves in tucked-away communities scattered among the hills. Their

Year upon year of swirling springtime floodwaters have sculpted the limestone cliffs along the Buffalo River into unusual rock formations such as this vast hollow at aptly named Skull Bluff.

In the hilly Ozarks, level valleys often gave rise to small farms and towns like Boxley (above). The original Baptist church, now used as a community center, stands near the cemetery. The new church is across the road.

unchanging ways led to a century of stereotyping — an image of a hillbilly sitting on the sagging porch of a rough-hewn shanty, a scrawny, slouching hound nearby — but also kept alive old music and folk crafts that are celebrated today at the Ozark Folk Center in Mountain View. The peace and quiet have also made the Ozarks a magnet for retirees and others who simply would like a little distance from the hustle and bustle of city life. Today the Ozarks are among the fastest growing rural areas in America.

A FACE TO THE SOUTH

But not all of Arkansas is uplands. Along the flat and fertile floodplains of the Mississippi River — the Delta region — a different way of life developed. Cotton made this country, as it did so much of the antebellum South, bringing with it enormous plantations and a slow-paced, genteel society. Riverboats glided down the Mississippi into ports like Helena, which Mark Twain said had "one of the prettiest situations on the river." Now rice and soybeans have replaced cotton as the staple

crops, and Arkansas produces more rice than any other state. In the Delta town of Stuttgart, towering grain elevators often confuse out-of-towners, who think they are approaching a city filled with skyscrapers.

HOT SPRINGS AND PINELANDS

Southwest of the Delta lie the Timberlands, a region of gentle hills cloaked in dense pine forests. Spiritually, the region is more akin to the West than to the South. The town of Washington was a stopping place for Sam

HEATING THE HOT SPRINGS

Ghostly vapors rise in the Zig Zag Mountains of Arkansas, hovering above an eerie landscape encrusted in white. Their source, however, is far from otherworldly. The vapors rise where water from hot springs emerges after centuries inside the earth. The white crust surrounding the springs is tufa, a calcium carbonate deposit built up by the slow and endless flow of these steaming mineral-rich waters.

For centuries people have attributed marvelous healing powers to these springs. No less marvelous is the story of why they are hot and bubbly.

Whenever rain falls northeast of what is now the town of Hot Springs, it trickles down through the mountains' sedimentary rock, absorbing carbon dioxide and calcium carbonate, which gives the water its bubbles and distinctive taste. After 4,000 years the water reaches its maximum depth of 8,000 feet within the earth. Throughout this journey it has been warmed: as a result of the decay of radioactive elements, the average temperature in the earth's crust grows 3° to 5° F hotter every 100 yards.

Joints and fractures in the sandstone deep beneath Hot Springs allow the water to gush back to the earth's surface in as little as a year. Bubbling with gases that have been trapped within it for 40 centuries, the water bursts forth at 47 different springs at an average temperature of 143° F and a daily volume of 850,000 gallons.

Perched some 700 feet above the Buffalo River valley, Whitaker Point commands a magnificent view of the Upper Buffalo Wilderness Area. The spectacular vista from this crag overlooking an oak-hickory forest has attracted so many tourists in recent years that their very numbers have done damage.

Houston, Stephen Austin, and many of the other men who wrested Texas from Mexico in the 1830's. And here too, legend has it, Jim Bowie had a local artisan fashion his fearsome knife, dubbed the Arkansas toothpick. An oil boom in the 1920's around El Dorado further cemented the region's ties to Texas.

To the north, the craggy heights and steep valleys of the Ouachita Mountains initially discouraged permanent settlers, who often sought flatter lands for farming. However, the region's many natural springs, both hot and cold, were becoming a major tourist attraction as early as the first decades of the 1800's. Veiled in vapor, the bubbling hot springs here were hallowed by local Indians for their supposed healing powers long before white settlers built the bathhouses that made the town of Hot Springs a world-renowned health spa.

FRONTIER JUSTICE

Fort Smith was established in 1817 where the Ouachita Mountains met the Indian Territory that is now Oklahoma. It would become the state's most notorious town. Although tribal courts had legal authority over Indians, no one had jurisdiction over whites in the territory until Judge Isaac C. Parker arrived in 1875. Over the next 21 years Parker tried some 13,000 cases and sentenced 160 men to death, thus achieving a lasting place in western lore as the Hanging Judge.

But Arkansas is better known for its natural beauty than its history. It has been tagged the Wonder State and the Natural State, and both names fit. Nurtured by the natural barriers that once thwarted its development, Arkansas remains one of the most unspoiled sections of America.

Lying four miles west of the Mississippi River, Wapanocca National Wildlife Refuge is a major stopping place for ducks and geese during their north-south migrations. Some 600 of the refuge's 5,485 acres are covered with stands of cypress, like that above, which take root in the swamplands. Although many swamps have been drained, this terrain is typical of the landscape pioneers encountered along the river as they moved west into Arkansas in the early 1800's.

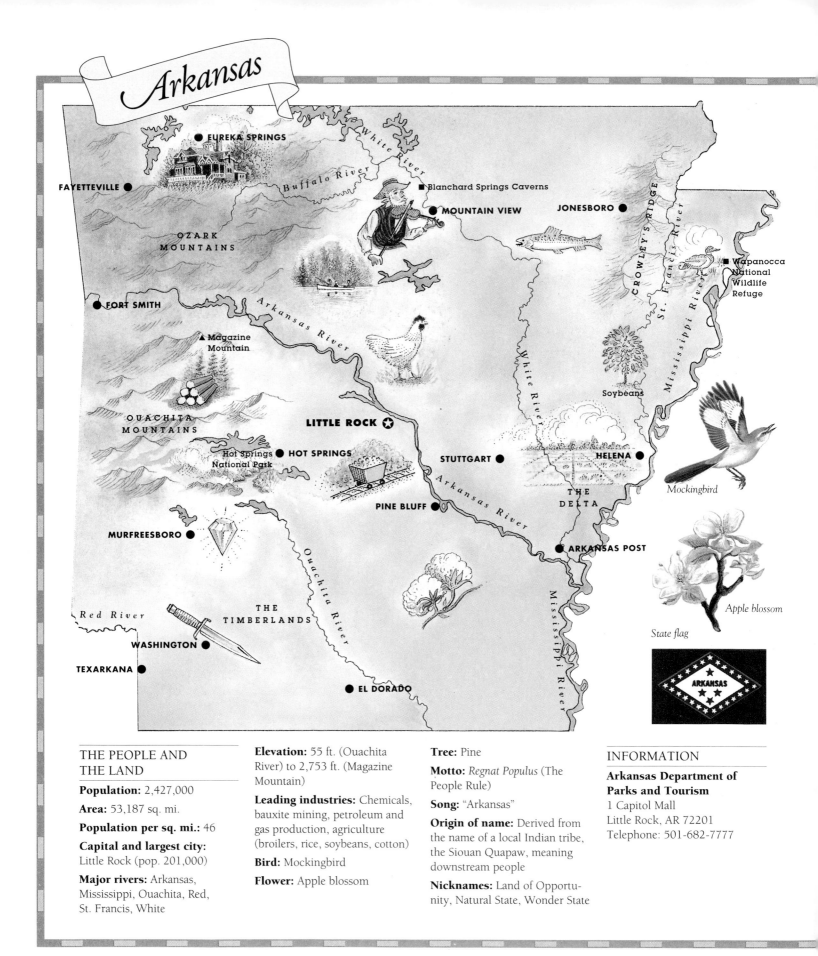

Arkansas

EUREKA SPRINGS

FAYETTEVILLE

White River

Buffalo River

Blanchard Springs Caverns

MOUNTAIN VIEW

JONESBORO

OZARK MOUNTAINS

CROWLEY'S RIDGE

St. Francis River

Mississippi River

Wapanocca National Wildlife Refuge

FORT SMITH

Arkansas River

▲ Magazine Mountain

Soybeans

OUACHITA MOUNTAINS

White River

LITTLE ROCK ★

Hot Springs National Park ● HOT SPRINGS

STUTTGART

HELENA

THE DELTA

Mockingbird

MURFREESBORO

PINE BLUFF

Arkansas River

ARKANSAS POST

Ouachita River

Apple blossom

Red River

THE TIMBERLANDS

State flag

WASHINGTON

TEXARKANA

Mississippi River

EL DORADO

ARKANSAS

THE PEOPLE AND THE LAND

Population: 2,427,000

Area: 53,187 sq. mi.

Population per sq. mi.: 46

Capital and largest city: Little Rock (pop. 201,000)

Major rivers: Arkansas, Mississippi, Ouachita, Red, St. Francis, White

Elevation: 55 ft. (Ouachita River) to 2,753 ft. (Magazine Mountain)

Leading industries: Chemicals, bauxite mining, petroleum and gas production, agriculture (broilers, rice, soybeans, cotton)

Bird: Mockingbird

Flower: Apple blossom

Tree: Pine

Motto: *Regnat Populus* (The People Rule)

Song: "Arkansas"

Origin of name: Derived from the name of a local Indian tribe, the Siouan Quapaw, meaning downstream people

Nicknames: Land of Opportunity, Natural State, Wonder State

INFORMATION

Arkansas Department of Parks and Tourism
1 Capitol Mall
Little Rock, AR 72201
Telephone: 501-682-7777

HISTORICAL HIGHLIGHTS

1541 Hernando de Soto crosses the Mississippi to become the first European on Arkansas soil.

1686 Frenchman Henri de Tonti founds Arkansas Post, the first white settlement in the lower Mississippi Valley.

1817 The U.S. builds Fort Smith to keep peace between Indian tribes and to protect westward-moving settlers.

1836 Arkansas is admitted to the Union as the 25th state.

1861 State conventions vote first to reject secession, then to secede. Some 9,000 whites and 5,000 blacks join Union Army.

1887 Bauxite is discovered near Little Rock; by 1918 Arkansas produces almost all bauxite mined in the U.S.

1921 Discovery of oil near El Dorado leads to a boom, and in 1924 Arkansas is fourth among states in oil production.

1927 Flooding of Mississippi River leaves one-fifth of state underwater.

1957 Defying a federal court order, Gov. Orval Faubus blocks integration of Central High School in Little Rock. President Eisenhower sends troops to enforce the order.

1971 After an expenditure of $1.2 billion to dredge and to build dams, the Arkansas River opens to commercial navigation from the Mississippi River to Tulsa, Okla., making Little Rock an inland port.

1985 Arkansas starts a national trend by requiring teachers to pass basic tests in reading and math to retain their jobs.

FAMOUS SONS AND DAUGHTERS

Hattie Caraway (1878 – 1950). The first woman elected to the U.S. Senate, Caraway won office in 1932, only 12 years after women got the right to vote.

Dizzy Dean (1911 – 74). The son of a sharecropper, Dean became one of baseball's great pitchers. He led the National League in strikeouts for four consecutive years (1932 – 35) and was elected to the Baseball Hall of Fame in 1953.

J. William Fulbright (1905 –). A longtime U.S. senator (1945 – 74), Fulbright chaired the Foreign Relations Committee from 1959 to 1974 and sponsored the act that established the Fulbright Scholarships for student exchange with other countries.

Douglas MacArthur (1880 – 1964). His most famous words were "I shall return" — a promise he made and kept to recapture the Philippines from the Japanese in World War II. Commander of U.S. forces in the Far East from 1941, he headed the Allied occupation of Japan and later the United Nations military forces in Korea.

Edward Durell Stone (1902 – 78). An architect of international fame, Stone designed the Museum of Modern Art in New York City, the Kennedy Center in Washington, D.C., and the U.S. Embassy in New Delhi.

Sam Walton (1918 –). Perhaps the wealthiest man in America, Walton opened his first Wal-Mart store, in Rogers, in 1962.

ODDITIES AND SPECIALTIES

The oldest continuously published newspaper west of the Mississippi River is the *Arkansas Gazette,* founded in 1819.

As much as 500 feet high, 1 to 12 miles wide, and running half the length of the state, Crowley's Ridge was built up over millennia from fine windblown soil.

The city of Texarkana straddles the Arkansas-Texas border. So that neither state will feel slighted, the post office building is divided by the state line and has three doors, one leading to each state and a main door right on the boundary.

In 1925 the citizens of Winslow elected a woman, Maud Duncan, mayor and an all-female city council. Two years later, announcing that they had proved women could do the job as well as men, the women all resigned.

The only diamonds ever mined in the U.S. were discovered in Murfreesboro in 1906. Mined from 1908 to 1925, the site became part of Crater of Diamonds State Park in 1972.

At Hot Springs you can enjoy the purity of bottled spring water that fell as rain in the mountains here some 4,000 years ago.

Parking meters used worldwide are made in Harrison and Russellville.

PLACES TO VISIT, THINGS TO DO

Bass fishing The Arkansas River is among the best for bass anywhere in the U.S.

Blanchard Springs The limestone caverns of Blanchard Springs are filled with water-sculpted stalactites and stalagmites. The temperature remains a constant 58° F, and the relative humidity near 100 percent.

Buffalo River Flowing scenically through the Ozarks for 132 miles, the Buffalo was designated the country's first national river in 1972. It is ideal for canoeing, shoreline hiking, and small-mouth-bass fishing.

Eureka Springs With winding streets and Victorian homes, this popular Ozarks spa exudes the charm of the late 1800's.

Fort Smith Downtown Fort Smith is a national historic site. You can visit the old jail and the courtroom where "Hanging Judge" Isaac Parker presided.

Hot Springs National Park (Hot Springs). In 1832 part of the Hot Springs area was made the country's first national preserve. In the 1880's the park became a fashionable spa; in the 1940's the town was a gathering place for gangsters.

Ozark Folk Center (Mountain View). All the folk arts on display are handmade and reflect traditional skills. Local musicians play Ozark music.

California

Soaring mountains, vast deserts, and jagged cliffs at the continent's edge

When Spanish seafarers first sighted the golden hills of North America's western coastal range in 1532, the view reminded them of the mythical land described in *The Exploits of Esplandian,* a popular romance of the time — "an island called California, very near to the Terrestrial Paradise." The Spaniards' geography was imperfect — what they had found was not an island, but a 760-mile-long peninsula now called Baja (Lower) California. Nevertheless, the land that stretched north from those hills was indeed a paradise, undeniably blessed.

DIVERSE AND DRAMATIC

California is unmatched in its abundance and diversity. Its 500-mile-long Central Valley, lying between the Coast Ranges and the Sierra Nevada, is the most productive agricultural land in the entire Western Hemisphere, with an output of $11.5 billion in cash crops and livestock each year. The mist-covered forests of the north are home to the world's tallest living things: the coast redwoods (*Sequoia sempervirens*), which reach heights of more than 350 feet and can live for 1,000 years. A mere two hours' drive east from the balmy beaches of the Pacific is an enormous desert whose rock carvings are visual reminders of past civilizations that have disappeared as surely as the silver mines of a more modern era. Towering above all these wonders is the state's granitic spine, the Sierra Nevada, a range of rugged mountains larger in area than the Swiss, Italian, and French alps combined.

With tree lupines blooming in the foreground, the mountains and rolling pasturelands of the Coast Ranges meet the sea in Sonoma County.

A foxtail pine, cousin of the ancient bristlecone, stands like a sentinel at the edge of Kern Canyon in Sequoia National Park.

Equally grand is California's 760-mile coastline of jagged cliffs and sandy beaches. This dramatic rim of the continent has been a source of inspiration ever since Franciscan friars from Spain began building missions along the coast and linking them with the Camino Real (Royal Road) more than 200 years ago. Today the Pacific Coast Highway closely follows that early *camino*, and generations of poets and painters have traced every mile of it in their efforts to capture the beauty of Big Sur, the power of breakers crashing against the northern coast, and the twilight glow that transforms the evening sky above southern California into a palette of pastels.

California's population is as diverse as its landforms. The state's natural bounty has made it a 20th-century Ellis Island. One out of every four immigrants who enter the United States eventually settles here. Hispanics, mainly from Mexico and Central and South America, make up 28 percent of the population of Los Angeles County. And more than a third of all Asians living in the United States in 1990

Weathered sandstone bluffs tower over the ocean at Torrey Pines State Reserve near San Diego. The rare Torrey pine grows only here and on Santa Rosa Island, 175 miles away.

In a relatively peaceful stretch of California coastline, waves wash the beach at Drake's Bay, part of Point Reyes National Seashore north of San Francisco.

A light fog cloaks a grove of California black oaks in Yosemite National Park.

Spring-flowering trillium adorns the woods of Humboldt County in northern California.

called California home. The new arrivals have joined with native Californians to build a state that leads the nation not only in agriculture, but in computer science, aerospace, biotechnology, and entertainment.

A WORK IN PROGRESS

For most Americans, however, California is still defined by its scenery, from the lofty peak of Mount Whitney to the barren floor of Death Valley. Most of North America was molded eons ago by retreating Ice Age glaciers that scoured the Great Plains, scooped out the Great Lakes, and shaped the course of rivers. California, by comparison, remains a work in progress, a place where grinding pressures deep within the earth continue to uplift mountains, trigger volcanic eruptions, and rearrange the landscape.

Millions of years ago these tectonic forces brought forth the Sierra Nevada (called by Californians simply the Sierra or High Sierra), a bold 400-mile link in the mountain chain running from Central America to Alaska. The mountains contained the gold that drew a rush of miners and led to California's settlement and statehood. Though time has softened the wounds left by the hydraulic mining of gold rush territory, it has also claimed many of the towns cobbled together by forty-niners out to strike it rich. Those that have survived — places like Copperopolis, Chinese Camp, El Dorado, Jenny Lind, and Sutter Creek — are booming again because of a steady influx of retirees.

The coming of the "flatlanders" has not diminished the Sierra's sense of tradition. Saloons in the town of Columbia still offer a choice of whiskey or sarsaparilla just as they did a century ago, and the legendary Calaveras Jumping Frog contest has not changed since the days of Mark Twain. Nevertheless, gentrification is an undeniable and unavoidable fact of life. Old Wells Fargo offices more often than not sell designer cookies now, while hitching posts along Main Streets mark the spots where realtors park their cars.

But the Sierra offers a gift even greater than gold: water. In winter, moisture carried by prevailing westerlies blowing off the Pacific

The sun catches El Capitan, one of the world's largest granite monoliths, in Yosemite National Park on a November morning.

turns to snow when it hits the mountain range. Then, during the long months of summer, water from melting snow recharges the rivers, irrigates the Central Valley, and fills the swimming pools of Southern California, carried there by a system of aqueducts.

The heart of the Sierra is Yosemite National Park. Yosemite was originally carved out by streams cascading down the western face of the mountains. Later, glaciers moved through and ground away at the bedrock. The result is a breathtaking seven-mile-long valley from which rise sheer granite walls 3,000 to 4,800 feet high. Discovered by gold rush pioneers, the valley was saved from herdsmen and timber companies by John Muir, the pioneer environmentalist. Today Yosemite's exquisite alpine meadows, tumbling waterfalls, and trees that started life when ancient Greece was flourishing attract tens of thousands of visitors. Crowds and commercialization notwithstanding, the person who sees the mist hovering above Mirror Lake on an early autumn morning finds it is difficult to describe Yosemite as anything other than paradise.

VINEYARDS AND REDWOODS

West from Yosemite, across the Central Valley and beyond the capital city of Sacramento, lies the densely populated Bay area of northern California, with San Francisco as its cosmopolitan center. Just north of the city are the Napa and Sonoma valleys, home to hundreds of the vineyards that produce California's celebrated wines. Farther north, in Mendocino County, forests close in on the highway. Buffeted by salt winds and blanketed by fog, tiny towns cling to the barren coast or take shelter amid the towering redwoods.

Before man began cutting them down, the giant redwoods of California's northwest corner were virtually indestructible. Their wood is naturally resistant to water, their thick bark impervious to disease, parasites, and even fire. These qualities made the trees ready for the taking — for the wood used in Nob Hill mansions, for railroad ties, and for the planking in clipper ships carrying tea and silk from China to San Francisco. Today, to the alarm of conservationists, the demand is greater than

Giant sequoias rise from the western slopes of the Sierra Nevada. The species is one of the last survivors of an ancient family of trees that flourished in the time of the dinosaurs.

ever, and many stands of old-growth trees are scheduled for cutting. The original 2 million acres of primeval forest have been reduced to less than 100,000. Fortunately, some 80,000 acres of the ancient forest are protected in Redwood National Park and elsewhere.

"A LOVELY AND TERRIBLE WILDERNESS"

For all of the favored green land of the north, most of California's south is arid. The stark mountains and plateaus east of the Sierra Nevada form part of the Great Basin, the largest and most desolate desert in North America. Nearby is the vast Mojave Desert, an area author Wallace Stegner described as "a lovely and terrible wilderness . . . harshly and beautifully colored, broken and worn until its bones are exposed."

Though home to the dry basin that early settlers named Death Valley, the Mojave is full of life, especially in the spring when flowers fed by winter rains bloom briefly before the heat of summer. Panamint chipmunks, Death Valley sage, turkey vultures, and sprucebush all call the Mojave home. Perhaps its most famous resident is the Joshua tree, a towering yucca that was named by a colony of Mormon pioneers who, while traveling west in search of a new Jerusalem, thought the plant's armlike branches beckoned to them like an Old Testament prophet.

But Southern California — especially the green, warm edge of the state that extends from Los Angeles southward to San Diego — has always beckoned to people. Los Angeles' vast network of towns exploded in mid-century into the nation's second largest metropolis, and the city took its place as a symbol of the fast-living, car-based culture that typifies America in the eyes of much of the world.

Because growth continues unabated (California has been the nation's most populous state since 1963), conservationists, like John Muir a century ago, seek to preserve their state's distinctive treasures: the virgin redwoods of the north, the haunting Mojave Desert of the south, the waters off the majestic rock-strewn coast. Enduring still, after a century of intense development, these treasures seem more valuable than ever.

JOHN OF THE MOUNTAINS

In 1863, John Muir, a native of Scotland, left the University of Wisconsin to explore the country's wilderness areas on his own. After treks through the Midwest, Canada, and into the Deep South, accompanied only by his knapsack, he made his way to California. There he was overwhelmed by the glory of the landscape — and outraged by the wholesale destruction of forests and meadows by timber companies and grazing sheep (animals he called "hoofed locusts").

In those days most Americans considered the land valuable only for the economic rewards it could offer. Muir, in writings and lectures, argued that the wilderness, its beauty, and the life it harbored were of value in themselves. And as his fame spread, so did his influence. Largely due to Muir's urgings, Yosemite was made a national park in 1890.

The bearded man whom Californians came to know as John of the Mountains continued to hike away for months at a time, only to return, like a Moses from Mount Sinai, to exhort Americans to preserve their remaining wilderness.

President Theodore Roosevelt invited the environmentalist on a camping trip to Yosemite in 1903. Muir, who by then had founded the Sierra Club, later said: "I stuffed him pretty well regarding the timber thieves . . . and other spoilers of the forests." Roosevelt must have listened, for by the time he left office his administration had created five national parks and added more than 140 million acres to the national forest system.

Cactus flowers bloom in Anza-Borrego Desert State Park, 90 miles east of San Diego.

Blanketed in grass and pine, the Santa Lucia range recedes into the mist along the ragged Big Sur coastline. The dramatic scenery, visible along Route 1 between San Simeon and Carmel, has long been an inspiration for writers and artists.

AMERICA: LAND OF BEAUTY AND SPLENDOR

THE ACCIDENTAL SEA

Last century, the Salton Sink straddling the California-Mexico border was a desolate, furnace-hot basin choked with mesquite and tumbleweeds. Today the sink is the Salton Sea, the result of an accident on a massive scale.

In 1901, land developers, eager to see if the wasteland could be made to bloom, cut into the bank of the nearby Colorado River and built a short canal and a series of irrigation ditches to channel water into the basin. Their feat was immediately proclaimed a success. The newly irrigated land was so productive that speculators renamed the area the Imperial Valley.

For three years the towns of Brawley, Calexico, and El Centro boomed. No one, however, realized the power of the Colorado, an untamed 1,450-mile-long dynamo that, in those days, carried one of the heaviest silt loads of any river in the world. By the summer of 1904, silt was starting to plug the main irrigation canal along the Mexican border, and farmers were getting nervous as their water supply dwindled. To assure continued irrigation, a second cut was made in the riverbank. But when spring floods hit in the following year, the weakened embankment collapsed, sending the entire flow of the Colorado roaring into the basin and creating an instant sea almost 50 miles long and 15 miles wide.

Although the towns were spared, hundreds of farms were inundated. By 1907 the embankment was patched, and the Colorado resumed its regular course. But the Salton Sea, though now shrunk to 30 miles long and 10 miles wide, still laps at the desert — the curious result of man challenging nature and getting more than he bargained for.

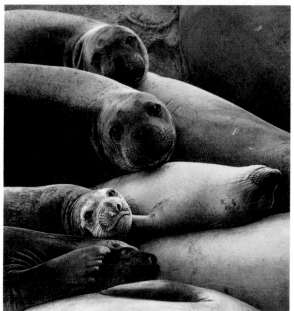

Mount Ritter looms over a sylvan meadow in the Ansel Adams Wilderness, part of Inyo and Sierra national forests. The naturalist John Muir was the first to climb the mountain and study its glaciers.

Northern elephant seals can be seen up and down the California coast. Here, young seals lounge sociably on the beach. Elephant seals get their name from the large size of the males — up to 5,500 pounds — and for the elongated snouts the males will grow as adults.

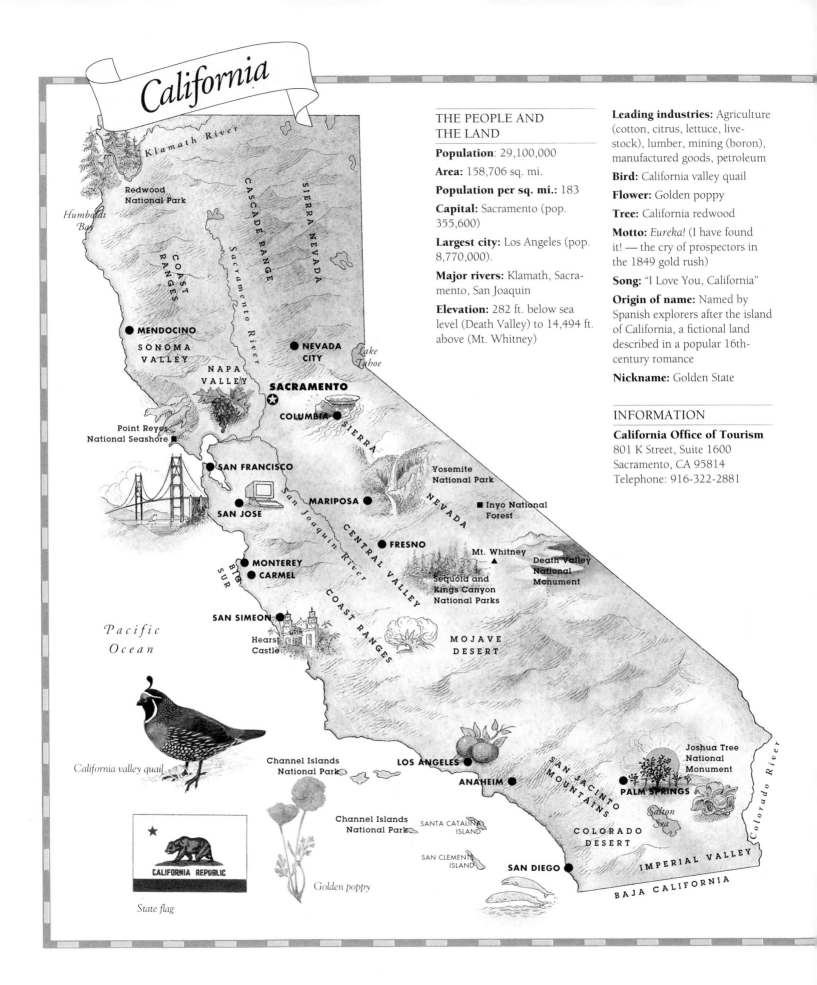

California

THE PEOPLE AND THE LAND

Population: 29,100,000

Area: 158,706 sq. mi.

Population per sq. mi.: 183

Capital: Sacramento (pop. 355,600)

Largest city: Los Angeles (pop. 8,770,000).

Major rivers: Klamath, Sacramento, San Joaquin

Elevation: 282 ft. below sea level (Death Valley) to 14,494 ft. above (Mt. Whitney)

Leading industries: Agriculture (cotton, citrus, lettuce, livestock), lumber, mining (boron), manufactured goods, petroleum

Bird: California valley quail

Flower: Golden poppy

Tree: California redwood

Motto: *Eureka!* (I have found it! — the cry of prospectors in the 1849 gold rush)

Song: "I Love You, California"

Origin of name: Named by Spanish explorers after the island of California, a fictional land described in a popular 16th-century romance

Nickname: Golden State

INFORMATION

California Office of Tourism
801 K Street, Suite 1600
Sacramento, CA 95814
Telephone: 916-322-2881

Klamath River

Redwood National Park

Humboldt Bay

COAST RANGES

CASCADE RANGE

SIERRA NEVADA

Sacramento River

MENDOCINO

SONOMA VALLEY

NEVADA CITY

Lake Tahoe

NAPA VALLEY

SACRAMENTO

COLUMBIA

SIERRA NEVADA

Point Reyes National Seashore

SAN FRANCISCO

Yosemite National Park

SAN JOSE

MARIPOSA

Inyo National Forest

SAN JOAQUIN RIVER

CENTRAL VALLEY

FRESNO

Mt. Whitney

Death Valley National Monument

MONTEREY

CARMEL

BIG SUR

Sequoia and Kings Canyon National Parks

Pacific Ocean

SAN SIMEON

Hearst Castle

COAST RANGES

MOJAVE DESERT

California valley quail

Channel Islands National Park

LOS ANGELES

SAN JACINTO MOUNTAINS

Joshua Tree National Monument

PALM SPRINGS

ANAHEIM

Salton Sea

Channel Islands National Park

SANTA CATALINA ISLAND

SAN CLEMENTE ISLAND

COLORADO DESERT

Colorado River

CALIFORNIA REPUBLIC

State flag

Golden poppy

SAN DIEGO

IMPERIAL VALLEY

BAJA CALIFORNIA

HISTORICAL HIGHLIGHTS

1542 Juan Rodríguez Cabrillo, a Portuguese navigator sailing under the flag of Spain, arrives in San Diego Bay.

1579 Sir Francis Drake lands on California coast and claims the area for England.

1769 After Spain gains control of the region, Franciscan priest Junípero Serra founds a mission near present-day San Diego.

1821 Mexico revolts against Spain and the following year claims California as its own.

1848 Mexico cedes California to U.S. after the Mexican War. James W. Marshall finds gold at Sutter's Mill in the Sierra Nevada.

1849 Thousands of "forty-niners" rush to California in search of gold.

1850 California joins Union as 31st state.

1869 The first transcontinental railroad provides a direct link from West Coast to East.

1906 An earthquake destroys buildings and causes raging fires that devastate San Francisco. At least 3,000 people die.

1910 The first film made in Hollywood — D.W. Griffith's *In Old California* — is released.

1937 Golden Gate Bridge, connecting San Francisco and Marin County, opens to traffic.

1960 California Water Project makes it possible to direct water from northern mountains to arid areas, turning desert into productive farmland.

1965 Race riots break out in Los Angeles suburb of Watts. Before they end after five days, 34 people die.

1978 In a grass-roots taxpayers' rebellion, voters ratify Proposition 13, cutting property taxes by more than half.

1989 An earthquake with an epicenter near Santa Cruz shakes San Francisco Bay and nearby areas, causing 67 deaths.

FAMOUS SONS AND DAUGHTERS

Joe DiMaggio (1914 –). "Joltin' Joe" was a superb center fielder and hitter who hit safely in 56 consecutive games. He was elected to the National Baseball Hall of Fame in 1955.

Isadora Duncan (1878 – 1927). Duncan's expressionistic dancing, done barefoot in flowing garb, made her one of the best-known artists of her day.

William Randolph Hearst (1863 – 1951). Hearst became phenomenally wealthy and influential after amassing a huge empire of newspapers, magazines, and radio stations.

Jack London (1876 – 1916). The adventurous journalist, essayist, and fiction writer chronicled the Pacific Northwest in *The Call of the Wild* and other works.

Richard Milhous Nixon (1913 –). The 37th president, who resigned from office in 1974 after the Watergate scandal, grew up in Whittier and was graduated from Whittier College.

George S. Patton, Jr. (1885 – 1945). In World War II, Patton commanded the Third Army, which swept through Europe from Normandy to Czechoslovakia in 1944 – 45.

John Steinbeck (1902 – 68). This novelist won both the Pulitzer and Nobel prizes. His best-known work, *The Grapes of Wrath,* traced the migration of poor Okies to the promised land of the West.

ODDITIES AND SPECIALTIES

In only four years, 1848 – 52, the gold rush swelled California's population from 15,000 to 250,000 in one of the largest migrations in history.

If California were a nation, it would have the sixth strongest economy in the world.

North America's largest bird, with a wingspan of 10 feet, is the endangered California condor.

Yosemite Falls are 13 times higher than Niagara Falls.

With more than 25 million cars, trucks, and buses, California has the most motor vehicles per square mile in the world.

Inyo National Forest's bristlecone pine trees, estimated to be 4,600 years old, may be the earth's oldest living organisms.

PLACES TO VISIT, THINGS TO DO

Death Valley National Monument This parched desert basin of canyons, sand dunes, and salt flats is the lowest, hottest, and driest spot in the U.S.

Disneyland (Anaheim). The huge amusement park was the first to use high technology in exhibits and rides.

Gold Country (Mariposa to Nevada City on Highway 49). Visitors can pan for gold in the old mining towns that dot Highway 49, the road known as the Golden Chain.

Hearst Castle (San Simeon).

William Randolph Hearst's lavish and eccentric home, filled with art from around the world, is open daily for tours.

Point Reyes National Seashore This rugged peninsula north of San Francisco has scenic cliffs, meadows, lakes, woods, and long beaches pounded by surf.

Redwood National Park (near Crescent City). This park in the northwest corner of the state has 76,862 acres of old- and new-growth coast redwoods, the tallest trees on earth. Wild beaches edge the forests along the Pacific.

Sequoia and Kings Canyon National Parks (Three Rivers). The sequoias in these adjoining parks are not as tall as coast redwoods but are larger in sheer bulk. Looming above them is Mt. Whitney, tallest peak in the contiguous U.S.

Wineries (Napa, Sonoma, Lake, and Mendocino counties). Tastings are available throughout California wine country, which has more than 700 wineries.

Yosemite National Park This awe-inspiring stretch of the Sierra Nevada is a wonderland of waterfalls, granite formations, forests, cliffs, and mountains.

Colorado

America's rooftop,
the state nearest heaven

Colorado bestrides the Rocky Mountains with a foot in two different Americas. Its eastern edge is firmly planted in the rolling plains of the nation's agricultural heartland. Yet at its western border, 385 miles away, Colorado is a land of lonely buttes and mesas amid the picturesque plateaus of the desert. In between is the mountainous terrain where the Rockies, which stretch all the way from New Mexico into Canada, reach their greatest height. Colorado has an average elevation of 6,800 feet, with some 1,100 peaks soaring more than 10,000 feet high, and 53 peaks above 14,000 feet — making it literally the state nearest heaven. And although its scenery has made it a magnet for tourists from all over the world, until the 1860's it was hardly known.

THE FORBIDDING LAND

For many years Colorado seemed too stark and desolate to attract even the hardiest of explorers and settlers. As early as the 17th and 18th centuries, French trappers moved west from the Mississippi and Spaniards north from Santa Fe. But both groups were turned away by the proud and warring Indians of the Colorado plains and in the mountain valleys by the powerful Utes.

In 1820, when Maj. Stephen H. Long led an expedition across the high plains in the eastern part of the state, he pronounced it a useless desert, unfit for cultivation. The writer Washington Irving, commenting on the report of Capt. Benjamin L. E. de Bonneville's explorations in 1837, said that the Rocky

In a burst of beauty high in the San Juan Mountains, Ice Lake basin comes to life each summer with blue columbines, the Colorado state flower.

Mountains would always remain a wilderness because "there is nothing to tempt the cupidity of the white man."

THE GLINT OF GOLD

Irving was wrong. There was temptation aplenty in 1858, when William Green Russell saw the glint of gold in Cherry Creek at a site that is now in modern Denver. Within a year some 100,000 hopeful souls poured into the territory, and the slogan of the day was "Pikes Peak or Bust!" Miners kept their eyes peeled for that landmark mountain because it was the first of the Rockies visible from the plain: when they sighted it, they were sure gold would soon be in their grasp. But often prospectors headed home broke, grumbling that the reports of gold were a hoax. Then a fresh strike brought

Mountain environments vary with elevation and the direction they face. Spruce and fir trees, such as those above, grow at altitudes of 6,000 to 9,000 feet on slopes that face north. At the same elevation, south-facing slopes are sunnier, drier, and covered with junipers and ponderosa pines. Coniferous forests help prevent erosion by shading the winter's snow so that it melts slowly, thus limiting torrential spring run-offs.

the rush to a new fever. Denver sprouted up to serve the miners, becoming the "Queen City of the Plains," a rough-edged town with an overlay of gentility.

"AN ATMOSPHERE OF ELIXIR"

By the 1860's the supposedly useless eastern part of the territory — dry plains covered with endless grasslands — was coming into its own as a cattle range. Herds were driven north from Texas into Colorado, and investors from the East and Europe, particularly England, put up huge sums to finance what was to become a thriving cattle industry.

Many of these investors came to inspect the territory where they were spending their money. Only then were the mountains appreciated for something more than their commercial potential; their astonishing physical beauty and purity of air were enough in themselves. "An atmosphere of elixir," proclaimed the New England journalist Samuel Bowles in his book *The Switzerland of America*, published in 1869. Colorado, he wrote, was the place where the jaded traveler could find "new and exhilarating scenes."

Colorado's climate was called "the very quintessence of perfection"; the air was said to be like champagne and so healthful that it not only cured but actually prevented disease. Colorado Springs, a resort then referred to as "Newport in the Rockies," attracted throngs of visitors seeking rejuvenation. Vacationers there looked so healthy that P. T. Barnum quipped, "Two thirds of them came here to die, and they can't do it."

The railroad between Durango and Silverton was built in 1881 – 82 to transport gold and silver ore from the San Juan Mountains. Today it carries tourists into an area that is still a wilderness, otherwise accessible only on horseback or on foot.

BLOWIN' IN THE WIND: COLORADO'S GREAT SAND DUNES

The tallest sand dunes in North America lie hundreds of miles from the nearest ocean — in the Colorado Rockies. When the glaciers melted at the end of the last ice age — about 12,000 years ago — the swollen Rio Grande carried millions of tons of silt and sand into the San Luis Valley. Once the waters subsided, the prevailing southwest winds blew the sand northward against the Sangre de Cristo Mountains in a process that continues to this day. As the wind collides with the mountains, it loses its speed and dumps the sand at their base. Today, these mammoth hills of sand are nearly 700 feet high and cover 55 square miles.

The wind also sculpts the crests of the dunes. Swirling upward across a dune, it gains speed and strength and picks up more sand. As the wind clears the peak, much of the sand drops suddenly, giving the dune a steeper far side.

Although the crests may shift several feet a day, the bulk of the dunes is stationary, in part because the mass of sand retains so much moisture that only the top few inches are dry enough to be carried off by the wind.

The bizarre rock formations of the Garden of the Gods, near Colorado Springs, were formed, the Ute Indians believed, when manitou, a supernatural force, turned the giants who invaded their land into stone. In the view at right, masses of weather-worn sandstone frame Pikes Peak in the distance.

The brilliant yellow of an aspen forest glows in Snowmass Canyon near the town of Aspen. Fall foliage is one of the splendors of the mountains.

While cattle barons and vacationers were civilizing the eastern plains and the Rockies, the part of Colorado west of the Rocky Mountains remained relatively untouched. Here, the convoluted land slopes down to the vast Colorado Plateau — a desolate but beautiful terrain of formidable gorges, jagged rock towers, and mesas jutting into a cobalt-blue sky. Ending in sagebrush flats that stretch into central Utah on the west, the land is host not only to the mighty Colorado River but also to the Gunnison, which over millions of years has cut a startling 53-mile-long gash in the earth — the awe-inspiring Black Canyon of the Gunnison. This gorge is such a fearsome sight that Indians and settlers alike believed that no one who entered it could come out alive. The walls are so sheer and the canyon so

Rocky Mountain meadows abound in fireweed and other wildflowers during the summer.

Sandstone pinnacles carved by thousands of years of erosion dominate the harsh wilderness of the Colorado National Monument, near Grand Junction. The highest of these natural spires is Independence Rock, pictured above, which towers to a height of 565 feet.

LAND OF THE GIANTS

Some 140 million years ago the desolate mountains on the Colorado-Utah border were a verdant plain crisscrossed with shallow rivers. Dinosaurs lived there then: the lumbering stegosaurus, with bony plates along its spine; the vegetarian camarasaurus (left); and the meat-eating allosaurus.

Millions of years later floods buried scores of these dinosaurs in muddy riverbanks. Slowly, the ocean inundated the plain and covered the dinosaur remains with thousands of feet of sediment that eventually turned to sandstone.

Then, about 65 million years ago, after the waters had retreated, the sandstone buckled upward, part of the same movement of the earth's crust that created the Rocky Mountains. Exposed as craggy ridges, the stone began to erode, ultimately revealing its fossil record.

Dinosaur remains have been found throughout western Colorado at such places as Grand Junction and Rangely. The best place to see them is at Dinosaur National Monument, which straddles the Colorado-Utah border north of the town of Dinosaur.

deep that the sun shines into it for only a few minutes each day, leaving parts of the interior in a perpetual gloom.

THE MAKING OF THE ROCKIES

For all of the stark beauty of western Colorado, the high ground of central Colorado is the state's real treasure. The Rocky Mountains were created when an older, worn-down mountain range was pushed upward, causing cracking and folding in the layers of sandstone, shale, and limestone that had formed in the bed of an ancient sea. In this phase of mountain building 70 to 10 million years ago, scenery was fashioned that remains almost unequaled anywhere else.

In some parts of the state, the land was shaped more abruptly. The San Juan Mountains, which extend over some 10,000 square miles of southwestern Colorado, were formed by volcanoes. This range presents some of the wildest beauty in the state, with vividly colored formations of striking, needlelike spires and jumbled piles of fallen rock.

Ice also helped to sculpt the landscape, as glaciers formed in the Rockies ground out U-shaped valleys, sheered off the faces of the mountains to form cliffs, and carved out depressions that filled up with water to form lakes. Five small glaciers can still be seen in Rocky Mountain National Park.

THE FIVE RANGES

The Colorado Rockies created by this geological turmoil are actually five separate ranges: the Front, Park, and Sawatch ranges, and the San Juan and Sangre de Cristo mountains.

The Front Range is the easternmost, running in a north-south direction more than halfway down the center of the state. More than 80 percent of the state's 3.4 million inhabitants live east of this range, in a strip not much more than 30 miles wide and 150 miles long. Three of Colorado's most populous cities lie here: Colorado Springs, Pueblo, and Denver, the capital and a major financial center.

The Front Range is paralleled to the west by the Park Range, which is itself paralleled farther west by the Sawatch Mountains, where the resorts of Aspen and Vail nestle.

The massive grandeur of the Rockies is most apparent from above, as in this early autumn view of Mount Sneffels near Ouray in the San Juan Mountains.

High in the Sangre de Cristo Mountains, a climber pits his courage and endurance against a craggy rock face as Crestone Needle looms in the background. Challenging peaks attract climbers from all over the world to Colorado.

In the southwestern part of the state, the last two ranges, the Sangre de Cristo Mountains and the San Juans, enclose the San Luis Valley, the largest of Colorado's four "parks" — high valleys walled by mountains. The Rio Grande, which springs forth as a stream in the San Juans, meanders through the valley on its voyage to the Gulf of Mexico, providing drinking water for livestock and irrigation for sprawling fields of potatoes, sorghum, alfalfa, corn, and peppers.

MOUNTAINS OR MIRAGE?

Beyond their scenic splendor, the five ranges of the Rockies form a great geographic and climatic barrier: the Continental Divide, the towering north-south ridge that separates the raindrops that eventually flow to the Pacific Ocean from those that head for the Atlantic. The mountains also divert winds and storms from the Great Plains.

The cool, dry air of the divide — the air that drew the Europeans to this wilderness a mile and more above sea level — plays tricks on the eyes of lowlanders. The very mountains become mirages. Even Pikes Peak was seen from the plains as "a small, blue cloud" — a cloud that never moved — by Zebulon Pike and his party of explorers as they moved westward across the plains in 1806.

Years later, the panorama seen from the top of a now-familiar Pikes Peak inspired one of the country's most famous anthems. The author was Katherine Lee Bates, a professor of English literature at Wellesley College, who took a wagon ride to the top in the year of 1893. "Then and there," she wrote, "as I was looking out over the sealike expanse of fertile country spreading away so far under these ample skies, the opening lines of the hymn floated into my mind." The hymn was "America the Beautiful."

Glistening and twisting, Nellie Creek in the San Juan Mountains is typical of Rocky Mountain streams, many of which eventually swell into major rivers. The Arkansas, Colorado, North Platte, South Platte, and Rio Grande rivers all have their sources in the Colorado Rockies.

COLORADO

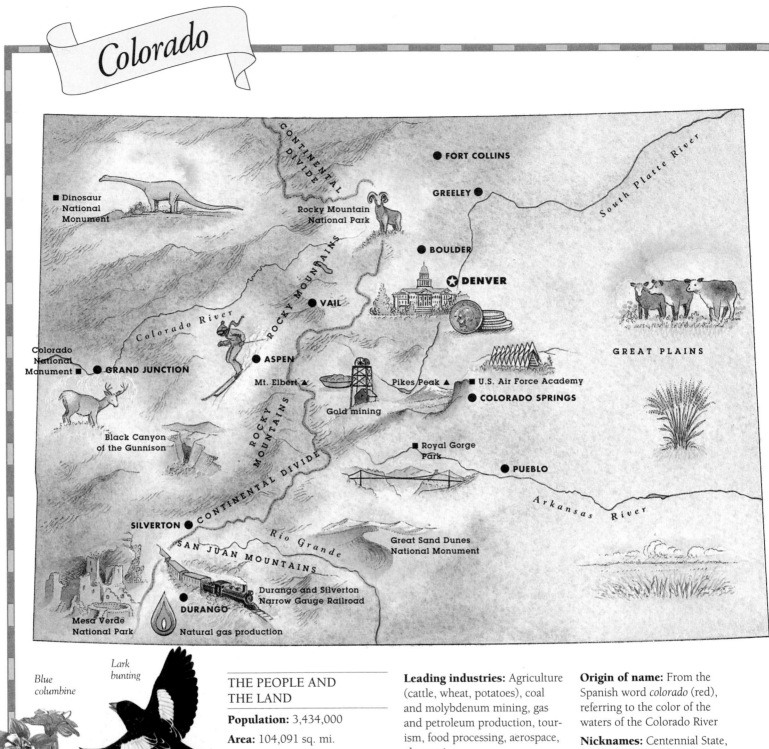

Blue columbine

Lark bunting

State flag

THE PEOPLE AND THE LAND

Population: 3,434,000

Area: 104,091 sq. mi.

Population per sq. mi.: 33

Capital and largest city: Denver (pop. 1,900,000)

Major rivers: Arkansas, Colorado, Rio Grande, South Platte

Elevation: 3,350 ft. (Arkansas River) to 14,433 ft. (Mt. Elbert)

Leading industries: Agriculture (cattle, wheat, potatoes), coal and molybdenum mining, gas and petroleum production, tourism, food processing, aerospace, electronics

Bird: Lark bunting

Flower: Blue columbine

Tree: Blue spruce

Motto: *Nil Sine Numine* (Nothing Without Providence)

Song: "Where the Columbines Grow"

Origin of name: From the Spanish word *colorado* (red), referring to the color of the waters of the Colorado River

Nicknames: Centennial State, Highest State, Rocky Mountain State, Switzerland of America

INFORMATION

Colorado Tourism Board
1625 Broadway
Suite 1700
Denver, CO 80202
Telephone: 303-592-5410

HISTORICAL HIGHLIGHTS

1706 Spain claims Colorado.

1803 After gaining control of the territory from Spain during Napoleonic Wars, France sells eastern Colorado to U.S. as part of Louisiana Purchase.

1806 Lt. Zebulon M. Pike's expedition sights Rocky Mountains.

1848 U.S. wins western Colorado as a result of victory in Mexican War.

1859 Gold rush! Discovery of gold at Cherry Creek lures prospectors by the thousands.

1876 Colorado enters Union as the 38th state.

1906 U.S. Mint in Denver distributes its first coins.

1915 Rocky Mountain National Park is established.

1958 U.S. Air Force Academy finds a permanent home near Colorado Springs.

1966 North American Aerospace Defense Command (NORAD) completes its underground headquarters in Cheyenne Mountain.

1985 The Frying Pan – Arkansas irrigation project, designed to carry water from the Rockies to Colorado's eastern plains, is completed.

FAMOUS SONS AND DAUGHTERS

Molly Brown (1867 – 1932). After surviving the *Titanic* disaster in the North Atlantic, Molly Brown declared herself "unsinkable." The legend of her life is told in the musical *The Unsinkable Molly Brown.*

M. Scott Carpenter (1925 –). In 1962 navy commander Carpenter became the second American astronaut to orbit the earth.

Jack Dempsey (1895 – 1983). Born in Manassa (and later known as the Manassa Mauler), Dempsey was a popular world heavyweight boxing champion from 1919 to 1926.

Douglas Fairbanks (1883 – 1939).

Handsome and athletic, the producer-actor played the swashbuckling hero in movies that made him "King of Hollywood" in the 1920's and 1930's.

Ouray (c. 1833 – 80). A Ute chief, fluent in English and Spanish, Ouray led his people in negotiations with settlers.

Byron R. White (1917 –). President Kennedy appointed this former professional football player and Rhodes scholar to the Supreme Court in 1962.

Paul Whiteman (1891 – 1967). By introducing jazz into orchestral music, Whiteman helped usher in the Jazz Age of the 1920's. He commissioned Gershwin's *Rhapsody in Blue* and conducted its premiere in 1924.

ODDITIES AND SPECIALTIES

Colorado's average elevation of 6,800 feet is the highest of any state. Three-quarters of the land in the U.S. that is more than 10,000 feet above sea level is in Colorado.

Colorado is emerging as the U.S. mountain bike capital, with ski trails serving as bike trails in summer. Ski lifts are convenient for transporting bikers and bikes to mountaintops.

A silver nugget found in Aspen in 1894 weighed 1,840 pounds — the largest ever discovered in North America.

The U.S. Mint in Denver makes up to 40 million coins a day.

PLACES TO VISIT, THINGS TO DO

Black Canyon of the Gunnison National Monument (Montrose). This 53-mile-long canyon carved by the Gunnison River is in places as much as 3,000 feet deep. Roads and foot trails on either side provide views of the chasm.

Colorado National Monument (Fruita). More than 20,000 acres of beautifully colored rock formations, some of them 500 feet high, are preserved here. The 23-mile-long Rim Rock Drive offers sweeping vistas.

Dinosaur National Monument (Dinosaur). Named for the dinosaur fossils discovered in the area, the monument contains 326 square miles of canyons and river country.

Durango and Silverton Narrow Gauge Railroad (Silverton). A 45-mile ride between old mining towns on this historic train allows magnificent views of mountain scenery.

Great Sand Dunes National Monument (Mosca). Here are the highest sand dunes in North America, rising up to 700 feet.

Mesa Verde National Park (Cortez). Indian cliff-top dwellings, some more than 1,000 years old, are preserved here. From one point visitors can see a panoramic view of four states.

Pikes Peak (Colorado Springs). Travel up one of the West's most famous mountains by foot, car, bus, or cog railway.

Rocky Mountain National Park (Estes Park). This nature-lover's paradise contains more than 400 square miles of spectacular mountain scenery — with pines and aspens, waterfalls and lakes, tundra and meadows, bighorn sheep and elks. Trail Ridge Road, 11 miles of which crosses country above 10,000 feet, is the highest through road in the U.S.

Royal Gorge Park (Canon City). The Royal Gorge plunges to a depth of 1,055 feet. North America's highest suspension bridge, built in 1929, spans the Arkansas River here.

Skiing This sport is synonymous with Colorado, which has two of the nation's most famous winter resorts — Vail and the Aspen/Snowmass area. More than 10 million lift tickets are issued in Colorado each year.

Connecticut

Rolling hills and old New England villages

T he only street in America more beautiful than North Street in Litchfield is South Street in Litchfield." So said writer Sinclair Lewis about two of the village's postcard-pretty streets. With their pleasant arrangement of clapboard houses, picket fences, steepled churches, and well-kept squares, Litchfield and other Connecticut towns are among New England's treasures. Puritans founded many of them, and even today the typical Connecticut village exemplifies order and simplicity — a legacy of the Puritan ways that prevailed in the state for more than 200 years, longer than anyplace else on the continent.

RELIGIOUS FREEDOM AND ELBOW ROOM

The quest for religious freedom is often said to have lured Thomas Hooker and his followers from Massachusetts Bay to the Connecticut Valley, but what the pioneers also sought was fertile soil and elbow room. Settling in Hartford, Wethersfield, and Windsor in the 1630's, the Puritans built their towns according to uniform plans, with a centrally located church and facing town green, or common, surrounded by the homes of the town's elite. Today Connecticut has 169 towns, many of them built on this pattern.

The third-smallest state, only 73 miles north to south and 100 miles east to west, Connecticut is shaped roughly like a rectangle, its jagged 253-mile southern boundary washed by Long Island Sound. In the densely populated southwestern corner, Darien, Greenwich, and other bedroom communities are home to

The pride of the reconstructed historic village at Mystic Seaport is the Charles W. Morgan, *an 1841 whaling bark that sailed to the Arctic and the South Pacific.*

Once part of a dense forest, the open fields of Connecticut's farmlands are a monument to the hard work of its early settlers. Orchards of pears, peaches, or apples, such as this one near Wallingford, are often seen amid the state's rolling hills. Fruit is Connecticut's fourth largest crop.

affluent suburbanites who commute to nearby New York City. Eastward, on the coast, are picturesque seafaring towns — Essex, Mystic, Stonington — where the pace is more leisurely and village life centers on boats.

STONE FENCES IN FORESTS

Rising from the busy coastal plain a series of low ranges and hills forms a classic rural setting. Stone fences solemnly mark property lines or retreat into forests — reminders of how mightily farmers once labored to clear the land. Even more bucolic is the far northwest corner, where the Litchfield Hills offer panoramic vistas into neighboring New York and Massachusetts. In fall, thousands of tourists, whom the locals call leaf peepers, journey to Litchfield, Kent, Cornwall, and their environs to see the dazzling red and yellow display offered by forests of maple and oak. Even today, more than half of Connecticut is forested, mainly with deciduous trees.

But the state's greatest natural asset is its splendid network of riverways that includes the Connecticut, Housatonic, Naugatuck, and Thames. Chief among them is the Connecticut, which rises in northern New Hampshire and sweeps down a 410-mile course to Long Island Sound, bisecting the state of Connecticut. The rich alluvial soil left in its wake was what the Puritans sought.

This fine river system, with its bounty of cheap water power, transformed Norwich, Waterbury, Bridgeport, and other towns into important manufacturing cities and made Connecticut a leading industrial state in the mid-19th century. Earlier, the people of Connecticut had discovered that most of the land outside the fertile river valleys was far too poor for farming. Industrious and enterprising, they turned to commerce — best represented by the Yankee peddlers who traveled across the young nation on wagons loaded with pots and pans, tools and nails, hats and

Throughout New England, stately maples line rural lanes, looking as if they have been standing on the land forever. In fact, most of the trees were planted as saplings to shade the byways after the forest was cleared. Many of these maples are now almost 200 years old.

Viewed from above on an autumn evening, Litchfield is the model of a well-ordered New England village centered on the Congregational Church and spacious town common.

THE CHARTER OAK — SYMBOL OF LIBERTY

In 1662 King Charles II of England granted Connecticut its own charter, entitling the colony to extensive self-government. Nonetheless, in 1687 not long after Sir Edmund Andros was appointed governor of all the New England colonies, he marched to Hartford and in the name of the new king, James II, demanded the charter back.

At the evening meeting where the document was to be relinquished, the lights suddenly went out. By the time they were relit, the charter had vanished. According to legend, Joseph Wadsworth, a Hartford resident, snatched the charter in the darkness and hid it in the hollow of a nearby oak.

The disappearance of the charter did not prevent Governor Andros from revoking it, but both his regime and that of James II were short-lived, and in 1689, after the Glorious Revolution in England, the colony's charter was restored to Connecticut.

The tree where Wadsworth had hidden the charter became a cherished local symbol of the struggle for self-government. Known as the Charter Oak, it had a circumference of 33 feet when it was felled by a storm in 1856. Afterward all sorts of objects were said to have been cut from its wood. Mark Twain once quipped that he had seen "enough Charter Oak to build a plank road from Hartford to Salt Lake City."

This painting of the oak was done about 1846 by Frederick Edwin Church, whose ancestors were among the original founders of Hartford.

combs. Still, it was not until the beginning of the American Industrial Revolution that Connecticut really came into its own.

YANKEE INGENUITY

Connecticut did not just benefit from the revolution; it helped create it. Hartford native Eli Whitney, inventor of the cotton gin, pioneered the use of interchangeable parts in the manufacture of firearms. His innovation was just one step away from the assembly line and mass production. American steel manufacturing began in Connecticut, and over the years Connecticut entrepreneurs invented or pro-

duced a mind-boggling number of other products: revolvers, clocks, bicycles, sewing machines, postage meters, shaving soap, jet engines, and nuclear submarines. Thus did Yankee ingenuity earn Connecticut a place among the nation's most prosperous states.

Hartford, the state capital since colonial times, has also been its economic center. Mark Twain made his home there, and although he traveled widely throughout the United States, Hawaii, Europe, and even to Egypt, he deemed Hartford "the prettiest town." Today its shiny glass and steel office towers are headquarters for some 50 companies whose business has

long been synonymous with the city — insurance. The city's insurance industry got its reputation for reliability in 1835, when a fire in New York City destroyed hundreds of buildings. Many insurance companies defaulted on their obligations, but one, the Hartford Insurance Company, paid every claim.

Connecticut residents, even those who live in Hartford or some other modern city, cherish their semirural surroundings and try to preserve them. That task has been easier since 1960, when local law was placed firmly in the hands of the villages and towns with which Connecticut is so closely identified.

Weathered farms like this one recall Connecticut's agricultural heritage. Although today Connecticut has only 3,800 farms — there were more than 20,000 fifty years ago — it has some 50,000 horses, giving it one of the greatest "equine densities" of any state, nearly 10 horses per square mile.

Connecticut

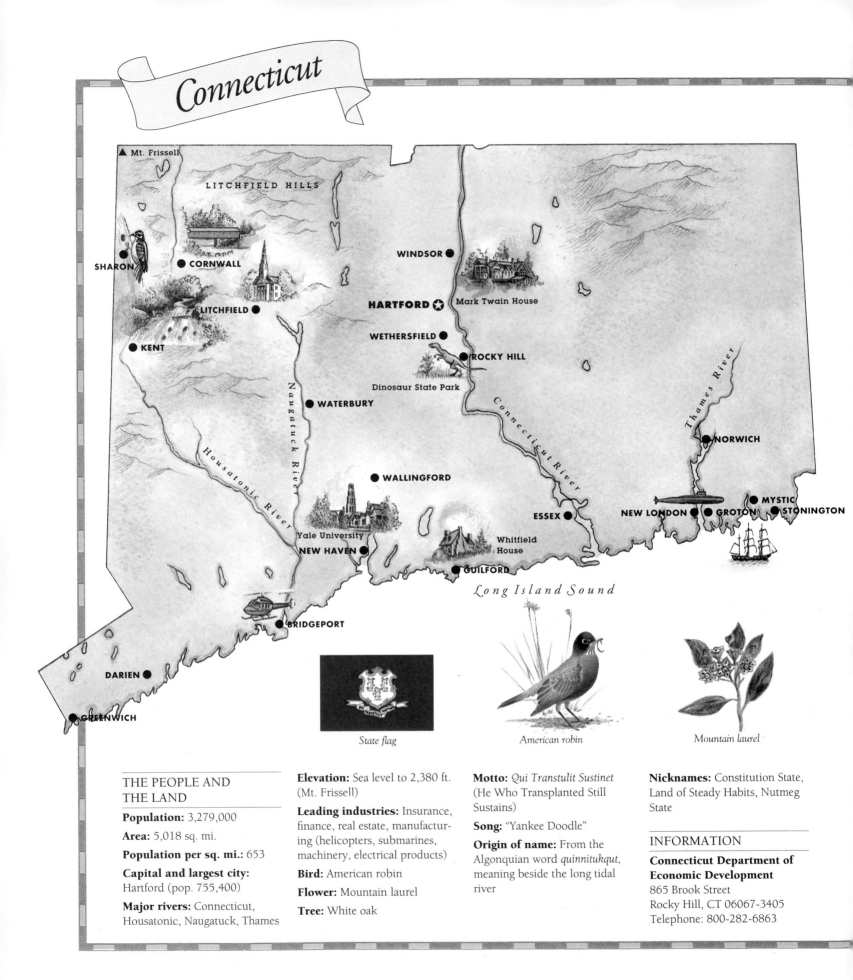

▲ Mt. Frissell

LITCHFIELD HILLS

SHARON

CORNWALL

WINDSOR

HARTFORD ☆ Mark Twain House

LITCHFIELD

WETHERSFIELD

KENT

ROCKY HILL

Dinosaur State Park

WATERBURY

Naugatuck River

Housatonic River

Connecticut River

Thames River

NORWICH

WALLINGFORD

MYSTIC

ESSEX

NEW LONDON GROTON STONINGTON

Yale University

Whitfield House

NEW HAVEN

GUILFORD

Long Island Sound

BRIDGEPORT

DARIEN

GREENWICH

State flag

American robin

Mountain laurel

THE PEOPLE AND THE LAND

Population: 3,279,000

Area: 5,018 sq. mi.

Population per sq. mi.: 653

Capital and largest city: Hartford (pop. 755,400)

Major rivers: Connecticut, Housatonic, Naugatuck, Thames

Elevation: Sea level to 2,380 ft. (Mt. Frissell)

Leading industries: Insurance, finance, real estate, manufacturing (helicopters, submarines, machinery, electrical products)

Bird: American robin

Flower: Mountain laurel

Tree: White oak

Motto: *Qui Transtulit Sustinet* (He Who Transplanted Still Sustains)

Song: "Yankee Doodle"

Origin of name: From the Algonquian word *quinnitukqut,* meaning beside the long tidal river

Nicknames: Constitution State, Land of Steady Habits, Nutmeg State

INFORMATION

Connecticut Department of Economic Development
865 Brook Street
Rocky Hill, CT 06067-3405
Telephone: 800-282-6863

HISTORICAL HIGHLIGHTS

1614 The explorer Adrian Block sails up Connecticut River and claims land for the Dutch.

1633 Dutch build fort and trading post at present-day Hartford.

1633 Colonists from Massachusetts establish first English settlement in Connecticut Valley.

1636 Thomas Hooker and his congregation from Massachusetts found Hartford.

1639 Representatives of Hartford, Wethersfield, and Windsor meet to adopt the Fundamental Orders, or laws — a written constitution establishing popular government.

1647 One Alse Young is "arraigned and executed at Hartford for a witch" — the first woman to be put to death as a witch in New England.

1662 Connecticut receives a charter from King Charles II.

1701 Collegiate School, later to become Yale College, is founded in Branford.

1784 Tapping Reeve establishes America's first law school at Litchfield.

1788 Connecticut becomes fifth state to ratify Constitution.

1806 Noah Webster publishes the first American dictionary at New Haven.

1878 The first telephone exchange in the world begins operation in New Haven with 21 subscribers.

1910 U.S. Coast Guard Academy moves to New London.

1954 The *Nautilus,* first atomic-powered submarine, is built and launched at Groton.

1979 Connecticut bans building of new nuclear power plants.

FAMOUS SONS AND DAUGHTERS

Phineas Taylor Barnum (1810 – 91). The man whose name is synonymous with showmanship began his career as an exhibitor of human oddities, including Siamese twins and the midget Commodore Nutt, and crowned it by creating his famous circus "The Greatest Show on Earth."

Samuel Colt (1814 – 62). Inventor of the revolving barrel pistol, Colt built up a successful armament business after selling 1,000 revolvers to the government during the Mexican War.

Charles Goodyear (1800 – 60). The inventor of the process for vulcanizing rubber — which prevents it from melting and sticking in the heat — saved the failing rubber industry but died in poverty himself.

Nathan Hale (1755 – 76). This Revolutionary War spy was only 21 years old when he was captured by the British with plans of their fortifications. From the gallows he said, "I only regret that I have but one life to lose for my country."

J. Pierpont Morgan (1837 – 1913). Founder of a legendary financial and industrial empire, Morgan was both criticized and credited for saving the U.S. economy in the Panic of 1907.

Harriet Beecher Stowe (1811 – 96). Her desire to help American slaves prompted her to write the best-selling, antislavery novel *Uncle Tom's Cabin* (1852).

Noah Webster (1758 – 1843). His *Elementary Spelling Book* won enduring fame. The "blue-backed speller" sold 15 million copies between 1792 and 1837 and standardized American spelling. His monumental *American Dictionary of the English Language* (1828) included 12,000 words never before recorded.

Eli Whitney (1765 – 1825). His invention of the cotton gin (1793) gave the South a profitable crop, while his use of interchangeable parts in gunmaking foreshadowed assembly-line mass production.

ODDITIES AND SPECIALTIES

Connecticut has no less than 1,000 colonial landmarks.

Ever since the U.S. Patent Office opened in 1790, Connecticut citizens have filed more patents per capita than inhabitants of any other state.

In 1901 Connecticut legislators enacted the first U.S. auto law: speed limit, 12 miles per hour, 8 miles per hour in cities.

The football tackling dummy was invented at Yale in 1889 by Amos Alonzo Stagg, who also introduced the T-formation.

Connecticut produced many pioneers who won prominence in other states. In the 1831-33 Congress, one third of the senators were Connecticut-born.

PLACES TO VISIT, THINGS TO DO

Dinosaur State Park (Rocky Hill). Here are some of the best-preserved dinosaur tracks anywhere, plus a nature trail.

Kent Falls State Park (near Kent). Besides the scenic falls, there is a trail leading to a view of the Housatonic Valley.

Litchfield This village seems almost untouched by the 20th century. On the second Saturday in July visitors can tour some of the houses.

Mark Twain House (Hartford). The author wrote his most famous books, *Huckleberry Finn* and *Tom Sawyer,* in this redbrick Victorian fantasy, which he built.

Mystic Seaport (Mystic). Old-time sailing ships and a restored 19th-century whaling village recreate Connecticut's colorful maritime heritage.

Northeast Audubon Center (Sharon). Nearly 700 protected acres in northwestern Connecticut offer a sanctuary for plants and wildlife and foot trails for nature lovers and walkers.

Peabody Museum, Yale University (New Haven). One of the largest and oldest natural history museums, it houses a world-famous collection of dinosaur remains.

U.S.S. *Nautilus* Memorial (Groton). The decommissioned nuclear submarine, the world's first nuclear-powered vessel, is open to visitors.

Whitfield House (Guilford). The home of Rev. Henry Whitfield, this 1639 house is the oldest stone house in New England.

Delaware

A thimbleful of scenic beauty and serenity

Delawareans relish their state's nickname Small Wonder, taking as much pride in the small as in the wonder. Yellowstone National Park, they point out, is larger than diminutive Delaware, as are two Alaskan islands. Despite its tiny size, however — only Rhode Island is smaller — Delaware offers a wealth of beauty and a bonus of serenity. Even though it edges the populated corridor between Washington, D.C., and New York City, Delaware retains areas as unblemished today as they were a century ago.

UPSTATE, DOWNSTATE

In the north and west, Delaware is part of the hilly Piedmont province of the Appalachians. Here old fields break the rhythm set by rolling woodland knolls. During the 19th century, the rushing streams of these foothills powered flour and paper mills, whose efficiency prompted the Frenchman Éleuthère Irénée du Pont to set up a black gunpowder mill along the Brandywine Creek.

Today northern Delaware, in large part because of the Du Pont company's successes, is a bustling urban center with Wilmington at its hub. The outskirts of the city, however, offer the beauty of sprawling historic estates, many of which, like the Du Pont estate Winterthur, north of Wilmington, are now museums. This region, so like a quiet French watercolor, is called Château Country.

Northern Delaware comprises only one-sixth of the state. It is separated from southern Delaware by the Chesapeake and Delaware Canal, which links the Chesapeake Bay to the

A winter sun highlights snow-covered barrier dunes near Indian River Inlet, south of Cape Henlopen.

Giant bald cypress trees, which thrive in wet conditions, reach the northern limit of their range in Delaware's Great Cypress Swamp.

Delaware River. Southward from this busy shipping channel spread the farming tracts of central Delaware. The modern poultry industry was born here in Sussex County in 1923, when Mrs. Wilmer Steele raised a brood of 500 chicks for quick sale.

Delaware's expansive farmland (50 percent of the state is still agricultural) ends in the east, where the waters of Delaware Bay lap into the fertile tidal marshes of the Atlantic flyway. In autumn, the piercing calls of migrating wigeons, teals, mallards, and geese fill the air above two national wildlife refuges, Bombay Hook and Prime Hook .

Tucked behind the barrier island that stretches along Delaware's Atlantic coast, the Rehoboth, Indian River, and Little Assawoman bays finger their way through low-lying land that offers tranquil sanctuaries for skyscraping loblolly pines and white-tailed deer. The waters of these bays are a playground, dotted with the colorful sails of pleasure boats.

THE DELAWARE COAST

Where the rolling waves of the Atlantic meet the more serene waters of Delaware Bay a crook of land called Cape Henlopen protrudes. It is the northernmost point of Delaware's 25-mile coastline. Each May, hundreds of thousands of migratory shorebirds stop here, lured by newly laid horseshoe crab eggs. Bobbing their long bills into the sand, they dart, stilt-legged and chattering, along the beach. Many have flown here nonstop from South American wintering grounds. Above pinelands and cranberry bogs, an observation tower in Cape Henlopen State Park overlooks the Great Dune — at 80 feet the highest sand dune between Cape Hatteras and Cape Cod.

Not far from Cape Henlopen, Rehoboth Beach, the "nation's summer capital," for years has provided a haven for refugees from the oppressive summer heat of Washington, D.C. Most Delaware beaches are state-owned — the creeping shadows of late afternoon are from protective dune fencing, not multistoried hotels. Laughing gulls fill the sky, while human visitors share the sands with cottontail rabbits and hermit crabs. It is something Delaware does well, packing a lot into a little.

Hand-gathered bundles of cornstalks surround an Amish farm west of Dover after the harvest.

Bombay Hook National Wildlife Refuge, near Smyrna, is a major stopping place for birds migrating along the Atlantic flyway. Hundreds of great egrets feed here each August as they travel from their northern summer haunts to winter homes in the Southeast.

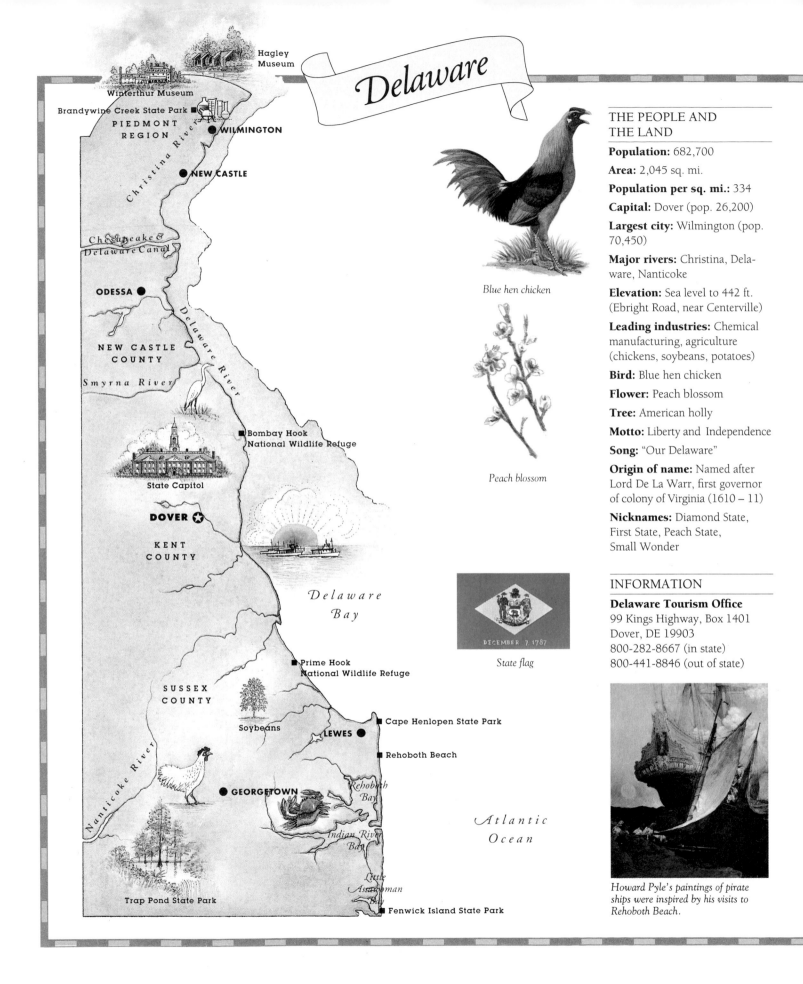

Delaware

Hagley Museum

Winterthur Museum

Brandywine Creek State Park

PIEDMONT REGION

Christina River

● **WILMINGTON**

● **NEW CASTLE**

Chesapeake & Delaware Canal

● **ODESSA**

Delaware River

NEW CASTLE COUNTY

Smyrna River

■ Bombay Hook National Wildlife Refuge

State Capitol

DOVER ✪

KENT COUNTY

Delaware Bay

■ Prime Hook National Wildlife Refuge

SUSSEX COUNTY

Soybeans

■ Cape Henlopen State Park

LEWES ●

■ Rehoboth Beach

● **GEORGETOWN**

Rehoboth Bay

Nanticoke River

Atlantic Ocean

Indian River Bay

Little Assawoman Bay

Trap Pond State Park

■ Fenwick Island State Park

THE PEOPLE AND THE LAND

Population: 682,700

Area: 2,045 sq. mi.

Population per sq. mi.: 334

Capital: Dover (pop. 26,200)

Largest city: Wilmington (pop. 70,450)

Major rivers: Christina, Delaware, Nanticoke

Elevation: Sea level to 442 ft. (Ebright Road, near Centerville)

Leading industries: Chemical manufacturing, agriculture (chickens, soybeans, potatoes)

Bird: Blue hen chicken

Flower: Peach blossom

Tree: American holly

Motto: Liberty and Independence

Song: "Our Delaware"

Origin of name: Named after Lord De La Warr, first governor of colony of Virginia (1610 – 11)

Nicknames: Diamond State, First State, Peach State, Small Wonder

Blue hen chicken

Peach blossom

DECEMBER 7, 1787

State flag

INFORMATION

Delaware Tourism Office
99 Kings Highway, Box 1401
Dover, DE 19903
800-282-8667 (in state)
800-441-8846 (out of state)

Howard Pyle's paintings of pirate ships were inspired by his visits to Rehoboth Beach.

HISTORICAL HIGHLIGHTS

1609 Searching for a trade route for a Dutch company, Henry Hudson explores Delaware Bay.

1631 A Dutch group establishes first European settlement on site of present-day Lewes.

1638 Swedes establish first permanent settlement, later taken over by the Dutch.

1664 English capture the Dutch holdings.

1682 The duke of York gives Delaware to William Penn. It becomes known as the Lower Three Counties of Pennsylvania.

1704 Penn lets Delaware have its own legislature.

1787 Delaware is first state to ratify U.S. Constitution.

1829 A canal connecting the Delaware River with Chesapeake Bay links Delaware farmers with urban markets.

1861 Though a slave-holding state, Delaware supports Union.

1935 Dr. W. H. Carothers, a Du Pont chemist, develops nylon.

1940 The Alfred I. du Pont Institute, one of the world's leading orthopedic hospitals, opens near Wilmington.

1951 Delaware Memorial Bridge links Delaware with New Jersey.

1971 Delaware passes Coastal Zone Act to protect wetlands against industrialization.

1983 University of Delaware celebrates its 150th anniversary.

FAMOUS SONS AND DAUGHTERS

Thomas Francis Bayard (1828 – 98). Like his grandfather and father, Bayard held office in the U.S. Senate (1869 – 85). He also served as Cleveland's secretary of state and as ambassador to Great Britain.

Henry Seidel Canby (1878 – 1961). A writer and critic, Canby was a founder of *The Saturday Review of Literature*. His books include *The Brandywine*.

Annie Jump Cannon (1863 – 1941). An astronomer known as the census taker of the sky, Cannon discovered and cataloged hundreds of stars while working at Harvard College.

John Dickinson (1732 – 1808). Called the penman of the Revolution, Dickinson wrote political articles and attended the Federal Constitutional Convention.

Éleuthère Irénée du Pont (1772 – 1834). A Parisian by birth, Du Pont started a gunpowder mill near Wilmington in 1802. His business developed into E. I. du Pont de Nemours & Company, now a leading manufacturer of chemicals and chemical products.

Thomas Garrett (1789 – 1871).

Garrett made his home part of the abolitionists' underground railroad that helped slaves travel to freedom.

Howard Pyle (1853 – 1911). A popular magazine illustrator, Pyle also wrote and illustrated books for young people. His work, which was inspired by the beauty of Delaware's piedmont, helped establish the Brandywine school of art.

Caesar Rodney (1728 – 84). Rodney rode all night to get to the Second Continental Congress in time to cast his tie-breaking vote for independence.

ODDITIES AND SPECIALTIES

The arc that bounds Delaware in the north was drawn in colonial days so that no part of Delaware's boundary with Pennsylvania would be closer than 12 miles to New Castle.

Wilmington's Old Swedes Church, built in 1698, is the oldest U.S. Protestant church still to hold regular services.

Swedish immigrants in southern Delaware built the first log cabins in the country.

Delaware was nicknamed the Peach State in the 1800's when orchards on the peninsula supplied nearby cities with the lush fruit. By 1900, however, the peach trees were gone, victims of a disease called the yellows.

In 1911 T. Coleman du Pont, fascinated by the automobile, spent $40 million to build a four-lane highway, then the most modern in the U.S., that ran the length of Delaware.

PLACES TO VISIT, THINGS TO DO

Bombay Hook National Wildlife Refuge (near Smyrna). More than 16,000 acres, mostly tidal salt marsh, are a haven for great egrets, snow geese, white-tailed deer, river otters, and other wildlife.

Brandywine Creek State Park (near Wilmington). Nature lovers can enjoy 784 acres of forests, meadows, and marshlands with a wide variety of flora and fauna, as well as the creek.

Fishing For saltwater fishermen Delaware Bay yields mackerel, bluefish, weakfish, and tautog. Rehoboth Bay and Indian River Bay are good for crabbing and clamming.

Hagley Museum and Eleutherian Mills (near Wilmington). The museum and E. I. du Pont's stone house are located on the banks of Brandywine Creek, on the site of Du Pont's first mill. Exhibits trace the evolution of industry in this region.

Lewes This historic city has a colorful historic district that includes the Zwaanendael Museum, a replica of a Dutch town hall.

Odessa Historic District Named for the Russian seaport, Odessa has fine examples of 18th- and 19th-century architecture, including the Brick Hotel with its famous collection of Victorian furniture.

Prime Hook National Wildlife Refuge (22 miles southeast of Dover). These coastal wetlands along Delaware Bay provide a breeding and winter habitat for migratory waterfowl.

Trap Pond State Park (Laurel). This park boasts the country's northernmost public natural stands of bald cypress.

Winterthur Museum and Gardens (near Wilmington). Henry Francis du Pont's exquisitely landscaped former country home has nearly 200 period rooms and a large collection of American decorative arts.

Florida

The exotic treasure of America's subtropics

Florida's destiny has been molded by water. Jutting into the Atlantic for 450 miles, this most celebrated of America's peninsulas has no point more than 60 miles from its coastline. Rainfall averages more than 50 inches a year, making Florida one of the wettest states. As a result, some 30,000 lakes are scattered throughout its interior, ranging from pint-sized ponds to the 700-square-mile Lake Okeechobee, the second largest natural freshwater body entirely within the United States after Lake Michigan. Water draining from Okeechobee flows slowly southward, creating the vast marshlands of the Everglades. A ribbon of islands, sandbars, and coral reefs festoons the coast, culminating 150 miles off the southern shore at the tip of the Keys.

These warm and sheltered waters attract one of the most astounding arrays of wildlife found anywhere in the world. Alligators, crocodiles, manatees, sea turtles, more than 350 species of birds, and 700 species of fish can be found in or around Florida's ponds and coastal waters. Since the turn of the century, Florida has also attracted another sort of inhabitant, whose numbers constantly grow. More than 40 million tourists now savor the state each year, most of them headed for the good life on its sunny coast.

AN 8,OOO-MILE COASTLINE

Curving 1,350 miles down the Atlantic and back up the Gulf of Mexico, Florida's coastline expands to over 8,000 miles when the shores of islands, bays, and lagoons are included.

Huge flocks of ibises and egrets — just two of Florida's more than 350 bird species — probe for fish and other food in the shallow waters of the Everglades.

Skin diving is popular along south Florida's reefs, a colorful, complex underwater world built from living and dead coral.

AMERICA: LAND OF BEAUTY AND SPLENDOR

The protected waters between these islands and the shore make an ideal habitat for wildlife, especially fish-eating birds such as herons, ibises, and pelicans. Coastal swamps, estuaries, and saltwater marshes create inviting environments for crabs, conches, clams, and oysters. Fertile shoals yield shrimps, lobsters, and scallops. Offshore waters also offer some of the world's best deep-sea fishing.

The Gulf Stream bestows its favors on Florida. A subtropical climate reigns over the southern end of the peninsula and the Keys, while the rest of the state is temperate. The climate has also made Florida a spectacular year-round playground and a magnet for business. As a result, Florida has become one of the fastest growing states.

MIAMI, CITY AMONG THE PALMS

The ever-burgeoning symbol of this boom is Miami. Yet just over 100 years ago, its site was a jungle of alligator-infested swamps. The persistence of an ebullient woman from Ohio touched off the explosive change.

Julia Tuttle owned considerable property in what is now downtown Miami. For years, she had tried unsuccessfully to persuade railroad magnate Henry Flagler to extend his rail lines south from the tony resort of Palm Beach. In 1894 disaster came to her aid.

An exceptionally harsh winter that year froze out tourists and blackened the citrus crop all the way down to Flagler's estate in Palm Beach. Farther south in Miami, however, fruit trees were still blooming. Cannily, Mrs. Tuttle sent Flagler a sprig of Miami orange blossoms and offered to give him half her property if he brought in the train. Within six years, Miami had its rail link.

At first development was slow; money was tight and World War I dominated national attention. But with the coming of the exuberant 1920's all that changed. Across the bay on a sandbar known as Miami Beach, millionaire developer Carl Fisher bulldozed the mangroves, filled in the lowlands, and laid the foundation for one of the most famous resort areas of the century. Tourism continues to thrive today, and contemporary Miami has ripened into a global metropolis.

Floating in a shallow slough, this alligator is probably basking in the sun rather than searching for its next meal, which may be a large fish, a turtle, a racoon, or an otter. One of the largest reptiles in North America, alligators are dangerous and can move quickly when approached.

The leaflike sea fan that seems to float beside this colorful queen angelfish is not an underwater plant but coral. The reefs along the Florida Keys abound in tropical fish, and their waters are so clear that divers can at times see 60 feet away.

Nine Mile Creek, above, is just one of the many waterways that wend through Ocala National Forest, a "wet desert" of porous sand that is covered with shallow pools and subtropical vegetation. The area offers outstanding largemouth-bass fishing.

Florida panthers, right, are the last cougars in the eastern United States. Equally at home in the pine forests, grassy wetlands, or tree-shaded hammocks of south Florida, they were hunted nearly to extinction before being protected as an endangered species. Today, they are rarely seen in the wild.

THE DEEP SOUTH OF FLORIDA'S NORTH

Northern Florida, on the other hand, exudes the leisurely aura of the Deep South, replete with pine forests and lofty oaks draped in Spanish moss above flowering dogwoods and brilliant azaleas.

The upper half of Florida's panhandle region is an area of gently rolling red clay hills where the state reaches its highest elevation — 345 feet above sea level. The Suwannee River rises in the north, in the Okefenokee Swamp on the Georgia border, and flows southwestward to the Gulf. When Stephen Foster composed his song about the "Old Folks at Home" on the "Swanee River," he never foresaw that in the next century more people would retire to Florida than to any other state.

From north to south, the interior is covered with lakes and swamps. In some places, underground rivers rise through caverns to create sparkling artesian springs. Of the 75 largest in the United States, 27 gush from Florida's depths. They are often of such crystalline purity that plants and fish can be seen clearly 80 feet below.

THE RIVER OF GRASS

Covering almost the entire tip of Florida south of Lake Okeechobee, the Everglades are the largest subtropical wilderness in the United States. Driving through the heart of Everglades National Park, one is struck by its flatness and openness. Vast grasslands, which look like the African savanna, stretch to the horizon. In fact, this is freshwater marshland and sloughs, a "river of grass" 100 miles long, 50 miles wide, and rarely more than a few inches deep. The land is so level that the water creeps southward at a rate of only half a foot per day.

Standing a few feet above the high-water level are hammocks, small islands covered with trees and shrubs. Their slight elevation, which holds them above summer floods, is the key to their different environment. In an area often only a few feet square, gumbo limbo trees (called tourist trees because their bark is red and peeling) rise beside hardwoods such as mahogany and live oaks.

Everglades wildlife is diverse. Lime-green tree frogs and colorfully banded tree snails

FLORIDA'S UNLIKELY MERMAIDS

Even in a state renowned for its exotic wildlife, manatees are objects of curiosity. Distantly related to elephants, these large and lumpy gentle giants belong to the only order of mammals other than whales that spend their entire lives in the water. The average adult — about 10 feet long and weighing 1,000 pounds — spends as much as eight hours a day grazing, during which it devours about 100 pounds of sea grass and other aquatic vegetation. With their voluminous appetites, manatees have occasionally been pressed into service to clear weed-choked waterways.

Floating just below the surface, manatees can look almost human. When Christopher Columbus explored Caribbean waters he mistook them for mermaids, reporting with disappointment on their lack of beauty. A thick, wrinkled hide all but covers the manatee's small eyes, and bristly hair covers its lips. Nevertheless, beauty in manatees, too, is only hide deep, and these amiable sea cows are also known for their graceful movement.

Sensitivity to water temperature limits the manatee's range. Although a few are found as far north as the Carolinas in summer, winter's chill drives them south. Yet even during the colder months there are perhaps no more than 1,200 manatees in all of Florida. Since 1973 they have been officially designated an endangered species. The chief threat to these slow-moving mammoths comes not from any natural predator but from their collisions with barges and the propellers of powerboats.

can be spied among the foliage. Lingering in the shade, a deer sniffs the air. Rare and endangered, the powerful cougar, or Florida panther, prowls the higher ground of the hammocks and pinelands.

In sloughs and waterholes, stately great blue herons stalk frogs and fish, while white ibises probe the shallows. After spearing a fish underwater, the long-necked anhinga spreads its black wings in the sun to dry so that it can fly again. From heights up to 100 feet, ospreys and bald eagles swoop down to snatch some wriggling fast food. Stubby white-plumed night herons, paddle-beaked roseate spoonbills, and purple gallinules augment the palette of the area's colorful bird species.

Also fishing, but from below, is the powerful reptile known as the keeper of the Everglades — the alligator, which despite its fearsome reputation, helps preserve wildlife. During the dry winter season, alligators burrow into the boggy muck, clearing out debris and creating waterholes that serve other animals. Once headed toward extinction, alligators now flourish to the point where they often turn up as uninvited backyard guests.

On the south and west coasts, mangrove forests seem to clamber into the sea atop their tangled roots, their foliage bristling over the myriad islands that dot Florida Bay. Here bottle-nosed dolphins cruise, and 1,000-pound manatees graze contentedly in nearby sheltered waterways.

The barred owl above is perched in its favorite habitat, a thick, wet woodland. Common in Florida, barred owls also are found as far away as western Canada. Generally, they feed on birds and small mammals, but they also may wade into pools to catch fish.

TROPICAL JEWELS

South of the mainland, a 150-mile-long necklace of islands curves between the Atlantic and the Gulf of Mexico. Known as the Keys from the Spanish word *cayo* meaning small island, the last of these landfalls peeks above the ocean only 90 miles from Cuba.

Commencing off Key Biscayne, the Florida Keys are North America's largest coral reef system. More than 40 species of coral thrive here together with hundreds of species of neon-hued tropical fish.

Here in the Keys, Florida literally wades out to sea — a fitting endpoint for a place whose beauty is so fully tied to the subtle balance between the land and water.

Among the most striking-looking of Florida's wading birds, roseate spoonbills hunt by touch rather than sight. Swinging their bills slowly back and forth in long arcs through the water, they scoop up small fish, shellfish, and crustaceans.

THE TREE THAT BUILDS NEW LAND

Throughout Florida's southern tip, dense mangrove forests blanket the coast, sheltering the shore from storm damage and serving as nurseries for fish, crabs, shrimps, and oysters. Unlike most trees, these broad-leaved evergreens are able to grow in salt water, making them ideal for the coastal environment. Of the three types of mangroves — red, black, and white — the red is the basis for their successful proliferation.

Called walking trees by the Seminole Indians, red mangroves seem to be marching along on a tangled bundle of roots. These not only provide the trees with food, water, and oxygen, they also build land. Each year, the average acre of red mangrove forest sheds about 7,000 pounds of leaves and twigs, which drop among the roots and are caught there. Shells and other ocean-carried debris are also swept in and snared. All of this organic material gathers around the dense root system and eventually decays, forming new land.

As the land builds up, the sturdy black mangroves take root, identifiable by the vertical tubes that grow from their roots. Farther inland, where the land is still higher and drier, the tall white mangroves find a home.

Since saltwater-hardy red mangrove seedlings can float unharmed for up to a year, experts believe that the Florida forests may have originated from seeds that drifted from Africa across the Atlantic.

At Cayo Costa, a barrier island on the Gulf coast outside Fort Myers, a lone whelk shell sparkles on the beach where the land and water gently merge to create a peaceful refuge. Even the clouds enhance the island's tranquil beauty.

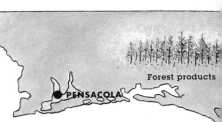
HISTORICAL HIGHLIGHTS

1513 After landing on coast, the explorer Ponce de León claims Florida for Spain.

1564 French Huguenots build Fort Caroline on St. Johns River.

1565 Pedro Menéndez de Avilés drives out French and founds city of St. Augustine.

1763 Spain gives Florida to Britain in exchange for Cuba.

1783 Spain takes Florida from Great Britain.

1821 After years of dispute, Spain cedes Florida to U.S.

1832 Seminole Indians refuse to leave their homeland for reservations in the West. This leads to Seminole Wars, which Indians lose 10 years later.

1845 Florida enters Union as 27th state.

1920 – 25 Land speculation leads to an unprecedented real-estate boom and greatly increases state's population.

1947 Everglades National Park is established.

1950 Newly established space center at Cape Canaveral sends off its first rocket.

1969 *Apollo 11* astronauts, launched from Cape Canaveral's Kennedy Space Center, become first people to walk on moon.

1971 Walt Disney World opens.

1983 – 85 Freezing weather and a fungus ruin the citrus crops.

1986 Space shuttle *Challenger* explodes, killing the entire crew on board.

1988 Space shuttle *Discovery* is launched successfully.

FAMOUS SONS AND DAUGHTERS

Mary McLeod Bethune

(1875 – 1955). The 17th child of emancipated slaves, Bethune became cofounder of Bethune-Cookman College. During the 1930's and 1940's she organized the National Council of Negro Women and served as President Franklin Roosevelt's special adviser on minority affairs.

Osceola (c. 1800 – 38). A brilliant guerrilla fighter, Osceola led the Seminole Indians during the Second Seminole War. Lured to a peace meeting, he was arrested by U.S. military officers. He died in prison.

Claude Pepper (1900 – 89). A stalwart champion of the rights of the elderly, Pepper served in the U.S. Senate (1936 – 51) and in the House of Representatives from 1963 until his death.

Marjorie Kinnan Rawlings (1896 – 1953). After a career as a journalist, Rawlings settled in rural Florida. Her novel *The Yearling*, about a boy's love for his deer, won a Pulitzer Prize in 1939.

Joseph W. Stilwell (1883 – 1946). Known as Vinegar Joe for his bluntness, Stilwell fought in both world wars and became an army general. During World War II he was U.S. commander in the China-Burma-India theater.

ODDITIES AND SPECIALTIES

Florida has possibly the world's largest and deepest spring: Wakulla Springs, near Tallahassee.

Florida's weather is so consistently fair that the St. Petersburg *Evening Standard* did not charge for its newspaper if the sun was not shining by press time. This "sunshine offer" remained in effect from 1910 until the paper closed in 1986.

Key limes, which grow in the Keys and other tropical areas, are the tangy basis of Key lime pie, a creamy dessert.

Florida's tourist population outnumbers its year-round residents by more than 3 to 1.

PLACES TO VISIT, THINGS TO DO

Biscayne National Park (near Homestead). Visitors can explore this marine preserve, with its living coral reefs, from glass-bottomed boats, or make a short trip to Elliott Key for swimming or a nature walk.

Walt Disney World (near Orlando). Combining the Magic Kingdom, Epcot Center, and the Disney – MGM Studios Theme Park, this extraordinary amusement center offers scores of rides, shows, and pavilions.

Everglades National Park (near Homestead). A unique subtropical wilderness, the Everglades are larger than Delaware. Their southern section has been preserved in this park where boardwalks and tour boats provide easy access to varied habitats and an astounding array of wildlife.

Key West Famous for its sunsets, this tiny island has long been an artists' and writers' haven. The historic district includes the homes of Ernest Hemingway and John James Audubon.

Kennedy Space Center (near Titusville). Historic spacecraft and launch sites as well as exhibits and movies are on view.

John and Mabel Ringling Museum of Art (Sarasota). The legacy of circus owner John Ringling, the complex includes art and circus galleries, a mansion, and a playhouse.

St. Augustine The nation's oldest city, founded in 1565, features a living history museum in the restored Spanish Quarter.

Seashell collecting

Sanibel and Captiva islands along with the rest of the Gulf coast abound in unusual shells. Go at low tide.

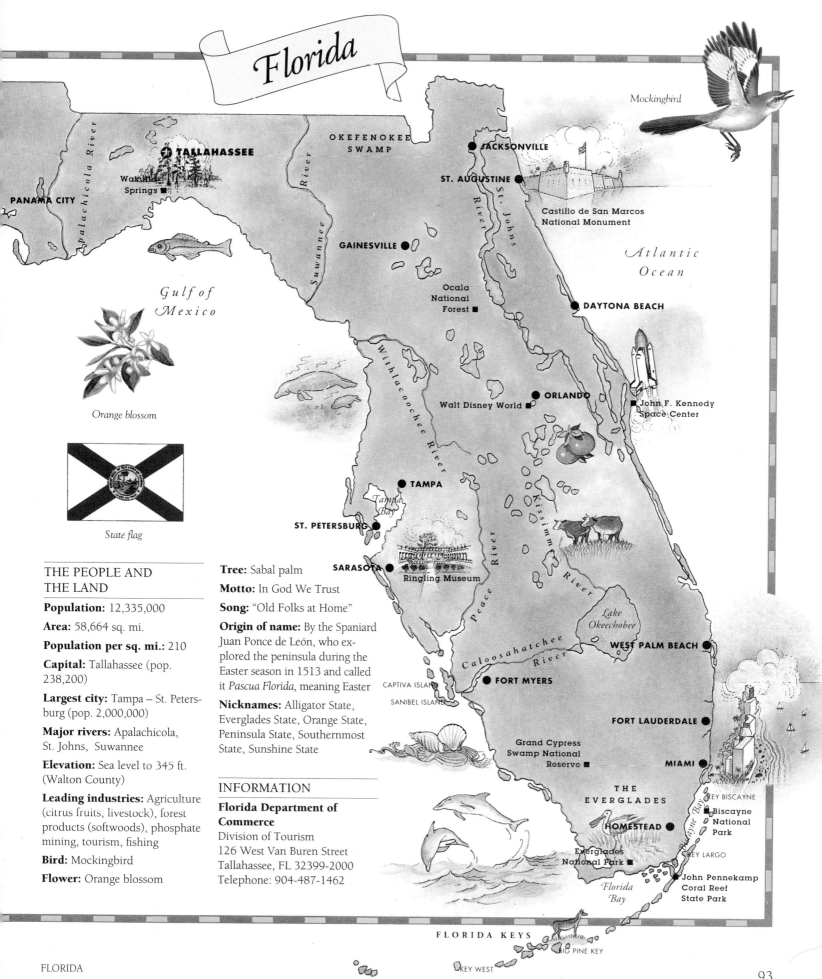

Florida

Mockingbird

OKEFENOKEE SWAMP

PANAMA CITY

Apalachicola River

⊛ **TALLAHASSEE**

Wakulla Springs ■

Suwannee River

JACKSONVILLE

ST. AUGUSTINE

St. Johns River

Castillo de San Marcos National Monument

Atlantic Ocean

GAINESVILLE

Gulf of Mexico

Ocala National Forest ■

DAYTONA BEACH

Orange blossom

State flag

Withlacoochee River

Walt Disney World ■ **ORLANDO**

John F. Kennedy Space Center

TAMPA

Tampa Bay

Kissimmee River

ST. PETERSBURG

Peace River

SARASOTA

Ringling Museum

Lake Okeechobee

WEST PALM BEACH

Caloosahatchee River

CAPTIVA ISLAND

FORT MYERS

SANIBEL ISLAND

Grand Cypress Swamp National Reserve ■

FORT LAUDERDALE

MIAMI

THE EVERGLADES

KEY BISCAYNE

HOMESTEAD

Biscayne National Park

Everglades National Park ■

KEY LARGO

Florida Bay

John Pennekamp Coral Reef State Park

FLORIDA KEYS

BIG PINE KEY

KEY WEST

THE PEOPLE AND THE LAND

Population: 12,335,000

Area: 58,664 sq. mi.

Population per sq. mi.: 210

Capital: Tallahassee (pop. 238,200)

Largest city: Tampa – St. Petersburg (pop. 2,000,000)

Major rivers: Apalachicola, St. Johns, Suwannee

Elevation: Sea level to 345 ft. (Walton County)

Leading industries: Agriculture (citrus fruits, livestock), forest products (softwoods), phosphate mining, tourism, fishing

Bird: Mockingbird

Flower: Orange blossom

Tree: Sabal palm

Motto: In God We Trust

Song: "Old Folks at Home"

Origin of name: By the Spaniard Juan Ponce de León, who explored the peninsula during the Easter season in 1513 and called it *Pascua Florida,* meaning Easter

Nicknames: Alligator State, Everglades State, Orange State, Peninsula State, Southernmost State, Sunshine State

INFORMATION

Florida Department of Commerce
Division of Tourism
126 West Van Buren Street
Tallahassee, FL 32399-2000
Telephone: 904-487-1462

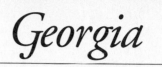

Georgia

Red clay hills and golden isles in the Empire State of the South

In 1733 the new colony of Georgia spread all the way from the marshy islands of the Atlantic coast to the banks of the Mississippi. James Edward Oglethorpe, an idealistic member of Parliament, had obtained a charter that would make the vast expanse of forested land a refuge for Britain's destitute and religious dissidents — a place for a second chance.

Exotic and virtually tropical in the eyes of the English, Georgia also held promise as a place to produce the spices, silks, and wines needed by the mother country. Soon it was evident that those commodities would never materialize — but the land was rife with other possibilities. The marshes along the coast were ideal for growing rice, and the land farther west would quickly yield a bounty of cotton and peaches. The earth would also give up marble, granite, and even gold (Dahlonega was the site of the nation's first gold rush in 1828, beating California by two decades).

BLUE RIDGE TO PIEDMONT

The city Oglethorpe laid out on the Savannah River was sultry and mosquito-infested, but it was also a model of town planning. Savannah's two-square-mile original quarter, with buildings clustered around leafy squares, remains one of the South's most romantic places. Spanish moss hanging from gnarled oaks brushes the sidewalks, and grand old houses suggest the graciousness with which the South, and Georgia in particular, are identified.

Not all of Georgia is so typically Southern. Cool mountains slope down into the northern reaches, part of the Blue Ridge of the

A live oak, heavy with vines and Spanish moss, frames a path through the forest on Wassaw Island.

Sharptop and Oglethorpe, two of the peaks in the Appalachian Mountains that reach into northern Georgia, blaze with color in autumn. Hollows and valleys in the mountains have been home to people of Scotch-Irish descent since the early 19th century.

Appalachians. Still more characteristic are the pine-covered red clay hills, known as the Piedmont, in the central part of the state. It was here that Georgians would eventually make good — both by mining the region's bedrock of granite and by turning its gentle slopes into the cotton fields that would become the basis for Georgia's first great industry.

A railway hub established in the Piedmont in the 1830's grew into the city of Atlanta. In the Civil War, Union General Sherman reduced most of it to ashes. Today, some 130 years later, the shimmering skyscrapers of the resurrected city rise like monuments to Georgians' initiative and enterprise.

Atlanta may be the pride of Georgia, but back roads fan out in every direction to what locals think of as the "real Georgia" — green expanses of field and forest interspersed with tiny towns with such remarkable names as Enigma and Between. Along the way, roadside entrepreneurs sell peaches, cold cider, and boiled peanuts, a Southern specialty served up from a bubbling caldron.

LAND OF THE TREMBLING EARTH

South of the Piedmont, the land becomes lower and flatter toward the coastal plain. Much of this part of the state is fertile farmland where wheat, soybeans, and still more cotton

A white water stretch of the Chattooga River challenges a kayaker in north Georgia.

are grown. Peach trees fill the flats south of Macon, while the town of Vidalia considers itself the onion-growing capital of the world.

One part of southern Georgia, however, is not arable. In the southeastern corner and extending into Florida is the Okefenokee Swamp, with its patchwork of cypress groves, glassy black water, and spongy islands of peat — a 770-square-mile wetland that the native Creek Indians called Land of the Trembling Earth. Unappreciative of its rare beauty or its value as a refuge for alligators and other swamp life, a determined group of agriculturists of the 1890's actually tried to drain the whole scenic morass into the Atlantic Ocean 120 miles away.

Near Springer Mountain, a hiker treks the southernmost portion of the Appalachian Trail, the mountain footpath that stretches 2,050 miles from Georgia to Maine.

Water runoff from farms in the mid-1800's created Providence Canyon, a huge gully carved into the soft red clay and sand near Lumpkin.

CRADLES OF A CULTURE

As more of the marshy, palmetto-studded barrier islands off the coasts of Georgia and South Carolina are developed into chic resorts, the longtime inhabitants — African-Americans known as Gullahs — have all but disappeared.

The same isolation that makes the islands attractive to tourists and retirees also turned Cumberland, Hilton Head, and other islands into cradles of the unique Gullah culture and language. Bridges from the mainland were not built until the 1920's, and many of the islands are still accessible only by boat.

The roots of Gullah culture go back to the 1700's, when West African slaves were put to work on the islands' rice plantations. After the Civil War, the land was ceded to the newly freed slaves. Cut off from the mainland, they lived self-sufficient lives, casting nets for fish along the shore and growing their own crops, and gradually developing their own distinctive dialect.

While most Gullahs have sold their land to developers and moved away, a few have stayed put. African culture lives on in their crafts (handwoven baskets are virtually identical in style to those from Sierra Leone), their food, and especially their musical language, which even today includes more than 6,000 words of African origin.

THE GOLDEN ISLES

Sprinkled along the Atlantic coast are the barrier islands Georgians call the Golden Isles for the warm color of their sands. Some developed and some not, these languorous havens are a wonderland of constantly evolving marshes, beaches, and palmetto trees.

The islands have admitted the modern world to differing degrees. Eight of them, still largely unspoiled, have been sold or donated to various government or conservation organizations. Four more — Tybee, St. Simons, Jekyll, and Sea islands — are resorts, outfitted with golf courses and five-star hotels.

Of the islands preserved in their natural state, Cumberland is the largest and wildest. Even today wild horses roam there, descendants of the steeds brought to the area by the Spanish in the 16th century. With its verdant marshes and wind-warped oaks, Cumberland Island seems caught in time — a lovely remnant of the exotic Georgia that greeted the first fleet of settlers more than 250 years ago.

Wisteria cascades from a cypress in the Okefenokee. The swamp, a haven for birds, also harbors the country's largest alligator population.

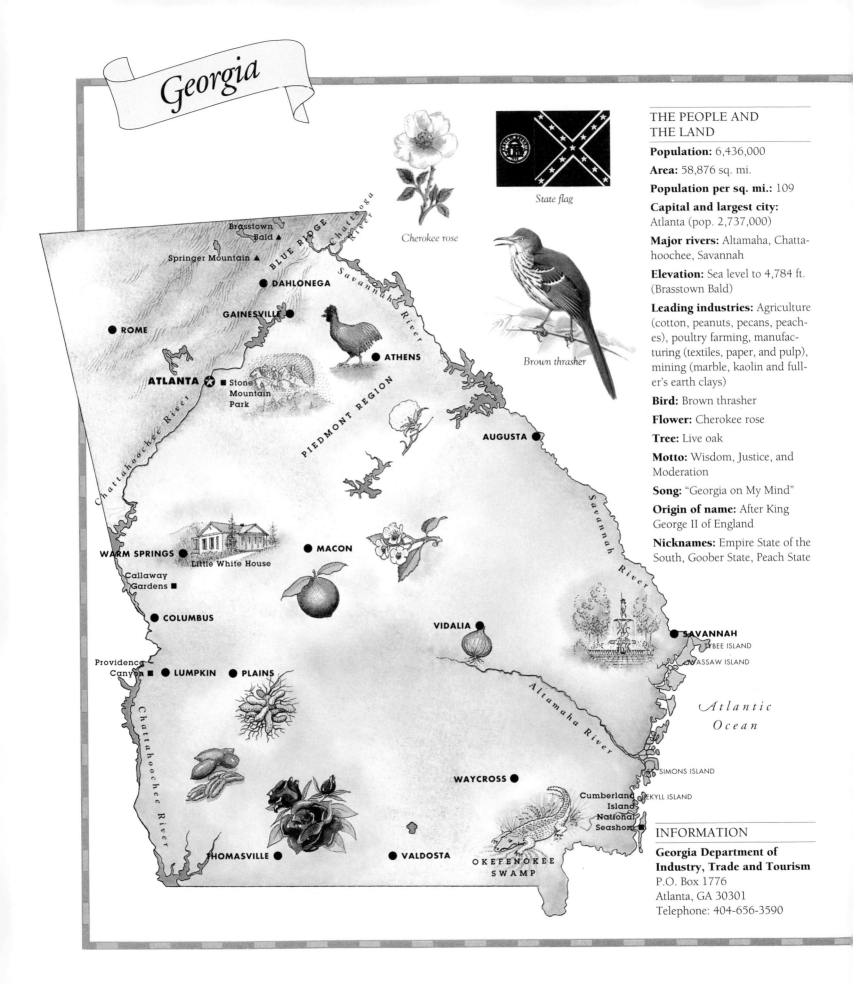

Georgia

Cherokee rose

State flag

Brown thrasher

THE PEOPLE AND THE LAND

Population: 6,436,000

Area: 58,876 sq. mi.

Population per sq. mi.: 109

Capital and largest city: Atlanta (pop. 2,737,000)

Major rivers: Altamaha, Chattahoochee, Savannah

Elevation: Sea level to 4,784 ft. (Brasstown Bald)

Leading industries: Agriculture (cotton, peanuts, pecans, peaches), poultry farming, manufacturing (textiles, paper, and pulp), mining (marble, kaolin and fuller's earth clays)

Bird: Brown thrasher

Flower: Cherokee rose

Tree: Live oak

Motto: Wisdom, Justice, and Moderation

Song: "Georgia on My Mind"

Origin of name: After King George II of England

Nicknames: Empire State of the South, Goober State, Peach State

Brasstown Bald ▲

Springer Mountain ▲

BLUE RIDGE

Chattooga River

Savannah River

● DAHLONEGA

GAINESVILLE ●

● ROME

● ATHENS

ATLANTA ✪ ■ Stone Mountain Park

PIEDMONT REGION

Chattahoochee River

AUGUSTA ●

Little White House

WARM SPRINGS ●

Callaway Gardens ■

● MACON

Savannah River

● COLUMBUS

VIDALIA ●

● SAVANNAH

TYBEE ISLAND

WASSAW ISLAND

Providence Canyon ■

● LUMPKIN ● PLAINS

Chattahoochee River

Altamaha River

Atlantic Ocean

SIMONS ISLAND

WAYCROSS ●

JEKYLL ISLAND

Cumberland Island National Seashore ■

THOMASVILLE ●

● VALDOSTA

OKEFENOKEE SWAMP

INFORMATION

Georgia Department of Industry, Trade and Tourism
P.O. Box 1776
Atlanta, GA 30301
Telephone: 404-656-3590

HISTORICAL HIGHLIGHTS

1540 Hernando de Soto leads Spanish expedition into the area.

1732 King George II's charter establishes Georgia, the last of the 13 colonies.

1733 British colonists, led by James Edward Oglethorpe, found town of Savannah.

1742 The British defeat the Spanish, who have also claimed Georgia, on St. Simons Island.

1788 Georgia ratifies U.S. Constitution, becoming fourth state.

1793 Eli Whitney invents the cotton gin near Savannah.

1838 Last of Georgia Cherokees are forced to take "Trail of Tears" to reservations in the West.

1861 Georgia secedes from Union, joins Confederacy.

1864 General Sherman's troops burn Atlanta and ravage state in their "March to the Sea."

1881 Rebuilt, Atlanta holds International Cotton Exposition.

1921 Boll weevils destroy much of the state's cotton crop.

1943 Georgia becomes the first state in U.S. to give 18-year-olds the vote.

1973 Maynard Jackson, Jr., of Atlanta becomes first black mayor of a major southern city.

1986 Carter Presidential Center opens in Atlanta as museum, library, and think tank for international issues such as human rights and the environment.

FAMOUS SONS AND DAUGHTERS

Jimmy Carter (1924 –). Elected president in 1976, the peanut farmer from Plains brought an unaffected style to the White House. During his term Carter negotiated the Camp David accord between Israel and Egypt.

Ty Cobb (1886 – 1961). The phenomenal ability of this baseball player, known as the Georgia Peach, earned him a charter membership in the National Baseball Hall of Fame.

Joel Chandler Harris (1848 – 1908). Fascinated by black folklore, this newspaperman wrote the Uncle Remus tales. Many of the stories were inspired by slaves Harris had known as a young man.

Martin Luther King, Jr.

(1929 – 68). A Baptist minister, King became leader of the civil-rights movement and was awarded the Nobel Peace Prize in 1964. In 1968 he was assassinated in Memphis while there to support a strike.

Sidney Lanier (1842 – 81). One of the most accomplished poets of his time, Lanier took much of his inspiration from his home state, with such works as "Song of the Chattahoochee."

Juliette Gordon Low (1860 – 1927). Low started the Girl Scouts of America. Today there is an extensive collection of Girl Scout memorabilia on display at her Savannah home.

Carson McCullers (1917 – 67). This novelist and playwright wrote *The Heart Is a Lonely Hunter* and *The Member of the Wedding*.

Margaret Mitchell (1900– 49). Mitchell's story of Georgia in the Civil War, *Gone With the Wind*, is one of the most widely read novels in history and a motion picture classic.

Jackie Robinson (1919 – 72). Born in the town of Cairo, Robinson was the first black to play major-league baseball and the first to be inducted into the National Baseball Hall of Fame.

ODDITIES AND SPECIALTIES

Beneath modern Atlanta lies the original city, which was rebuilt in the 1960's as Underground Atlanta. It comprises 12 acres of museums, shops, restaurants, and nightclubs.

Gainesville, the self-proclaimed poultry capital of the world, has an ordinance against using utensils, instead of fingers, to eat the local fried chicken.

The Cherokee alphabet was invented in New Echota. Later, the first newspaper in an American Indian language, the *Cherokee Phoenix,* was printed there.

Macon boasts more cherry trees than any other U.S. city.

PLACES TO VISIT, THINGS TO DO

Callaway Gardens (Pine Mountain). This pine-swathed, 2,500-acre resort has hiking trails, lakes, and a huge greenhouse open for tours.

Stephen C. Foster State Park (Okefenokee National Wildlife Refuge). Boat tours and the Trembling Earth Nature Trail offer the best views of the 770-sq.-mi. Okefenokee Swamp, one of the largest freshwater wetlands in North America.

Jekyll Island Once the winter home of the nation's wealthiest families, including the Rockefellers and Vanderbilts, this barrier island is now a resort. Several of the former family homes are open to the public.

Savannah National Historic District The nation's largest urban historic district is made up of restored 18th- and 19th-century homes and public buildings, many of them facing picturesque squares. Old cotton warehouses along the Savannah River now house galleries, restaurants, and shops.

Stone Mountain Park

(Stone Mountain). The world's largest bas-relief sculpture — a tableau of Jefferson Davis, Robert E. Lee, and Stonewall Jackson on horseback — is carved into the face of the world's largest granite outcropping. Other attractions include a railroad, an antebellum plantation, and a riverboat.

Warm Springs After contracting polio, Franklin D. Roosevelt was a frequent visitor to this town's therapeutic springs. He built his home, the Little White House, nearby and died there in 1945. The house, now open to the public, is as he left it.

Hawaii

*America's tropical paradise
in the Pacific*

More than 2,000 miles from the nearest continent, and not even part of North America, Hawaii is the newest state both historically and geologically. Islands are being added to the 1,500-mile chain of 132 islands in a thrilling process of creation that can actually be observed. While lava spills hot and glowing down the slopes of Kilauea on the island of Hawaii, a new island is rising up offshore; although it is still half a mile underwater, it has a name, Loihi.

New, isolated, and on the same latitude as central Mexico, Hawaii is a tropical paradise, seductive and exotic. Plants and animals native to the islands are found nowhere else on earth, while some introduced species have taken on strange forms.

THE BEAUTIFUL WORLD

The inhabitants are relative newcomers, too. About A.D. 300, a group of Polynesians, navigating outrigger canoes by the sun, wind, ocean currents, and stars, arrived at this remote string of islands, and according to tradition named them after their homeland Hawaiki, but called them affectionately Ke Ao Nani ("The Beautiful World"). Though the Hawaiians descended from these settlers now account for less than 20 percent of the state's population, their culture has made a distinct and permanent imprint.

Collectively, the Hawaiian Islands are nicknamed the Aloha Islands. But *aloha* is not just a mellifluous word of greeting. It also means love. The warm and outgoing nature of Ha-

The Kilauea Lighthouse crowns an isolated promontory on the north shore of Kauai. The adjoining parkland is a wildlife sanctuary for seabirds.

waiians has made this state a melting pot that works. While a movement is on to preserve the Hawaiian language, culture, and traditions, Polynesians, Orientals, Caucasians (*haoles* in Hawaiian), and other racial and ethnic groups live together harmoniously, with an intermarriage rate of more than 40 percent.

ISLANDS FROM THE SEA

Millions of years ago the Hawaiian Islands erupted from a hot spot on the Pacific Ocean floor. Layers of lava rose over time, formed undersea mountains, and 70 million years ago emerged from the sea as fiery volcanoes. They spread out in a line, northwest to southeast, more than 1,500 miles from end to end.

Once the volcanoes emerged from the ocean, the erosion process began as the forces of waves, wind, and rain did their work. The youngest and least eroded of the volcanoes are the eight major islands that constitute the state of Hawaii — Hawaii, Maui, Oahu, Kauai, and Molokai; privately owned Lanai and Niihau; and uninhabited Kahoolawe. The 124 smaller points of land are among the older, more eroded volcanoes.

HAWAII: THE BIG ISLAND

Hawaii, the Big Island, lends its name to the entire state. Big though it is, with two-thirds of the state's total land surface, a better description might be the Volcano Island. Five volcanoes have contributed to its formation, two of which, Mauna Loa and Kilauea, remain active. Mauna Loa is the largest mountain in the world, a massive hunk of 10,000 cubic miles. Kilauea has the distinction of being the world's most active volcano. A third volcano, Mauna Kea, though its summit is a mere 13,796 feet above sea level, is the world's tallest mountain, measuring over 33,000 feet from the ocean floor.

Because of its geographical diversity, some parts of the island are drenched by constant rainfall while others are almost as dry as desert. Near Hilo lush stands of rain forest bloom with brilliant tropical flowers while waterfalls tumble into serene pools — exotic images that have long inclined people to think of Hawaii as paradise. On the other side of the island, a light blanket of snow may cover the cold-

Near Hilo, on the island of Hawaii, Rainbow Falls spill over a lava ledge into a pool fringed by red torch ginger.

An 'apapane, a native species of honey creeper found on most of the main islands, feeds on the nectar of lehua blossoms.

shouldered summits of Mauna Loa and Mauna Kea. Meanwhile, the sun always shines on the dry, sunny beaches of the Kona Coast. If you like, you can swim and ski on the same day on the Big Island.

Despite its natural wonders and tourist attractions, the Big Island is largely agricultural. At the Parker Ranch, the largest individually owned cattle ranch in the United States, more than 50,000 head of cattle graze on nearly 225,000 acres in the shadow of old volcanoes. The island's rich soil also bears Kona coffee, macadamia nuts, orchids, and anthuriums.

OAHU: THE GATHERING PLACE

Archeologists have been unable to pinpoint the first Hawaiian landing site, but some of the earliest identified settlements are on Oahu, long ago nicknamed the Gathering Place for its large population — which at more than 800,000 today is the largest of any Hawaiian island. Honolulu, on the southeastern coast, is the state's largest city, capital, and business center, as well as the site of Waikiki Beach.

While much of the island is a modern metropolis with urban skyscrapers, suburban homes nestled in mountains and valleys, and

Gulches etch the leeward slopes of the island of Molokai, site of one of Hawaii's few remaining drylands. Seemingly as barren as the moon when seen from afar, the gulches harbor a rich assortment of dryland plant species.

The remnant of an ancient volcanic crater, Hanauma Bay forms a perfect crescent 10 miles down the coast from Honolulu. Once the favored retreat for Hawaiian royalty, the picturesque bay is now a marine reserve whose waters support more than 90 species of fish.

KILAUEA: THE ISLAND BUILDER

In early 1990 the world watched on television as the volcano Kilauea consumed a village on the island of Hawaii and displaced hundreds of people. The fiery spectacle offered a graphic geology lesson in the power of volcanoes and their role in shaping the land.

Because the lava oozing from Kilauea is thin and fluid, it flows quickly away from the volcano's vents, or rift zones, before it solidifies. As a result, Kilauea (which means "much spreading" in Hawaiian) has never become the steep-sided cone that would have formed if its lava were thicker. Instead, the mountain rises gradually to an elevation of 4,560 feet.

Visitors to Hawaii Volcanoes National Park, which includes both Kilauea and the larger but less active Mauna Loa, can watch as the lava flows, steams, and hardens. In fact, in the 19th century, it was fashionable for tourists to lower postcards into the hot cracks to scorch the edges before mailing the souvenirs to envious friends back home.

Since 1955, volcanic activity at Kilauea has periodically produced unusually heavy flows of lava to the sea. Geologists estimate that since 1986 alone, the molten rock has extended the Big Island's mass at sea level by about 40 acres a year.

interstate highways (connected to no other state), Oahu retains its tropical allure. Overlooking Waikiki is Diamond Head, the extinct volcano that is Hawaii's most familiar landmark. (Early explorers gave the volcano its name after finding calcite crystals that looked like diamonds on its slopes.) Off Waikiki Beach are the waters where ancient Hawaiians developed the sport of surfing to an art, and 20th-century Hawaiians and *haoles* continue the search for the perfect wave. Up along the Windward Coast is idyllic Hanauma Bay, formed by the erosion of another old volcanic crater, its peaceful waters a haven for tropical fish and a heaven for snorkelers. The steep green mountains of the Koolau Range drop into the Windward Coast in the east.

In downtown Honolulu stands a heroic bronze statue of Kamehameha the Great, one hand holding a spear and the other outstretched in a greeting of aloha. Around his shoulders is his royal cape, which was originally made from thousands of yellow feathers from the now-extinct mamo bird. When Capt. James Cook made the European discovery of the Hawaiian Islands in 1778 (naming them the Sandwich Islands), he found no single ruler. One of the leaders he met, however, was the young warrior chief Kamehameha.

In 1795, Kamehameha united the islands (except Kauai and Niihau) and founded the Kingdom of Hawaii. He thus became the first of eight monarchs to rule Hawaii — the only state to have been an independent kingdom.

Queen Liliuokalani, beloved by the Hawaiian people, was deposed in 1893 by American business interests and held virtual prisoner in her own Iolani Palace. A provisional government was established, which worked for annexation to the United States. Its efforts were finally successful in 1898. The Victorian palace, with its empty thrones, still stands.

KAUAI: THE GARDEN ISLAND

Kauai, the Garden Island, is known for its lush vegetation, the result of a potent mixture of sunshine and rainfall. It was here that Captain Cook first anchored and came ashore in Hawaii. Mount Waialeale, whose volcanic activity formed Kauai, is the wettest spot on earth,

Irrigated fields of taro spread over the Keanae Peninsula on Maui. The starchy root vegetable, a staple in Hawaii and the rest of Polynesia, grows for seven months before being harvested.

A thicket of tulip trees and royal palms surrounds Nanaue Falls on the island of Hawaii.

Early morning sun strikes Iao Needle, a 1,200-foot volcanic cinder cone on Maui.

averaging more than 450 inches of rain a year. Rolling farmlands dominate the landscape, and sugarcane is the major crop.

Waimea Canyon — over 2,800 feet deep, a mile wide, and 10 miles long — is one of Kauai's most dramatic landforms. Weather and erosion have painted the high cliff walls with a palette of soft earth colors. Equally dramatic is the Na Pali Coast, where green, ridged mountains descend to the sea. It is with beaches, however, that Kauai is associated in the popular imagination — this island was the setting for the motion picture *South Pacific*.

Just southwest of Kauai lies Niihau, the Forbidden Island, where all outsiders are

barred and the Hawaiian language and culture are preserved. The island is owned by a family who operate it as a cattle and sheep ranch.

MAUI: THE VALLEY ISLAND

Maui was formed from two volcanoes, connected by an isthmus, the "valley" in its nickname. In the eastern half lies the awe-inspiring Haleakala, whose crater is 21 miles in circumference, 19 square miles in area, and 3,000 feet deep. Cattle graze and flowers and vegetables are grown on its cool slopes. Nearly 30 miles of trail wind down from the crater rim into the barren lava landscape (U.S. astronauts did some training here for their moon mis-

sions). This part of the island is the site of the little town of Hana, known to Hawaiians as the Land of Mist and Low-Lying Cloud and to others simply as Heavenly Hana.

Eruptions from the western volcano created the valleys and peaks of the West Maui Mountains. This is the highly developed part of the islands, often compared to California. But there is also a bit of New England on the western coast — the town of Lahaina, complete with clapboard houses, widow's walks, and false-front buildings. In the 19th century Lahaina welcomed not only Yankee whalers by the thousands but New England missionaries, come to convert the natives.

The Koolau Range parallels the eastern coast of Oahu for 37 miles and forms a dramatic backdrop for the city of Honolulu. Suburbs creep right up into foothills of the mountains.

HAWAII'S WINTER VISITORS

Like sensible tourists, from one-half to two-thirds of the northern Pacific herd of humpback whales migrate from the chilly waters off Alaska each year to spend the winter in Hawaii. Here, these long-flippered and highly acrobatic mammals mate and give birth to their young in successive years.

The whales seem particularly fond of the waters of Maui's calm Maalaea Bay as a birthing ground. A few weeks after birth, small groups of baby whales and adults can be seen cavorting in the waters off Maui, Molokai, and other islands. Boatloads of whale-watchers find the creatures most spectacular when they breach, or leap partly out of the water and fall back with a great splash. In late April, the whales begin the swim to their Alaskan home.

Humpbacks average about 40 feet in length, can weigh 40 tons or more, and sing "songs" that are audible underwater for miles. At the turn of the century there were an estimated 15,000 of them in northern Pacific waters. By the early 1970's, the population had dwindled to 1,000 or less. Since that time, as a result of strict protective measures taken by the International Whaling Commission, the Pacific population may have grown to 3,000. Still, the frolicsome whales remain an endangered species.

West of Maui lies Lanai, site of a large pineapple plantation. Kahoolawe, the smallest of the major islands, lies southwest of Maui and is uninhabited.

MOLOKAI: THE FRIENDLY ISLAND

Molokai adopted its nickname, not just because its people are friendly, but to bury its past. It was here, during the 1860's, that the government started shipping leprosy patients into exile on the Kalaupapa Peninsula, separated from the rest of Molokai by steep perpendicular cliffs. The recent history of Kalaupapa is dominated by the saintly figure of Father Damien, a Belgian priest who volunteered in 1873 to serve the colony, knowing full well that he might catch the disease himself. That is exactly what happened, and Father Damien died in 1889.

Molokai is the only island, except Niihau, whose population is mainly Hawaiian. Everywhere remnants of Hawaiian culture are evident. Temple ruins, petroglyphs, and derelict ponds once stocked with fish for kings are historic reminders of the Hawaiian heritage that happily still pervades the islands.

Looking like a misplaced fragment of the American West, Waimea Canyon plunges almost 3,000 feet into the earth of Kauai. The canyon was formed as the Waimea River cut through layers of old lava flows.

The sun sets on the Na Pali Coast, a remote chain of cliffs and coves on Kauai. The beaches are accessible by land only on a footpath cut by ancient Hawaiians.

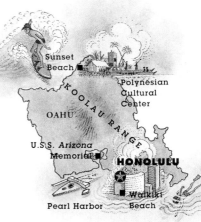

Pacific Ocean

HISTORICAL HIGHLIGHTS

c. A.D. 300 Polynesians, probably from the Marquesas, migrate to islands.

1778 British naval captain James Cook lands on islands and names them Sandwich Islands.

1795 Hawaii is unified under Kamehameha I.

1820 Missionaries arrive from New England.

1835 Americans establish the islands' first permanent sugarcane plantation on Kauai.

1885 Hawaiian pineapple industry gets its start when plants are imported from Jamaica.

1887 King Kalakaua allows U.S. Navy to occupy Pearl Harbor.

1893 Revolution led by Americans and backed by U.S. Marines abolishes monarchy.

1894 Republic of Hawaii is established.

1898 U.S. annexes Hawaii.

1941 Japanese attack Pearl Harbor, propelling U.S. into World War II.

1959 Hawaii enters Union as 50th state.

1982 Hurricane Iwa devastates Kauai and Oahu, causing over $300 million worth of damage.

1990 Eruptions of Kilauea destroy town of Kalapana, about 20 miles east of volcano's crater.

FAMOUS SONS AND DAUGHTERS

Hiram Bingham (1789 – 1869). Born in Vermont, Bingham, a missionary, helped to put the Hawaiian language into written form, and then to translate the Bible into Hawaiian.

Sanford Ballard Dole (1844 – 1926). The son of missionaries, Dole became president of the new Hawaiian republic in 1894. His efforts to attain U.S. annexation succeeded, and he was named governor.

Hiram L. Fong (1907 –). Fong's parents left China to work on a plantation on Oahu. Fong became a U.S. senator in 1959 — the first person of Chinese ancestry in the Senate.

Kamehameha I (c. 1758 – 1819). This legendary hero unified the islands through conquest. The dynasty he founded lasted until 1893.

Liliuokalani (1838 – 1917).

Queen Liliuokalani reigned from 1891 to 1893, when she was deposed during a bloodless revolution that ended the kingdom. The last monarch of Hawaii wrote the song "Aloha Oe."

ODDITIES AND SPECIALTIES

The southernmost point in the U.S. is Ka Lae, meaning south point, located on the Big Island.

More than 90 percent of Hawaii's plants and wildlife are found no place else on earth.

Hawaii's famous luaus feature kalua pig, which is roasted in an underground oven called an imu. Another essential food is poi, a paste made from taro whose virtues are not always perceived on first taste.

Coffee beans grown on the Kona Coast of the Big Island are the only commercial coffee beans produced in the U.S.

In Hilo, on the Big Island, orchids are raised in fields for shipment worldwide.

The distinctive sound of Hawaiian music comes primarily from the steel guitar, invented by a Hawaiian student in 1895.

Maui and the Big Island of Hawaii have black sand beaches, formed when hot lava hit the cool sea water, exploded into small pieces, and was gradually reduced to grains of sand.

The Hawaiian alphabet has 12 letters: *a, e, h, i, k, l, m, n, o, p, u, w.*

PLACES TO VISIT, THINGS TO DO

Akaka Falls (Hawaii). In a lush green gorge, a waterfall plunges 442 feet over a cliff.

Haleakala National Park (Maui). Haleakala means House of the Sun, a name whose appropriateness is apparent to anyone who stands at the top of the 10,023-foot dormant volcano, Haleakala, at sunrise.

Hawaii Volcanoes National Park (Hawaii). This 344-square-mile park boasts the only active volcanoes on the islands, Kilauea and Mauna Loa.

Kokee State Park (Kauai). This forested park is the place to go for hiking and for a spectacular view of Waimea Canyon from the 4,000-foot-high Kalalau Lookout.

Na Pali Coast (Kauai). The northwest shore's jagged mountains, sea caves, waterfalls, and beaches are breathtaking, whether seen by boat, helicopter, or — by the hardy — on foot.

Pearl Harbor National Historic Landmark (Oahu). The U.S.S. *Arizona* Memorial stands over the place where the *Arizona* was sunk on the morning of December 7, 1941.

Polynesian Cultural Center (Oahu). Seven Polynesian villages, re-created as once found on Fiji, Hawaii, the Marquesas, New Zealand, Samoa, Tahiti, and Tonga, can be toured on foot at this center operated by the Mormon Church.

Snorkeling The island waters off many beaches offer close viewing of brightly hued fish, such as parrot and butterfly fish, and coral reefs.

Hawaii

THE PEOPLE AND THE LAND

Population: 1,112,000

Islands: Hawaii, Maui, Kahoolawe, Lanai, Molokai, Oahu, Kauai, Niihau, and 124 islets

Area: 6,471 sq. mi.

Population per sq. mi.: 172

Capital and largest city: Honolulu (pop. 841,600)

Elevation: Sea level to 13,796 ft. (Mauna Kea, on island of Hawaii)

Leading industries: Tourism, defense, agriculture (sugar, pineapples, flowers, nursery products)

Bird: Hawaiian goose (nene)

Flower: Hibiscus

Tree: Candlenut (kukui)

Motto: *Ua Mau ke Ea o ka Aina i ka Pono* (The Life of the Land Is Perpetuated in Righteousness)

Song: "Hawaii Ponoi" ("Our Hawaii")

Origin of name: Traditionally held to be named after an ancient Polynesian homeland, Hawaiki

Nicknames: Aloha State, Paradise of the Pacific, Pineapple State

INFORMATION

Hawaii Visitors Bureau
2270 Kalakaua Avenue
Suite 801
Honolulu, HI 96815
Telephone: 808-923-1811

Hibiscus

State flag

Hawaiian goose (nene)

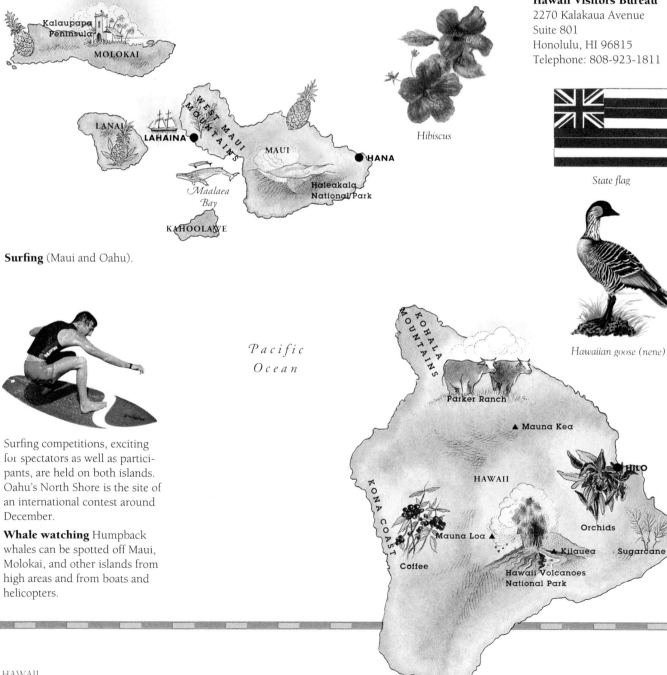

Surfing (Maui and Oahu).

Surfing competitions, exciting for spectators as well as participants, are held on both islands. Oahu's North Shore is the site of an international contest around December.

Whale watching Humpback whales can be spotted off Maui, Molokai, and other islands from high areas and from boats and helicopters.

Idaho

From wilderness to farmland, a grand mix of western scenery

Geographers cannot seem to agree on whether to call Idaho part of the Pacific Northwest, the Rocky Mountain West, or the Intermountain West — not surprising, since a topographical map of the state looks something like a crazy quilt patched together with odd pieces of mountain and prairie, desert and lakeland, forest and plain.

First part of Oregon Country, then Washington Territory, present-day Idaho — home to only about a million people — is what was left over when Montana was eventually shorn away. But if Idaho is a scrap, it is a gloriously scenic one, from its 45-mile-wide panhandle on the Canadian border to its mountainous wilderness areas and vast plains farther south. Cobbled in along the way are rolling prairies, snowy peaks, and sage-covered flatlands.

BRIGHT FIELDS OF THE GRASSLAND

Hugging the western edge of the panhandle and curving partway down the Snake River is Idaho's grassland — Camas Prairie (named for the star-shaped blue flowers whose bulbs were a staple food of the region's Nez Perce Indians) and the fertile Palouse Hills. The cultivated fields in this part of Idaho could have been lifted from Pennsylvania Dutch country. Rustic barns dot oceans of rippling wheat and flowering rape, while poplars edge bright green fields of barley, beans, and peas. (Potatoes, Idaho's most famous commodity, belong to the Snake River Valley, a distant 300 miles to the south). The city of Lewiston, market center for the prairie and once the capital of

A country road in the Palouse Hills cuts a swath between fields of peas and flowering yellow rape.

An onion field blooms in Ada County in southwestern Idaho. Once a wasteland, the region became productive with the advent of large-scale irrigation.

Idaho Territory, ships grain from the surrounding farmland down the Snake and Columbia rivers to the coast. Thus Lewiston has become an important port, even though it lies 470 miles from the Pacific Ocean.

BLUE LAKES AND WHITE PINES

Rising at the eastern edge of the prairie are the Clearwater Mountains, ore-rich slopes that drew gold-seekers and miners in the 1870's. One of 81 mountain ranges that steeple the state from corner to corner, the Clearwater and other ranges of the north — the Cabinets, Selkirks, and Purcells — ascend to little more than 8,000 feet. But their valleys embrace the greatest concentration of lakes in the West. Lake Coeur d'Alene, which even well-seasoned travelers consider to be one of the most beautiful lakes in the world, is a stunning expanse of blue water surrounded by lush forest. Mosses and ferns grow in the cool, moist air of the forest floor, and brilliant

In the Selway-Bitterroot Wilderness of northern Idaho, a moose wades in the shallows of a river. Some 3.8 million acres of wilderness are protected in the state.

RAPTORS ON THE WIND

The roughcast basalt cliffs that rise up to 700 feet along an 80-mile stretch of river are the focal point for visitors to the Snake River Birds of Prey Area in southwestern Idaho. Here, 483,000 acres are set aside for the country's largest nesting population of falcons, eagles, hawks, and turkey vultures.

Three features attract these raptors: nesting sites in the cliffs, an abundance of small animals on the plains above, and the convenient topography of the location. The birds' nests are lower than their hunting ground, but the raptors can easily rise above the cliffs on updrafts and then soar on warm air currents across the sagebrush-covered plains in search of prey. Once they have swooped down and captured a squirrel or rabbit, they take their prey home effortlessly by gliding down to the cliffs.

Visitors using binoculars or a spotting scope on the banks of the Snake River can see the birds nesting in the cliffs. On the plain above, prairie falcons skim along the top of the sagebrush at breakneck speed and golden eagles zig-zag skyward on the rising air.

Although typical of the yawning chasms of the West in this section of its 70-mile length, Bruneau Canyon narrows to only 30 feet wide in some places.

wildflowers bloom on the open slopes. Also nestled in the northern ranges is Lake Pend Oreille, 43 miles long, more than 1,000 feet deep, and an irresistible lure for fishermen.

Blanketing these northern ranges are western white pines — some of them 200 feet tall. Relentless logging, a disastrous fire in 1910, and the ravages of blister rust have reduced much of the virgin growth to a memory, but 80 percent of northern Idaho is still forested. The cedar-hemlock forest of the Selkirks shelters the country's last remaining herd of woodland caribou. And from many overlooks in this lakeland, only the wake of a holiday fisherman's boat suggests that anything has changed in the last 200 years.

In central Idaho, the Salmon River cuts through the loftier Lemhi, Lost River, and Sawtooth ranges. This storied "River of No Return" was the one that Indians convinced Lewis and Clark to detour. From its birthplace in the Sawtooths — mountains sharpened to points by glaciers — the 400-mile Salmon traverses a 2-million-acre wilderness. Today adventurous river runners in kayaks, canoes, and rafts test its waters and give new life to isolated towns like Stanley and Salmon.

LAND OF ABRUPT CHANGE

South of the Sawtooths the land is arid and flat, with the Snake River swinging in a graceful arc across sagebrush-covered plains. But irrigation of the Snake River Valley has turned more than 2 million acres into flourishing farmland. Seventy percent of all Idahoans live within 50 miles of the river; most are concentrated in the cities of Boise, Pocatello, and Idaho Falls, but many live on farms, growing sugar beets, beans, and enough potatoes to account for a full quarter of the nation's output.

With fertile fields cheek by jowl with arid plains, southern Idaho is not easily categorized. But that is true of the rest of the state as well, where the land is wont to change all the more abruptly — from plain to mountain, from prairie to forest. Within the jigsaw borders of this piece of western terrain, nature has created a splendid patchwork.

With the sunlit Sawtooth Mountains in the background, a solitary sculler glides through the mist on Little Redfish Lake.

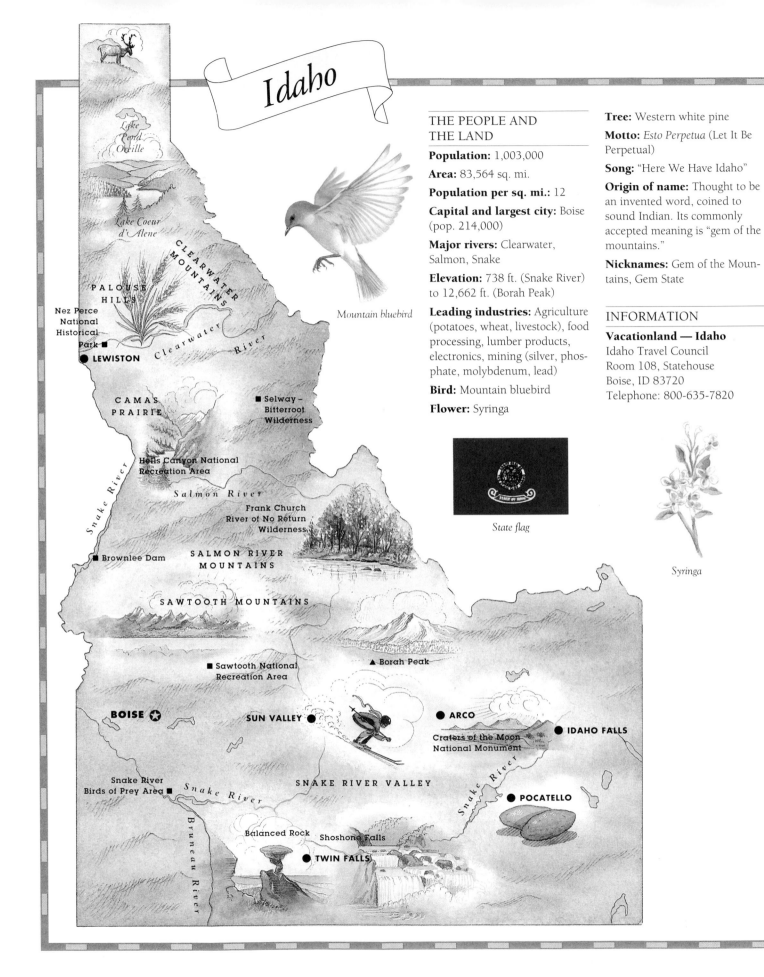

Idaho

THE PEOPLE AND THE LAND

Population: 1,003,000

Area: 83,564 sq. mi.

Population per sq. mi.: 12

Capital and largest city: Boise (pop. 214,000)

Major rivers: Clearwater, Salmon, Snake

Elevation: 738 ft. (Snake River) to 12,662 ft. (Borah Peak)

Leading industries: Agriculture (potatoes, wheat, livestock), food processing, lumber products, electronics, mining (silver, phosphate, molybdenum, lead)

Bird: Mountain bluebird

Flower: Syringa

Tree: Western white pine

Motto: *Esto Perpetua* (Let It Be Perpetual)

Song: "Here We Have Idaho"

Origin of name: Thought to be an invented word, coined to sound Indian. Its commonly accepted meaning is "gem of the mountains."

Nicknames: Gem of the Mountains, Gem State

INFORMATION

Vacationland — Idaho
Idaho Travel Council
Room 108, Statehouse
Boise, ID 83720
Telephone: 800-635-7820

Mountain bluebird

State flag

Syringa

Map labels

Lake Pend Oreille
Lake Coeur d'Alene
CLEARWATER MOUNTAINS
PALOUSE HILLS
Nez Perce National Historical Park
LEWISTON
Clearwater River
CAMAS PRAIRIE
Selway – Bitterroot Wilderness
Hells Canyon National Recreation Area
Salmon River
Frank Church River of No Return Wilderness
Snake River
Brownlee Dam
SALMON RIVER MOUNTAINS
SAWTOOTH MOUNTAINS
Sawtooth National Recreation Area
BOISE
SUN VALLEY
▲ Borah Peak
ARCO
IDAHO FALLS
Craters of the Moon National Monument
SNAKE RIVER VALLEY
Snake River Birds of Prey Area
Snake River
Bruneau River
Balanced Rock
Shoshone Falls
TWIN FALLS
POCATELLO

HISTORICAL HIGHLIGHTS

1805 Explorers Lewis and Clark cross Idaho on their way to the West Coast.

1809 Trading post is established on the shore of Lake Pend Oreille.

1834 Fort Hall and Fort Boise, which later became stops on Oregon Trail, are built.

1860 Mormons from Utah found Franklin, the first permanent settlement. Gold is discovered on Clearwater River.

1863 Congress makes Idaho a U.S. territory.

1877 U.S. troops defeat Nez Perce Indians.

1880 Silver is discovered in the Wood River area.

1890 Idaho becomes 43rd state.

1892 Martial law is imposed and federal troops are dispatched during a violent miners' strike in northern Idaho.

1905 Former governor Frank Steunenberg is assassinated.

1907 In a famous trial, two union miners, represented by Clarence Darrow, are acquitted of the Steunenberg murder.

1927 Northern and southern Idaho are linked by-land for the first time with completion of U.S. Highway 95.

1955 Arco, site of first U.S. nuclear power plant, becomes first town on earth to be lighted solely by atomic power.

1959 Brownlee Dam, first of three private power dams on the Snake River, is completed, making Idaho fourth among states in irrigated land area.

1972 Mine fire kills 92 workers.

1975 New waterway connects Snake and Columbia rivers to Pacific Ocean.

1976 Collapse of Teton Dam kills 11 people and causes extensive damage.

1980 Frank Church River of No Return Wilderness, at 2.3 million acres the largest wilderness preserve in the contiguous U.S., is established.

FAMOUS SONS AND DAUGHTERS

William Edgar Borah (1865 – 1940). The Lion of Idaho, a U.S. senator for 33 years, was best known for his fight to keep the U.S. from joining the League of Nations after World War I.

Gutzon Borglum (1867 – 1941). A sculptor on a monumental scale, Borglum designed and carved the spectacular Mt. Rushmore National Memorial in North Dakota.

Vardis Fisher (1895 – 1968). Fisher, a popular novelist who lived his entire life in Idaho, wrote stories about frontier life in the West. One of his best known, *Tale of Valor*, recounted the Lewis and Clark expedition.

Joseph (1840? – 1904). As chief of Idaho's Nez Perce Indians, Joseph was renowned for his brilliant, though ultimately unsuccessful, military tactics during the Indian wars.

Ezra Pound (1885 – 1972). This influential modern poet, the author of *Cantos*, was born and raised in Idaho, but lived much of his life in Italy. Charged with treason by the U.S. during World War II, he was found mentally unfit to stand trial.

Sacagawea (1787 – 1812?). A Shoshoni Indian, Sacagawea, or "Bird Woman," became a guide and interpreter for the Lewis and Clark expedition.

ODDITIES AND SPECIALTIES

Idaho comes honestly by its nickname of Gem State, since at least 70 kinds of precious and semiprecious stones are found there. One mine produced a 10.5-carat diamond — the nation's largest to date.

In Payette National Forest, archeologists were astonished to find hills cleared and terraced in the manner of Chinese agriculture — until they learned that Chinese miners grew subsistence crops there between 1865 and the mid-1920's.

Idaho has more unroaded townships and more allocated wilderness than any state except Alaska.

Inhabited by Indians for 12,000 years, Idaho was the last part of the country explored by whites. Lewis and Clark were the first outsiders to set foot there.

Appaloosa horses, originally from Asia, owe their existence in the U.S. to the Nez Perce Indians of Idaho, who bred their favorite horses into a huge herd and kept them from extinction.

PLACES TO VISIT, THINGS TO DO

Balanced Rock (near Buhl). This mushroom-shaped rock, at the rim of Salmon Falls Creek Canyon, is perched precariously atop a 40-foot-high base.

Craters of the Moon National Monument (near Arco). Astronauts have studied the rocks, similar to the moon's, of this stark landscape. The park is composed of black lava formations once spewed from a number of small volcanoes.

Hells Canyon National Recreation Area (Riggins). The steep basaltic walls of this deepest chasm in North America rise up to 8,000 feet above the turbulent Snake River.

Nez Perce National Historical Park and Museum (Spalding). This park consists of 24 sites scattered across north central Idaho. Attractions include a fort, battlefields, and a museum focusing on Nez Perce Indians.

Sawtooth National Recreation Area (Stanley). The sharp peaks of the Sawtooth Mountains seem to puncture the sky. Forests and alpine lakes draw hikers, anglers, and boating buffs.

Shoshone Falls (near Twin Falls). Called the Niagara of the West, these falls descend 212 feet into Snake River Canyon.

Sun Valley This famous ski resort in the Sawtooths is home to Bald Mountain, deemed the greatest mountain in the world by many skiers.

Illinois

The spirit of the prairie, the heart of America

Illinois was the place where the sky began, the place where new settlers emerged from the shadows of the eastern woodlands into a vast, sun-drenched plain. Here, standing at the edge of an ocean of grass, Americans got their first, awestruck glimpse of the immense fertility of the continent, the abundance that lay like God's promise over the land. At last freed of the forest, the sky unfurled and the land rolled on to infinity — flat, free, destined for the plow. Here, they knew, the East ends and the West begins.

PROSPECT OF THE PRAIRIE

"One of the most delightful prospects I have ever beheld," wrote an amazed traveler describing the prairie in 1791, "all the low grounds being meadow, and without wood, and all of the high grounds being covered with trees and appearing like islands; the whole scene seemed an Elysium." The land was then thickly covered with tall grass, the big bluestem that rises higher than a man can reach, with roots lodged 15 feet into the earth. The depth of the grass roots was the key to the life of the prairie. Periodic fires raged over the land, burning off dead grass on the surface and leaving the roots intact to sprout anew from the ashes.

Over thousands of years this process of fiery death and regrowth created soil of unsurpassed fertility. From A.D. 900 to 1450 the land nurtured an advanced American Indian culture, known to us today by the fascinating remnants of a large city, the Cahokia Mounds, near present-day Collinsville. The largest urban Indian settlement north of Mexico, this

The rocky land at the southern tip of Illinois remains wooded, as in this scene at Ferne Clyffe State Park.

The rolling midwestern prairie, its tough grass tamed by the plow, presents a classic American panorama. The farms shown here lie in the northwest corner of Illinois.

city and its surrounding communities housed some 20,000 people who had an extensive trading and agricultural economy. The 70-odd surviving earthworks, most of them burial mounds, cover six square miles.

So rich was the soil of the prairie that the first white settlers who farmed it did not have to work very hard to survive. It took only 50 days of plowing, planting, cultivating, and harvesting to bring in a 10-acre corn crop. One traveler thought that Illinoisans "do the

least work I believe of any people in the world." In Illinois in 1837, a transplanted Vermonter named John Deere made farming still easier, manufacturing a steel plow that cut through the tough grass roots and became known as "the plow that broke the plains."

Deere's plow ushered in the age of large-scale agriculture. Today, 80 percent of the state's land is devoted to farming, and Illinois produces much of the nation's corn, soybeans, and wheat. The taming of the prairie has not

Streams feeding the Illinois River eroded 18 canyons through Starved Rock State Park, near Utica. The park takes its name from the 125-foot butte where, according to legend, a band of Illinois Indians died of hunger after a battle with the Ottawa-Potawatomi tribes.

Geese wander the grounds at Lincoln's New Salem State Historic Site, a re-creation of the village where Abraham Lincoln lived in the 1830's. The village, with its rustic log buildings, is located near the central Illinois town of Petersburg.

come without cost (huge amounts of topsoil arc washed away each year), but it has brought a different kind of beauty to Illinois — the sight of impeccably straight rows of corn stretching to the horizon across a patchwork of farms, the very image of abundance.

A MINGLING OF NORTH AND SOUTH

The first lands to be settled in Illinois were the less arable plains along the rivers in the south. Cairo, the city that grew up at the confluence

The dramatic sweep of the prairie inspired not only the poetry of Carl Sandburg and the paintings of realists like Grant Wood, but also an architecture that is emphatically American in style. Frank Lloyd Wright, who lived and worked in Chicago for some 30 years, saw in the prairie a particular kind of beauty that he believed its dwellings should reflect. The result was his elegantly simple design for "prairie houses," countless examples of which sprang up in Illinois and neighboring states. The houses were particularly prized in the more affluent suburbs of Chicago, where the specimens that remain true to their original designs are given landmark status today.

With their low, horizontal lines and expansive rooms, prairie houses blended into the endless horizon of the plains. Porches, terraces, and balconies served to bring the outdoors inside, and indigenous construction materials and mellow earth colors further integrated the houses with their surroundings.

Wright constructed his most famous example of the style, Robie House, in Chicago in 1909. Now open to the public, the graceful structure stands as a telling reminder of Wright's lasting influence on American domestic architecture, and, in turn, of his primary inspiration — the distinctive landscape of the great American Midwest.

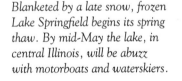

Blanketed by a late snow, frozen Lake Springfield begins its spring thaw. By mid-May the lake, in central Illinois, will be abuzz with motorboats and waterskiers.

of the Mississippi and Ohio rivers — the arteries that carried foodstuffs and manufactured goods through inland America — seemed destined for greatness as a marketplace. But Cairo waned, while a city on a patch of marshland to the north grew to splendor — Chicago. Railroads, meatpacking, steel, banking, commerce, and a host of other enterprises drew millions of immigrants, creating the mighty "City of the Big Shoulders."

This contrast between industrialized north and rural south is one of the aspects that gives Illinois its dynamism. From its early days this midwestern state has been a crossroads of cultures, politics, religions, and economic forces. Not only was it the meeting place of East and West, it was the place where the people and attitudes of North and South mingled. Chicago is almost as far north as Boston, Cairo as far south as Richmond. And Illinois is so long that it has the climate and flora of both North and South — fir trees flourish in the cool northern reaches while peaches grow in the warmth of the south.

ORCHARDS AND WILDFOWL

Not all of Illinois is prairie. A glacier-made ridge in the southernmost part of the state, the Shelbyville moraine, marks a dividing line between the grasslands and forests. South of the ridge the hills are thick with trees. Farmers cultivate lush orchards of plums, apples, peaches, cherries, and pears, and the landscape is dotted with crystalline lakes that sustain rare and endangered wildfowl. The wild turkey, once virtually extinct in Illinois, has been coming back in increasing numbers in the southern counties. And near Shawnee National Forest, more than 100,000 Canada geese come to spend the winter each year at Crab Orchard National Wildlife Refuge and Horseshoe Lake Wildlife Refuge.

Still, for all the beauty of the southern counties, it is the spirit of the state's northern rolling prairie that suffuses Illinois. Carl Sandburg, a native of the state, evoked that spirit in one of his poems:

The prairie sings to me in the forenoon and I know in the night I rest easy in the prairie arms, on the prairie heart.

Tower Rock is the highest of the limestone bluffs that loom over the Ohio River in southern Illinois. The scenic overlook is part of the 263,000-acre Shawnee National Forest.

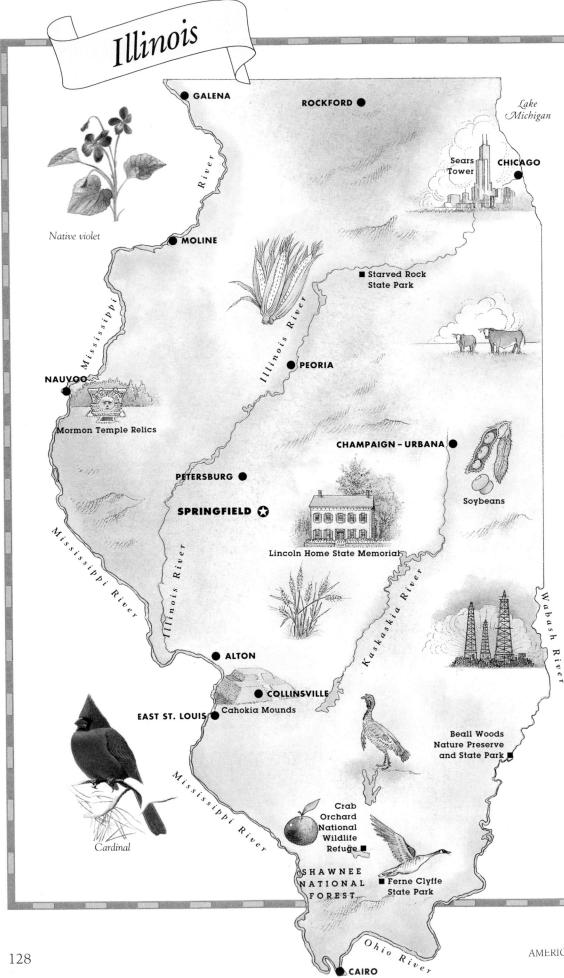

Illinois

Native violet

Cardinal

Mormon Temple Relics

Lincoln Home State Memorial

Soybeans

Cahokia Mounds

GALENA

ROCKFORD

Lake Michigan

Sears Tower

CHICAGO

MOLINE

■ Starved Rock State Park

Illinois River

PEORIA

NAUVOO

CHAMPAIGN – URBANA

PETERSBURG

SPRINGFIELD ✪

Mississippi River

Kaskaskia River

Wabash River

ALTON

COLLINSVILLE

EAST ST. LOUIS

Beall Woods Nature Preserve and State Park ■

Crab Orchard National Wildlife Refuge ■

■ Ferne Clyffe State Park

SHAWNEE NATIONAL FOREST

Ohio River

CAIRO

THE PEOPLE AND THE LAND

Population: 11,325,000

Area: 56,345 sq. mi.

Population per sq. mi.: 201

Capital: Springfield (pop. 191,700)

Largest city: Chicago (pop. 6,216,200)

Major rivers: Illinois, Kaskaskia, Mississippi

Elevation: 279 ft. (Mississippi River) to 1,235 ft. (Charles Mound)

Leading industries: Agriculture (corn, soybeans, wheat, livestock), coal mining, petroleum, manufacturing (farm machinery, electronics, railroad equipment)

Bird: Cardinal

Flower: Native violet

Tree: White oak

Motto: State Sovereignty — National Union

Song: "Illinois"

Origin of name: From the French version of an Indian word, *illiniwek*, meaning men or warriors

Nicknames: Corn State, Land of Lincoln, Prairie State

INFORMATION

Illinois Department of Commerce and Community Affairs
Division of Tourism
620 East Adams Street
Springfield, IL 62701
Telephone: 217-782-7139

ILLINOIS

State flag

HISTORICAL HIGHLIGHTS

1673 French explorers Jolliet and Marquette, exploring the Mississippi River, reach Illinois.

1699 French priests found the first settlement, Cahokia, just across the Mississippi from present-day St. Louis.

1763 France cedes Illinois to Great Britain.

1783 Treaty ending Revolutionary War gives Illinois to U.S.

1818 Illinois joins the Union as the 21st state.

1832 Last of Sauk and Fox Indians are driven from state by white settlers.

1848 Illinois and Michigan Canal opens, linking Great Lakes to Illinois River.

1858 Abraham Lincoln and Stephen Douglas, vying for U.S. Senate, argue the abolition of slavery in seven debates.

1860 Abraham Lincoln is elected president.

1871 Great Chicago Fire kills 300 and destroys much of city.

1886 Laborers assemble in Haymarket Square in Chicago to protest police intervention in a strike. In the ensuing riot, eight people are killed.

1893 Chicago hosts the World's Columbian Exposition, displaying America's technological and scientific advances.

1908 Springfield race riots, in which several blacks are killed, leads to founding of NAACP.

1933 Century of Progress Exposition, also known as Chicago World's Fair, showcases U.S. industrial achievements.

1968 Hordes of demonstrators clash violently with police during Democratic national convention in Chicago.

1983 Harold Washington is Chicago's first black mayor.

FAMOUS SONS AND DAUGHTERS

Jane Addams (1860 – 1935). This social worker founded Hull House, a prototype for settlement houses, in Chicago. She was awarded the Nobel Peace Prize in 1931.

Saul Bellow (1915 –). A Chicago author who has often used the city as the setting for his novels, Bellow won a Pulitzer Prize for *Humboldt's Gift*. In 1976 he was awarded the Nobel Prize in literature.

Jack Benny (1894 – 1974). The penny-pinching, fiddle-playing comedian, forever 39, had his own radio program for 23 years, then moved to television.

William Jennings Bryan (1860 – 1925). Bryan received the Democratic nomination for president three times but never won. After serving as secretary of state, Bryan, an antievolutionist, led the prosecution in the Scopes "Monkey Trial."

Walt Disney (1901 – 66). After studying at the Academy of Fine Arts in Chicago, Disney made his name as an innovative animated cartoonist, creating characters beloved around the world. He founded his own movie studio and later created Disneyland.

Ernest Hemingway (1899 – 1961).

Hemingway captured the spirit of a "lost generation" of expatriate Americans in his short stories and novels. Among his works are *The Sun Also Rises* and "The Snows of Kilimanjaro."

Ronald Reagan (1911 –). Born in Tampico, Reagan became an actor and president of the Screen Actors Guild. Beginning in 1967, he served two terms as California's governor. In 1980 he won the presidential election and in 1984 was reelected.

Carl Sandburg (1878 – 1967). Sandburg captured the soul of the Midwest in such poems as "Chicago" and "Smoke and Steel." He also wrote a six-volume, Pulitzer Prize-winning biography of Lincoln.

Adlai Stevenson (1900 – 65). A Chicago lawyer, Stevenson was elected governor of Illinois in 1948. He ran for president in 1952 and 1956 but was defeated both times by Eisenhower. In 1961 President Kennedy named him ambassador to the U.N.

ODDITIES AND SPECIALTIES

The atomic age began when, in 1942, Enrico Fermi and other University of Chicago scientists produced the first self-sustaining nuclear reaction.

In 1885 the first metal-framed skyscraper, the 10-story Home Insurance Building, was built in Chicago. Today the city has the world's tallest building, the Sears Tower, 1,454 feet high.

Soybeans are grown in every one of the 102 counties in Illinois.

The world's most devastating tornado struck the Midwest on March 18, 1925, killing 689 people — 234 of them in the town of Murphysboro.

PLACES TO VISIT, THINGS TO DO

Art Institute of Chicago As well as an outstanding collection of impressionist paintings, this museum has an exhibit of ornamental fragments from demolished Chicago buildings.

Beall Woods Nature Preserve and State Park (near Mt. Carmel). Situated along the scenic Wabash River, this is one of the largest virgin deciduous forests in the nation.

Lincoln Home State Memorial (Springfield). Lincoln and his family lived in this modest frame house from 1844 to 1861, when they left for the White House.

Museum of Science and Industry (Chicago). Exhibits explaining the principles of science and technology are housed in a mammoth Greek revival structure built for the World's Columbian Exposition in 1893.

Nauvoo Mormons settled here in 1839 but were driven out five years later. Today the restored town offers historic craft demonstrations and tours of 19th-century homes.

Indiana

Historic, homey, and Hoosier

At a turkey shoot during pioneer days, the typical Indiana frontiersman would hang back, leaning on his long rifle, while the visitors and city folk did all the talking. Then he would prime his piece, step up to the line, and win the turkey. Hoosiers, as Indianans like to be called, remain much the same today: calm, competent, and competitive — colorful, too, just not flamboyant.

The same can be said of the state that is their home. It is a green, leafy, unpretentious sort of place, with plenty of trees in the cities and towns, patches of woods scattered here and there across the rural countryside, and dense forests in the south.

FROM FOREST TO FARMLAND

When Indiana entered the Union in 1816 almost the entire state was part of a great hardwood forest stretching from the Mississippi River to the Appalachians. Today only 19 percent of the state is wooded and three-quarters of the land is devoted to agriculture.

The southern hills were the first part of Indiana to be settled as backwoodsmen, mainly from similar areas in Tennessee, Kentucky, and Virginia, crossed the Ohio River in search of new land. Typical of these yeoman farmers were Abraham Lincoln's parents, who arrived from Kentucky in 1816, the year Indiana became a state and the future president was seven years old. Even today the region retains its heritage, giving Indiana perhaps the most southern character of any northern state.

Glimpses of the original landscape can still be seen in southern Indiana, especially its

The East Fork of the White River wends its way across Hoosier National Forest south of Bedford.

Circular barns like the one above became the rage in Fulton County around 1900 as farmers sought to lessen their labors by using a central feeding area for livestock. The barns proved difficult to heat and light, however, and the last one was built in 1924.

Brown County is pretty all through the year, but each autumn the colorful foliage of mixed hardwoods turns this unspoiled terrain into one of nature's grand spectacles. Generally, people flock to Brown County State Park, which comprises some 15,500 acres and has 27 miles of picturesque country roads. Also in the county are Yellowwood State Forest and Hoosier National Forest, equally beautiful and not as crowded.

central part — an area of steep bluffs and scenic outlooks, tranquil river bottoms, limestone caves, and wandering deer.

By contrast, the northern half of the state is flat, dotted with lakes and crossed by an intertwining system of rivers that served the Indians and early explorers as highways. The Miami Indian stronghold of Kekionga, for example, stood on the site of present-day Fort Wayne, guarding the short overland portage between the Maumee River and a tributary of

the Wabash and ultimately connecting Lake Erie with the Gulf of Mexico.

Settlers from the East began entering Indiana in significant numbers during the 1830's, when the National Road (the main pioneer roadway west, now paralleled by Route 40) reached Indianapolis. Their first task was to clear the vast tracts of level, fertile land for farms. After the Civil War, lumbering operations began, and in a matter of decades the great forest had disappeared, to be replaced by the farms, country roads, quiet villages, and amiable tree-lined streets that have become Indiana's hallmarks.

A TREACHEROUS SWAMP

The wetlands of Indiana's northern plains were among the last places to be cleared. It was here that the young writer and naturalist Gene Stratton Porter came in the late 1890's, encountering what she called "a treacherous swamp and quagmire filled with every plant,

Sixty-foot-high Big Clifty Falls is the most spectacular of the many cascades in Clifty Falls State Park near Madison. The most thrilling time to hike the trails of this hilly, 1,360-acre preserve is during the spring, when the water level is highest.

animal, and human danger known in the worst of such locations in the Central States." Yet it was also, as she realized, a place of surpassing beauty, teeming with birds, moths, butterflies, and wildflowers — and it was vanishing as lumbermen felled trees and developers pushed through drainage ditches.

In best-selling novels published between 1903 and 1923, Porter brought national attention to the fragility and transient loveliness of this world. Today, Indiana protects its northern wetlands with a series of fish-and-wildlife preserves where migrating mallards, blue herons, and sandhill cranes still swoop down to rest among the cattails and water hemlock, just as they did in Porter's time.

HOOSIERS ALL

Occupying a patch of flat land in the exact geographic center of the state is Indianapolis, the state capital. Laid out in 1820, the planned city is the epitome of tree-lined urban orderliness in its older neighborhoods and downtown. Cornfields and orchards lie well within its borders — the result of a move to extend the city's boundaries in 1969 — while residents enjoy such urban amenities as art museums, a symphony orchestra, and professional sports, as well as the running of the world-famous Indianapolis 500-mile auto race.

Its big-city ways notwithstanding, Indianapolis is typically Hoosier, and it is Hoosier character that gives this state its style. These days that character is no longer exemplified by the cool and competent frontiersman at the turkey shoot, but it still may have much to do with sharpshooting. Every March in cities and towns throughout Indiana, excitement mounts as Hoosiers breathlessly follow the playoffs for the statewide high-school basketball championship. It always seems to come down to a tie score with only seconds left on the clock. Then some lanky Hoosier calmly steps to the line and drops in a free throw — and, like the pioneers before him, wins it all. It is a ritual Indianans never tire of.

Flat-topped black buggies are a sign of devotion to tradition in the Amish villages of northeastern Indiana.

AMERICA'S QUARRY

Walk around New York, Chicago, Washington, D.C., or many other American cities and you will be looking at bits of Indiana. Much of the architectural limestone used on building exteriors in this country comes from a strip of Indiana ground 50 miles long, a few miles wide, and 60 feet deep near the towns of Bedford and Bloomington. Stone from this belt — the Salem Outcrop — was used in Rockefeller Center and the Empire State Building in New York City, the Tribune Tower in Chicago, the Pentagon and the Lincoln Memorial in Washington, and in 14 state capitols.

The limestone was created some 330 million years ago when water covered the Midwest. Like most limestone, it is made from the decomposed bodies and shells of ancient sea creatures. But the Indiana beds are especially free of other ocean debris, which would have flawed the rock. This purity makes the Hoosier stone prized building material. It can be worked in smooth architectural slabs of 10 to 20 tons and quarried in mammoth blocks weighing up to 10 times that much.

Autumn brings both bounty and beauty to Conner Prairie, a 55-acre restoration of an 1830's pioneer village and farm north of Indianapolis.

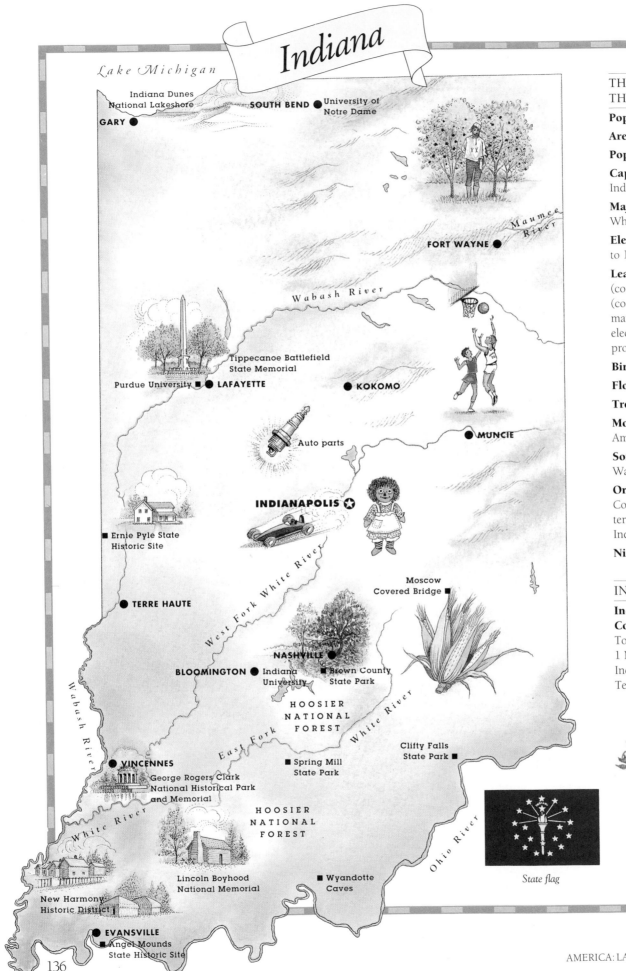

Indiana

Lake Michigan

Indiana Dunes
National Lakeshore

SOUTH BEND ● University of
Notre Dame

GARY ●

Maumee River

FORT WAYNE ●

Wabash River

Tippecanoe Battlefield
State Memorial

Purdue University ■ ● **LAFAYETTE**

● **KOKOMO**

Auto parts

● **MUNCIE**

■ Ernie Pyle State
Historic Site

INDIANAPOLIS ☆

West Fork White River

● **TERRE HAUTE**

Moscow
Covered Bridge ■

NASHVILLE ●

BLOOMINGTON ● Indiana
University ■ Brown County
State Park

East Fork

HOOSIER
NATIONAL
FOREST

White River

Clifty Falls
State Park ■

● **VINCENNES**
George Rogers Clark
National Historical Park
and Memorial

■ Spring Mill
State Park

Wabash River

HOOSIER
NATIONAL
FOREST

White River

Lincoln Boyhood
National Memorial

■ Wyandotte
Caves

Ohio River

New Harmony
Historic District ■

● **EVANSVILLE**
■ Angel Mounds
State Historic Site

State flag

THE PEOPLE AND THE LAND

Population: 5,499,000

Area: 36,185 sq. mi.

Population per sq. mi.: 152

Capital and largest city:
Indianapolis (pop. 1,236,600)

Major rivers: Ohio, Wabash, White

Elevation: 320 ft. (Ohio River) to 1,257 ft. (Wayne County)

Leading industries: Agriculture (corn, tomatoes, hogs), mining (coal, limestone, petroleum), manufacturing (steel, auto parts, electrical equipment), lumber products

Bird: Cardinal

Flower: Peony

Tree: Tulip poplar

Motto: The Crossroads of America

Song: "On the Banks of the Wabash, Far Away"

Origin of name: Name given by Congress when it established the territory, referring to the original Indian population

Nickname: Hoosier State

INFORMATION

Indiana Department of Commerce
Tourism Development Division
1 North Capitol, Suite 700
Indianapolis, IN 46204-2288
Telephone: 800-782-3775

Peony

Cardinal

HISTORICAL HIGHLIGHTS

c. 1732 French establish first permanent settlement, Vincennes.

1763 Victorious in French and Indian War, Great Britain gains control of Indiana area.

1778 American troops under George Rogers Clark take Vincennes from the British.

1811 Indians are routed at the Battle of Tippecanoe.

1816 Indiana is admitted to Union as 19th state.

1905 The U.S. Steel Corporation founds the town of Gary, leading to development of Indiana's Lake Michigan shore.

1911 The first running of Indianapolis 500 auto race takes place on Memorial Day.

1937 Ohio River reaches record heights. Flood damage is extensive in southern Indiana.

1965 Studebaker auto company closes after 63 years.

1988 Indiana's junior senator, J. Danforth Quayle, is elected vice president.

FAMOUS SONS AND DAUGHTERS

James Dean (1931 – 55). Killed in an auto crash when he was only 24, this talented actor remains famous for his portrayals of troubled teenagers.

Eugene V. Debs (1855 – 1926). An influential labor leader, Debs ran for president five times on the Socialist ticket.

Virgil (Gus) Grissom (1926 – 67).

One of NASA's seven original astronauts, Grissom was killed in a fire during a flight simulation.

Eli Lilly (1838 – 98). The drug company Lilly founded in 1876 grew into a pharmaceutical giant, producing insulin in the 1920's and polio vaccine in the 1950's.

Cole Porter (1893 – 1964). "Night and Day," "You're the Top," "Begin the Beguine" . . . Porter remains unsurpassed as a composer for the American musical stage.

Knute Rockne (1888 – 1931). Born in Norway, Rockne came to Indiana as an undergraduate at Notre Dame, where he first won fame as a football player and then as the team's head coach from 1918 to 1931. During his reign, Notre Dame won 105 games, tied 5, lost 12, and had 5 undefeated seasons.

Madame C. J. Walker (1867 – 1919). Born Sarah Breedlove in Louisiana, the daughter of former slaves, Madame Walker settled in Indianapolis in 1910. There she built a successful business in cosmetics for black women and

became the nation's first black female millionaire. She willed much of her fortune to charity.

ODDITIES AND SPECIALTIES

The origin of the nickname Hoosier is unclear. It may derive from "Who's here?" — once a common reply to a knock at the door; from *hoozer*, early English dialect for something large; or from Samuel Hoosier, a contractor who favored Indiana workers for building a canal along the Ohio River in 1825.

Far out of proportion to its size, Indiana has produced a prodigious number of well-known writers, among them novelists Theodore Dreiser, Lew Wallace, Kurt Vonnegut, and Booth Tarkington; poet James Whitcomb Riley; journalist Ernie Pyle; and cartoonist Jim Davis, creator of *Garfield*.

John Chapman (1774 – 1845), the legendary Johnny Appleseed, who traveled the Midwest planting fruit trees and spreading the Swedenborgian religion, is buried in Fort Wayne.

Indiana is renowned for covered bridges. Parke County alone has more than 30. The 330-foot Moscow covered bridge in Rush County is the longest in the state.

Raggedy Ann was born in Indianapolis in 1914, when a little girl asked her father, cartoonist John Gruelle, to fix up an old doll.

PLACES TO VISIT, THINGS TO DO

Angel Mounds State Historic Site (near Evansville). Prehistoric Indian burial mounds and relics dating from 1200 to 1450 are preserved here.

Brown County State Park (near Belmont). Changing foliage in these hills attracts thousands

of visitors each autumn. Historic buildings in the nearby town of Nashville retain the ambience of Indiana in the 1870's to 1920's.

Hoosier National Forest (near Bedford). Bounded on the south and southeast by the Ohio River, these 155,000 acres of forested hills offer lakes and streams for boating and fishing.

Indiana Dunes National Lakeshore (Porter). Miles of sandy beach along Lake Michigan invite swimmers and sunbathers. Nearby bogs, marshes, and swamps contain a variety of plants and wildlife.

Lincoln Boyhood National Memorial (Lincoln City). A re-created 19th-century farm surrounds a replica of the log cabin where the president spent his youth.

New Harmony Historic District In 1814 George Rapp founded Harmonie for the Harmony Society and awaited the apocalypse. A decade later, Robert Owen bought the town to form a utopian colony of scholars. Many buildings from that era are open for viewing.

Spring Mill State Park (near Mitchell). This park features a restored pioneer village, a memorial to astronaut Gus Grissom, and several caverns. Boat rides are available on the subterranean river at Twin Caves.

Wyandotte Caves (Leavenworth). The larger of these two caves contains the biggest underground room in any known cave.

Iowa

*Cornfields green and gold,
proclaiming a fertile land*

In the popular movie *Field of Dreams,* a long-dead legendary baseball player returns to life and steps onto a baseball diamond a farmer has built on his cornfield. Surveying the scene of agrarian beauty, the baseball player asks, "Is this heaven?"

"No," the farmer replies. "It's Iowa."

In Iowa movie theaters this brief exchange produced bursts of applause as well as hoots of laughter. The mixed reaction reflects the two-sided feeling Iowans have for their state: on the one hand, a self-deprecating awareness of Iowa's reputation as a place where corn and hogs reign supreme, and on the other, a deep conviction that Iowa, a magnificently fertile land between two great rivers, really is the next thing to heaven.

RURAL HEART AND SOUL

The very word *Iowa* stands as a virtual synonym for America's agricultural heritage and bounty. Only California and Texas, which are several times Iowa's size, exceed the state in the value of farm products. And more than any other state, Iowa still represents Thomas Jefferson's ideal nation of well-educated farmers. It boasts both the greatest number of farms of any state except Texas and the highest literacy rate in the nation.

Despite its image as a state of farmers, Iowa's town- and city-dwellers outnumber farm residents by almost 10 to 1. They live in places like Des Moines, Iowa's capital and a major center for the insurance industry; Cedar Rapids, home of one of the nation's largest

Cattle and cornfields under a broad Iowa sky are the picture of American agriculture. This farm is in the eastern part of the state, near Iowa City.

Plowing furrows across the slope of the land helps to prevent water erosion.

In full bloom during summer, lavender wild bergamot brightens a thicket near Decorah.

cereal mills; and Dubuque, a picturesque Mississippi River town where one can find both a greyhound track and a monastery nearby. But the heart and soul of Iowa resides in its rural towns — more than 1,000 of them, scattered more or less uniformly across the state.

THE GREAT AMERICAN BICYCLE RIDE

A rolling celebration of Iowa's small towns occurs each July, when about 10,000 bicyclists from all over the country ride clear across the state. The week-long event, called Ragbrai (an acronym for the sponsoring Des Moines Register's Annual Great Bicycle Ride Across

Iowa), serves up a smorgasbord of midwestern specialties. Ragbrai riders are apt to encounter, say, a pig roast in Pisgah, Danish pancakes in Kimballton, a beer tent in Belle Plaine, and corn on the cob in Exira.

The Ragbrai route changes every year, but always proceeds from west to east, along with the prevailing breezes. Near the western border, most of it formed by the Missouri River, looms a newcomer's first sign that Iowa (to quote one bicyclist) "is emphatically *not* flat." Grassy ridges, called loess hills, rise 100 to 200 feet above the surrounding landscape. Indians and French fur trappers once gath-

ered in these hills to trade goods. This pre-pioneer era is memorialized in the name of Iowa's seventh-largest city, Council Bluffs, situated just across the Missouri from Omaha.

The Iowa landscape east of Council Bluffs rolls up and down through dense networks of streams and rivers. Here, in river valleys lacing the eastern and southern sections of the state, are most of Iowa's woodlands — some 1.5 million acres forested mainly with hardwoods such as elms, oaks, maples, hickories, and walnuts.

The topography flattens out suddenly as one travels northeast. An invisible boundary

Dry, golden stalks of corn glisten in the sunlight at harvest time. Iowa's fertility is legendary. Poet Robert Frost, who had struggled to farm less generous ground in New England, said that Iowa soil "looks good enough to eat without putting it through vegetables."

Dusted with snow, a farm in Clayton County in northeastern Iowa sparkles in the clear, cold winter air. The sunlight reflected on the clouds creates such vivid colors that they seem almost painted.

THE RIGS THAT WORKED THE PRAIRIE

The conversion of Iowa's prairie into productive farmland in the mid-19th century coincided with rapid advances in the implements used to plow, reap, and thresh. In addition to John Deere's famous steel plow, new machines drawn by horses (but still requiring a man to operate the moving parts) provided a level of efficiency that only a couple of decades before had been unimaginable.

The new horse-drawn rake did the work of 10 men with hand rakes. Horse-drawn reapers processed six times more acreage than men with hand-held grain cradles or scythes could. And a mechanical hay loader, such as the one shown here, did the work in a fraction of the usual time.

Some of these old rigs are still working in Iowa today — not on the modern farms seen from the highway, but at a unique outdoor museum, Living History Farms, on the edge of Des Moines. This 600-acre site includes three working farms that rely entirely on implements used, respectively, in 1700,

1850, and at the turn of the century. Visitors can mark the progression of 19th-century agriculture as farmers in period clothing use the vintage machines to perform tasks exactly the way their forebears did a century or more ago.

delineates a peninsulalike lobe extending down from the north and deep into central Iowa, as far south as Des Moines. This region, the Des Moines Lobe, is where the Wisconsinan glacier lopped off the hills and filled in the valleys of north-central Iowa some 20,000 to 25,000 years ago. This is Iowa as the world knows it, relatively flat and very fertile.

FROM PRAIRIE TO FARMLAND

The Woodland and Plains Indians knew the territory that became Iowa as a vast, rolling expanse carpeted with prairie vegetation. This included such native grasses as big and little bluestem, switchgrass, sideoats grama, and buffalo grass. The grasses mingled with scores of wildflowers, such as pasqueflowers, prairie violets, gentians, blazing stars, and asters. All told, some 300 different plant species supported a similar diversity of insects and animals, from honeybees to bison. Here and there groves of burr oak trees dotted the grasslands.

Fewer than 10,000 of the original 30 million acres of Iowa prairie remain, much of it in railroad rights-of-way, abandoned pioneer cemeteries, or state-maintained prairie preserves.

Iowa's earliest pioneers, who made their homes in wooded bottomlands near the Mississippi in the 1830's, had no idea of the agricultural potential that the prairies held. But when John Deere's all-steel plow became available to them, farmers were able to penetrate the thick prairie loam, and the region was settled in a quick burst of westward expansion. The most enduring images of Iowa may be those created by the artist Grant Wood, who ranks among Iowa's most famous natives. Wood chose the land and people of his native state as his subjects in such paintings as "Fall Plowing" and "American Gothic."

Iowa has changed a great deal since Wood painted his popular canvases of the state in the 1930's. Iowans have endured the worst family-farm crisis in their history, and are now struggling to bring industrial farming practices into line with environmental and food-safety concerns. But through it all, Iowa holds fast to its special place in the American imagination as the quintessence of rural life, symbol of the nation's bounty.

An east coast wildflower, New Jersey tea, is well established in Turin Loess Hills Preserve.

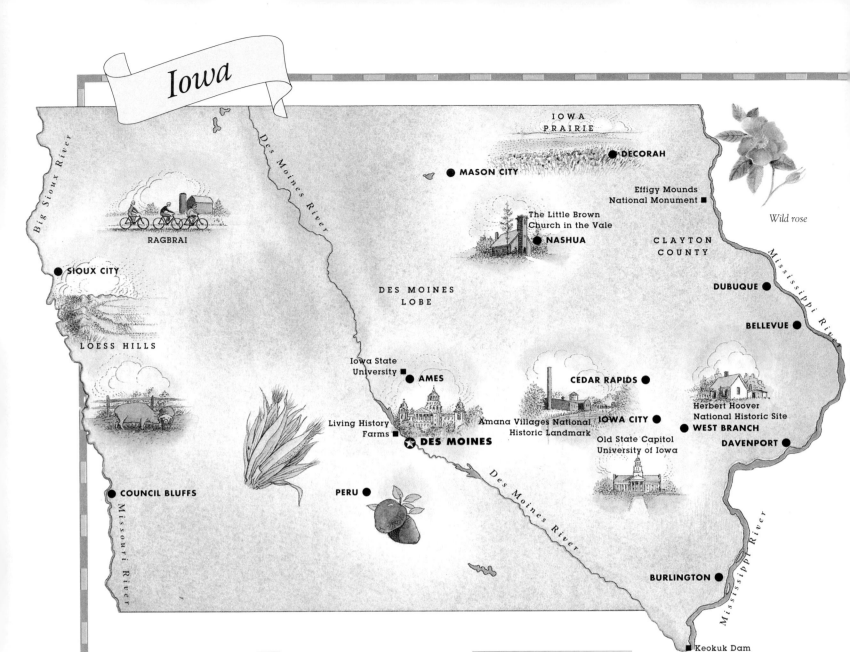

Iowa

IOWA PRAIRIE

● DECORAH

● MASON CITY

Effigy Mounds
National Monument ■

The Little Brown
Church in the Vale

● NASHUA

CLAYTON COUNTY

DES MOINES LOBE

Big Sioux River

Des Moines River

Missouri River

Wild rose

DUBUQUE ●

Mississippi River

BELLEVUE ●

RAGBRAI

● SIOUX CITY

LOESS HILLS

Iowa State University ■

● AMES

CEDAR RAPIDS ●

Herbert Hoover
National Historic Site

Living History Farms

★ DES MOINES

Amana Villages National
Historic Landmark

IOWA CITY ●

● WEST BRANCH

Old State Capitol
University of Iowa

DAVENPORT ●

● COUNCIL BLUFFS

PERU ●

Des Moines River

BURLINGTON ●

Mississippi River

■ Keokuk Dam

THE PEOPLE AND THE LAND

Population: 2,766,600

Area: 56,275 sq. mi.

Population per sq. mi.: 49

Capital and largest city: Des Moines (pop. 391,800)

Major rivers: Big Sioux, Des Moines, Mississippi, Missouri

Elevation: 480 ft. (Mississippi River) to 1,670 ft. (near Sibley)

Leading industries: Agriculture (livestock, corn, soybeans), manufacturing (tires, farm machinery, appliances), mining (gravel, shale)

Bird: Eastern goldfinch

Flower: Wild rose

Tree: Oak

Motto: Our Liberties We Prize, and Our Rights We Will Maintain

Song: "The Song of Iowa"

Origin of name: From *ayuxwa,* an Iowa Indian word translated as "beautiful land" and "This is the place"

Nicknames: Corn State, Hawkeye State, Land Where the Tall Corn Grows, Nation's Breadbasket

INFORMATION

Iowa Department of Economic Development
Division of Tourism
200 East Grand Avenue
Des Moines, IA 50309
Telephone: 800-345-IOWA

State flag

Eastern goldfinch

HISTORICAL HIGHLIGHTS

1673 The European explorers Jolliet and Marquette pass through Iowa.

1682 La Salle claims Iowa region for France.

1788 The first settler, French Canadian Julien Dubuque, mines lead near what is now Dubuque.

1803 U.S. receives region as part of Louisiana Purchase.

1832 U.S. Army defeats Chief Black Hawk, leading the Sauk and Fox Indians.

1833 Several permanent settlements — Bellevue, Burlington, and Peru — are founded.

1838 Congress makes Iowa, formerly part of Wisconsin, a separate territory.

1846 Iowa is admitted to Union as 29th state.

1867 The first railroad to cross Iowa is finished.

1913 The new Keokuk Dam on Mississippi River supplies power to midwestern cities.

1929 Herbert Hoover becomes 31st president, the first born west of the Mississippi.

1936 In an effort to hold onto their land during the Depression, farmers form cooperatives.

1948 Iowa is first in production of corn, hogs, oats, poultry, eggs, and cattle.

1959 Soviet premier Nikita Khrushchev visits Iowa farm to learn about American agricultural methods.

1985 Recognizing the economic hardship faced by many farmers, U.S. government orders a moratorium on farm foreclosures.

FAMOUS SONS AND DAUGHTERS

Bix Beiderbecke (1903 – 31). Born in Davenport, jazz cornetist and composer Beiderbecke influenced many musicians despite his early death.

Buffalo Bill Cody (1846 – 1917).

Buffalo Bill's exploits as a Pony Express rider, frontier scout, and buffalo hunter led to a career in show business, most notably in his Wild West Show.

Herbert Hoover (1874 – 1964). Although his presidency (1929 – 33) was sullied by the Great Depression, Hoover is honored for his organization of European relief following World War I and for heading commissions to study governmental reorganization in the 1940's and 1950's.

John L. Lewis (1880 – 1969). President of the United Mine Workers of America (1920 – 60), Lewis founded the Committee for Industrial Organization (CIO) in 1935 in order to unionize mass-production industries.

Lillian Russell (1861 – 1922). Called the American Beauty, Russell — an opera singer who also appeared in revues and plays — was famous for her relationship with the high-living financier "Diamond Jim" Brady.

James Van Allen (1914 –). This astrophysicist discovered the Van Allen radiation belts, which surround the earth, while studying the *Explorer* and *Pioneer* findings at his laboratory at the University of Iowa.

Henry A. Wallace (1888 – 1965). A pioneer in agricultural economics, Wallace was named secretary of agriculture in 1933. He served as Franklin Roosevelt's vice president from 1941 to 1945.

John Wayne (1907 – 1979). This star of western and other action movies became a symbol of the rugged he-man and patriot that he portrayed in such films as *The Green Berets* (1968).

Meredith Willson (1902 – 84). Willson composed symphonies, movie scores, and musical comedies. His hit Broadway musical, *The Music Man,* was inspired by Mason City, his hometown.

Grant Wood (1891 – 1942). An artist in the realistic mode, Wood painted "American Gothic" and other works that depict Iowa farm people.

ODDITIES AND SPECIALTIES

The first electronic digital computer was built in 1939 at Iowa State University, at Ames, by Dr. John Vincent Atanasoff.

Once home to 30 million acres of prairie, Iowa today has less than 10,000 acres of this unique ecosystem, but these are vigorously protected.

Abolitionist John Brown trained his men for the attack on Harper's Ferry, W. Va., in Springdale.

America's favorite apple, the Red Delicious, first appeared in 1872 as a genetic mutation in the orchard of Jesse Hiatt of Peru.

Near Nashua each year, hundreds of couples are wed at the Little Brown Church in the Vale, the 19th-century church immortalized in the popular hymn "The Church in the Wildwood."

PLACES TO VISIT, THINGS TO DO

Amana Villages National Historic Landmark (near Cedar Rapids). In the mid-1800's the religious Amana Society founded seven colonies in Iowa. Visitors can see original and restored buildings, museums, and craft and furniture shops.

Effigy Mounds National Monument (McGregor). This beautiful, rustic area has Indian burial mounds shaped like bears, birds, and other animals.

Herbert Hoover National Historic Site (West Branch). The site includes the cottage where Hoover was born, his father's blacksmith shop, a Quaker meetinghouse, and Hoover's grave.

Iowa State Fair (Des Moines). Every August, Iowa's state fair celebrates the state's bounty with big-name entertainment as well as livestock, produce, and other farm exhibits. A 160-acre campground is open to fairgoers.

Kansas

A windswept state of prairies, wheat fields, and cottonwoods

The original inhabitants of this land called themselves the *Kansa,* "people of the south wind." So when the name of the Indian tribe was applied to the whole territory that became Kansas, it was appropriate. Far from the gentling influence of any ocean, Kansas is beset by extremes of weather brought in by constant wind. Hot southerly winds ripple the prairie grasses all summer, until autumn reverses them and the winds sweep back through as freezing blasts from the north.

A GENTLY RISING STATE

Early European visitors here were like the wind: they passed through Kansas, seeing little reason to stay. Zebulon Pike, leading an expedition in 1806 across what would become Kansas, likened the land to the Sahara. Nearly two centuries later, motorists speeding through on the interstates might still brand the landscape as flat and desolate, lacking in variety. They, like Pike before them, would be wrong.

Although the land is occasionally flat, it is nowhere level. The rectangle that is Kansas is on a slant, sloping upward from the southeastern corner toward the northwest, rising at an average of about eight feet per mile. And there is nothing desertlike about the Chautauqua Hills of southeastern Kansas, covered by forests of oak and hickory. During the warmer months rose-red summer tanagers sing from the blackjack oaks all day, and the nighttime woods echo with the throaty chants of the chuck-will's-widow — the same bird sounds that one might hear in the Carolinas.

Almost ready for the October harvest, sunflowers grow in a farmer's field in eastern Kansas. The plants' seeds will be used for foodstuffs and oil.

On the plains south of Dodge City, a wheat field is whipped by wind as clouds churn overhead. Kansas is given to extremes of weather because it is located midway across the continent, where warm southerly air collides with cold currents from the north.

These southern sounds were unfamiliar to the pioneers who rushed to Kansas from New England in the 1850's, making haste to help install enough antislavery voters to ensure that Kansas would become a free state. They, like later settlers, were people of strong convictions, leaders in a variety of causes: abolition, prohibition, and woman suffrage.

Eastern Kansas has other wooded regions, each with its own special mix of trees. But along the edges of rivers everywhere, in the arid west as well as the rainier east, the typical tree is the cottonwood. Named the official state tree in 1937, the cottonwood was the perfect choice. In parts of central and western Kansas, it is practically the only tree. Tough

Designed for the aerial view, the works of artist Stan Herd are planted into Kansas farmland. The "canvas" for the piece above is the soil of Douglas County, near Eudora.

and fast-growing, it sends down deep taproots for water and assumes a stately form. It can grow along rivercourses where the flow is far underground in dry seasons. Many a Kansas pioneer must have blessed the cottonwood for its cool shade; many a traveler must have spied it from afar as a sign of water in dangerously dry country.

Konza Prairie in the Flint Hills is part of the largest remaining tall-grass prairie in the country.

Startling rock formations, called both Monument Rocks and the Kansas Pyramids, rise from the flat valley of the Smoky Hill River in northwest-central Kansas.

AMERICA: LAND OF BEAUTY AND SPLENDOR

Toward Kansas's western boundary, cottonwoods hug the banks of the sandy riverbeds. Behind them, stretching away for miles, lie the dry High Plains, a region of low rainfall and short-grass prairie. Wildflowers carpet the plains in spring — pink and purple locoweeds, white yarrow, yellow groundsel, and dozens more — but by midsummer the land is often brown and dry. Wide flats of blue grama and buffalo grass bake under the sun, waiting for rain. This is where long ago massive herds of buffaloes, or bison, roamed.

TURKEY RED WHEAT AND BLUESTEM GRASSES

Across the state, the land supports some 200 varieties of native grasses, and a few introduced species too. Chief among the imports is the hardy winter wheat, brought in by Mennonite immigrants from Russia. Arriving in 1874, the Mennonite farmers had packed in each family's luggage some handpicked Turkey Red wheat, a choice variety that is well adapted to the hard conditions of the Great Plains. Winter wheat transformed central Kansas into the breadbasket of America and created many typical Kansas scenes: wheat fields stretching to the horizon; tall grain elevators, visible for miles around; combines clanking across the fields at harvesttime.

But little wheat grows in the most distinctive of Kansas landscapes: the Flint Hills, a rocky, rugged region running north and south through the middle of the eastern half of the state. Too formidable even for tough and resourceful Kansas farmers, much of the land here was never broken by the plow, and it remains one of the largest tall-grass prairies in North America.

To walk in the Flint Hills in summer is to see the Great Plains through the eyes of the pioneers. Gently sloping hills covered with bluestem grasses roll away toward the horizon, mile after green mile. Birdsong echoes softly on all sides. Down in a narrow draw, where springwater seeps from the rocks, may stand a lone cottonwood. But in all other directions, the deep blue sky is unbroken save for the occasional tall thunderhead sailing on the south wind — the same south wind that gave Kansas its name.

PRAIRIE DANCE

Spring on the Kansas prairie is ushered in by an ancient ritual: the mating dance of prairie chickens. At a traditional site — often a slight rise, surrounded by a wide sweep of grassland — male prairie chickens gather in the blackness before dawn. There may be only a few or there may be a flock of 40 or more, but all are there in the hopes of attracting females.

Under normal conditions, the male prairie chicken is not an impressive sight. Merely the size of a small barnyard rooster, he is heavily marked with narrow brown bars, a dull cryptic pattern that serves as a camouflage in dry grass. But when the mating dance begins, this drab brown member of the grouse family is transformed. He raises his long neck feathers above his head, lifts his tail, drops his wings, and inflates a pair of orange air sacs on his neck. Stamping his feet rapidly on the ground, he sends out his mating call — a sound like a distant foghorn with hiccups. The ghostly noise may carry a mile across the plains. Sometime during the spring, every female prairie chicken within earshot will come to the display site to select a mate.

Two kinds of prairie chickens are found in Kansas. The more common greater prairie-chicken is found over much of the eastern and north-central sections, and sometimes in the northwest. The lesser prairie chicken, a smaller and paler denizen of drier country, favors the sagebrush-covered flats of southwestern Kansas.

Bison wander the Maxwell Game Refuge in central Kansas. Before hunters virtually wiped them out in the 19th century, bison inhabited the Great Plains from Canada to central Texas.

Kansas

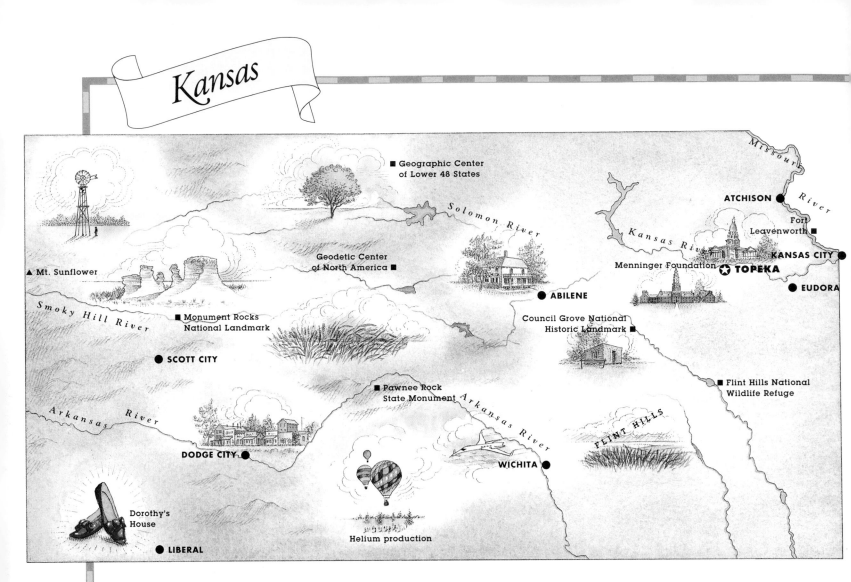

- Geographic Center of Lower 48 States
- **ATCHISON**
- Fort Leavenworth
- *Missouri River*
- *Solomon River*
- *Kansas River*
- Menninger Foundation
- **KANSAS CITY**
- ☆ **TOPEKA**
- ● **EUDORA**
- ▲ Mt. Sunflower
- Geodetic Center of North America
- ● **ABILENE**
- *Smoky Hill River*
- Monument Rocks National Landmark
- ● **SCOTT CITY**
- Council Grove National Historic Landmark
- Flint Hills National Wildlife Refuge
- Pawnee Rock State Monument
- *Arkansas River*
- *FLINT HILLS*
- *Arkansas River*
- ● **DODGE CITY**
- ● **WICHITA**
- Helium production
- Dorothy's House
- ● **LIBERAL**

THE PEOPLE AND THE LAND

Population: 2,467,000

Area: 81,781 sq. mi.

Population per sq. mi.: 30

Capital: Topeka (pop. 164,800)

Largest city: Wichita (pop. 483,100)

Major rivers: Arkansas, Kansas, Missouri

Elevation: 680 ft. (Verdigris River) to 4,039 ft. (Mt. Sunflower)

Leading industries: Agriculture (wheat, beef cattle, sorghum), manufacturing (aircraft, processed foods), helium, petroleum, and natural gas production

Bird: Western meadowlark

Flower: Sunflower

Tree: Cottonwood

Motto: *Ad Astra per Aspera* (To the Stars Through Difficulties)

Song: "Home on the Range"

Origin of name: From the Sioux Indian word *kansa*, meaning people of the south wind

Nicknames: Breadbasket of America, Cyclone State, Jayhawker State, Squatter State, Sunflower State, Wheat State

INFORMATION

Kansas Department of Commerce
Travel and Tourism Division
400 SW 8th Street, 5th floor
Topeka, KS 66603-3957
Telephone: 800-2-KANSAS

Western meadowlark

Sunflower

State flag

HISTORICAL HIGHLIGHTS

1541 Searching for gold, the Spanish explorer Coronado comes to Kansas.

1682 The explorer La Salle claims the area for France.

1762 After the French and Indian War, France cedes Kansas to Spain.

1800 Crippled by wars, Spain gives region back to France.

1803 U.S. receives most of Kansas as part of Louisiana Purchase.

1822 William Becknell takes wagons on Santa Fe Trail, establishing it as trade route. Two-thirds of route crosses Kansas.

1827 Col. Henry Leavenworth founds Fort Leavenworth to protect travelers on Santa Fe Trail.

1854 Congress names Kansas a U.S. territory.

1854 – 59 Fighting between pro- and antislavery groups becomes so intense that territory is called Bleeding Kansas.

1860 First railroad reaches Kansas from the east.

1861 Kansas enters Union as 34th state.

1863 Confederate raiders led by Capt. William Quantrill burn the town of Lawrence, killing more than 150 persons.

1867 Abilene becomes first major center for Texas cattle drives.

1874 Mennonite immigrants from Russia introduce a hardy winter wheat, called Turkey Red.

1880 Kansas becomes first state to enact a constitutional ban on alcohol.

1932 – 39 Years of drought, dry topsoil, and Kansas winds combine to make much of the state a dust bowl.

1948 Prohibition is repealed by state legislature.

1951 The landmark school desegregation case, *Brown v. Board of Education of Topeka,* is filed.

1986 Voters approve sale of liquor by the drink, although some counties remain dry.

FAMOUS SONS AND DAUGHTERS

Charles Curtis (1860 – 1936). Part Indian himself, Curtis fought for Indian rights. He served as Herbert Hoover's vice president beginning in 1929.

Amelia Earhart (1898 – 1937).

Earhart made aviation history as the first woman to fly solo across the Atlantic and the first person to fly solo from Hawaii to California. She was attempting to fly around the world when her plane disappeared in the Pacific.

Dwight David Eisenhower (1890 – 1969). Eisenhower's impressive military career, especially during World War II, brought him national attention,

and he easily won the presidential election in 1952 and again in 1956. As president, he helped end the Korean War and worked against Communist expansion.

Charles Menninger (1862 – 1953). He and his sons **Karl** (1893 – 1990) and **William** (1899 – 1966) founded the Menninger Clinic for psychiatric patients in Topeka in 1925, and the Menninger Foundation for research, training, and public education in psychiatry in 1941.

Carry Nation (1846 – 1911). While she was living in Kansas Nation's tactics as a temperance advocate — destroying saloons with a hatchet — advanced the cause of national prohibition.

Charlie Parker (1920 – 55). Parker was a jazz saxophonist who, with Dizzy Gillespie, made the first bebop recordings.

ODDITIES AND SPECIALTIES

Sometimes called Midway, U.S.A., Kansas is located at the geographic and geodetic center of the contiguous states. The geodetic center, in Osborne County, is used in mapmaking as the prime reference point for North American maps.

Golden wheat billows through every county in the state, whose production of that grain is surpassed only by entire countries.

Kansas doesn't quite want to stay on the ground. It is the leading producer of helium in the U.S. And Wichita, called the Air Capital of the World, has three major aircraft companies, which make two-thirds of the world's general aviation planes.

Dodge City is known not only for its onetime lawlessness but for its winds, which have the highest average speed in the U.S. — 13.4 miles per hour.

PLACES TO VISIT, THINGS TO DO

Council Grove National Historic Landmark At this major staging point of the Santa Fe Trail, a mission school, a tavern, a jail, and an Indian home are preserved.

Dodge City Front Street in The Wickedest Little City in America looks today almost as it did in the wild 1870's.

Dorothy's House (Liberal). *Wizard of Oz* fans can visit this museum, an early 20th-century farmhouse restored to represent the era in which the story takes place. It has the original model house used in the 1939 movie.

Eisenhower Center (Abilene). Adjacent to Eisenhower's childhood home are a museum and library. Eisenhower and his wife are also buried here.

Flint Hills National Wildlife Refuge (Hartford). Lying in the Neosho Valley, these 18,500 acres provide a haven for migrating ducks and geese. Beavers, muskrats, coyotes, and bobcats live there too.

Monument Rocks National Landmark (25 miles north of Scott City). These rocks, remnants of ancient undersea chalk beds, contain an extraordinary accumulation of marine fossils.

Pawnee Rock State Monument This park features a huge red sandstone cliff, called the Citadel of the Prairie, which provided a landmark and meeting spot on the Santa Fe Trail.

Kentucky

Surpassing beauty in the land of Daniel Boone

Kentucky was one of America's legendary frontiers, thrown open when Daniel Boone blazed the Wilderness Road through Cumberland Gap just as the American Revolution was beginning. Until then, the formidable Appalachian Mountains had discouraged the colonists from even attempting to explore the virgin territory extolled by a few intrepid trappers and hunters — a land of deeply forested hills and valleys roamed by bears, buffaloes, and elk.

Kentucky was also a land of surpassing beauty and natural abundance, and Boone's expedition suddenly made it attainable. Following his trail or traveling down the Ohio River, settlers poured into the new frontier from Virginia, the Carolinas, and Pennsylvania — 12,000 of them by the end of the Revolutionary War.

BLUEGRASS AND PENNYROYAL

Pushing on past the jagged ridges and narrow valleys of the Cumberland and Pine mountains, many of the early pioneers planted their corn and hemp in the promising bluegrass meadows of north-central Kentucky. Others farmed the fertile Pennyroyal, or "Pennyrile," to the south, a region named for the aromatic herb that flourishes there. Civilization advanced so rapidly in the Bluegrass region that prospering farmers soon replaced their sturdy log houses with elegant Georgian and Greek revival estates, where they grew fine tobacco, bred fast horses, and distilled bourbon whiskey. Lexington, founded in 1775, was proudly pointed out as the "Athens of the West" to such

Few horse farms are as handsome as those in the Bluegrass, where Thoroughbreds are raised for racing.

Fog settles in the hollows of the western foothills of the Appalachian Mountains. This view is from Pilot Knob, a lookout near Berea.

19th-century tourists as the marquis de Lafayette, who may well have thought the whole of Kentucky was as aristocratic as its Bluegrass.

KENTUCKY CONTRASTS

In fact, Kentucky was then and is today a region of extreme contrasts created by the state's unique geography. The Bluegrass owes its prosperity both to the Ohio River, which made Louisville an important port, and to the rich limestone soil that nourishes the famous blue-tinged grasses so relished by Thoroughbreds. The beautiful farmland of the Pennyroyal, with its rolling hills and rivers —the Green, the Cumberland, the Tennessee —is dotted with geological oddities: sinkholes, subterranean streams, and a vast labyrinth of caverns culminating in Mammoth Cave.

In the west, the hilly land of the western coalfield region is rich in mineral deposits and dotted with hardscrabble mining towns. Yet the Purchase — a tract of alluvial bottomlands and loess uplands at the extreme western tip of Kentucky that was purchased from the Chickasaws in 1818 — was settled by

southern planters and still looks like a remnant of the romantic Old South today.

At the other end of the state, the eastern highlands are another world. With spectacular waterfalls, towering hardwood forests, and cliffsides scarred by strip-mining but massed with rhododendrons, the highlands reflect both the heartbreaking beauty and back-breaking challenge of Appalachia. Here weathered cabins cling to ridges, swaying bridges span dizzying heights across gorges, Canada warblers sing from shady thickets, and the sound of the dulcimer drifts through the hollows on summer evenings.

But this, too, is Kentucky, as authentic a part of the state's heritage as the Bluegrass horse farms. It was from these mountains the settlers first saw the land they would call home. "Stand at Cumberland Gap," wrote historian Frederick Jackson Turner in 1893, "and watch the procession of civilization, marching single file — the buffalo following the trail to the salt springs, the Indian, the fur-trader and hunter, the cattle-raiser, the pioneer farmer — and the frontier has passed by."

Sky Bridge, a rock arch spanning 90 feet, is one of more than 80 natural arches in the Red River Gorge Geological Area. The area, part of Daniel Boone National Forest in eastern Kentucky, was overlaid with erosion-resistant sandstone millions of years ago. Arches were created when weaker rock underneath the narrow sandstone ridges was gradually worn away.

HISTORICAL HIGHLIGHTS

1750 Thomas Walker explores eastern Kentucky for a Virginia land company.

1767 Daniel Boone first crosses Cumberland Gap into Kentucky.

1774 James Harrod and others found Harrodsburg, the first permanent settlement.

1775 Boone blazes Wilderness Road and builds Fort Boonesborough in central Kentucky.

1775 – 83 During Revolutionary War, pioneers defend settlements against British-instigated Indian attacks.

1792 Kentucky joins Union as the 15th state.

1798 – 99 State legislature passes Kentucky Resolutions, denouncing restrictive federal Alien and Sedition Acts.

1815 First steamboats travel between Louisville and New Orleans, facilitating the export of Kentucky products.

1861 Though neutral, Kentucky is invaded by both Yankee and Rebel forces during Civil War.

1875 First Kentucky Derby horse race is held.

1904 – 09 In "Black Patch War," disgruntled farmers break tobacco monopoly by burning warehouses and fields.

1918 State begins to build an extensive road system.

1936 U.S. government installs a gold depository at Fort Knox.

1964 Land Between the Lakes recreation area opens.

1970 Coal mine explosion near Wooton kills 38.

FAMOUS SONS AND DAUGHTERS

Muhammad Ali (1942 –). The popular boxer (born Cassius Clay) won an Olympic gold medal in 1960 and the world heavyweight championship four times from 1964 to 1978.

Cassius Marcellus Clay (1810 –1903). Clay founded the antislavery paper *True American* in Lexington in 1845. He was an early supporter of the Republican Party and served as ambassador to Russia.

D. W. Griffith (1875 – 1948). The pioneer director and producer originated a number of cinematic techniques, including tracking shots, intercutting, and backlighting.

Abraham Lincoln (1809 – 65). The 16th president was born in Hodgenville and lived in Kentucky until age seven, attending a log schoolhouse. Thereafter he moved with his family to Indiana. At 21, Lincoln moved to Illinois, where he studied law and began his political career.

Jesse Stuart (1907 – 84). Author of more than 30 volumes, Stuart wrote novels, short stories, and poetry about the mountain folk of eastern Kentucky, where he was born. *God's Oddling* describes his own childhood there.

Zachary Taylor (1784 – 1850). Old Rough-and-Ready's distinguished army career won him a popular following. He became president in 1849.

Robert Penn Warren (1905 – 89). Born in Guthrie, Warren was a novelist, poet, and literary critic. He won the Pulitzer Prize in 1947 for his novel *All the King's Men*.

ODDITIES AND SPECIALTIES

Central Kentucky's famous bluegrass is, of course, green, but its tiny buds lend a slight blue-purple cast in spring.

Cumberland Falls boasts a moonbow, a rare atmospheric phenomenon similar to a rainbow but generated by moonlight. The ethereal spectrum appears in the mist above the water.

The Reverend Elijah Craig created bourbon whiskey in 1789 in Kentucky, which now ranks first in the world for bourbon production. Bourbon is the key ingredient in the state's famous drink, the mint julep.

The Kentucky Derby, held every May since 1875 at Churchill Downs in Louisville, is the oldest continuously run horse race in the country.

The origin of the famous Hatfield-McCoy feud is unclear, but the two families, who lived near the Kentucky-West Virginia border, fought for 14 years. The feud, which began in 1878, resulted in more than 40 deaths.

Mother's Day was conceived in the little town of Henderson, the brainchild of schoolteacher Mary S. Wilson in 1887.

PLACES TO VISIT, THINGS TO DO

Abraham Lincoln Birthplace National Historic Site (Hodgenville). A granite and marble memorial building shelters the one-room log cabin believed to be Lincoln's birthplace.

Cumberland Gap National Historical Park (Middlesboro). The Cumberland Gap, a natural rift in the mountains, provided a passageway for pioneers. The park encompasses 20,273 acres in the Cumberland Mountains in Kentucky and Tennessee.

Kentucky Horse Park (Lexington). This unique park pays tribute to the state's favorite animal with museums, films, and horse shows. A farm tour and horseback rides are available.

Kentucky

COVINGTON ●

Ohio River

Kentucky River

Appalachian dulcimer

☆ **FRANKFORT**

LOUISVILLE ● Kentucky Derby

■ Kentucky Horse Park

LEXINGTON ●

Ohio River

■ Fort Knox

THE BLUEGRASS

HARRODSBURG ● Shaker Village of Pleasant Hill ● **RICHMOND**

Hatfield-McCoy Feud

HODGENVILLE ●

Abraham Lincoln Birthplace

DANIEL BOONE NATIONAL FOREST

BEREA ●

APPALACHIAN MOUNTAINS

Mammoth Cave National Park ■

THE PENNYROYAL

Lake Cumberland

▲ Black Mountain

PINE MOUNTAIN

OWLING GREEN

■ Cumberland Falls State Park

CUMBERLAND MOUNTAIN

Cumberland Gap National Historical Park ■

Land Between the Lakes (Golden Pond). This 40-mile peninsula between Barkley and Kentucky lakes offers boating, woodland hiking, and a living history farm that re-creates an 1850's homestead.

Mammoth Cave National Park (Cave City). Explored passages of the world's longest known cave system extend over 300 miles, with 12 miles open for tours, including a boat trip on the underground Echo River.

Shaker Village of Pleasant Hill (Harrodsburg). Shakers maintained a community here for about 100 years, beginning in 1805. Today this National Historic Landmark includes restored original buildings with furniture of Shaker design.

State flag

Cardinal

Goldenrod

THE PEOPLE AND THE LAND

Population: 3,665,200

Area: 40,409 sq. mi.

Population per sq. mi.: 91

Capital: Frankfort (pop. 27,000)

Largest city: Louisville (pop. 967,000)

Major rivers: Kentucky, Ohio

Elevation: 257 ft. (Mississippi River) to 4,145 ft. (Black Mountain)

Leading industries: Manufacturing (machinery, electronics, automotive assembly), agriculture (tobacco, soybeans, livestock), coal mining, lumber

Bird: Cardinal

Flower: Goldenrod

Tree: Kentucky coffee tree

Motto: United We Stand, Divided We Fall

Song: "My Old Kentucky Home"

Origin of name: From the Wyandot Indian word meaning grand meadow

Nicknames: Bluegrass State, Tobacco State

INFORMATION

Kentucky Department of Travel Development
500 Mero Street
Frankfort, KY 40601
Telephone: 800-225-TRIP

Louisiana

A spicy potpourri of people, cultures, and wildlife

Louisiana is nothing less than exotic — a land of steamy swamps and lazy bayous, regal old mansions and tumbledown fishing shacks, Cajuns and Creoles, jambalaya and bouillabaisse. Its lush landscapes — fields engulfed by honeysuckle, kudzu, and wisteria, endless marshes that shimmer in the heat like mirages, swamps where towering bald cypresses are veiled in Spanish moss — are just as remarkable as Louisiana's culture, which is well known for its distinctive foreignness. Though largely the legacy of the region's French past, Louisiana's language, folklore, and cuisine, particularly in the southern half of the state, are strongly seasoned by other influences — Spanish, African, West Indian, American Indian — and each lends its own special accent to Louisiana's cultural potpourri.

ON THE BANKS OF THE MISSISSIPPI

The state's unique character also owes much to its lakes, bayous, lagoons, marshes, swamps — and, above all, the majestic, meandering Mississippi River. (Even Shreveport, far to the west and north, connects to the Mississippi via the Red River.) As it snakes down from Arkansas, the Mississippi serves as Louisiana's eastern border, flowing past cottonfields, stands of loblolly pine, and oxbow lakes formed from the river's own abandoned loops. Farther south, near Baton Rouge and New Orleans, the river sweeps by the impressive lawns and white columns of plantation homes built two centuries ago by cotton and sugarcane planters. Farther along, the river skirts Lake Pontchartrain, with its sailboats and shining

Sunbeams streaming through morning mist accent the mysterious beauty of the luxuriant Atchafalaya swamp.

Thousands of egrets, herons, ibises, and other elegant birds nest in the trees at Lacassine National Wildlife Refuge, one of several giant wildlife havens situated within Louisiana's extensive coastal wetlands.

causeway, and swings around New Orleans in the broad curve that inspired the town's nickname — the Crescent City.

CREOLE CHARM AND CULTURE

New Orleans began in 1718 as a neat square which French engineers laid out in the river's swampy curve and filled in with oyster shells and cypress logs — an area known today as the Vieux Carré, or French Quarter. Here the

French and Spanish built their charming houses and courtyards, decorated them with lacy wrought iron, entertained at balls and banquets, intermarried, and over the years created the rich hybrid culture known as Creole.

New Orleans remains diverse and intriguing — a city where life is one marvelous parade. During the world-famous Mardi Gras season the city hosts colorful festivities that culminate in a raucous, gorgeous parade. And

ISLANDS IN THE MARSH

Louisiana's coastal marshland seems endlessly flat. But in the western half of the state the expanse is elegantly punctuated by long, narrow "islands" called cheniers. Rising from 2 to 10 feet above the surrounding marsh, cheniers consist of sand, silt, and shells anchored by shrubs and live oaks. The massive oaks, gnarled by the wind and draped with Spanish moss, inspired the name *chenier* — derived from a French word meaning the "place where the oaks grow."

Ranging in length from a few yards to 30 miles or so, the cheniers are, in fact, old stretches of shoreline. They were formed when clay and silt were carried westward from the Mississippi delta and deposited by the sea. Over thousands of years, as the marshland extended farther out into the Gulf, these sections of shore were left behind, becoming ridges of solid ground amid a sea of marsh. In some areas, parallel rows of cheniers extend inland for 10 miles; those closest to the open waters of the Gulf are the youngest, about 300 years old, while those farthest inland are up to 3,000 years old.

The largest cheniers, Pecan Island and Grand Chenier, provide a splendid habitat for wildlife. Here warblers and scarlet tanagers perch in thickets, and egrets feed among the bordering reeds. Marsh deer rest amid wildflowers such as yellow flag and blue iris, while raccoons and horned owls nap high in the twisted, moss-covered limbs of the live oaks.

in this town, even such solemn occasions as funerals call for a parade, with a jazz band playing dirges on the way to the cemetery.

Once past the Crescent City, the Mississippi turns south, gradually losing its identity in the labyrinth of bayous, bays, lagoons, and marshes that make up its delta. A road follows the river as best it can past Barataria Bay, where Jean Lafitte once plotted with his pirate band, past groves of tangerines, fishing shacks on stilts, crumbling forts, sulfur mines, and oil rigs. When the land begins to dissolve into marsh, the road stops — still miles from the place where the muddy river meets and merges with the gray-green swells of the Gulf.

SWAMPS AND BAYOUS

West of New Orleans, in the south-central part of the state, lies Acadiana, a unique region of bayous. It was named for the French peasants

Lavish displays of azaleas grace 4,700-acre Hodges Gardens in west-central Louisiana.

Hundreds of lazy bayous meander through the lush, soggy swampland of southern Louisiana.

who made their way there via the Mississippi River after being exiled from Acadia (an early name for Nova Scotia) in 1755 for refusing to swear loyalty to the British crown. Called Cajuns (from "Açadians"), the people clung to their own language and customs, but adapted to their swampy home by living in raised cottages, growing what crops they could on higher ground, and carving dugouts called *pirogues* to explore the giant Atchafalaya swamp.

Within this enormous swamp, silence usually reigns amid moss-draped bald cypresses and rafts of water hyacinths growing in the

tea-colored water. The stillness is broken only by the flapping wings and noisy squawk of a night heron taking flight or by the distant hammering of a pileated woodpecker.

WHERE MIGRATORY BIRDS MEET

Although abundant in the swamps, bird life is most spectacular in Louisiana's coastal wetlands — a vast sea of marshland stretching from the Texas border to the Mississippi delta. Here migratory birds of every kind — waterfowl, shorebirds, songbirds, and birds of prey — gather to spend the winter months in such

great wildlife refuges as Sabine, Lacassine, and Rockefeller. On November evenings at sunset, half a million waterfowl and thousands of ibises, egrets, and avocets can be seen overhead. The sky is filled with long straight lines of pelicans and cormorants, V-formations of geese, and loosely scribbled patterns of ibises. At night, the birds' noisy honking, squawking, flapping, and splashing can be heard for miles around, mingled with choruses of croaking frogs and bellowing alligators. Such sights and sounds epitomize Louisiana: a place both strange and wonderful.

An elegant allée *(or alley) of overarching, 200-year-old oaks frames the long approach road at Rosedown Plantation. On either side of the road, paths wind through gardens adorned with statues and fountains.*

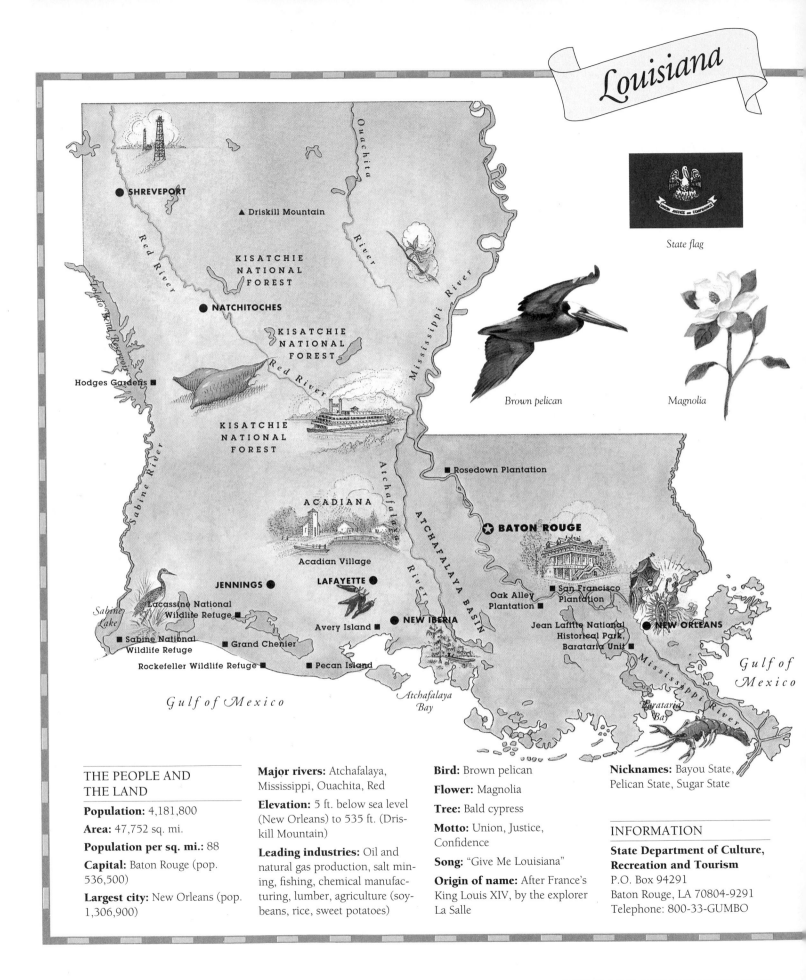

State flag

Brown pelican

Magnolia

SHREVEPORT

▲ Driskill Mountain

KISATCHIE NATIONAL FOREST

NATCHITOCHES

KISATCHIE NATIONAL FOREST

Hodges Gardens ■

KISATCHIE NATIONAL FOREST

Rosedown Plantation ■

ACADIANA

Acadian Village

★ BATON ROUGE

Oak Alley Plantation ■

San Francisco Plantation ■

JENNINGS ●

LAFAYETTE ●

Lacassine National Wildlife Refuge ■

Sabine Lake

Sabine National Wildlife Refuge ■

Grand Chenier ■

Avery Island ■

NEW IBERIA ●

Jean Lafitte National Historical Park, Barataria Unit ■

● NEW ORLEANS

Rockefeller Wildlife Refuge ■

Pecan Island ■

Gulf of Mexico

Atchafalaya Bay

Barataria Bay

Gulf of Mexico

THE PEOPLE AND THE LAND

Population: 4,181,800

Area: 47,752 sq. mi.

Population per sq. mi.: 88

Capital: Baton Rouge (pop. 536,500)

Largest city: New Orleans (pop. 1,306,900)

Major rivers: Atchafalaya, Mississippi, Ouachita, Red

Elevation: 5 ft. below sea level (New Orleans) to 535 ft. (Driskill Mountain)

Leading industries: Oil and natural gas production, salt mining, fishing, chemical manufacturing, lumber, agriculture (soybeans, rice, sweet potatoes)

Bird: Brown pelican

Flower: Magnolia

Tree: Bald cypress

Motto: Union, Justice, Confidence

Song: "Give Me Louisiana"

Origin of name: After France's King Louis XIV, by the explorer La Salle

Nicknames: Bayou State, Pelican State, Sugar State

INFORMATION

State Department of Culture, Recreation and Tourism
P.O. Box 94291
Baton Rouge, LA 70804-9291
Telephone: 800-33-GUMBO

HISTORICAL HIGHLIGHTS

1519 Alonso Alvarez de Piñeda discovers a great river, presumably the Mississippi.

1541 Hernando de Soto explores the region.

1682 La Salle claims the Louisiana region for France.

1714 Louis Juchereau de St. Denis establishes the first permanent settlement at present-day Natchitoches.

1718 New Orleans is founded.

1762 France secretly cedes Louisiana to Spain.

1788 A fire nearly destroys the city of New Orleans.

1795 Jean Etienne de Boré invents a method for granulating large quantities of sugar.

1800 Spain cedes Louisiana back to France.

1803 U.S. buys Louisiana.

1812 Louisiana becomes the 18th state. The first steamboat to ply Mississippi arrives in New Orleans from Pittsburgh.

1815 Andrew Jackson defeats British in the Battle of New Orleans, the last battle of the War of 1812.

1838 New Orleans has its first Mardi Gras.

1861 Louisiana secedes from Union and flies the flag of an independent nation for 55 days before joining the Confederate States of America.

1862 Union soldiers capture New Orleans.

1901 Oil is discovered near town of Jennings.

1927 The Mississippi floods much of the state.

1935 The powerful U.S. senator Huey P. Long is assassinated by a political enemy.

1960 School integration begins amidst rioting.

1963 The Mississippi River – Gulf Outlet, a shortcut shipping channel, opens.

1965 Hurricane Betsy causes 61 deaths and extensive damage in southeastern Louisiana.

1975 Louisiana adopts a new state constitution.

1984 The Louisiana World Exposition opens in New Orleans.

FAMOUS SONS AND DAUGHTERS

Louis Armstrong (1900 – 71). Born in New Orleans, Satchmo was a world-renowned jazz trumpeter, singer, and bandleader.

Jean Baptiste le Moyne, sieur de Bienville (1680 – 1768?). This explorer and three-term governor of the colony of Louisiana was the founder of New Orleans.

George Washington Cable (1844 – 1925). Cable's fiction depicted life in New Orleans and especially the world of antebellum Creoles.

Truman Capote (1924 – 84). Born in New Orleans, Capote set his early novels in the South. His works include *Breakfast at Tiffany's* and *In Cold Blood.*

Lillian Hellman (1907 – 84). Author of *The Little Foxes, Toys in the Attic,* and other plays, Hellman was known for her profound insights into themes both political and psychological.

Jean Lafitte (1780 – 1826?). This pirate and smuggler helped Americans defeat the British in the Battle of New Orleans during the War of 1812.

Huey Pierce Long (1893 – 1935). A Louisiana governor and U.S. senator, the folksy and flamboyant Kingfish championed the poor but took on nearly dictatorial powers to wield control of the state. He was assassinated in 1935.

Edward Douglass White (1845 – 1921). After serving as a Louisiana judge and a U.S. senator, White was appointed to the U.S. Supreme Court in 1894. He became chief justice in 1910.

ODDITIES AND SPECIALTIES

The spicy Cajun and Creole cuisines of Louisiana include such distinctive dishes as gumbo (a soup thickened with okra) and jambalaya (a rice dish).

Louisiana ranks first in the world for its crayfish harvests and first in the nation for salt production.

Around the turn of the century, New Orleans became the birthplace of jazz, one of America's greatest contributions to music. More recently, zydeco, the lively music of French-speaking blacks in southwest Louisiana, has become widely popular.

Louisiana has an official state dog — the Catahoula leopard dog, a breed native to Louisiana.

The Mardi Gras draws thousands of tourists to New Orleans each year. Held since 1838, the carnival includes parades, masked balls, floats, marching bands, and street dancing.

PLACES TO VISIT, THINGS TO DO

Acadian Village (Lafayette). The Acadian (Cajun) way of life in the last century is preserved in this museum-village, set on 10 acres of gardens and woods.

Avery Island (near New Iberia). Sitting atop a salt dome, this forested island features a botanical garden, an egret sanctuary, and fields of hot red peppers.

French Quarter (New Orleans). The oldest section of New Orleans, the Vieux Carré, with its ornate buildings, narrow streets, and lovely courtyards, is saturated with Old World charm.

Jean Lafitte National Historical Park, Barataria Unit This section of the park, located in the Mississippi delta area, includes bayous, swamps, and marshlands. Trails allow hikers to view Spanish-moss-covered bald cypresses, as well as egrets, otters, and alligators.

Kisatchie National Forest Located at six different sites in central and northern Louisiana, these vast woodlands include scenic bayous, lakes, and mesas.

Oak Alley Plantation (Vacherie). The "alley," made by two parallel rows of live oaks, leads to a splendid Greek revival mansion built by a French sugar planter in 1839.

Maine

The land that greets the sunrise

Katahdin ("highest land, nearest to the gods") is the Abnaki Indian name for Maine's loftiest mountain. And the name is apt, for Katahdin, nearly a mile high, dominates the surrounding hills and is the centerpiece of the state's vast woodlands.

This majestic peak is but one example of Maine's natural beauty — a beauty that does indeed seem near to the gods, or at least divinely inspired. Seven chains of lakes, more than 2,500 in all, spill across dark green forests like sparkling blue sapphires. In the northeast, vast fields of potato plants carpet the earth with white blossoms. In the southeast, the coastline twists and turns through an intricate network of coves, inlets, and islands at the edge of the indigo sea. And in the center of the state, densely forested mountains, Katahdin among them, cut an awe-inspiring profile against the azure sky.

DOWN EAST

Maine's jagged coast meets the Atlantic Ocean with long peninsulas, spray-soaked granite cliffs, and more than 2,000 off-shore islands. Some of these islands are no more than rocky resting places for gulls. Others, such as Vinalhaven, have sizable and flourishing communities, and the largest, Mount Desert Island, contains the town of Bar Harbor and much of Acadia National Park. The names of the islands often provide a clue about the origin of the people who lived there: Monhegan was named by American Indians, Isle au Haut by the French, and Beals Island by Yankees.

Crashing surf at craggy Portland Head creates a quintessential image of Maine. Built in 1791, the lighthouse here rises more than 100 feet above the shore.

The tranquillity of a sunlit cove at Acadia National Park belies the violence of its history. Maine's jagged coastal cliffs are the legacy of glaciers that passed over the region 20,000 years ago. Moving southward, the massive ice sheets smoothed slopes that faced north and tore rock from those that faced south, leaving the southward-facing coast rough-hewn and rugged.

It seems reasonable to say that Maine is located "up north," but ever since early New England mariners sailed downwind in an easterly direction from Boston to reach its coast, Maine has been dubbed Down East. Earlier residents, the Abnakis, called the region Dawnland because they saw it as near the rising sun. More realistic than poetic was the Algonquian name, which translates as Land of the Frozen Ground. Its truth is echoed by present-day Mainers, who joke that their state has two seasons: July and winter.

The Maine coast is a world of quiet, sea-worn villages tucked into sheltered harbors where sailboats are moored. From Kittery north to Eastport, lobstermen ply their trade, and kayakers explore the rocky coves of protected archipelagoes. When the fog rolls in, it can be so thick that the ocean seems to disappear. At moments like this, the coastal cottages have a timeless charm, their shuttered windows, weathered clapboard siding, and gabled roofs seeming to peek through the mist from yesteryear. Often the only sounds are the cries of gulls and the forlorn moaning of a distant foghorn.

At other times, the sun shines so brightly and the air is so clear and crisp that the whole coast seems to sparkle. It is not hard to understand why so many painters — among them Winslow Homer, Rockwell Kent, Edward Hopper, John Marin, and three generations of Wyeths — have sought inspiration here for more than a century.

DEEP IN THE WOODS

From its border on the Atlantic Ocean, the state extends north to Canada, embracing vast woodlands that become increasingly wild and undisturbed the farther north one goes. This is the domain of moose, deer, bears, and owls, where humans are merely intruders in a primeval land that still belongs to nature.

Nearly 90 percent of Maine is still blanketed with forest — maple, oak, spruce, fir, hemlock, and especially white pine, the state's official tree. When explorer Henry Hudson sailed into Penobscot Bay in 1609 with a broken mast, he found that a white pine, with its tall, straight trunk, made a perfect replacement. In 1691 the British government decreed that all white pines more than 24 inches in diameter growing within three miles of the shore belonged to the British navy.

Surprisingly, in this century of vanishing wilderness, the forests of Maine are still so undeveloped that over half the woodland is divided into large townships identified solely by numbers and often accessible only by the deeply rutted, unpaved roads connecting isolated logging camps. No wonder, then, that the wry advice of Maine natives to lost motorists is "You can't get there from here."

In this wild domain — stretching from Rangeley Lakes near the New Hampshire border northeast to Fort Kent — people are scarce and moose can seem as common as squirrels. The forest seems to go on forever, ornamented by rocky outcrops, glistening lakes, and winding rivers. Moosehead Lake, Maine's largest, lies here, and not far away are Mount Katahdin and the scenic trails of Baxter State Park.

Solitude and serenity reign in the Maine woods. Camped by a sun-dappled stream, where a gentle breeze brings the scent of pine and the chirping of songbirds, the visitor cannot help but feel that Maine is the place to rediscover the world as nature made it.

Fog invades Monhegan Island with stealth, robbing it of sunshine but not serenity.

Lean and stark, the trunks of paper birches contrast sharply with the vibrant palette of autumn foliage at Grafton Notch State Park in Maine's western mountains.

A purity accompanies winter on the Maine coast, as the coves are dusted with snow, shrouded in mist, and abandoned by their summer visitors.

CLOWN PRINCE OF THE NORTH ATLANTIC

One of Maine's most colorful residents is the puffin, or sea parrot. With black and white feathers, triangular orange bills, and short, plump bodies, puffins look like a cross between a parrot and a penguin. In fact they are members of the auk family, which includes other deep-diving seabirds.

Puffins are superb fishermen. They dive underwater and "fly" after fish, propelled by their strong, stubby wings. When they emerge on the surface, they often carry their catch — as many as 30 small fish at a time — clamped firmly in their bills.

When it comes to flying in the air, however, puffins are less successful. Unless there is a brisk wind to give them a boost, the portly birds splash along in the water, wings flapping madly, in order to get aloft. Once airborne, they continue their arduous pumping in a clumsy flight that has been called a triumph of will over physique.

Puffins nest in colonies by burrowing into seaside cliffs. The female generally lays only one egg, and after it hatches both parents care for the offspring until it is about six weeks old. Then the chick is abandoned in the protection of the burrow. A week later, driven by instinct and, presumably, hunger, the young bird flutters off the cliff and into the sea, where it develops the skills to fish and fly.

Mount Katahdin dominates Baxter State Park, a 200,000-acre wilderness named for Gov. Percival P. Baxter, who donated the land to the state.

Maine

White pine cone and tassel

ST. JOHN RIVER
● FORT KENT

Allagash Wilderness Waterway

AROOSTOOK
COUNTY

Lumber industry

Baxter
State
Park ▲ Mt. Katahdin

Moosehead
Lake

● MILLINOCKET

St. Croix River

Rangeley
Lakes

River

Penobscot River

● CALAIS

● OLD TOWN

EASTPORT ●

● BANGOR

■ Grafton Notch
State Park

● MACHIAS

Androscoggin River

Kennebec River

● BAR HARBOR
MT. DESERT ISLAND
Acadia National Park

★ AUGUSTA

Penobscot
Bay

● ROCKLAND

VINALHAVEN
ISLAND

Pemaquid
Point Light

*Atlantic
Ocean*

BOOTHBAY HARBOR ●

PORTLAND ●

Gulf of Maine

PROUTS NECK ● ■ Portland
Head Light

OGUNQUIT ●

KITTERY ●

Chickadee

State flag

THE PEOPLE AND THE LAND

Population: 1,218,000

Area: 33,265 sq. mi.

Population per sq. mi.: 37

Capital: Augusta (pop. 22,000)

Largest city: Portland (pop. 212,200)

Major rivers: Androscoggin, Kennebec, Penobscot, St. Croix

Elevation: Sea level to 5,268 ft. (Mt. Katahdin)

Leading industries: Manufacturing (paper and other forest products, electronics), agriculture (potatoes, apples, blueberries, livestock), fishing and lobstering

Bird: Chickadee

Flower: White pine cone and tassel

Tree: White pine

Motto: *Dirigo* (I Direct)

Song: "State of Maine Song"

Origin of name: Possibly after the French province Le Maine or from the word *mainland*

Nicknames: Border State, Lumber State, Pine Tree State

INFORMATION

The Maine Publicity Bureau
97 Winthrop Street
Hallowell, ME 04347-2300
Telephone: 207-289-6070

HISTORICAL HIGHLIGHTS

c. 1000 Norsemen believed to land on Maine coast.

1604 French establish a colony but migrate to Nova Scotia after a hard winter.

1622 An English royal grant gives Maine territory to John Mason and Ferdinando Gorges.

1677 Massachusetts buys Maine from Gorges's heirs.

1726 Settlers make treaty with 40 of Maine's Indian chiefs, improving trade and relations.

1775 In first naval battle of the American Revolution, Maine patriots capture British schooner *Margaretta* near Machias.

1788 Maine abolishes slavery.

1816 Record cold wave grips Maine. Year is dubbed "eighteen hundred and froze to death."

1820 As part of Missouri Compromise, Maine enters Union as 23rd state.

1842 Maine's border dispute with Canada is resolved.

1851 Maine adopts country's first law prohibiting sale of liquor. Not until 1934 is this prohibition repealed.

1863 Confederates hijack a ship from Portland. Pursued at sea, they are captured.

1919 Acadia National Park is created by act of Congress.

1948 Winning election to the U.S. Senate, Representative Margaret Chase Smith becomes first woman to serve in both houses of Congress.

1972 Edmund S. Muskie is a leading contender for the Democratic presidential nomination.

1980 Federal government grants $81.5 million to Passamaquoddy and Penobscot Indians in compensation for land taken from tribes around 1800.

FAMOUS SONS AND DAUGHTERS

Winslow Homer (1836 – 1910). Famous for his powerful paintings of the sea, Homer drew much of his inspiration from the Maine coast at Prouts Neck, where he settled in 1884.

Henry Wadsworth Longfellow (1807 – 82). Among America's best-loved poets, Longfellow often used historical themes, as in "Paul Revere's Ride" and *The Song of Hiawatha*.

Edna St. Vincent Millay (1892 – 1950). A popular poet, Millay was admired as much for defying social conventions in the 1920's as for her lyrical sonnets. Her book *The Ballad of the Harp Weaver* won the Pulitzer Prize for poetry in 1923.

Edmund S. Muskie (1914 –). Muskie helped build Maine's weak Democratic Party. Four years after winning the governorship in 1954, he became the first Democrat in Maine's history to be elected to the U.S. Senate. Later, he served as secretary of state under President Carter.

Robert E. Peary (1856 – 1920). Peary was one of the greatest arctic explorers, acclaimed for being the first to reach the North Pole, on Apr. 6, 1909.

Andrew Wyeth (1917 –). One of America's most popular painters, Wyeth often depicts coastal Maine or rural Pennsylvania. His father, N. C. Wyeth, also painted in Maine, as does his son, James.

ODDITIES AND SPECIALTIES

Maine is the only state in the Union that borders just one other state, New Hampshire.

The Appalachian Trail, the world's longest hiking path, runs from Mt. Katahdin to Springer Mountain in Georgia.

Sixty lighthouses line Maine's rocky coast. Portland Head Light, one of the oldest in the U.S., was commissioned by George Washington.

Maine is the nation's largest producer of lobster (around 20 million pounds a year), low-bush blueberries (around 50 million pounds a year), and toothpicks.

Now a delicacy, lobster was considered so ordinary in colonial times that some indentured servants had clauses in their contracts stipulating that they could be served the shellfish at no more than five meals a week.

Maine is the third-largest producer of potatoes in the U.S. Potatoes mean so much to the economy in Aroostook County that children are excused from school to help with the harvest.

PLACES TO VISIT, THINGS TO DO

Acadia National Park (Bar Harbor). The oldest national park east of the Mississippi, Acadia encompasses 41,642 acres of the Maine coast and islands, containing cliffs, mountains, lakes, springs, woods, caves, and coves. A roadway leads to the top of Cadillac Mountain, from which there are breathtaking views of the ocean speckled with offshore islands.

Baxter State Park (Millinocket). The centerpiece of this 200,000-acre wilderness is 5,268-foot Mt. Katahdin, whose rocky upper peaks are in an alpine zone where arctic plants grow. This is one of the best places for seeing bears and moose in Maine.

Fishing Anglers will especially enjoy the Rangeley Lakes in western Maine, the remote Allagash Wilderness Waterway, and Grand Lake Stream, west of Calais.

Flying with a bush pilot Many of the remote lakes in Maine are accessible only by plane. Bush pilots offer sightseeing tours over woodlands as well as transportation to outposts.

Ogunquit This coastal town boasts beautiful beaches, a summer theater, and an art colony. Nearby is 100-foot-high Bald Head Cliff, which reaches out into the ocean for 300 feet.

Old Town Canoe Company (Old Town). Tours through this factory offer a glimpse of the way canoes are made.

Portland Museum of Art The museum contains a fine collection of American realist art, specializing in Maine painters.

Sailing You can sail as a guest on a windjammer from many coastal towns. Cruises last from a few hours to a week.

White water rafting The Dead, Kennebec, and Penobscot rivers (West Branch) are among the best rafting spots in the country.

Maryland

A pocket-size portrait of America

Small though it is, Maryland has such a dazzling variety of natural and man-made features — remote mountains, crowded urban areas, fertile farmlands, scenic shorelines, modern industrial centers, old tobacco plantations — that the state has been called an America in miniature. It seems fitting, then, that America's national anthem, "The Star-Spangled Banner," was written in Maryland, and that its capital, Washington, D.C., was built on land donated by the state.

THE BOUNTIFUL CHESAPEAKE BAY

The most striking of Maryland's natural features — and a great national treasure in itself — is the Chesapeake Bay. This 200-mile-long estuary, which bisects the state, has so many arms, inlets, and islands that its total shoreline is greater than the distance from Maryland to California. It is also a mammoth nursery and feeding ground for wildlife, so replete with birds, fish, shellfish, and other creatures that Baltimore writer H. L. Mencken once facetiously dubbed it a protein factory.

A giant peninsula (called the Delmarva Peninsula because it is shared by Delaware, Maryland, and Virginia) separates the Chesapeake Bay from the Atlantic Ocean. While throngs of vacationers are drawn to beaches in and around Ocean City, on the Atlantic, the rest of Maryland's share of the peninsula, called the Eastern Shore, manages to preserve the flavor of its agricultural and maritime past. On the Bay side, major highways pass through expansive fields of wheat, corn, and

At this exhilarating overlook in western Maryland's Garrett County, mountains surround the Cove, a natural amphitheater of rolling, contour-plowed fields.

As the light of dawn creeps eastward from the Chesapeake Bay Bridge in the distance, a sloop makes its way down Whitehall Creek toward open water.

soybeans, and smaller country roads wind through old villages whose names — Oxford, Cambridge, St. Michaels — reflect the area's British heritage. The countryside's gracious brick mansions and venerable churches, some more than 200 years old, cannot, however, match the age of a local tree, the magnificent Wye Oak, which has been casting its ample shade for some four centuries.

When the Wye Oak was a mere century old, a visiting Dutchman remarked on "a great storm coming through the trees," a thunderous sound made by the flapping wings of thousands of ducks. He was, of course, an early witness to one of the huge migrations of waterfowl, shorebirds, and songbirds that —

attracted by the abundant food, water, and shelter provided by the Chesapeake Bay — pause here every spring and fall.

GRACEFUL MOUNTAINS, GENTEEL TOWNS

Western Maryland, a narrow strip of land bordered by the historic Mason-Dixon line on the north and the Potomac River on the south, contrasts dramatically with the flat coastal plain. Here the scenic Blue Ridge and Allegheny mountains, where wealthy Americans once built idyllic retreats, now draw hikers, skiers, and white-water rafters.

In southern Maryland, just west of the Chesapeake, are miles of tobacco fields that have been a part of the landscape since colo-

nial days. The tobacco crop built the elegant town houses and mansions of Annapolis, just to the north, which in its 18th-century heyday was called the genteelest town in North America by an English visitor.

In the next century it was Baltimore that grew and prospered, becoming a preeminent center of shipping and manufacturing. Even so, the city retained what visiting author Henry James called a perfect felicity. Though linked by commerce to the North and to ports throughout the world, Baltimore even today manages to preserve the gentle airs of the South — not surprising in a state where so many contrasting elements blend to form a miniature America.

Catoctin Mountain Park, west of Thurmont, contains 25 miles of scenic woodland trails. It is also the site of Camp David, the presidential retreat.

Wild ponies are among the most charming and conspicuous residents of Assateague Island, situated on the Atlantic Coast south of Ocean City. Though the precise origin of the ponies is uncertain, they have lived on the island for centuries and are believed to be descended from small domestic horses kept here by early settlers.

HISTORICAL HIGHLIGHTS

1608 British captain John Smith explores Chesapeake Bay.

1632 King Charles I grants charter to the second Lord Baltimore, Cecil Calvert.

1634 The ships *Ark* and *Dove* carry first settlers to Maryland.

1649 Maryland passes Toleration Act, guaranteeing religious freedom to all Christians.

1729 Baltimore Town is founded.

1767 Mason and Dixon's survey sets the Delaware-Maryland-Pennsylvania boundaries.

1776 Maryland asserts its independence and adopts a state constitution.

1783 Annapolis is made the temporary national capital.

1784 At Annapolis, Congress approves Peace of Paris, ending Revolutionary War.

1788 Maryland becomes the seventh state.

1791 Maryland donates land for the District of Columbia.

1828 Construction of nation's first railroad, the Baltimore & Ohio, begins.

1829 Chesapeake-Delaware Canal connects the Bay with the Delaware River.

1845 U.S. Naval Academy is founded at Annapolis.

1862 Union troops defeat Confederates at Antietam.

1919 – 33 Maryland refuses to enforce Prohibition and becomes known as the Free State.

1952 The Chesapeake Bay Bridge opens to automobiles.

1980 Harborplace, an enclosed complex of restaurants and stores, brings new life to Baltimore Harbor.

FAMOUS SONS AND DAUGHTERS

Frederick Douglass (c. 1818 – 95). After escaping slavery, Douglass became an influential spokesman for black rights. He published the *North Star*, an abolitionist newspaper.

Johns Hopkins (1795 – 1873). A banker, businessman, and philanthropist, Hopkins founded a free hospital and a university, both of which bear his name.

Thurgood Marshall (1908 –). As chief counsel of the NAACP, Marshall advanced the cause of civil rights. He became the first black associate justice of the U.S. Supreme Court in 1967.

H. L. Mencken (1880 – 1956). A Baltimore journalist, editor, and essayist known for his biting social criticism, Mencken also wrote the monumental, multivolume study of words entitled *The American Language*.

Babe Ruth (1895 – 1948). The first great home run hitter, and a remarkable pitcher as well, Ruth started out with the Baltimore Orioles but is best known for his years with the New York Yankees.

Elizabeth Ann Seton (1774 – 1821). A convert to Catholicism, Seton became a nun and founded the Daughters of Charity. In 1975 her canonization made her the first saint born in America.

Upton Sinclair (1878 – 1968). A novelist concerned with social ills, Sinclair wrote *The Jungle*, which exposed the conditions of the Chicago stockyards and led to important reforms.

Harriet Tubman (c. 1820 – 1913). An escaped slave, Tubman helped some 300 other slaves gain freedom via the Underground Railroad. She also aided Union troops as a nurse and spy during the Civil War.

ODDITIES AND SPECIALTIES

Maryland is the only state with an official sport — medieval jousting.

Baltimore's Preakness Stakes, an annual horse race, is part of the famous Triple Crown, along with the Kentucky Derby and the Belmont Stakes.

The Chesapeake Bay is one of the nation's most bountiful sources of seafood, especially blue crab. Maryland is so proud of its blue crab that it publishes tips on how to catch, cook, and eat it.

America's first umbrella factory — with the slogan "Born in Baltimore, raised everywhere" — began production in 1828.

Doc Holliday, the notorious western outlaw, attended dental school in Baltimore.

Margaret Brent, who emigrated from England to Maryland in 1638, was the first woman in America to own land, pay taxes, practice law, and advocate woman suffrage.

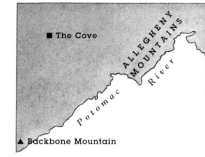

Mason – Dixon Line

■ The Cove

ALLEGHENY MOUNTAINS

Potomac River

▲ Backbone Mountain

PLACES TO VISIT, THINGS TO DO

Antietam National Battlefield (Sharpsburg). Here Union and Confederate forces clashed in one of the bloodiest battles of the Civil War.

Baltimore Harbor This popular area includes shops and restaurants, a science museum, an aquarium, and an early naval ship. Here also is Fort McHenry, where a battle fought during the War of 1812 inspired "The Star-Spangled Banner."

Chesapeake and Ohio Canal National Historical Park (Sharpsburg). The historic canal closed in 1924, but visitors can tour a museum and take a mule-drawn boat ride along a restored section of the canal.

Chesapeake Bay Maritime Museum (St. Michaels). Focusing on Bay life, the museum includes a floating exhibit of boats, an aquarium, and a lighthouse.

Fishing and crabbing Many freshwater lakes, streams, rivers, and reservoirs offer bass, trout, and pike, while the Chesapeake Bay and its tidewater tributaries supply flounder, bluefish, croaker, and blue crab.

Pocomoke River State Forest and Park (Snow Hill). This area, embracing some 13,000 acres, includes loblolly pines and the Pocomoke Cypress Swamp.

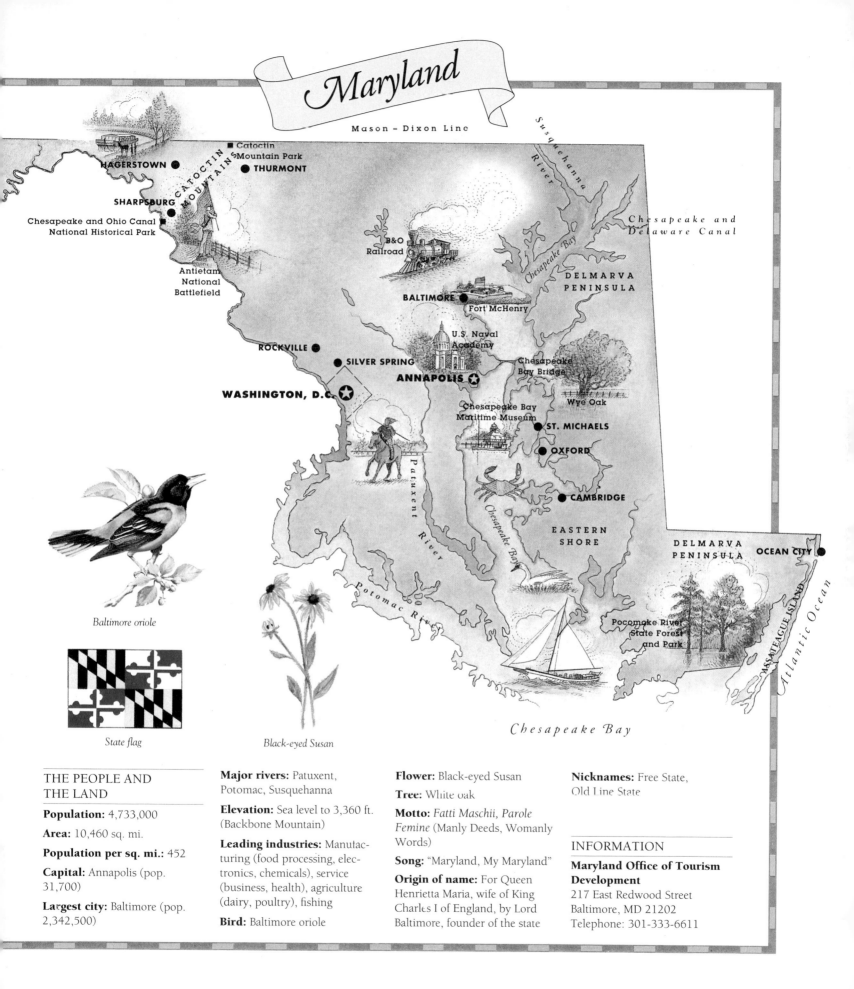

Maryland

Mason – Dixon Line

Baltimore oriole

State flag

Black-eyed Susan

Susquehanna River

Chesapeake and Delaware Canal

DELMARVA PENINSULA

Chesapeake Bay

Catoctin Mountain Park

HAGERSTOWN

THURMONT

SHARPSBURG

Chesapeake and Ohio Canal National Historical Park

Antietam National Battlefield

CATOCTIN MOUNTAINS

B&O Railroad

BALTIMORE

Fort McHenry

ROCKVILLE

U.S. Naval Academy

SILVER SPRING

ANNAPOLIS

Chesapeake Bay Bridge

WASHINGTON, D.C.

Wye Oak

Chesapeake Bay Maritime Museum

ST. MICHAELS

OXFORD

Patuxent River

CAMBRIDGE

EASTERN SHORE

DELMARVA PENINSULA

OCEAN CITY

Potomac River

Pocomoke River State Forest and Park

ASSATEAGUE ISLAND

Atlantic Ocean

Chesapeake Bay

THE PEOPLE AND THE LAND

Population: 4,733,000

Area: 10,460 sq. mi.

Population per sq. mi.: 452

Capital: Annapolis (pop. 31,700)

Largest city: Baltimore (pop. 2,342,500)

Major rivers: Patuxent, Potomac, Susquehanna

Elevation: Sea level to 3,360 ft. (Backbone Mountain)

Leading industries: Manufacturing (food processing, electronics, chemicals), service (business, health), agriculture (dairy, poultry), fishing

Bird: Baltimore oriole

Flower: Black-eyed Susan

Tree: White oak

Motto: *Fatti Maschii, Parole Femine* (Manly Deeds, Womanly Words)

Song: "Maryland, My Maryland"

Origin of name: For Queen Henrietta Maria, wife of King Charles I of England, by Lord Baltimore, founder of the state

Nicknames: Free State, Old Line State

INFORMATION

Maryland Office of Tourism Development
217 East Redwood Street
Baltimore, MD 21202
Telephone: 301-333-6611

Massachusetts

*Sandy shores, gentle hills, and
our nation's heritage*

Massachusetts abounds in images that
have helped to form our sense of
America's past: the Pilgrims landing at
Plymouth Rock, the first Thanksgiving, the
Boston Tea Party, the midnight ride of Paul
Revere, the minutemen at the battles of Lexington and Concord. Yet the state that looms so
large in our nation's story is not very big at all.
Only five states are smaller, and three hours is
all it takes to drive from the Atlantic coast to
the ski slopes of the Berkshires in the west.

THE CAPES

Massachusetts seashores are among New
England's finest, with rocky coves and inlets as
well as vast stretches of sandy beach. Some of
the best beaches are preserved in the 44,000-
acre Cape Cod National Seashore, which covers almost the entire outer cape from Orleans
north to Provincetown. Its eastern shore is
pummeled by the swirling surf of the open
Atlantic, while its western coast is swept by the
gentler waves of sheltered Cape Cod Bay.

Walking the streets of the cape's seaside
villages evokes a rich sense of the area's maritime past, from the stately captains' houses in
Sandwich to the fishing shanties on Sandy
Neck in Barnstable and the colorful harbors
at Chatham and Provincetown. Nowhere is
this feeling of nautical history stronger than
on Martha's Vineyard and Nantucket, the islands just south of the cape whose fortunes
were founded on 19th-century whaling. It
was Nantucket that Herman Melville depicted
in his classic novel *Moby Dick*.

*As the Green Mountains of Vermont stretch southward
into Massachusetts, they become the Berkshire Hills,
where scattered farms recall New England's past.*

Elegant homes peek from tree-covered dunes between Scargo Lake and Cape Cod Bay in Dennis. The lake is named for a local Nobscusset Indian chief's daughter. According to legend, the tribe's squaws dug the pond for the girl's pet fish.

North of Boston lies another maritime center — Cape Ann, where the town of Gloucester stands, the nation's oldest active fishing port. Boats from here still head out to Georges Bank in search of cod and haddock, just as they have since the time of the Pilgrims.

THE RIVER AND THE HILLS

Inland, beyond the broad coastal plain, lies a wide swath of uplands — a southward extension of the White Mountains of New Hampshire. From these heights, the land slopes gently down to the banks of the Connecticut River, New England's longest and most important waterway.

To the west of the Connecticut Valley the land rises again to form the Berkshire Hills. They are not imposing by most standards; Mount Greylock, the tallest peak, tops out at only 3,491 feet. But their gentle slopes are among the most beautiful areas in the state, drawing droves of vacationers not just to the

scenery but to the summer arts colonies that present theater, music, and dance.

Beyond the Berkshires the land rolls down to a narrow valley before rising once again in the Taconic Range along the Massachusetts-New York border. Much of this area is woodland, as is more than half of the entire state. Efforts to restock these forests with animals have succeeded to the point that bears and wild turkeys now roam the woods much as they did in earlier centuries.

Blankets of snow add elegance to the grandeur of the Connecticut River valley in winter.

The marshes along the Ipswich River are not only picturesque, but ecologically important because they offer a resting spot for migrating birds.

AMERICA: LAND OF BEAUTY AND SPLENDOR

Much of the farm country in western Massachusetts is a patchwork of ridges and valleys where meadows intermingle with woodlands.

RECYCLED CITIES

Massachusetts was among the first states to experience the rapid growth of cities, and today it is one of America's most urbanized and industrialized regions. From Lowell and Fall River to Worcester and Springfield, its cities have persevered by adapting to changing times.

Few places better illustrate this than New Bedford, which once ranked among the most prosperous whaling ports in the world. In the mid-19th century, when whale oil gave way to kerosene for lighting, New Bedford transformed itself into a busy textile-manufacturing center. Some hundred years later, when most of the great mills had closed or moved away, Yankee ingenuity again came to the rescue: New Bedford was reborn as home port to the largest fishing fleet on the East Coast. Since then the city has gained new luster by restoring its historic district, where the streets are lined with mansions that once belonged to well-to-do sea captains and the ambience of the 19th century still prevails.

SQUANTO, PLAGUE, AND THE PILGRIMS

When the Pilgrims landed in Massachusetts in December 1620, they had few of the practical skills needed to survive in the North American wilderness. Fortunately for them, Squanto, a Pawtuxet Indian, came to their settlement at Plymouth and served the newcomers as guide and mentor, showing them, among other things, the Indian trick of using dead fish as fertilizer when planting corn.

Squanto had little trouble communicating with the Pilgrims because, unlikely as it may seem, he already spoke English. He had been kidnapped several years earlier by a British adventurer and sold into slavery in Spain. Escaping, he made his way to London, where he lived for a time before hiring on as a hand on a ship bound for New England.

By late 1619 Squanto had made his way back to his home village at Plymouth, where he found that the entire Pawtuxet tribe had been wiped out by the plague — one of many epidemics that rat-infested European ships brought to America's shores. According to one estimate, 90 percent of the coastal Indians from Rhode Island to Maine succumbed to disease in the early 1600's. Finding himself the last of the Pawtuxets, a man without a tribe, Squanto joined the Pilgrims who now inhabited his homeland.

From the 1880's through the 1920's, the village of Magnolia — now part of Gloucester — was a summer haven for the wealthy, who built mansions along its rocky shore. Although most of these grand estates have now been converted to condominiums, the area's magnificent vistas of the open ocean remain unchanged.

WALKING THROUGH HISTORY

Massachusetts residents everywhere have learned to live in comfortable proximity with history, and many places are so authentically preserved and restored that they bring the past to life. In Salem, site of the notorious 17th-century witch trials, a walking tour highlights a happier era in the city's history — the days when three-masted ships called East Indiamen, designed and built by Salem shipwrights, sailed around the globe to trade with Europe and the Orient.

In Boston the Black Heritage Trail features landmarks of the city's black community. Among them are the Abiel Smith School on Beacon Hill, the first public school for black children, and on Boston Common a monument by sculptor Augustus Saint-Gaudens commemorating the 54th Regiment, the first black regiment recruited by the Union Army during the Civil War.

The Freedom Trail, Boston's most famous stroll through the past, winds among such landmarks as Paul Revere's home, the oldest surviving house in the city; King's Chapel, an Anglican church that became the first Unitarian church in the nation; and Faneuil Hall, a meeting place for revolutionaries in colonial times and now part of a bustling new commercial center called Quincy Market.

What characterizes not only Boston, but all of Massachusetts today, is more than the mixing of old and new; it is the invigorating blend of diverse ethnic groups: Irish, Portuguese, Italian, Greek, Jewish, Chinese, French Canadian, and most recently, Indian, Korean, and Japanese. Whatever their native origins, these new residents have been quick to adopt the spirit of independence that made the citizens of Massachusetts leaders in the American Revolution — a spirit that has inspired Bay Staters ever since.

THE SACRED COD

In Massachusetts, the Sacred Cod, as residents still call it, is no ordinary fish; in fact, since 1784 a golden replica of a codfish has hung in the State House in Boston as a memorial to "the importance of the Cod-fishery to the welfare of the Commonwealth."

As early as the 1490's, John Cabot and other explorers had alerted Europeans to the existence of vast schools of cod in the North Atlantic. By 1580 there was a veritable armada of fishing vessels off the North American coast — as many as 350 ships in a single season.

Early settlers were quick to note this natural bounty: the rocky soil of New England convinced many that fishing would be far better than farming as a way of life. Three years after the Pilgrims landed in Plymouth, an outpost was established at Gloucester, and by the 1770's it was one of New England's busiest fishing ports. Indeed, fishing and trans-atlantic trading became the bases of many early New England fortunes.

The typical Cape Cod cottage, like this one on Nantucket, has well-weathered cedar shingles and a white picket fence festooned with flowers.

HISTORICAL HIGHLIGHTS

1620 Pilgrims on the *Mayflower* land at Plymouth.

1630 Puritans found Boston.

1676 Settlers defeat Indians in King Philip's War.

1692 Twenty people executed at Salem Village for witchcraft.

1775 The Revolutionary War begins at Lexington and Concord.

1788 By ratifying Constitution, Massachusetts becomes sixth state to enter Union.

1831 William Lloyd Garrison publishes antislavery newspaper, the *Liberator*, giving birth to abolitionist movement.

1891 Basketball is invented by Dr. James Naismith at Springfield School for Christian Workers.

1897 Nation's first subway system opens in Boston.

1903 Boston hosts first baseball World Series.

1927 After a sensational trial, anarchists Nicola Sacco and Bartolomeo Vanzetti are executed for murder.

1942 Fire at Cocoanut Grove nightclub in Boston kills 492 people and leads to improved fire laws nationwide.

1960 Senator John F. Kennedy is elected president.

1974 – 75 Boston erupts in racial violence over busing to achieve racial balance in schools.

1980's Growth of computer industry revives state's economy.

FAMOUS SONS AND DAUGHTERS

The only father and son U.S. presidents, **John Adams** (1735 – 1826) became the second U.S. president in 1797 and his son **John Quincy Adams** (1767 – 1848) became the sixth in 1825.

Leonard Bernstein (1918 – 90). The dashing musical director (1958 – 70) of the New York Philharmonic also left a legacy of compositions, including the musical *West Side Story*.

Emily Dickinson (1830 – 86). Often brief, Dickinson's poems are filled with insights and imagery. She lived her entire life in her father's house in Amherst.

W.E.B. Du Bois (1868 – 1963). A distinguished scholar, Du Bois helped found the National Association for the Advancement of Colored People in 1909.

Nathaniel Hawthorne (1804 – 64). Descended from a judge at the Salem witch trials, Hawthorne criticized the Puritan past in such works as *The Scarlet Letter*.

Oliver Wendell Holmes, Jr. (1841 – 1935). Known as the Great Dissenter, Holmes served on the U.S. Supreme Court from 1902 to 1932.

John F. Kennedy (1917 – 63).

At the age of 42, Kennedy became the youngest person to be elected president. He was assassinated in Dallas.

Edwin H. Land (1909 –). Inventor of the instant camera, Land founded the Polaroid Corporation in Cambridge in 1937.

Norman Rockwell (1894 – 1978). Technical skill and a wry sense of humor made Rockwell one of America's favorite illustrators. His studio in Stockbridge is now a museum.

Henry David Thoreau (1817 – 62). An iconoclast who championed individual integrity and the beauty of nature, Thoreau is best remembered for the time he spent living alone at Walden Pond and for his essay "Civil Disobedience."

ODDITIES AND SPECIALTIES

Cape Cod and the area around Plymouth produce nearly half of the nation's cranberries.

Massachusetts is famous for its colleges — 106 in all. Harvard, the oldest college in the nation, was founded at Cambridge with a colonial government grant in 1636. Mount Holyoke, the oldest women's college, was established at South Hadley in 1837.

Boston baked beans, made with molasses, have been a staple since colonial times.

A lake near Webster has the remarkable Indian name of *Chargoggaggoggmanchauggagogg-chaubunagungamaug,* which means "I fish on my side of the lake, you fish on yours, and no one fishes in between." The fainthearted call it Lake Webster.

PLACES TO VISIT, THINGS TO DO

Cape Cod National Seashore (South Wellfleet). Preserving nearly 50 miles of Cape Cod's shoreline, as well as marshland, the refuge is a haven for wildlife and beach lovers alike.

Mt. Greylock State Reservation (North Adams). Mt. Greylock's summit, which can be reached by car, offers a view of five states. Enjoy the autumn foliage here.

Mt. Washington State Park (Mt. Washington). Hiking through the woodlands of the Taconic Range offers stunning vistas of surrounding farmlands. Eighty-foot-high Bash Bish Falls is one of the state's most spectacular sights.

Old Sturbridge Village (Sturbridge). Forty historic buildings have been moved to this 200-acre site to re-create a New England village in the early 1800's.

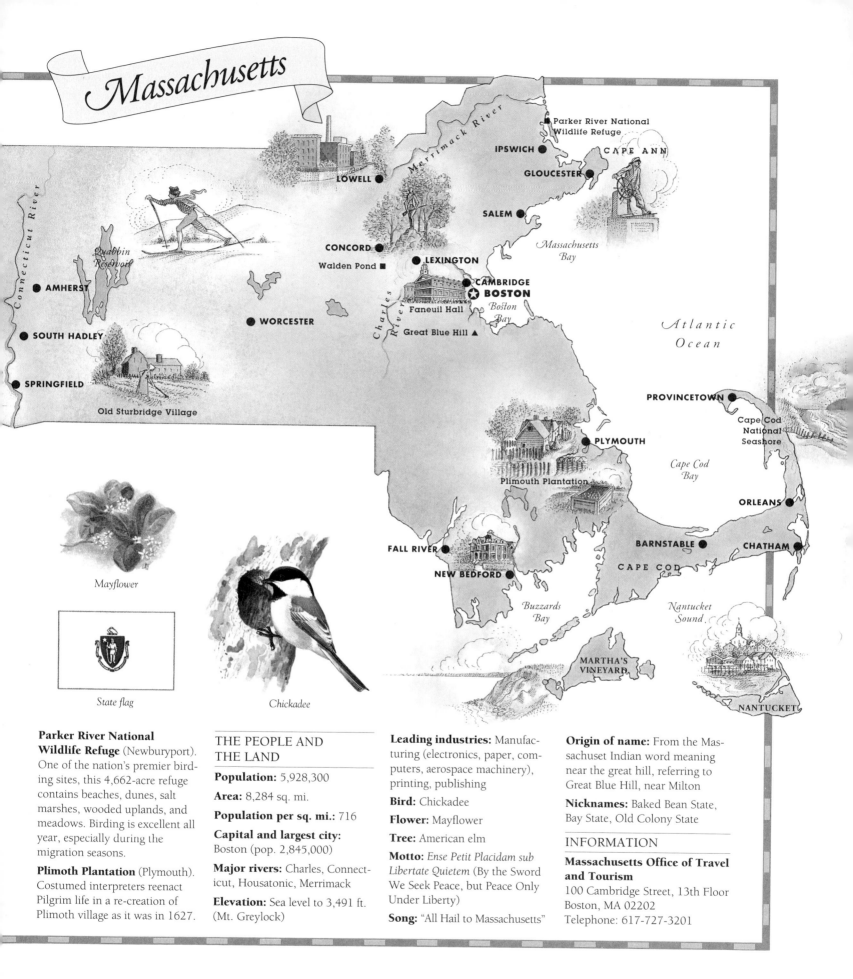

Massachusetts

LOWELL

IPSWICH

CAPE ANN

GLOUCESTER

Parker River National Wildlife Refuge

Merrimack River

SALEM

Massachusetts Bay

Connecticut River

Quabbin Reservoir

CONCORD

Walden Pond

LEXINGTON

CAMBRIDGE

AMHERST

WORCESTER

Faneuil Hall

★ **BOSTON**

Boston Bay

Charles River

Great Blue Hill ▲

Atlantic Ocean

SOUTH HADLEY

SPRINGFIELD

Old Sturbridge Village

PROVINCETOWN

Cape Cod National Seashore

PLYMOUTH

Plimouth Plantation

Cape Cod Bay

ORLEANS

FALL RIVER

BARNSTABLE

CHATHAM

NEW BEDFORD

CAPE COD

Buzzards Bay

Nantucket Sound

Mayflower

Mayflower

State flag

Chickadee

MARTHA'S VINEYARD

NANTUCKET

Parker River National Wildlife Refuge (Newburyport). One of the nation's premier birding sites, this 4,662-acre refuge contains beaches, dunes, salt marshes, wooded uplands, and meadows. Birding is excellent all year, especially during the migration seasons.

Plimoth Plantation (Plymouth). Costumed interpreters reenact Pilgrim life in a re-creation of Plimoth village as it was in 1627.

THE PEOPLE AND THE LAND

Population: 5,928,300

Area: 8,284 sq. mi.

Population per sq. mi.: 716

Capital and largest city: Boston (pop. 2,845,000)

Major rivers: Charles, Connecticut, Housatonic, Merrimack

Elevation: Sea level to 3,491 ft. (Mt. Greylock)

Leading industries: Manufacturing (electronics, paper, computers, aerospace machinery), printing, publishing

Bird: Chickadee

Flower: Mayflower

Tree: American elm

Motto: *Ense Petit Placidam sub Libertate Quietem* (By the Sword We Seek Peace, but Peace Only Under Liberty)

Song: "All Hail to Massachusetts"

Origin of name: From the Massachuset Indian word meaning near the great hill, referring to Great Blue Hill, near Milton

Nicknames: Baked Bean State, Bay State, Old Colony State

INFORMATION

Massachusetts Office of Travel and Tourism
100 Cambridge Street, 13th Floor
Boston, MA 02202
Telephone: 617-727-3201

 Michigan

Romantic landscapes at the heart of the Great Lakes

Perhaps because the waters that virtually surround Michigan lack the salty tang of the ocean, most people do not think of it as a place defined by water. And yet it is. Lying at the heart of the Great Lakes, the state is embraced by four of these five inland seas — Lakes Michigan, Superior, Huron, and Erie.

The lakes are everywhere an inescapable presence: no point in Michigan is more than 85 miles from one of their shores. And the waters also divide the state into two distinct parts. The five-mile-wide Straits of Mackinac separate the Lower Peninsula, with its familiar mitten shape, from the lushly forested Upper Peninsula, which juts out from the northeastern border of Wisconsin.

LEGACY OF THE GLACIERS

The Great Lakes were formed at the end of the last ice age, when meltwater from a vast continental ice sheet filled five enormous basins that had earlier been hollowed out by the ice. The glaciers also left smaller watery scars throughout Michigan. Scattered across the state are more than 11,000 lakes, many of them laced together by miles of sparkling rivers that slice through dark forests and spill over countless rapids and waterfalls. The largest falls, Tahquamenon, are the centerpiece of a state park northwest of Sault Ste. Marie. A torrent of dark water stained by tannin from a tamarack swamp upstream, they tumble down in a cascade 48 feet high and 200 feet wide.

Another souvenir of the Ice Age, though of quite a different sort, is preserved at Sleeping Bear Dunes National Lakeshore. There, on

Pictured Rocks is the name given to the fantastic sandstone cliffs that run along part of Lake Superior's shore.

Indian legend says that this arch on Mackinac Island was formed when the tears of a maiden pining for her lover washed away the stone.

In the wilds of the Upper Peninsula, the Presque Isle River winds through a gorge at Porcupine Mountains State Park.

the eastern coast of Lake Michigan, winds have piled up enormous dunes of glacier-made sand. Some of the dunes tower more than 450 feet above the lake and command majestic views of the twin Manitou Islands far offshore. According to Indian legend, the area took shape when a mother bear and two cubs tried to flee a forest fire by swimming across Lake Michigan. The mother, it is said, made it to shore, where, transformed into a gigantic dune, she still awaits her offspring. But the hapless cubs drowned before reaching land, and can be seen today as the two islands.

FORESTS AND FARMLANDS

Most of Michigan's lake-strewn terrain is gently rolling. Virtually all of it used to be covered with dense forests that long ago attracted the attention of loggers, who began arriving in Michigan in the mid-19th century.

Especially prized were the stands of towering white pines, which could easily be milled into building material. Huge amounts of pine were harvested to build houses, first for French settlers in Detroit (later to become one of the most industrialized cities in the world), then for settlers who poured into Michigan from the East after the opening of the Erie Canal in 1825. The pines also supplied building material for the cities that began to spring up on the treeless Great Plains. By the turn of the century, the state's woodlands started to disappear. Timber barons soon transferred operations to the Pacific Northwest and left the exposed earth of Michigan to the farmers.

But some areas proved to be unsuitable for anything but forest. The farmers departed too, leaving much of the woodland to restore itself. Only in the southern half of the Lower Peninsula did agriculture thrive. Farmers who

The red squirrels that inhabit Michigan's woods store pine and spruce cones for the winter.

Forming a delicate veil of water, Munising Falls are among the most exquisite of the 150 waterfalls of the Upper Peninsula. Visitors can walk on a ledge behind the falls.

had abandoned the thin soil of New England settled here and built Yankee farmhouses. Thus visitors to the area may feel they have somehow strayed into a corner of Vermont.

LAND OF HIAWATHA

The Upper Peninsula remains a place apart, even though it has been linked to the Lower Peninsula since 1957 by a bridge that gracefully leaps the Straits of Mackinac (pronounced Mackinaw). If the peninsula is bitterly cold for much of the year, the languorous summers there are enchanting. The romantic landscape became one of the most famous locales in American literature as the "shores of Gitche Gumee," the setting for Longfellow's narrative poem *The Song of Hiawatha*, which he based in part on the legends of Indians in this region.

A highlight of the area is also one of Michigan's greatest natural splendors — Pictured Rocks National Lakeshore. Extending for miles along the southern coast of Lake Superior, it is a realm of spectacular, multi-colored rock cliffs sculpted by the elements into caves, arches, and other fantastic shapes.

Poised between the two peninsulas is Mackinac Island. The British built a fort, now restored, on the island in 1780, and after the War of 1812 John Jacob Astor's fur company established a post there. In the words of the poet William Cullen Bryant, "the manifest destiny of Mackinac Island is to be a watering place." In the second half of the 19th century Mackinac did indeed become one of the nation's premier resorts, attracting the cream of midwestern society. Their favorite stopping place was the Grand Hotel, which opened in 1887 and is noted especially for its 880-foot-long veranda overlooking Lake Huron and the Straits of Mackinac.

With spectacular vistas rivaling those of the seaboard states, Mackinac Island is a place where the vastness of the Great Lakes is most apparent. But there is another spot with an equally commanding view — although it is a bit less accessible than the Grand Hotel's veranda. Astronauts traveling to the moon discovered that among the few terrestrial features visible to them were these five lakes, earthly mirrors shining into the infinity of space.

Icy winds from Lake Michigan turn the North Pier Lighthouse at St. Joseph, near the southwest corner of the state, into a winter sculpture.

AN ECOLOGICAL BALANCING ACT

Isle Royale, the largest island in Lake Superior, is more than a scenic national park. It is also a unique natural laboratory where animals, cut off from the mainland, play out the drama between predator and prey and, in the process, enable scientists to observe nature's ecological balancing act.

As late as the 1940's, foraging herds of moose on the island had no natural enemies. As a result, they multiplied so rapidly that they almost wiped out the stands of yew and balsam that provided their food.

When the animals' very existence seemed threatened, salvation came along in an unexpected form: a pack of predatory wolves that crossed the frozen lake to the island around 1949. Since then, wolves have consistently thinned the moose population, usually attacking those weakened by age or disease. At the same time, healthy moose have kept the wolves in check with their lethal hooves. The result: naturally controlled populations of moose and wolves, with survival assured for both.

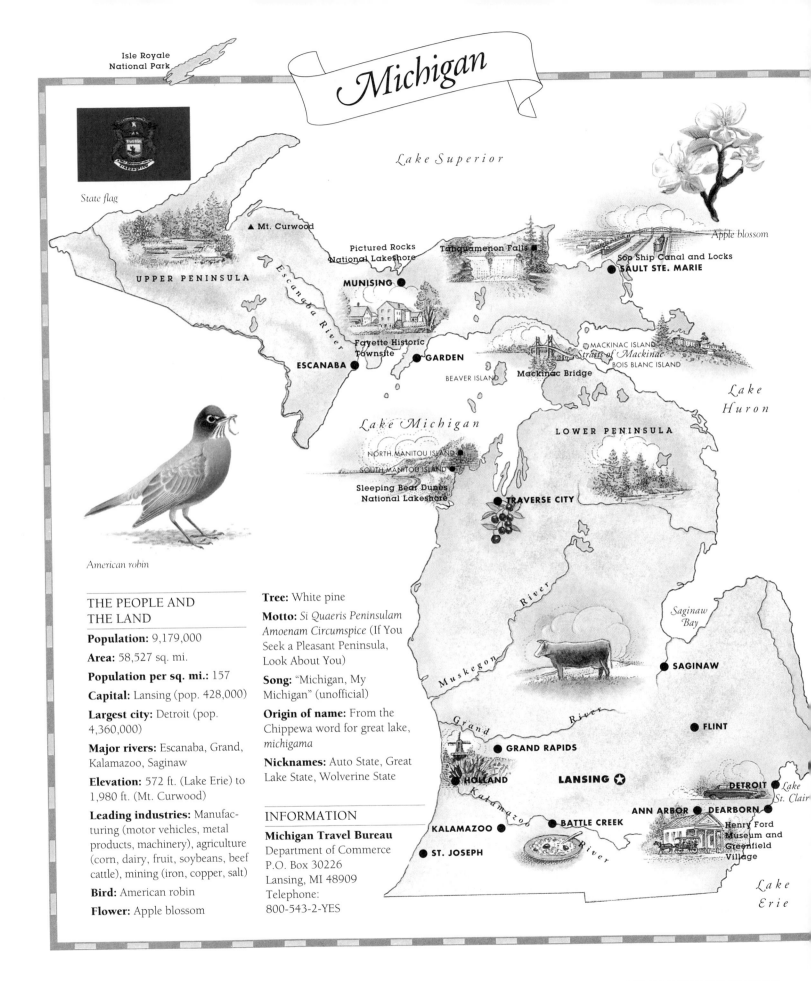

Michigan

Isle Royale National Park

Lake Superior

State flag

Apple blossom

▲ Mt. Curwood

UPPER PENINSULA

Escanaba River

Pictured Rocks National Lakeshore

Tahquamenon Falls

Soo Ship Canal and Locks
● SAULT STE. MARIE

MUNISING

Fayette Historic Townsite

● GARDEN

● ESCANABA

BEAVER ISLAND

MACKINAC ISLAND
Straits of Mackinac
BOIS BLANC ISLAND

Mackinac Bridge

Lake Huron

Lake Michigan

LOWER PENINSULA

NORTH MANITOU ISLAND

SOUTH MANITOU ISLAND

Sleeping Bear Dunes National Lakeshore

● TRAVERSE CITY

American robin

River

Saginaw Bay

Muskegon River

● SAGINAW

Grand River

● FLINT

● GRAND RAPIDS

Kalamazoo River

● HOLLAND

LANSING ✪

● DETROIT ● Lake St. Clair

ANN ARBOR ● DEARBORN

● KALAMAZOO

● BATTLE CREEK

Henry Ford Museum and Greenfield Village

● ST. JOSEPH

Lake Erie

THE PEOPLE AND THE LAND

Population: 9,179,000

Area: 58,527 sq. mi.

Population per sq. mi.: 157

Capital: Lansing (pop. 428,000)

Largest city: Detroit (pop. 4,360,000)

Major rivers: Escanaba, Grand, Kalamazoo, Saginaw

Elevation: 572 ft. (Lake Erie) to 1,980 ft. (Mt. Curwood)

Leading industries: Manufacturing (motor vehicles, metal products, machinery), agriculture (corn, dairy, fruit, soybeans, beef cattle), mining (iron, copper, salt)

Bird: American robin

Flower: Apple blossom

Tree: White pine

Motto: *Si Quaeris Peninsulam Amoenam Circumspice* (If You Seek a Pleasant Peninsula, Look About You)

Song: "Michigan, My Michigan" (unofficial)

Origin of name: From the Chippewa word for great lake, *michigama*

Nicknames: Auto State, Great Lake State, Wolverine State

INFORMATION

Michigan Travel Bureau
Department of Commerce
P.O. Box 30226
Lansing, MI 48909
Telephone:
800-543-2-YES

HISTORICAL HIGHLIGHTS

c. 1620 Étienne Brulé is believed to be the first European explorer to reach Michigan.

1668 Father Jacques Marquette establishes a permanent settlement at Sault Ste. Marie.

1701 Antoine Cadillac establishes the fur-trading post that will eventually become the city of Detroit.

1763 Britain acquires Michigan from France in treaty that ends French and Indian Wars.

1796 American flag is raised in Michigan for the first time as British leave Detroit.

1805 Congress establishes Michigan as a territory.

1837 Michigan joins Union as the 26th state.

1855 Soo Ship Canal and Locks, linking Lakes Huron and Superior, open at Sault Ste. Marie.

1900 Detroit's first automobile plant is built.

1914 Automobile industry accounts for 37 percent of state's manufacturing.

1942 Automobile factories convert to war production.

1957 Mackinac Bridge, between towns of St. Ignace and Mackinaw City, joins Upper and Lower Peninsulas.

1974 Coleman A. Young becomes first black mayor of city of Detroit.

1987 People Mover monorail, spanning almost three miles, opens in downtown Detroit.

FAMOUS SONS AND DAUGHTERS

Ralph Bunche (1904 – 71). A political scientist, Bunche became the first black division head at the U.S. State Department. His work on the United Nations Palestine Commission earned him the 1950 Nobel Peace Prize.

Edna Ferber (1887 – 1968). Born in Kalamazoo, Ferber wrote novels about American life. Her books include *Show Boat,* the basis for the famous Broadway musical, and the Pulitzer Prize-winning *So Big.*

Gerald R. Ford (1913 –). Longtime congressman, then vice president, Ford succeeded Richard M. Nixon as president in 1974. A candidate for the office in 1976, he was defeated by Jimmy Carter.

Henry Ford (1863 – 1947). Ford revolutionized the auto industry when he began mass-producing the moderately priced Model T in 1913.

Ring Lardner (1885 – 1933). Lardner's fine ear for the vernacular contributed to his success as a writer and satirist. Among his best-known short stories are "Haircut" and "Champion."

Sojourner Truth (1797? – 1883). Born Isabella Baumfree in New York, the evangelist spent the last 30 years of her life in Battle Creek, counseling freed slaves and working for women's rights.

ODDITIES AND SPECIALTIES

When Dr. John H. Kellogg of Battle Creek created cornflakes to serve as a nutritious dish for sanitarium patients, he started an industry. Today Battle Creek is the world's leading producer of breakfast cereals.

The southwest Michigan town of Holland is the only place in the U.S. where Dutch-originated delftware pottery is made.

Northern Michigan is the site of the National Mushroom Hunting Championship every May, when mushroom fanciers take to the woods to search out the prized morel mushrooms that grow there in profusion.

Despite its novelty, the reason for the naming of the Be Good to Your Mother-in-Law Bridge (built in 1880 across the Black River in Croswell) has been lost in the mists of time.

Although Michigan is nicknamed the Wolverine State, the small, bearlike creatures are exceedingly rare there. The only ones most Michiganders ever see are in the Detroit Zoo.

PLACES TO VISIT, THINGS TO DO

Fayette Historic Townsite (Garden). This iron-smelting village on Lake Michigan was abandoned more than a century ago. Restored buildings, including the opera house, are open for tours.

Henry Ford Museum and Greenfield Village (Dearborn). This 14-acre museum chronicles the nation's shift from agriculture to industry, with exhibits of cars, trains, furniture, and machinery. Adjacent is Greenfield Village, a collection of historic structures, some reconstructed. Included is the courthouse where Lincoln practiced law.

Hiawatha National Forest (Escanaba). The landscape immortalized in Henry Wadsworth Longfellow's poem, *The Song of Hiawatha,* has islands, swamps, and pine forests.

Isle Royale National Park (Houghton). The isolation of Lake Superior's largest island, 9 miles wide and 45 miles long, has made it a naturalist's paradise. Among the wildlife are moose, wolves, beavers, and loons.

Mackinac Island Rising from Lake Huron like the great turtle it was named for, this island is home to caves, natural bridges, and historic Fort Mackinac.

National Cherry Festival (Traverse City). This eight-day event, held every July, celebrates Michigan's status as the nation's leading cherry producer. Parades, live entertainment, sporting events, and cherry pies are the main attractions.

Pictured Rocks National Lakeshore (Munising). As well as beaches and waterfalls, the Lake Superior shoreline boasts 15 miles of dramatic rock cliffs that have been eroded into unusual shapes.

Sleeping Bear Dunes National Lakeshore (Glen Arbor, Glen Haven, Empire). Part of Lake Michigan's shoreline, this scenic area has two islands, vast sand dunes, beaches, and forests.

Minnesota

Cool forests, fertile farms, and a multitude of lakes

A remote lake in northern Minnesota, so hidden by the surrounding wilderness that it took explorers 130 years to find it, is the serene but rather unspectacular origin of the longest river in North America — the mighty Mississippi. When at last a party of indefatigable searchers led by Henry Rowe Schoolcraft and an Ojibwa Indian guide found the boggy headwaters of the great river in 1832, they named the lake Itasca.

It sounds like an American Indian word, but *Itasca* is in fact Latin — or truncated Latin, anyway — for the name was created by lopping off the first and last syllables of the phrase *veritas caput,* or "true source." Today the true source — together with the surrounding area of lakes, bogs, and evergreen forests — is protected and enshrined in beautiful Itasca State Park.

FROM TOPSOIL TO TWIN CITIES

The waters of Minnesota — from the Mississippi and other major rivers to a multitude of streams, lakes, swamps, and bogs — have determined much of the state's destiny. The paths of glaciers, the courses of rivers, and the locations of lakes large and small have all influenced where people built their homes, towns, and cities, where they planted crops, developed industries, spent their leisure time, and even buried their dead.

Some 10,000 years ago, the glacial ice that bulldozed its way across the land deposited tons of rich, virgin topsoil. From the 1850's to the early 1900's, news of this bountiful soil,

Serenity prevails at Cherokee Lake, one of thousands of idyllic lakes and ponds that make up the Boundary Waters Canoe Area in northeastern Minnesota.

Thousands of Canada geese winter on Silver Lake in Rochester, Minnesota. Some raid nearby cornfields for food, while others accept handouts from bird lovers who visit the lake.

Steep cliffs topped with birches and evergreens line much of Minnesota's Lake Superior shoreline. Abutting the giant lake is Tettegouche State Park, some 50 miles northeast of Duluth.

ideal for farming, attracted swarms of Scandinavians, Germans, and other immigrants seeking a new life. The Nordic newcomers especially — whose icy homelands had prepared them for the cold winters — flourished and multiplied, as evidenced today by the proliferation of blond, fair-skinned folk in Minnesota and the legions of Andersons and Johnsons listed in its telephone books.

The agricultural way of life continues, and it explains a great deal about the nature of Minnesotans. Thrifty, practical, plain-spoken, cautious — these are traits assigned to Minnesotans both on and off the farm.

Rich farmland is not the only legacy of the ancient glaciers. Their enormous bulk gouged out pits that became the myriad lakes Minnesota is famous for. The figure 10,000 is usually touted by Minnesotans, but the true number of lakes is far greater. In any case, their sheer quantity has made Minnesota a "land of lakes," where one out of six people owns a boat, one out of three has a fishing license, and nearly everyone spends at least some part of the year relaxing by a lake.

Lakes are found even within the city limits of Minneapolis and St. Paul — the Twin Cit-

Surrounded by snowfall, silence, and some 3 million acres of wooded wilderness, a cross-country skier makes his way through Superior National Forest, located in the Arrowhead region of northeastern Minnesota.

Brightened by the dawning light, the labyrinthine waters of Kabetogama Lake snake through miles of evergreen forest in remote Voyageurs National Park.

ies area, which is the home of more than half the people of Minnesota. Located where the Mississippi and Minnesota rivers join together — a choice spot convenient for travel, trade, and recreation — the Twin Cities were built on land first occupied by prehistoric Indians. Some of their burial mounds can be seen today, as can the original Fort Snelling, a frontier outpost established in 1819. This fortress, now enveloped by freeways, was the seed from which the Twin Cities took root.

LAND OF TIMBER WOLVES AND VOYAGEURS

In northeastern Minnesota, which is called the Arrowhead because of its triangular shape, lakes also take center stage. Largest of all — a

virtual inland sea — is mammoth Lake Superior. Its shoreline, parts of which are lined with spectacular cliffs, serves as Minnesota's eastern border north of Duluth. (This great port city is connected to the Atlantic Ocean via the St. Lawrence Seaway).

Inland from the giant lake lies one of Minnesota's greatest natural treasures: the maze of rivers and streams, glacial lakes, and deep boreal woods that make up Superior National Forest and, to the northwest, Voyageurs National Park. This vast wilderness provides a refuge for moose, bears, and the largest population of timber wolves in the lower 48. But it is known mainly for its network of waterways — given such peculiar names as Stump,

JEWELS OF MINNEAPOLIS

On a bright summer day, the six sparkling lakes in the heart of Minneapolis — Cedar Lake, Lake of the Isles, Lake Calhoun, Lake Harriet, Lake Hiawatha, and Lake Nokomis — seem as blue as lapis lazuli, their shimmering surfaces spangled with rowboats, canoes, and sailboats. In winter, the lakes harden into diamonds, where bundled-up skaters slice figure eights across the glistening ice.

Fashioned by ancient glaciers, the lakes and their shores were once the domain of Dakota Indians. A sign near Lake Calhoun, which the Indians called Lake of the Loons, marks the location of one of their villages. By the 1850's the Indians were gone, but the lakes and their settings, thanks to wise city planning, were beautifully preserved as Minneapolis expanded around them.

Today a stroll along one of the winding lakeside paths offers a visual commentary on urban fitness, fashion, and courtship. But with a little imagination one can picture the Dakota Indians in their canoes, gathering wild rice in the shallows.

Fiddle, Stickle, Temperance, and Vermilion — which were for 200 years the thoroughfares of commerce and conflict for Dakota and Ojibwa Indians and their clients, the French, British, and Canadian fur traders.

The routes once taken by voyageurs, the scrappy souls who hauled beaver pelts out of the wilderness, are still intact today. These historic paths and waterways continue to be traversed — not by voyageurs, but by adventurous hikers, campers, canoers, and city-weary vacationers. Visitors can commune with nature and, accompanied by the lonely cries of loons, get a telescopic glimpse into the past — a past that unfolded, here as elsewhere in Minnesota, amidst a wealth of water.

At dawn and dusk, white-tailed deer forage for weeds, twigs, and nuts. The deer are common in Minnesota woodlands, but this particular sight — twin albino does — is rare indeed.

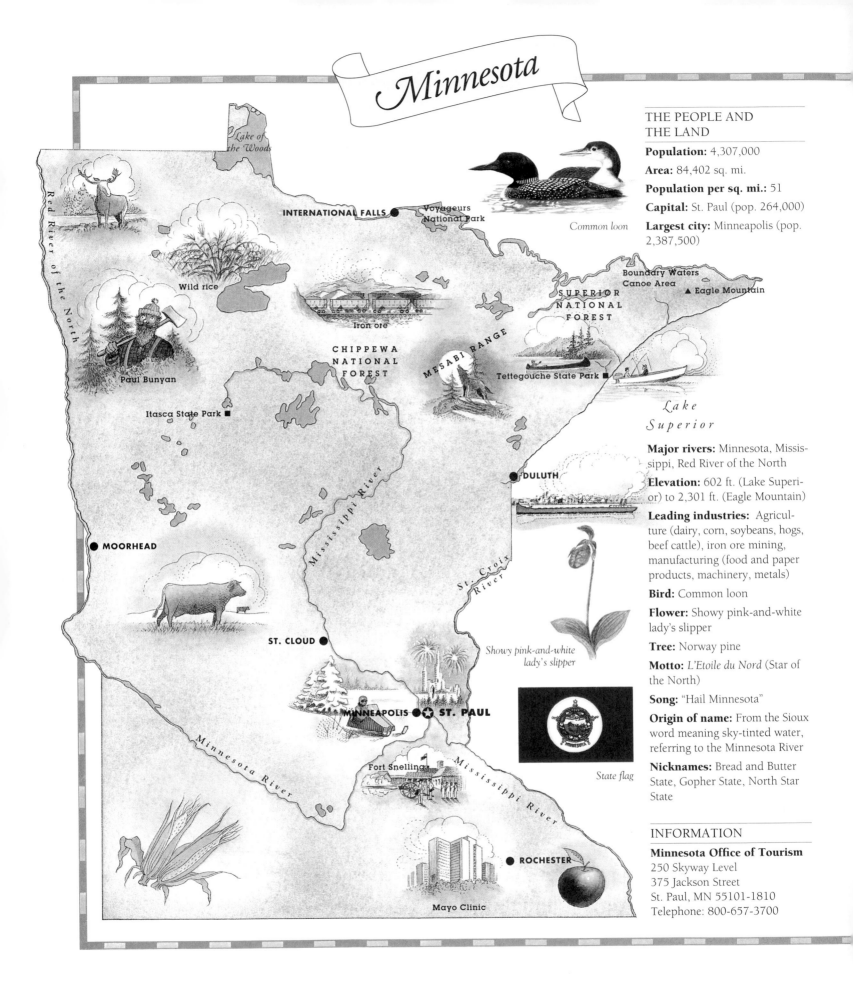

Minnesota

THE PEOPLE AND THE LAND

Population: 4,307,000

Area: 84,402 sq. mi.

Population per sq. mi.: 51

Capital: St. Paul (pop. 264,000)

Largest city: Minneapolis (pop. 2,387,500)

Common loon

Major rivers: Minnesota, Mississippi, Red River of the North

Elevation: 602 ft. (Lake Superior) to 2,301 ft. (Eagle Mountain)

Leading industries: Agriculture (dairy, corn, soybeans, hogs, beef cattle), iron ore mining, manufacturing (food and paper products, machinery, metals)

Bird: Common loon

Flower: Showy pink-and-white lady's slipper

Tree: Norway pine

Motto: *L'Etoile du Nord* (Star of the North)

Song: "Hail Minnesota"

Origin of name: From the Sioux word meaning sky-tinted water, referring to the Minnesota River

Nicknames: Bread and Butter State, Gopher State, North Star State

Showy pink-and-white lady's slipper

State flag

INFORMATION

Minnesota Office of Tourism
250 Skyway Level
375 Jackson Street
St. Paul, MN 55101-1810
Telephone: 800-657-3700

Map labels

Lake of the Woods

INTERNATIONAL FALLS

Voyageurs National Park

Wild rice

Iron ore

Boundary Waters Canoe Area

▲ Eagle Mountain

SUPERIOR NATIONAL FOREST

Paul Bunyan

CHIPPEWA NATIONAL FOREST

MESABI RANGE

Tettegouche State Park

Red River of the North

Itasca State Park

Lake Superior

DULUTH

MOORHEAD

Mississippi River

St. Croix River

ST. CLOUD

MINNEAPOLIS ★ ST. PAUL

Minnesota River

Fort Snelling

Mississippi River

ROCHESTER

Mayo Clinic

HISTORICAL HIGHLIGHTS

1679 Daniel Greysolon, sieur du Luth, explores area near present-day Duluth.

1783 U.S. acquires eastern Minnesota from Great Britain as part of Treaty of Paris.

1803 U.S. gains the western portion from France as part of the Louisiana Purchase.

1816 Congress passes law to ensure U.S. control of its fur trade.

1832 Henry Rowe Schoolcraft discovers source of the Mississippi at Lake Itasca.

1849 Congress creates Minnesota Territory.

1858 Minnesota becomes the 32nd state.

1862 U.S. troops squelch a bloody Sioux revolt.

1890 Huge iron-ore deposits are found in the Mesabi Range.

1959 St. Lawrence Seaway opens, making Duluth the westernmost Atlantic port.

1968 Minnesotan Hubert Humphrey loses presidential election to Richard Nixon.

1976 Native son Walter Mondale is elected vice president under Jimmy Carter.

1984 Mondale loses presidential election to Ronald Reagan.

FAMOUS SONS AND DAUGHTERS

Warren E. Burger (1907 –) This St. Paul lawyer became assistant U.S. attorney general and a U.S. judge before serving as chief justice of the United States from 1969 to 1986.

William O. Douglas (1898 – 1980). Appointed to the U.S. Supreme Court by Franklin D. Roosevelt in 1939, Douglas served as an associate justice until he resigned in 1975.

Bob Dylan (1941 –). Beginning in the early 1960's, Dylan's songs of social protest made him an icon of America's counterculture and one of the most magnetic performers of his generation.

F. Scott Fitzgerald (1896 – 1940). Fitzgerald spoke for the generation of the 1920's Jazz Age. His widely acclaimed novels include *The Great Gatsby* and *Tender Is the Night*.

Judy Garland (1922 – 69).

A child singer, Garland earned enduring fame as Dorothy in the motion picture *The Wizard of Oz*. As an adult she entertained millions of fans with her films, records, and concerts.

Hubert H. Humphrey (1911 – 78). After serving as mayor of Minneapolis, Humphrey became Minnesota's first Democratic senator. A champion of arms control and civil rights in the U.S. Senate, he later served as Lyndon Johnson's vice president and in 1968 ran for president himself.

Sinclair Lewis (1885 – 1951). The author of such novels as *Main Street*, *Babbitt*, and *Elmer Gantry*, Lewis waged war on parochialism and hypocrisy. He was the first American to win the Nobel Prize for literature.

Charles A. Lindbergh (1902 – 74). The shy aviator was celebrated worldwide after piloting the *Spirit of St. Louis* on the first nonstop solo flight from New York to Paris in 1927.

ODDITIES AND SPECIALTIES

Minnesota abounds in water — nearly 5,000 square miles of it, including well over 10,000 lakes and about 90,000 miles of lake and river shoreline.

Minnesota lumberjacks once entertained each other with tales of the mythic hero Paul Bunyan and his blue ox, Babe, whose gigantic feet and tail were said to have created the lakes and rivers.

Northern Minnesota grows about three-fourths of the world's native wild rice, and the southern part of the state produces over a dozen varieties of apples.

The abundant snow and ice in this state inspired the unusual sport of "smooshing," in which teams race not on skis but on two-by-four beams — four brave people to a pair.

Pipestone, quarried by Indians in southwestern Minnesota, is used to make the ceremonial peace pipes that were once smoked to seal treaties.

PLACES TO VISIT, THINGS TO DO

Fishing The lakes, rivers, and marshlands of Minnesota have an abundance of trout, walleye, muskellunge, and largemouth bass. Several rivers, such as the Baptism, Cascade, and French, have Chinook salmon.

The Guthrie Theater (Minneapolis). Founded by British director Tyrone Guthrie and opened in 1963, the theater, with its three-sided "thrust" stage and its remarkable productions, has received nationwide acclaim.

Itasca State Park (Lake Itasca). Here are the headwaters of the Mississippi River, as well as over 150 lakes and bogs, Indian mounds, and the forested Wilderness Sanctuary, which can be seen from Wilderness Drive.

Mayo Clinic Buildings National Historic Landmark (Rochester). This world-renowned clinic began as a family enterprise in 1889. Tours are available, and visitors may also view the Mayo Medical Museum and the mansion built by Dr. Charles Mayo in 1910 – 11.

St. Paul Winter Carnival Attracting thousands of visitors every year, the carnival features beautiful sculptures fashioned from blocks of ice and, every few years depending on the weather, the fabulous Ice Palace.

Superior National Forest (Duluth). This immense wilderness in the Arrowhead section of Minnesota contains millions of acres of lakes, streams, and woodland, including the Boundary Waters Canoe Area, which abuts the Canadian border.

Voyageurs National Park (International Falls). Just northwest of Superior National Forest, the park is crisscrossed with trails and waterways used by 18th-century fur traders.

Mississippi

*Magnolias and mockingbirds in
a land nobody wants to leave*

Lovely and languorous, Mississippi is the most traditionally southern of all the Deep South states. Here the legendary cotton fields sprawl in the sun beside sloping green levees. Here stand cool white-columned mansions shaded by magnolias that bear huge, creamy blossoms. Mockingbirds sing deliriously from the treetops. Aimless back-country roads meander past dogtrot cabins with swept-dirt yards and blue-tick hounds dozing under nearby chinaberry trees. Confederate cemeteries are still decorated with fresh flowers, and longleaf pine forests sweep grandly south to the splendid Gulf Coast beaches.

PATTERNS OF SETTLEMENT

Despite its accessibility by river and trail, Mississippi was settled relatively late in this country's history. Although Hernando de Soto had explored the region as early as 1540 and a French fort was built near present-day Ocean Springs in 1699, disputes among the French, Spanish, English, and Indians discouraged settlement for most of the 18th century.

Not until the turn of the 19th century did things begin to happen. The cotton gin was invented just at the time that planters were giving up on tobacco and indigo farming; and, in 1798, the U.S. Congress formally organized Mississippi as a territory. Then, as the Choctaw and Chickasaw Indians were sent to Oklahoma, leaving vast tracts of land behind, settlers poured in from South Carolina and Georgia, joining those who had already begun moving upriver from New Orleans and down the Natchez Trace from Tennessee.

Tangles of heavenly scented wisteria adorn a footbridge in Jackson's Mynelle Gardens.

Arranged as if for an exhibition of Deep South flora, palmettos and live oaks draped with Spanish moss grow on Point Clear Island, a mile-long sliver off the Gulf Coast.

Gulf Islands National Seashore is made up of six barrier islands a few miles off the Mississippi and Florida coasts. Here, sea oats sprout from the dunes of Horn Island.

Although they were often bound for the prosperous Natchez district, where planters were building fine houses, many pioneers settled down along the way, tempted by the sheltering pine woods, the rolling hill country, the rich soils along the Tombigbee River, or the level Mississippi floodplain. There, and along the Mississippi, they founded such towns as Vicksburg, Tupelo, Yazoo City, Holly Springs, and Le Fleur's Bluff — soon to be renamed for

Andrew Jackson and made the state capital. As the newcomers spread across the land, they established the pattern of fairly even population distribution that gives the Mississippi countryside an open, spacious look.

FROM COTTON COUNTRY TO GOLDEN COAST

Perhaps the most distinctive region of the state is the Delta, an elliptical floodplain lying between the Mississippi and Yazoo rivers in northwestern Mississippi. This is cotton country — flat, nearly treeless, home of the very rich and the very poor. It was this fertile land that made possible the leisurely and luxurious plantation lifestyle for which Mississippi has been both envied and censured.

East of the Mississippi floodplain, much of the state is a mix of undulating hills and prairies, forests, and farmland, interrupted here and there by ancient Indian mounds.

Travelers come upon landscaped driveways like this one as they explore the countryside around Natchez. This alluring tunnel of live oaks and azaleas arouses fantasies of what lies at the end — perhaps a glimpse of the Old South in the form of a white-columned mansion or a gazebo on a manicured lawn.

Grand 19th-century houses on the bluffs of the Mississippi River at Natchez overlook the river below. More than 600 houses built in Natchez at the turn of the century remain.

The highest elevations, in the northeastern corner of the state, are found among the outcroppings of the Tennessee River Hills, the southernmost ridges of the Appalachian Mountains. The best known of the prairie regions, just west of these hills, is the long, narrow Black Belt, so named for its dark and extremely fertile soil.

Most of the lower third of the state is known as the Pine Hills, or the Piney Woods. Once a forest of virgin longleaf and slash pine, it was severely cut during the timber boom of the early 1900's. But since then the area has been replanted and accounts for much of the state's 17 million acres of forestland.

Driving through these silvery-green pine woods, one comes at last to the coastal lowlands, where the Old Spanish Trail, now U.S. Highway 90, runs for 26 miles between the wide sandy man-made beaches of the Gulf of Mexico and the elegant antebellum and Victorian vacation homes of Bay St. Louis, Pass Christian, and Biloxi. Tall palms and ancient live oaks line the beach boulevard, shrimp boats crowd the harbors, black skimmers and least terns nest among the sea oats, and laughing gulls wheel noisily overhead.

A LOVE OF LAND

Such natural beauty, impressive all through the state, strengthens the love of land that makes Mississippi natives reluctant to leave. Nearly 90 percent of the people now living in Mississippi were born there, and many are eager to write about it, sing about it, or capture it on canvas. The blues, that uniquely American musical form, for instance, evolved from the work songs of the Delta slaves. William Faulkner modeled his mythical Yoknapatawpha County on Lafayette County in the north-central hill country. The Piney Woods nurtured opera star Leontyne Price, and the Black Belt produced Elvis Presley. Countless other musicians, poets, dancers, and painters have drawn inspiration from this land so rich in esthetic appeal. As the writer Willie Morris recalled his own childhood: "The beauty of the Mississippi land engulfed us — the smell of it in springtime, the katydids in the trees, the dark wetness of the shadows."

THE NATCHEZ TRACE

Originally a series of Indian footpaths extending over 500 miles across Mississippi, Alabama, and Tennessee, the Natchez Trace became a vital link between Natchez and Nashville. French explorers traversed the wilderness road, as did early settlers, itinerant preachers, soldiers, peddlers, government officials, postriders, outlaws, and, above all, Kentucky boatmen, who floated cargo down the Mississippi and then walked back home. Indian chiefs Pushmataha and Tecumseh, Meriwether Lewis, the marquis de Lafayette, Aaron Burr, Andrew Jackson, and John James Audubon all traveled the trace, stopping for food and rest at makeshift inns, known as stands, such as Pigeon Roost and French Camp. In 1806 Congress voted funds to improve this busy postal route, then deplored as "very devious and narrow." But only one year later the invention of the steamboat made going up the Mississippi possible, and by 1820 use of the trace began to decline. Today a handsome modern Natchez Trace Parkway closely follows the old route, serving 19 million travelers and sightseers every year.

Multicolored bluffs loom 200 feet over the Pearl River in southern Mississippi. Surrounding the sandy formations are woodlands of pine, oak, and hickory.

Mississippi

TENNESSEE
RIVER HILLS

Woodall Mountain ▲

Tennessee –
Tombigbee
Waterway

William
Faulkner

University of
Mississippi ■
● OXFORD

TUPELO ●

Magnolia

THE DELTA

COLUMBUS ●

BLACK BELT

● GREENVILLE

● YAZOO CITY

Vicksburg
National
Military Park

JACKSON ✪

● VICKSBURG

MERIDIAN ●

NATCHEZ ●

DESOTO
NATIONAL FOREST

PINEY WOODS

● HATTIESBURG

DESOTO
NATIONAL
FOREST

● OCEAN SPRINGS
GULFPORT ● ● BILOXI
PASS CHRISTIAN ●
BAY ST. LOUIS ●

Gulf Islands
National Seashore ■

Shrimp
festival

Gulf of Mexico

Fort Massachusetts

AMERICA: LAND OF BEAUTY AND SPLENDOR

THE PEOPLE AND THE LAND

Population: 2,534,800

Area: 47,716 sq. mi.

Population per sq. mi.: 53

Capital and largest city:
Jackson (pop. 396,200)

Major rivers: Big Black, Mississippi, Pearl, Yazoo

Elevation: Sea level to 806 ft.
(Woodall Mountain)

Leading industries: Agriculture
(chickens, cotton, soybeans, beef
cattle), transportation equipment,
electrical equipment, clothing,
wood products

Bird: Mockingbird

Flower: Magnolia

Tree: Magnolia

Motto: *Virtute et Armis* (By Valor
and Arms)

Song: "Go, Mississippi!"

Origin of name: Probably from
the Chippewa term *mici zihi,*
meaning great river. A lieutenant
of the French explorer La Salle
first wrote it as "Michi Sepe."

Nicknames: Bayou State,
Border-Eagle State, Eagle State,
Magnolia State, Mudcat State

INFORMATION

**Division of Tourism
Development**
P.O. Box 22825
Jackson, MS 39205-2825
Telephone: 800-647-2290

Mockingbird

State flag

HISTORICAL HIGHLIGHTS

1540 Spaniard Hernando de Soto explores Mississippi area.

1699 French establish first white settlement at Old Biloxi, present-day Ocean Springs.

1763 France cedes Mississippi to England in treaty ending French and Indian War.

1775 Mississippi remains loyal to the English crown during the Revolutionary War and becomes a loyalist haven.

1798 Congress creates Mississippi Territory.

1817 Mississippi is admitted to Union as 20th state.

1858 Program to drain Delta swamps for farming is initiated.

1861 Mississippi secedes from Union and joins Confederacy.

1863 Union troops capture Vicksburg and gain control of Mississippi River, a turning point in Civil War.

1874 Seventy blacks are killed in race riot in Vicksburg.

1927 The Mississippi's Great Flood leaves 100,000 homeless.

1936 The state enacts legislation to boost industry.

1939 Oil is discovered at Tinsley and Vaughan.

1962 Amid riots, James Meredith becomes first black to enroll in University of Mississippi.

1964 Three young civil rights workers are killed near town of Philadelphia.

1969 Federal courts order public schools to desegregate. In Fayette, Charles Evers is elected Mississippi's first black mayor since Reconstruction.

1973 Severe flooding causes extensive damage in 52 of Mississippi's 82 counties.

1976 Industrial employment in state reaches 80 percent.

1985 Tennessee-Tombigbee Waterway links Tennessee River and Gulf of Mexico.

FAMOUS SONS AND DAUGHTERS

Jefferson Davis (1808 – 89). A hero of the Mexican War (1846 – 48), Davis had been Franklin Pierce's secretary of war (1853 – 57) and was a U.S. senator when he resigned his seat in 1861 to join the Confederacy, which he later headed.

Medgar Evers (1925 – 63). The first field secretary of the NAACP in Mississippi, Evers was assassinated by a sniper's bullet.

William Faulkner (1897 – 1962). A resident of Oxford most of his life, Faulkner was one of America's great writers. The mythic Yoknapatawpha County, patterned after his home county, was the setting for his most famous novels, including *The Sound and the Fury* and *Absalom, Absalom!*, which explored the dark agonies of the South. He won the Nobel Prize in 1949.

Elvis Presley (1935 – 77).

Born in Tupelo, the King of Rock 'n' Roll dominated the airwaves in the late 1950's and early 1960's with songs influenced by rhythm and blues.

Leontyne Price (1927 –). Price's powerful soprano voice has graced such operas as *Aïda* and *Madame Butterfly* and has won her international renown.

Eudora Welty (1909 –). Welty's humorous, often fantastical, short stories and novels, such as *Delta Wedding,* are filled with Mississippi characters. In 1973 she won the Pulitzer Prize for *The Optimist's Daughter*.

Tennessee Williams (1911 – 83). Williams's searing plays, with their high tension and poetic dialogue, often take place in the South. Among the best known are *A Streetcar Named Desire* and *Cat on a Hot Tin Roof*.

Richard Wright (1908 – 60). Perhaps the most important black writer of his time, Wright wrote about racial injustice and his own life. *Native Son* and *Black Boy* are his most famous works.

ODDITIES AND SPECIALTIES

Mississippi leads the nation in producing upholstered furniture.

The Mississippi Delta area is known not only for cotton but for its music, in particular the blues. The University of Mississippi near Oxford holds the world's largest collection of this music.

The first lung and heart transplants took place in 1963 and 1964 at the University of Mississippi Medical Center in Jackson.

Women in Columbus helped inaugurate Memorial Day when, on Apr. 25, 1866, they decorated the graves of Confederate soldiers. Legend has it that they put aside wartime allegiance and placed flowers on the graves of Union men as well.

The nation's catfish capital, Mississippi devotes over 88,000 acres to watery farms for the whiskery fish.

PLACES TO VISIT, THINGS TO DO

Biloxi Shrimp Festival (Point Cadet). On the first weekend in June, scores of decorated shrimp boats pass before a priest to be blessed. Festivities include a parade, a seafood jamboree, and street dancing.

De Soto National Forest (Wiggins). This 500,000-acre forest offers the Big Biloxi River, as well as creeks, lakes, and hiking trails.

Faulkner Home National Historic Landmark (Oxford). William Faulkner wrote many of his famous novels here at Rowan Oak, which is open to visitors.

Gulf Islands National Seashore These barrier islands in the Gulf of Mexico, including four off Mississippi, contain 100 miles of beaches and the sites of five historic forts, among them Fort Massachusetts, off Biloxi.

Natchez The town's history is wonderfully preserved. On view are Indian mounds, 18th-century buildings, antebellum mansions, and magnificent gardens.

Natchez Trace Parkway (Entrance at points north of Natchez from Route 61). This scenic road virtually follows the route of the old Natchez Trace, many sections of which are preserved.

Vicksburg National Military Park The siege and capture of Vicksburg by the Union forces are memorialized by monuments marking army positions, remains of earthworks, and relics of war equipment.

Missouri

A serene landscape traversed by two mighty rivers

Missouri is a study in contrasts: mountain mists and prairie grasses, surging rivers and cloistered caves, genteel St. Louis and down-to-earth Kansas City, President Harry Truman and outlaw Jesse James. It is also a natural crossroads, for Missouri, located in the very heart of America, serves as a link between East and West, North and South.

PLAINS AND MOUNTAINS

Much of the state consists of rich farmland. North of the Missouri River, which bisects the state as it flows from Kansas City to St. Louis, fertile, rolling plains in a region once buried under glaciers are now covered by expanses of golden grain. South of the Missouri River and to the west lie the Osage Plains, where gentle streams meander through fields of wildflowers and where wheat and corn share the land with protected tracts of the original prairie.

In contrast, most of the state south of the Missouri River is taken up by the varied landscapes of the Ozark Mountain region — an area of forests, lakes, rivers, rugged hills, and low mountains that extends into neighboring Arkansas. The Ozarks contain some 10,000 springs, many of which gush with more than a million gallons of water per day. The area is also honeycombed with thousands of caves carved out of limestone by underground streams. These mysterious netherworlds, where labyrinthine passageways twist and turn for miles, are filled with beautiful rock formations and bizarre creatures, such as blind white cave fish, that spend their lives in total darkness.

The tortuous shoreline of mammoth, man-made Lake of the Ozarks is longer than the coast of California.

Autumn's color brightens the forested fringes of hayfields near the Current River in southeastern Missouri. Leased to farmers by the state, the fields encourage a greater variety of wildlife than is found in areas of uninterrupted woodland.

In the southeast corner a section of the state called the bootheel juts into Arkansas (when Missouri entered the Union, a few wealthy plantation owners from the region lobbied successfully to have it included in the state). Here the Mississippi alluvial plain, once covered by lush bald cypress swamps, was drained to expose its rich dark soil. The land now yields tons of soybeans and rice, as well as the most southern crop of all — cotton.

THE GATEWAY STATE

From the outset, the Mississippi and Missouri rivers, coursing through the state from top to bottom and from side to side, attracted explorers and fur traders. Early river towns such as St. Charles (the state's first capital) and the Town of Kansas (now Kansas City) became busy ports. In the 19th century the steamboats that chugged up and down the Mississippi were immortalized by Hannibal's own Mark Twain.

The Alley Spring Mill, built in 1894, sits on the scenic Jacks Fork River in Shannon County.

During America's years of exploration and growth, Missouri was the starting-off point to the vast, beckoning West. Lewis and Clark began and ended their famous expedition to the Pacific in St. Louis; both the Santa Fe and Oregon trails started in Independence; and the hardy riders of the pony express galloped out of St. Joseph toward Sacramento. This era of expansion is aptly memorialized in St. Louis by the world-famous Gateway Arch.

The giant boulders at Elephant Rocks State Park near Graniteville are over a billion years old.

Rising above the eroded limestone bedrock of the Mississippi River near Altenburg is massive, fortresslike Tower Rock.

THE WRY SAGE OF HANNIBAL

Samuel Langhorne Clemens was born in the little town of Florida, Missouri, but Mark Twain was born — fittingly enough — on the Mississippi River. The writer took his pen name from the words used by men on riverboats to call out the depth of the water. "Mark twain," which means two fathoms deep, was heard so often by Clemens during his exhilarating years as a steamboat pilot that he deemed it an apt nom de plume.

Later Mark Twain traveled around the world, speaking and writing on a dazzling variety of subjects, but he was considered at his best when reminiscing about his early years spent on the river.

Twain's connection with the Mississippi began when he was a small boy and his family moved to Hannibal, where the ever-present river shaped every aspect of life. Below the bluffs flowed "the great Mississippi, the majestic, the magnificent Mississippi, rolling its mile-wide tide along, shining in the sun." As a child, Twain could not have anticipated how significant his adventures on the river would become. Without them, Tom Sawyer would not have become a river "pirate," Huckleberry Finn would never have rafted the river with his friend Jim, and life on the Mississippi would be a much dimmer memory in the mind of America.

North and South also converged in Missouri. Abolitionists and slaveholders alike lived in the state, and during the long and bloody Civil War Missourians fought on both sides — some, tragically, against their own kin.

DIVERSE AND INDEPENDENT

As with all else about the state, Missourians themselves are a mixed bag. Ste. Genevieve, the oldest settlement, and Bonne Terre were founded by the French. Germans established such enclaves as Hermann and Rhineland, and the sons and daughters of Irish and Scottish settlers from the Smokies and Appalachia brought their ballads and lore to the Ozark hills.

Out of this mélange came a people known for their independence and skepticism, as was memorably expressed by Congressman Willard Vandiver in 1899: "Frothy eloquence neither convinces nor satisfies me. I am from Missouri. You have got to show me."

The state's many-faceted, contradictory nature was summed up in the 1950's by Irving Dilliard, who wrote: "Missouri is the abolitionist North with its belief in equal rights for all men and women. It is the plantation South with its old ideas of a leisure society. It is the industrial East, busy, noisy, mechanical, commercial. It is the grazing West, miles and miles of pasture and prize livestock in every direction." Missouri is also redbuds and blue phlox, cold bubbling springs and mysterious caves, ragtime and blues, towboats and showboats, and a high gleaming arch.

Delicate, downy seedballs catch the fading light in a field of thistles not far from Kansas City.

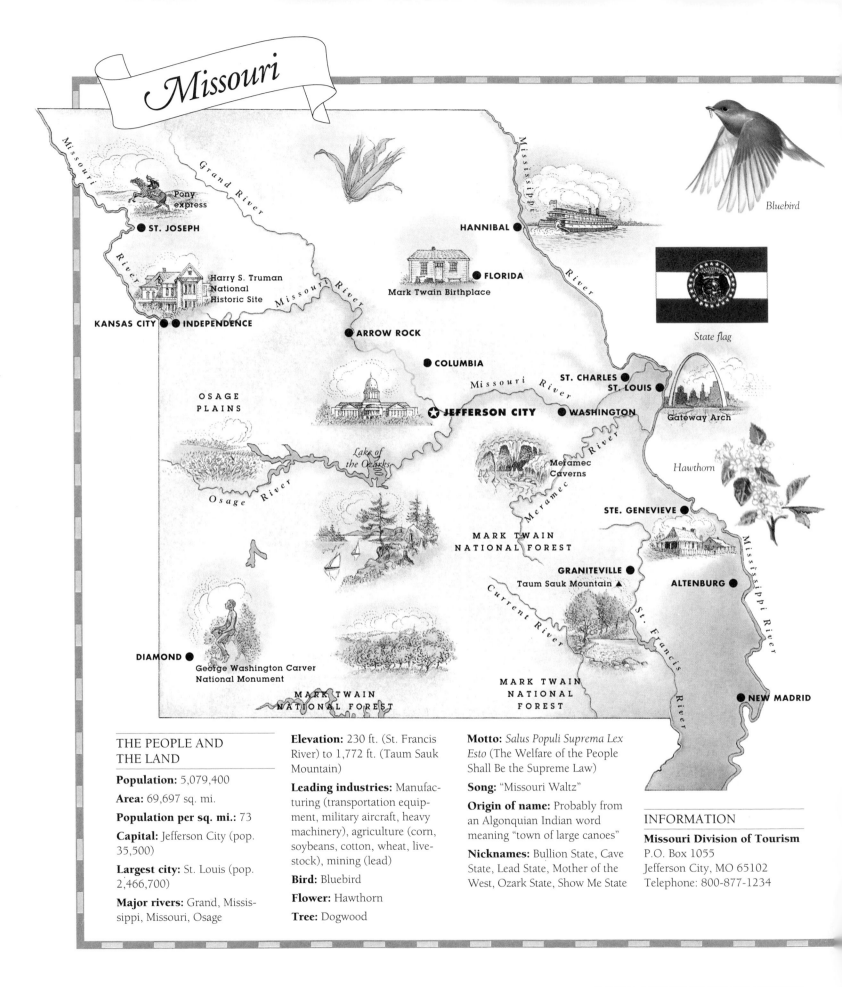

Missouri

Pony express

● ST. JOSEPH

Harry S. Truman
National
Historic Site

KANSAS CITY ● ● INDEPENDENCE

● ARROW ROCK

HANNIBAL ●

● FLORIDA
Mark Twain Birthplace

Bluebird

State flag

● COLUMBIA

OSAGE
PLAINS

★ JEFFERSON CITY

ST. CHARLES ●
ST. LOUIS ●

● WASHINGTON

*Lake of
the Ozarks*

Meramec
Caverns

Gateway Arch

Hawthorn

STE. GENEVIEVE ●

MARK TWAIN
NATIONAL FOREST

GRANITEVILLE ●
Taum Sauk Mountain ▲

ALTENBURG ●

DIAMOND ●
George Washington Carver
National Monument

MARK TWAIN
NATIONAL FOREST

MARK TWAIN
NATIONAL
FOREST

● NEW MADRID

THE PEOPLE AND THE LAND

Population: 5,079,400

Area: 69,697 sq. mi.

Population per sq. mi.: 73

Capital: Jefferson City (pop. 35,500)

Largest city: St. Louis (pop. 2,466,700)

Major rivers: Grand, Mississippi, Missouri, Osage

Elevation: 230 ft. (St. Francis River) to 1,772 ft. (Taum Sauk Mountain)

Leading industries: Manufacturing (transportation equipment, military aircraft, heavy machinery), agriculture (corn, soybeans, cotton, wheat, livestock), mining (lead)

Bird: Bluebird

Flower: Hawthorn

Tree: Dogwood

Motto: *Salus Populi Suprema Lex Esto* (The Welfare of the People Shall Be the Supreme Law)

Song: "Missouri Waltz"

Origin of name: Probably from an Algonquian Indian word meaning "town of large canoes"

Nicknames: Bullion State, Cave State, Lead State, Mother of the West, Ozark State, Show Me State

INFORMATION

Missouri Division of Tourism
P.O. Box 1055
Jefferson City, MO 65102
Telephone: 800-877-1234

HISTORICAL HIGHLIGHTS

1673 Explorers Marquette and Jolliet discover mouth of Missouri River.

1682 Robert Cavelier, sieur de La Salle, claims area for France.

c. 1735 Ste. Genevieve is the first permanent settlement.

1762 France yields Missouri region to Spain.

1763 Pierre Laclède selects site for St. Louis.

1800 Spain returns Missouri area to France.

1803 U.S. receives Missouri as part of Louisiana Purchase.

1804 Lewis and Clark set out on their famous western expedition from St. Louis.

1811 – 12 Three massive earthquakes hit sparsely populated New Madrid, permanently altering the southeastern Missouri landscape.

1812 Congress organizes the Missouri Territory.

1820 Missouri Compromise paves way for Missouri to enter Union as a slave state and Maine as a free state.

1821 Missouri becomes 24th American state.

1836 Platte Purchase adds six counties to the state.

1857 The U.S. Supreme Court denies freedom to Missouri slave Dred Scott, fueling controversy that leads to Civil War.

1860 Pony express service starts in St. Joseph.

1904 Louisiana Purchase Exposition (also known as the St. Louis World's Fair) opens in St. Louis.

1931 Bagnell Dam is completed, forming the Lake of the Ozarks.

1945 Harry S. Truman is inaugurated as 33rd president.

1965 Gateway Arch is completed in St. Louis.

1983 Dioxin, a toxic by-product of chemical manufacturing plants, contaminates Times Beach, forcing residents to leave.

1988 A severe drought causes major difficulties with river transportation.

FAMOUS SONS AND DAUGHTERS

Josephine Baker (1906 – 75). A black entertainer living in France, Baker achieved fame when she performed at the Folies-Bergére. By the late 1920's she was the toast of Paris.

Dale Carnegie (1888 – 1955). A lecturer and former salesman, Carnegie drew on experiences in his own life to write the hugely successful *How to Win Friends and Influence People*.

George Washington Carver (c. 1864 – 1943). Born a slave, Carver became an important scientist who discovered hundreds of uses for the peanut and sweet potato. His birthplace in the town of Diamond is now a national monument.

Jesse James (1847 – 82). Together with his brother Frank, Jesse James led a notorious outlaw gang that robbed banks and trains for more than a decade.

John J. Pershing (1860 – 1948). West Point graduate and former Indian fighter, Pershing was commander of the American Expeditionary Forces in World War I, during which he transformed the ill-prepared U.S. troops into effective combat units.

Joseph Pulitzer (1847 – 1911). Pulitzer, an immigrant from Hungary, published the St. Louis *Post-Dispatch* and the New York *World*. He also endowed the prestigious Pulitzer Prizes.

Virgil Thomson (1896 – 1989). A major figure in contemporary music, Thomson was an organist, composer, author, and music critic. His works include operas, ballets, chamber music, and scores for films.

Harry S. Truman (1884 – 1972). Raised in Independence, Truman served in the U.S. Senate before his election as vice president. When Roosevelt died in 1945, Truman became president.

ODDITIES AND SPECIALTIES

Missouri's central location and navigable rivers — notably the Mississippi and Missouri — made the state an important transportation center. Today St. Louis and Kansas City continue to serve as two of the nation's busiest inland ports.

More corncob pipes are produced in Washington, Mo., than anywhere else in the world.

A spelunker's heaven, Missouri in 1990 reported a record of 5,000 caves within its borders. Some of the creatures that live in them, such as the grotto salamander, can be found nowhere but in the Ozarks.

The ice-cream cone is believed to have been invented at the St. Louis World's Fair in 1904, when a vendor used a folded waffle to hold ice cream.

PLACES TO VISIT, THINGS TO DO

Arrow Rock An outfitting point for the Santa Fe Trail, this river town features a number of 19th-century buildings that have been carefully preserved.

Gateway Arch (St. Louis).

Located at the center of the Jefferson National Expansion Memorial, the 630-foot arch is the nation's tallest monument. It is also the highest freestanding arch ever built.

Hannibal The spirit of Mark Twain lives on in his childhood hometown, where one can visit his family home, a museum, and the famous Mark Twain Cave.

Lake of the Ozarks (60 miles southwest of Jefferson City). Covering 58,000 acres, with a shoreline of over 1,300 miles, this artificial lake is one of the world's largest. Set amid dense oak and hickory forests, the lake offers boating, fishing, and other recreational activities.

Mark Twain National Forest (Rolla). The rivers, springs, lakes, and caves of the Ozark woods create some of the most striking scenery in the state. Visitors can view it while hiking, driving, horseback riding, or taking a "float trip" down a river.

Meramec Caverns (Stanton). Once the hideout of Jesse James, the cave contains five levels of unusual rock formations.

Montana

*Fifty mountain ranges at
the edge of the Great Plains*

Although most of Montana belongs to
the Great Plains, it is mountains that
give the state its extraordinary beauty.
More than 50 majestic ranges — among them
the colorfully named Beaverhead, Big Belt,
Crazy, Flathead, and Tobacco Root — make
up Montana's share of the Rocky Mountains,
strung down the western third of the state.
Some were formed long ago by violent up-
thrust and volcanic eruption, others in more
recent geologic time by glacial activity. Faults
continue to grind away in western Montana
today, carrying on the age-long work of creating new mountains and demolishing old ones.

The mountains also helped give Montana
its Wild West image, for this was the territory
of rough-and-ready prospectors and opulent
copper barons. A gold strike in 1862 at
Grasshopper Creek first drew the miners, who
eventually found silver, coal, and copper as
well — and called Butte, the town they
founded on one of the world's largest copper
deposits, "the richest hill on earth."

THE ROAD TO BEARTOOTH PASS

Each of Montana's mountain ranges is a scenic
wonder in itself. The two-lane highway that
crosses the Beartooth range, for example, has
been called the most beautiful drive in America.
This 69-mile route, on U.S. 212, starts in the
little town of Red Lodge and traces a series of
steep zigzags, or switchbacks, along the Mon-
tana-Wyoming border to 10,974-foot-high
Beartooth Pass and beyond.

*Rocky Mountain goats live in places so remote and
precarious that the beasts have little to fear from predators. These two wander the rough terrain of Haystack
Butte in Glacier National Park.*

Horses graze in the meadows beneath Livingston Peak in the Absaroka Range. The Absaroka is one of the least barren of Montana's 50-odd ranges, with plenty of deep soil and a soft blanket of vegetation.

From Red Lodge to the first switchback the elevation rises from 5,200 feet to almost 8,000 feet in 12 miles. Along this stretch, a bear or two might be seen scrambling up the steep embankments. Farther on, at Beartooth Pass, travelers can look out over a mountainous terrain as large as all of the New England states combined. Then, on the descent, the highway skirts waterfalls and clear lakes. In the distance loom Pilot and Index peaks, whose jagged summits served as reference points for Indians, trappers, and prospectors. The drive ends at Cooke City, a gateway to Yellowstone National Park.

GOING TO THE SUN

Many other scenic ranges and subranges sweep down from northwestern Montana. Along the crest of some 20 of them — including the Boundary, Lewis, Anaconda, Mission, Bitterroot, Centennial, and Swan — runs the Continental Divide. Centered squarely on the divide at the northern border of the state is Glacier National Park, a breathtaking preserve of sharp peaks and icy lakes. The best view of the park's vast vertical walls of glacier-polished rock is from the Going-to-the-Sun Highway, a 55-mile-long road that traverses the park and crosses the divide at Logan Pass.

A rainbow appears as a storm clears over the broad Madison River valley in southwestern Montana. Here, sagebrush-covered foothills ascend to the mountains of the Madison Range.

Iceberg Lake in Glacier National Park is the perfect example of a tarn — a deep, round lake gouged out by a glacier. This lake's spectacular headwalls rise more than 3,000 feet.

With every 1,000-foot gain in elevation, the traveler encounters a climate equivalent to that 300 miles north; hence the presence of five life zones in the park — grassland, deciduous forest, coniferous forest, alpine tundra, and glacial ice. This range has endowed the park with an extraordinary variety of flora and fauna. Aromatic red cedars and hemlocks form dark, cathedrallike forests in the lower reaches, while glacier lilies bloom at the edges of receding snowfields above. Bighorn sheep and Rocky Mountain goats pick their way across the steep mountainsides as grizzly bears, cougars, and wolverines roam the woods.

The Musselshell River, here looking as tidy as an English stream, moves through the undulating terrain of central Montana.

AMERICA: LAND OF BEAUTY AND SPLENDOR

PAINTER OF THE PLAINS

No one documented the life of Montana's great northern plains better than Charles M. Russell, who was born in St. Louis, Missouri, in 1864. Drawn by the irresistible romance of the West, Charlie arrived in Montana as a 16-year-old; once there, he herded sheep, lived with a trapper, rode the range, and dwelled among the Indians. He also produced some 4,500 works of art before his death in 1926.

The self-taught artist's famous "Waiting for a Chinook," depicting the hard winter of 1886 – 87 that brought death to thousands of cattle, launched his career. His oil paintings, murals, watercolors, drawings, and bronze sculptures portray virtually every aspect of cowboy life, and his renderings of the Plains Indians are so detailed they can serve as historical records. But no matter how successful Charlie Russell became — a mural commission earned him $30,000 — his log-cabin studio was always open to his cowboy friends, with whom he indulged his legendary gift for storytelling. The studio and artist's house are now part of the C. M. Russell Museum Complex in Great Falls.

BIG SKY COUNTRY

Mountains give Montana its name and its grandeur, but the larger portion of the state is given over to sweeping plains — the majestic Big Sky Country. As in other parts of the West, a procession of immigrants put the land to different uses. Some succeeded and stayed, others failed and departed.

First, the Indians came for buffalo. The Blackfoot, Crow, and other Indian tribes tracked huge herds across the plains, using the animals for food and clothing, and sheathing tepees with their skins. Then, in the 1870's, white ranchers arrived to make use of the open range and its native grama and bunch grasses, which provide ideal food for cattle. They drove their herds from as far as Texas, more than 1,000 miles away, because grazing was free.

Soon after came professional buffalo hunters in search of animal hides to ship back east. By 1885 the seemingly inexhaustible buffalo herds had all but disappeared, and Montana's dozen-odd native Indian tribes, deprived of the animals that gave them sustenance (and now almost entirely dependent on the federal government), were relegated to six reservations by the end of the century.

The vast open range went the way of the buffalo in the early 20th century when hordes of sodbusters arrived to farm the land offered by the U.S. government. After staking out the range with barbed wire and bringing in a few good wheat crops in a run of unusually

Wagon wheels of old are brought to mind by the water pipes in a Montana wheat field. Grain covers much of the vast plain that lies east of the mountain ranges.

Nowhere is the beauty of Glacier National Park more apparent than at St. Mary, one of the largest of the park's 650 lakes. Visible in the center is tiny Wild Goose Island.

rainy years, most of the sodbusters abandoned their farms by 1920, defeated by grasshopper plagues, drought, and windstorms that blew away the topsoil.

Today many visitors come to Montana to enjoy a venerable western institution — the dude ranch. Such ranches got their start when railroads began bringing tourists, mainly from the East, to Yellowstone Park in the 1880's and nearby ranchers welcomed the strangers into their homes, charging a fee as a way to help keep things together in tough times.

Later, in the 1920's, a few drought-threatened cattle ranches were revived by doubling as vacation spots. A whole new tourist trade developed, and now more people than ever visit Montana's dude ranches. Some city dwellers choose working ranches where they can become part of the crew for a few days; others want only a little horseback riding or fishing. But all appreciate the truth in western artist Charlie Russell's words: "You can get in a car to see what man has made, but you have to get on a horse to see what God has made."

At the National Bison Range, 400 bison share the land with pronghorns, sheep, and elk.

Bear grass blooms at the Chinese Wall, a 13-mile-long cliff along the Continental Divide.

Whether seen on horseback or from the highway, the grandeur of Montana is undeniable — in any season. Spring brings the smell of fresh sagebrush to the plains and scatters brilliantly colored wildflowers across the mountainsides. Autumn turns forests of aspens to gold. The warm, dry wind that locals call a chinook may roll down from the mountains on a cold January day, while a sudden snowstorm can arrive in the middle of July. Even the weather is dramatic in this magnificent land of the Big Sky.

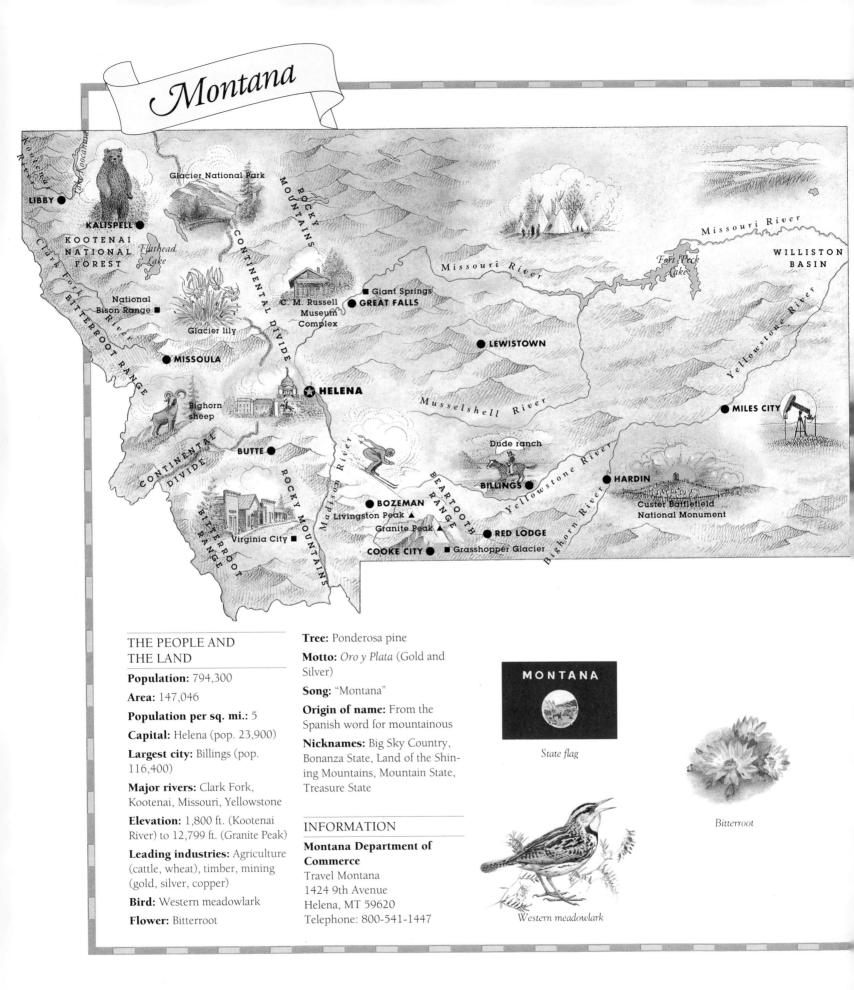

Montana

THE PEOPLE AND THE LAND

Population: 794,300

Area: 147,046

Population per sq. mi.: 5

Capital: Helena (pop. 23,900)

Largest city: Billings (pop. 116,400)

Major rivers: Clark Fork, Kootenai, Missouri, Yellowstone

Elevation: 1,800 ft. (Kootenai River) to 12,799 ft. (Granite Peak)

Leading industries: Agriculture (cattle, wheat), timber, mining (gold, silver, copper)

Bird: Western meadowlark

Flower: Bitterroot

Tree: Ponderosa pine

Motto: *Oro y Plata* (Gold and Silver)

Song: "Montana"

Origin of name: From the Spanish word for mountainous

Nicknames: Big Sky Country, Bonanza State, Land of the Shining Mountains, Mountain State, Treasure State

INFORMATION

Montana Department of Commerce
Travel Montana
1424 9th Avenue
Helena, MT 59620
Telephone: 800-541-1447

State flag

Bitterroot

Western meadowlark

HISTORICAL HIGHLIGHTS

1743 French explorers Pierre and François de La Vérendrye sight what they call the Shining Mountains, perhaps the Bighorn Mountains.

1803 With Louisiana Purchase, eastern Montana comes under jurisdiction of U.S.

1805 – 06 Lewis and Clark explore region on their way to and from Pacific Ocean.

1807 Manuel Lisa builds trading post at confluence of Yellowstone and Bighorn rivers.

1846 Treaty with Great Britain gives northwestern portion of Montana to U.S.

1862 Discovery of gold at Grasshopper Creek brings in thousands of prospectors.

1864 Congress passes bill declaring Montana a territory.

1876 Indians defeat George Armstrong Custer's cavalry troops in Battle of Little Bighorn.

1877 Indian fighting in Montana ends with surrender of Chief Joseph and Nez Perce Indians to federal troops.

1880 Railway line reaches Montana for first time.

1889 Montana enters Union as 41st state.

1910 Congress establishes Glacier National Park.

1940 Fort Peck Dam, the country's largest earth-filled hydraulic dam, is completed on Missouri River in northeastern Montana.

1951 Oil boom begins in Williston Basin in eastern Montana.

1975 Libby Dam, which created 90-mile-long Lake Koocanusa, begins operation.

1983 The Anaconda Company, whose mines yielded copper and other minerals worth nearly $4 billion, closes after a century of production in Butte.

FAMOUS SONS AND DAUGHTERS

John M. Bozeman (1835 – 67). This pioneer blazed the Bozeman Trail, a shortcut from the Overland Trail to the Montana goldfields. Today Bozeman Pass and a city are named after him.

Gary Cooper (1901 – 61).

The actor who epitomized the strong, silent type made more than 90 films and won Oscars for his performances in *Sergeant York* and *High Noon*.

A. B. Guthrie, Jr. (1901 –). After growing up on the Montana frontier, Guthrie wrote about the West in such works as the novel *The Big Sky* and the screenplay for *Shane*.

Mike Mansfield (1903 –). A U.S. representative for 10 years before being elected senator, Mansfield, a Democrat, was majority leader for a record 16 years. He served as ambassador to Japan from 1977 to 1988.

Jeannette Rankin (1880 – 1973). An outspoken pacifist who argued against U.S. participation in World Wars I and II, Rankin was the first woman to serve in the House of Representatives. She was the only legislator to vote against declaring war on Japan after the raid on Pearl Harbor in 1941 — a vote that effectively ended her political career.

ODDITIES AND SPECIALTIES

Only 201 feet long, the Roe River near Great Falls may be the shortest river in the world.

Millions of grasshoppers that were entombed in ice long ago can still be seen at Grasshopper Glacier in the Absaroka-Beartooth Wilderness.

An estimated 20 million buffalo roamed the Montana plains in the 1860's. Some 25 years later, hunters in pursuit of buffalo hides had reduced the population to fewer than 100.

In one of the greatest land rushes ever, the number of acres under cultivation in Montana jumped from 886 acres in 1900 to 30 million acres in 1919.

PLACES TO VISIT, THINGS TO DO

Custer Battlefield National Monument (near Hardin). Custer's Last Stand took place on this site in 1876, when Indians annihilated U.S. troops in the valley of the Little Bighorn River.

Flathead Lake (near Kalispell). The largest natural freshwater lake west of the Mississippi, Flathead reflects the surrounding mountains and forest in its waters, which offer fishing, boating, and swimming.

Giant Springs (near Great Falls). Located on the banks of the Missouri River, these springs are among the largest in the world, with a daily flow of nearly 390 million gallons of water.

Glacier National Park (West Glacier). This spectacular park in the Rocky Mountains features lofty peaks, sharp-edged ridges, clear lakes, dense forests, and alpine glaciers. Its streams are a favorite with fishermen; no license is required.

Kootenai National Forest (Libby). Rising above rivers, lakes, and evergreen trees are the snowy peaks of five mountain ranges in this vast forest.

Miles City Jaycee Bucking Horse Sale (Miles City).

Among the events centered on this annual sale of bulls and unbroken horses, held the third weekend in May, are pari-mutuel horse racing, dances, barbecues, and a rodeo.

National Bison Range (Moiese). The buffalo roam over some 19,000 acres of grassland at the base of the Mission Range. Visitors can either watch the bison in designated pastures or, in summer, take the 19-mile self-guided auto tour.

Virginia City This restored ghost town, now a national historic landmark, was the center of gold rush activity in the 1860's. Open for tours in the summer are an assay office, saloon, blacksmith shop, hotel, Wells Fargo office, general store, and the building that served as the territorial capitol from 1865 to 1875.

Nebraska

*Clear skies, rolling hills,
and the river road west*

Nebraska sweeps to the horizon in broad, gently undulating hills and open, sun-drenched vistas. These treeless expanses perplexed some of the first white people who ventured onto the prairie in the 19th century. Maj. Stephen H. Long, after exploring the region in 1819, concluded that it was "destined by the barrenness of its soil, the inhospitable character of its climate, and by other physical disadvantages, to be the abode of perpetual desolation." The lack of trees, however, belied the fruitfulness of the plain. Nebraska in actuality pulses with life.

RICHES OF THE PRAIRIE

Meriwether Lewis and William Clark on their 1804 expedition through this region were astonished by the immense herds of elk and antelopes they saw. Prairie potholes — shallow basins filled intermittently with water — supported untold numbers of ducks and geese, and the nutritious native grasses fed enormous herds of bison, or American buffalo. Estimated to have numbered between 60 and 70 million, the bison were perhaps the most abundant wild game animals in the world and a fundamental source of food for the Plains Indians.

What had been called "the abode of perpetual desolation" developed instead into the Cornhusker State, a realm of farms and ranches, livestock feedlots and towering grain elevators, where 95 percent of the terrain is given over to the production of corn, soybeans, wheat, sorghum, and other crops, and to the raising of beef cattle and hogs.

Winter frost bedecks the trees at the base of Scotts Bluff. A landmark for pioneers, the bluff was named for Hiram Scott, a fur trader who died nearby in 1828.

The classic badlands landscape of Toadstool Park, in northwest Nebraska, results from the erosion of the soft clay around the harder sandstone pillars.

In the eastern part of the state nature provides enough rain to sustain these crops and livestock. In the western reaches, however, where the rainfall dwindles, the water supply depends on human ingenuity. Networks of canals bring water from huge reservoirs in far western Nebraska and Wyoming, and deep wells tap underground aquifers for irrigation rigs that loom in the fields west of Cozad.

North-central Nebraska remains uncultivable, a 19,000-square-mile region of ancient sand dunes stabilized by the tenacious roots of prairie grass. These Sandhills of Nebraska, as they are called, were once the domain of nomadic Great Plains Indian tribes — especially the Cheyenne, Pawnee, and Sioux. Today the Sandhills are a kingdom of cattle ranches, for although the soil is too porous for irrigation, the dunes do support enough grass to feed cattle on the open range. Far removed from the din of urban civilization,

the Sandhills are exquisitely quiet, empty, and vast — a place of clear skies, stunning dawns and dusks, and jet black nights pricked with quadrillions of stars.

THE RIVER ROAD WEST

The name Nebraska comes from the Oto Indian word *nebrathka*, which means flat water. This is what the Otos called the great river that flows west to east across the state. It was a suitable name: before the river was harnessed for agricultural purposes, it was wide — three miles in places — and shallow, and rarely riled into swells or whitecaps. French traders concurred with the Oto assessment of this distinctly flat river and called it the Platte.

Indians navigated the Platte easily in small boats, but white expeditioners met the river with dismay. They found it too shallow for their larger craft, and its sandy bed shifted too often to provide a reliable transportation route.

Fremont Lakes State Recreation Area contains 20 ancient sandpits that now have been flooded to form lakes. Each is stocked with fish, such as bass and bullhead catfish.

Little changed from the way the early settlers found them, the Sandhills exude the vastness and solitude of open rangeland. The rolling hills here are in fact sand dunes held in place by grasses. Covering an area nearly the size of West Virginia, the Sandhills are the largest stable dune system in the Western Hemisphere.

Lt. John C. Frémont, who made a frustrating attempt to descend the Platte in 1842, reported: "The names given by the Indians are always remarkably appropriate."

Nonetheless, the river did lead the way west for the tide of overland migration that began in the 1840's. The hopeful masses included immigrant farm families heading for new land in Oregon, Mormons seeking freedom from religious persecution, and busting-to-strike-it-rich prospectors in eager pursuit of California gold. An estimated 350,000 people headed westward through the Platte Valley between 1840 and 1866. The proces-sion of wagon trains came to an end with the completion of the transcontinental railroad in 1869, which followed the same path along the Platte as the preceding pioneers. Today Interstate 80 parallels this pioneer route most of the way across Nebraska.

RITES OF SPRING

Migration to Nebraska has not been limited to humans. Every year in late March half a million sandhill cranes converge on the Platte in the central part of the state, pausing here on their northward migration to their mating grounds in the Arctic. At night they roost in tight

Each summer, the bold orange of wild sunflowers brightens the prairie vistas near Alliance.

huddles in the rippling shallows of the Platte. By day they scatter out to feed in nearby fallow cornfields. During this time of the year, the sky from Kearny to Grand Island, some 40 miles away, is flecked with cranes as phalanxes of the stately birds fly from field to field, their lovely flutelike calls spilling earthward.

The convocation of cranes is one of the great wildlife spectacles in North America. Here in the heart of the continent, a passerby who pauses to watch and listen to it can easily understand the wonder that Meriwether Lewis and William Clark felt as they crossed the Nebraskan Great Plains.

THE PIONEERS' LANDMARK

On the level land of the Great Plains, occasional geological irregularities — a towering rock spire or an unexpected canyon — provided unmistakable and welcome landmarks for pioneers headed west. The sight of these natural features not only assured the wagoners that they were on the right course, but also told them how far they had come and how far they had to go.

One such landmark on the Oregon Trail was mentioned more often in the diaries of pioneers than any other — Chimney Rock, the clay-and-sandstone spire that towers 470 feet above the North Platte Valley in Nebraska. Westward migrants, jostling across the plains in covered wagons at a speed of little more than a mile an hour, could see this steeplelike formation for days before they reached it. When they arrived, they knew that they had traveled 650 miles from St. Joseph, Missouri, and had 1,400 more to go before reaching the Pacific Ocean. They also could enjoy a pleasant campsite, for a reliable spring spouted from the base of the rock.

HISTORICAL HIGHLIGHTS

1541 Spanish explorer Francisco de Coronado probably reaches southern Nebraska while searching for legendary gold of Quivira.

1682 Moving down Mississippi River, Sieur de la Salle claims American interior for France.

1803 U.S. buys Nebraska from France as part of Louisiana Purchase, which includes lands from the Mississippi to the Rockies.

1804 Traveling along the Missouri River valley, Lewis and Clark explore eastern Nebraska.

1819 Maj. Stephen Long explores South Platte River valley.

1823 A trading post flourishes near present-day Bellevue, Nebraska's first permanent white settlement.

1830 Following the Platte and North Platte rivers, William Sublette leads a wagon train on a route that will become part of the Oregon Trail.

1854 An act of Congress creates Nebraska Territory.

1862 Congress passes Homestead Act to encourage settlement of West. The first person to claim one of the 160-acre homesteads is Daniel Freeman, who settles near Beatrice.

1865 Workers in Omaha begin laying track westward for the transcontinental railroad.

1867 Nebraska joins Union as 37th state.

1874 – 77 An invasion of grasshoppers devastates crops.

1877 Sioux warriors led by Crazy Horse surrender at Fort Robinson, ending Indian resistance in Nebraska.

1892 Omaha hosts first national convention of Populist Party.

1896 Democrat William Jennings Bryan makes first of three unsuccessful campaigns for president.

1933 During Great Depression, state protects farmers by declaring a moratorium on foreclosures of farm mortgages.

1946 The Strategic Air Command, the U.S. Air Force's long-range attack group, is established near Omaha.

1968 – 69 Meatpacking plants close in Omaha as the industry shifts to smaller regional centers.

1982 State prohibits corporations from buying farms.

1985 Defaulted farm loans cause 13 banks to fail.

FAMOUS SONS AND DAUGHTERS

Willa Cather (1873 – 1947). The renowned novelist grew up in Nebraska and used the state as a setting in her works, notably *O Pioneers!* and *My Antonia.*

Crazy Horse (c. 1842 – 77). As war chief of the Oglala Sioux, Crazy Horse led the Sioux and Cheyenne when they slaughtered Col. George Custer's troops at Little Bighorn River in 1876.

George W. Norris (1861 – 1944). During his 40 years in Congress, 30 as a senator, Norris championed the rights of labor unions and fathered the legislation that created the Tennessee Valley Authority, a vast water-management program.

Roscoe Pound (1870 – 1964). Distinguished both as a botanist and a legal philosopher, Pound argued that laws should be responsive to society's changing needs. He was dean of Harvard Law School from 1916 to 1936.

Darryl F. Zanuck (1902 – 79). Born in Wahoo, the trailblazing movie producer and cofounder of 20th Century-Fox introduced full-length "talkies" with *The Jazz Singer* and CinemaScope with *The Robe.* His many hits include *M*A*S*H* and *The Sound of Music.*

ODDITIES AND SPECIALTIES

Many entertainers have roots in Nebraska, among them Fred Astaire, Marlon Brando, Johnny Carson, Dick Cavett, Montgomery Clift, Sandy Dennis, Harold Lloyd, Dorothy McGuire, and Robert Taylor. Early in his career Henry Fonda worked at Omaha's Community Playhouse, where Brando's mother, Dorothy, appeared regularly in productions.

The first Arbor Day was Apr. 10, 1872, when Nebraska set aside a special day for tree planting.

Some 25,000 acres of woodland in the Nebraska National Forest were originally grassland. Trees were first planted there in 1902.

Nebraska had so few trees that settlers built homes from sod blocks, dubbed Nebraska marble.

Nebraska is the only state with a unicameral, or one-house, legislature. It was established by amendment to the state constitution in 1934.

PLACES TO VISIT, THINGS TO DO

Boys Town (Omaha). "He ain't heavy, father. He's m'brother." Founded in 1917 by Father Edward Flanagan (1886 – 1948),

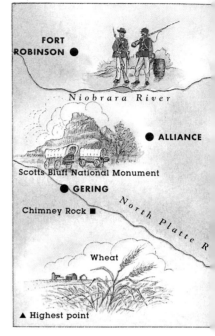

Boys Town gained renown as a home for children in distress. It began admitting girls in 1979.

Buffalo Bill Ranch State Historical Park (North Platte). Buffalo Bill Cody's ranch may be visited year-round. Rodeos are held in summer.

Omaha Indian Pow Wow (near Macy). Each August the Omaha Indians gather for a festival of traditional dance, arts, and ceremonies. Visitors are welcome.

Scotts Bluff National Monument (near Gering). Some 800 feet high, this bluff was a landmark for wagon trains. The museum here has exhibits about Oregon Trail pioneers.

Stuhr Museum of the Prairie Pioneer (Grand Island). A re-created late 19th-century railroad town evokes frontier life.

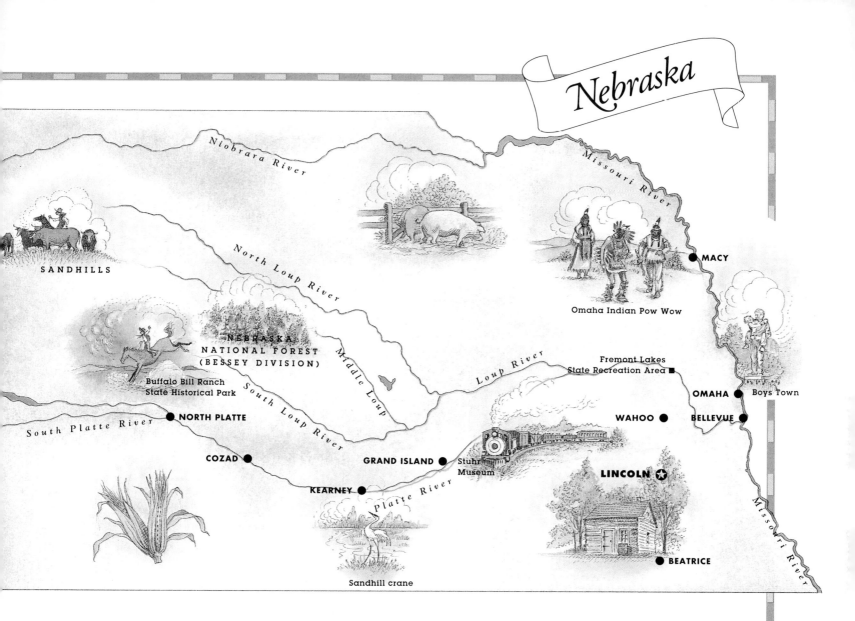

Nebraska

SANDHILLS

Niobrara River

North Loup River

NEBRASKA NATIONAL FOREST (BESSEY DIVISION)

Buffalo Bill Ranch State Historical Park

Middle Loup

South Loup River

Loup River

Omaha Indian Pow Wow

Missouri River

● MACY

Fremont Lakes State Recreation Area ■

Boys Town

South Platte River

● NORTH PLATTE

WAHOO ●

OMAHA ●

BELLEVUE ●

COZAD ●

GRAND ISLAND ● Stuhr Museum

LINCOLN ☆

KEARNEY ●

Platte River

Sandhill crane

BEATRICE ●

Missouri River

THE PEOPLE AND THE LAND

Population: 1,572,500

Area: 77,227 sq. mi.

Population per sq. mi.: 20

Capital: Lincoln (pop. 211,600)

Largest city: Omaha (pop. 621,600)

Major rivers: Loup, Missouri, Niobrara, North Platte, Platte, South Platte

Elevation: 840 ft. (Richardson County) to 5,426 ft. (Kimball County)

Leading industries: Agriculture (corn, soybeans, wheat, beef cattle, hogs), food processing, machinery manufacturing

Bird: Western meadowlark

Flower: Goldenrod

Tree: Cottonwood

Motto: Equality Before the Law

Song: "Beautiful Nebraska"

Origin of name: From the Oto Indian word meaning flat water, referring to the Platte River

Nicknames: Antelope State, Bug-Eating State, Cornhusker State, Tree Planters' State

INFORMATION

Nebraska Division of Travel and Tourism
P.O. Box 94666
Lincoln, NE 68509-4666
Telephone: 800-228-4307
800-334-1819 in Nebraska

State flag

Goldenrod

Western meadowlark

Nevada

Beauty in the desolate wasteland of the Great Basin

Well into the first half of the 19th century, the lonely land just east of the Sierra Nevada remained an enigma. While some explorers returned with stories of snow-covered mountains, pine forests, and rushing trout streams, others described the land as hell's antechamber.

People also wondered what became of all the snow from the Sierra Nevada when it melted. The first Spaniards to arrive in the region believed the snow drained into a mighty river that crossed present-day Nevada and linked the heart of the continent with the Pacific Ocean. But the hoped-for waterway, which they called the San Buenaventura, was never found. It was left to John Charles Frémont, assigned in 1844 to chart the desolate land between the Rocky Mountains and the Sierra Nevada, to discover the disappointing truth. Instead of feeding a great river, the snow from the Sierra Nevada drained onto the salt flats below, creating instant lakes and small rivers, many of which evaporated by summer. Left behind were shallow depressions filled with spiraling alkali dust. The enigma, it seemed, was solved: this land was little more than a forbidding desert.

GOLD AND SILVER

Proponents of Manifest Destiny — the idea that America's westward expansion was right and just — found it difficult to believe that the Almighty had burdened the Union with a chunk of worthless real estate. "I believe God never made anything without a purpose," said newspaper editor Horace Greeley after taking

The unearthly peaks of the Ruby Mountains smolder in the afternoon sun. This scene is at Liberty Lake.

Lake Tahoe, Nevada's oasis of water and woodland, is the largest alpine lake in North America. Its crystalline waters are cupped by the granite peaks of the Sierra Nevada on the Nevada-California border.

the Overland Trail through Nevada in 1859. "But the wilderness I have just crossed is certainly worthless for agriculture. Unless there shall prove to be great mineral wealth there, it has been created in vain."

Nevada's mineral wealth became uncontested fact that same year when two miners prospecting outside present-day Reno discovered what later became known as the Comstock Lode. Not only was there gold aplenty, but the bluish sand that kept clogging the miners' sifters that separated nuggets from sand turned out to be high-grade silver sulfide.

Gold and silver still contribute to Nevada's economy today. But the state's most valuable asset is its allure for tourists — the neon-lit casinos of Las Vegas, the resorts of Lake Tahoe, and the beauty of the very desert that early explorers deemed a wasteland.

WONDERS OF THE GREAT BASIN

The arid Great Basin within which Nevada lies extends into parts of California, Oregon, Idaho, Wyoming, and Utah. Once the basin was the bottom of a vast prehistoric sea called Lake Lahontan. As the lake slowly evaporated, repeated volcanic convulsions uplifted and fissured the earth, leaving more than 100 jagged mountain ranges running from north to south.

Only a few of the mountain valleys still contain viable lakes. Pyramid Lake and Walker Lake, once the deepest parts of ancient Lake

Lahontan, today are recreation areas, blue-green bodies of water eerily terraced with spongy calcium-based deposits called tufa. Many of the rivers in Nevada are shallow, and frequently run dry. Pioneers in covered wagons heading west along the route that has become Interstate 80 found only enough water in the Humboldt River to remind them of the fragility of their existence. "Here, on the Humboldt," a thirsty Horace Greeley noted in his journal, "Famine sits enthroned, and waves his scepter over a dominion expressly made for him."

Despite receiving less than 10 inches of rain a year, Nevada has an amazing diversity of plants and wildlife. Cactus, yucca, sage, and other brush plants blossom every spring.

Indigo blooms in the brick-red sands of southeastern Nevada, near Las Vegas.

Elephant Rock is one of the most curious of the eroded sandstone formations in Valley of Fire State Park.

AMERICA: LAND OF BEAUTY AND SPLENDOR

A field of wild lupines colors the scene in the Jarbidge Wilderness, a 65,000-acre preserve in the northeastern part of the state.

Mule deer frolic among the wind-scoured towers of red sandstone in the desolate Valley of Fire. When swollen with melted snow, Pyramid Lake provides a home for cormorants, white pelicans, and migrating waterfowl.

It is Lake Tahoe, however, that is Nevada's most precious gem. Set amid alpine meadows in the Sierra Nevada, the lake is surrounded by stands of ponderosa pine, piñon, and juniper. In 1861 Samuel Clemens (who would adopt the name Mark Twain a year later) arrived from Missouri to look for gold and discovered that Nevada's real treasure was the beauty and serenity of Lake Tahoe. "So singularly clear was the water . . . that the boat seemed floating in the air," he later reminisced in *Roughing It.*

The gold mines Twain wrote about are little more than rubble today. But the raw majesty of the snowcapped mountains and the stark drama of the desert remain undiminished.

GREAT LAKE OF THE DESERT

The driest state in the Union also boasts a lake that contains enough water to cover the entire state of New York to a depth of one foot — man-made Lake Mead in southeastern Nevada. The 550-mile shoreline of this enormous trough remains a harsh desert, but people flock here for the beauty of the blue-green water and the clarity of the desert air.

Lake Mead also boasts a more spectacular attribute — Hoover Dam, a colossus that contains enough concrete to build a two-lane highway from the Atlantic to the Pacific. Originally planned for Boulder Canyon, the dam was moved downstream where the harder rock offered a more solid footing. On its completion in 1935 President Franklin Roosevelt named the Depression's greatest public works project Boulder Dam, after its location on the original blueprints, rather than name it for his Republican predecessor, who had been a driving force in planning the dam. Nevertheless, two years after Roosevelt's death, Congress renamed the dam to honor Herbert Hoover, America's 31st president.

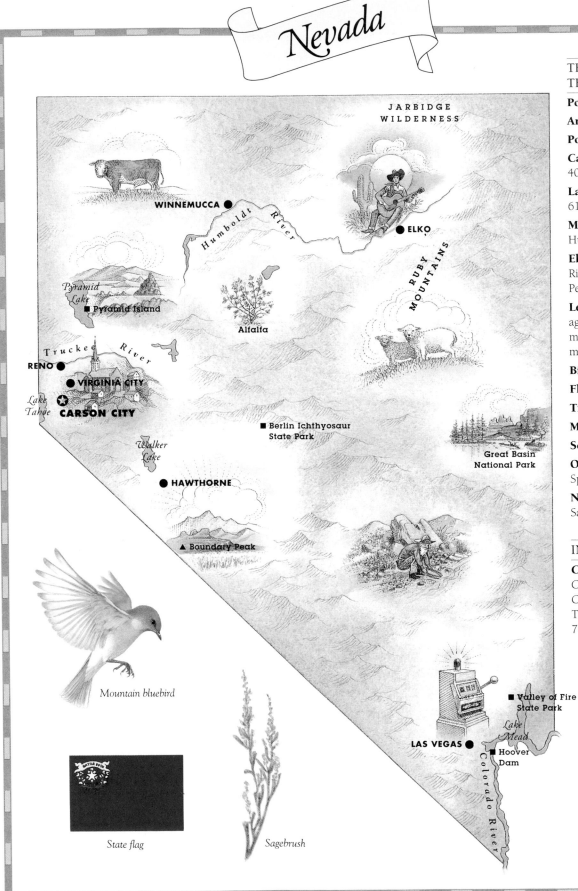

Nevada

THE PEOPLE AND THE LAND

Population: 1,193,000

Area: 110,561 sq. mi.

Population per sq. mi.: 11

Capital: Carson City (pop. 40,400)

Largest city: Las Vegas (pop. 612,600)

Major rivers: Colorado, Humboldt, Truckee

Elevation: 400 ft. (Colorado River) to 13,140 ft. (Boundary Peak)

Leading industries: Tourism, agriculture (cattle, sheep, alfalfa), mining (gold, silver), processed metals, processed foods

Bird: Mountain bluebird

Flower: Sagebrush

Tree: Single-leaf piñon

Motto: All for Our Country

Song: "Home Means Nevada"

Origin of name: From the Spanish word for snowcapped

Nicknames: Mining State, Sagebrush State, Silver State

INFORMATION

Commission on Tourism
Capitol Complex
Carson City, NV 89710
Telephone: 800-NEVADA
702-687-4322 in Nevada

Map labels

JARBIDGE WILDERNESS

WINNEMUCCA

ELKO

Humboldt River

RUBY MOUNTAINS

Pyramid Lake

Pyramid Island

Alfalfa

Truckee River

RENO

VIRGINIA CITY

Lake Tahoe

CARSON CITY

Walker Lake

Berlin Ichthyosaur State Park

Great Basin National Park

HAWTHORNE

▲ Boundary Peak

Mountain bluebird

Valley of Fire State Park

Lake Mead

State flag

Sagebrush

LAS VEGAS

Hoover Dam

Colorado River

HISTORICAL HIGHLIGHTS

1826 – 27 Fur trader Jedediah Smith and his party cross Nevada on their way to California.

1828 Peter Ogden, a Hudson's Bay Company employee, begins exploration of northern Nevada and discovers Humboldt River.

1844 John Frémont, with Kit Carson as his guide, begins to map Nevada.

1848 Mexico cedes Nevada to U.S. after Mexican War.

1849 Mormon Station, a trading post later renamed Genoa, is first permanent white settlement.

1859 With discovery of Comstock Lode, a rich silver and gold deposit, prospectors rush to the settlement that will become Virginia City.

1861 Congress establishes Nevada Territory.

1864 Nevada joins Union as the 36th state.

1868 Transcontinental railroad crosses Nevada.

1869 Gambling is legalized.

1873 Mining industry begins to wane as federal government limits use of silver in coins.

1874 Two Indian reservations, Pyramid Lake and Walker River, are created for Northern Paiutes, who were defeated in the Indian War of 1860.

1880 Population begins a 10-year decline as gold and silver mines peter out.

1907 Newlands Irrigation Project turns parts of west-central Nevada into agricultural land.

1909 State legislature declares gambling illegal.

1931 State legalizes gambling and lowers residency requirement for divorce to six weeks.

1935 Boulder Dam (now Hoover Dam), then the largest dam in U.S., is completed.

1951 Atomic Energy Commission tests nuclear weapons at Yucca Flat.

1970 U.S. census shows Nevada to have been fastest growing state in previous decade.

1980 State legislature passes antipollution laws to protect Lake Tahoe.

1986 Great Basin National Park, the first national park in Nevada, is established.

FAMOUS SONS AND DAUGHTERS

Walter van Tilburg Clark (1909 – 71). This writer set his psychological novels and short stories in the Old West. His most famous work, *The Ox-Bow Incident*, is the story of the lynching of three innocent men.

John W. Mackay (1831 – 1902). A "silver king," Mackay made his fortune mining the Comstock Lode. In 1886 he organized the Postal Telegraph Cable Company, which broke Western Union's monopoly in the U.S.

William Morris Stewart (1827 – 1909). As one of Nevada's first two U.S. senators, Stewart was author of the 15th Amendment, which guarantees equal voting rights, without regard to "race, color, or previous condition of servitude."

Sarah Winnemucca (1844? – 91). Daughter of a Paiute chief and wife of a U.S. Army officer, this interpreter and guide became one of the first Indians to write about Indian grievances. Her book was called *Life Among the Paiutes*.

Wovoka (1858? – 1932). This Paiute Indian was a leader of the 19th-century Ghost Dance religious movement, which sought to resurrect ancestors and restore a waning culture.

ODDITIES AND SPECIALTIES

Taxes from gambling provide nearly 40 percent of Nevada's general revenues.

The driest of all the 50 states, Nevada relies on a number of man-made lakes and underground sources to augment its meager water supply.

Outside of Alaska, the federal government owns more of Nevada than any other state — more than 85 percent.

Each year in Elko, thousands of cowboys and other ranch hands gather to perform poems and songs they have written to pass the time on the range.

Las Vegas is not only the nation's gambling capital but its marriage capital as well; the city boasts some 50 wedding chapels.

PLACES TO VISIT, THINGS TO DO

Berlin Ichthyosaur State Park (near Gabbs). This park has two attractions: the ghost mining town of Berlin and the fossils of ichthyosaurs, colossal reptiles that swam in an ancient inland sea.

Great Basin National Park The most spectacular part of the Great Basin is in this park — the southern part of the Snake mountain range, with forests (including ancient bristlecone pines), limestone caves, and Nevada's only glacier.

Lake Tahoe (near Carson City). Center of a year-round resort area, Lake Tahoe is renowned for the clarity of its water. Snowcapped mountain peaks surround the 72-mile shoreline.

Pyramid Lake (near Reno). A remnant of the prehistoric waters that covered northwest Nevada, this lake contains a pyramid-shaped island and abundant cutthroat trout.

Valley of Fire State Park (near Las Vegas). Striking sandstone formations of many colors stand in this desert valley.

Virginia City Looking almost as it did in 1870, when it was a rich mining town, Virginia City features boardwalks, Victorian mansions, churches, and an historic shortline railway.

NewHampshire

An old Yankee home, New England to the core

Nestled between Maine and Vermont, and extending from Massachusetts to the Canadian border, New Hampshire lies in the heart of New England. Since it is endowed with all the natural beauty of its neighbors — unspoiled forests, mammoth mountains, shimmering lakes, and scenic coastline — and is imbued with some 300 years of Yankee heritage, New Hampshire could easily lay claim to being the state most representative of New England.

WHITE MOUNTAIN WILDERNESS

Nature prevails in its northern reaches, where people are scarce and wildlife is not only plentiful but relatively undisturbed. Bears, moose, and bobcats roam the dense woods, while minks, beavers, and otters frolic in streams and ponds. In White Mountain National Forest, myriad trails wind through more than 1,000 square miles of woodland. Stands of pines, spruces, maples, and birches skirt breathtaking gorges and dramatic cliffs. One such craggy outcrop, at Franconia Notch, forms the famed profile of the Old Man of the Mountains. Nearby, the highest peaks in New England bear the names of American statesmen and presidents: Adams, Eisenhower, Franklin, Jackson, Jefferson, Madison, Monroe, Webster — and, most majestic of all, 6,288-foot Mount Washington.

The highest mountain north of the Carolinas and east of the Rocky Mountains, Mount Washington can be so ferociously windy at its snowy summit that the roofs of some of the

Looming over snow-covered buildings in Franconia are the massive slopes of the White Mountains, which extend from west-central New Hampshire into western Maine.

Spotlighted by sunbeams, winter hikers make their way along the Signal Ridge Trail on Mount Carrigain, located almost exactly in the center of gigantic White Mountain National Forest. A soupy mist envelops the mountainside to the rear of the hikers.

buildings there are chained to solid rock so they won't blow away. To get to the top of the mountain, visitors can hike, drive, or take a cog railway, completed in 1869, which huffs and puffs its way up slopes that seem impossibly steep. Among the rewards of the climb, besides the spectacular vistas, are the Lakes of the Clouds — two lovely pools so close to the sky that one can almost imagine the gods coming down to bathe.

South of White Mountain National Forest, in the state's midsection, lie many of New Hampshire's more than 1,000 crystal-clear lakes. Their names — Kanasatka, Winona,

Winnisquam, Ossipee — conjure up visions of the Indians who once plied their waters with birchbark canoes. Largest of the lakes is Winnipesaukee, whose name means "smile of the Great Spirit." Its shoreline snakes around some 280 miles of inlets and coves, and hundreds of islands, some looming 400 feet above the water's surface, dot the lake. Many are inhabited by people; others, by birds, squirrels, and raccoons. Just northwest of Winnipesaukee lies elegant Squam Lake, where Henry Fonda fished from his speedboat and, with Katharine Hepburn, contemplated old age in the celebrated film *On Golden Pond*.

From late September to early October, maple trees break out in a conflagration of color.

COVERED BRIDGES AND SALTY PIERS

The southwestern corner of New Hampshire is a serene and scenic land that time forgot, where classic New England villages, with general stores and white-steepled churches, are separated by miles of rolling countryside punctuated by red barns and covered bridges. Of all the covered bridges in New England, New Hampshire has more than half. It also has the longest — the 460-foot structure that spans the Connecticut River at Cornish.

Peterborough, not far from the Massachusetts border, could be called a typical, well-preserved New England town. In a sense it

This granite basin in Franconia Notch State Park was sculpted during the last ice age.

An early morning mist rises from a marshy pond near Lisbon, in west-central New Hampshire, where the trees are just beginning to turn.

AMERICA: LAND OF BEAUTY AND SPLENDOR

THE RETURN OF THE WILD TURKEY

The celebrated main course of the Pilgrims' first Thanksgiving dinner, the wild turkey also happened to be Benjamin Franklin's choice for America's national bird. (Franklin deemed the turkey a nobler and "more respectable bird" than the thieving, scavenging bald eagle.)

Quick, lean, and wary, the wild turkey is a far cry from the plump, ungainly domestic variety raised on farms for food. When threatened, the bird prefers simply to run away (it can nearly outrun a man), but if necessary it can take to the air, like its cousins the pheasant and grouse, with an abrupt flapping of wings.

Wild turkeys can swim, too. John James Audubon once reported seeing a group of them in a river, necks stretched forward, paddling "with great vigour" toward shore.

Before the 19th century, wild turkeys were a common sight all over New England, but hunting and habitat destruction took such a toll that by the mid-1800's the birds had all but disappeared. In recent decades, thanks to the efforts of wildlife conservationists, wild turkeys have been returned to many parts of the Northeast. They are now found in most counties of New Hampshire, with the main population located in the southwest corner of the state.

also represents the world at large, since it served as the model for Thornton Wilder's *Our Town,* the renowned play about life, death, and the human condition. Not far from Peterborough, 3,165-foot Grand Monadnock rises from the plain. Because its resistant rock held fast when, eons ago, the surrounding rock was worn away, it now stands alone.

Southeastern New Hampshire — between the Merrimack Valley and the Atlantic Coast — is where most of the state's residents live and work. Some are descended from the original British settlers; others, from European or Canadian immigrants. Whatever their ancestry, however, they proudly uphold the Yankee traditions of thrift, conservatism, and especially independence — as evidenced by the state's motto stamped on every New Hampshire license plate: "Live Free or Die"!

The Yankee spirit is perhaps most conspicuous in the historic old seafaring town of Portsmouth, which lies at the northern end of New Hampshire's 18-mile coastline. Long a center of naval shipbuilding, Portsmouth is also a city saturated with 18th-century charm, with venerable mansions, redbrick sidewalks, and elegant gardens. At the harbor, where scolding gulls glide on salt breezes and perch on pilings, fishing boats bring home their daily catch at sunset. This scene, like so many other aspects of New Hampshire, evokes the essence of New England.

The roof on a covered bridge protects its wooden trusswork from rain, snow, and ice.

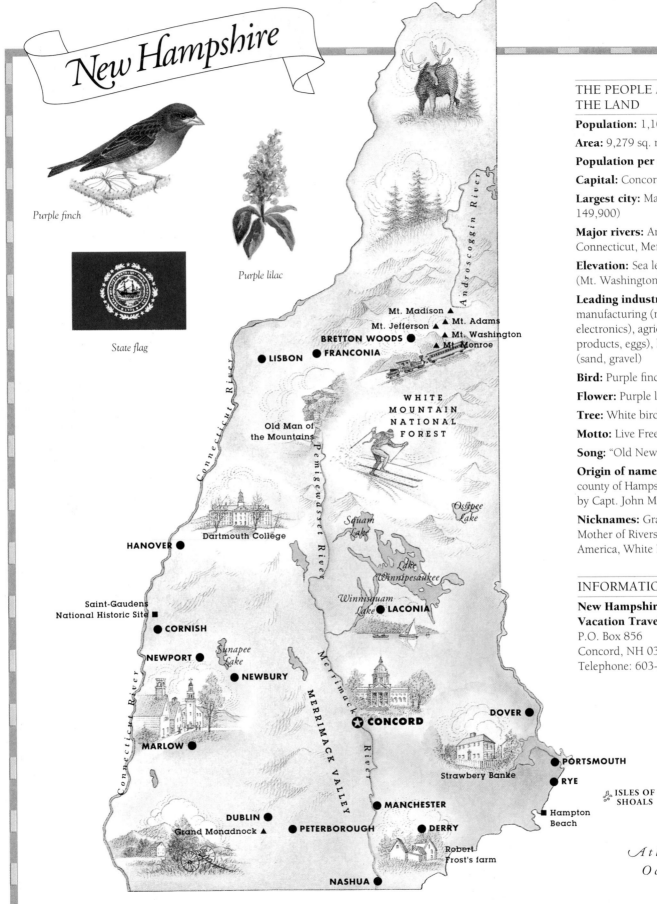

New Hampshire

Purple finch

Purple lilac

State flag

Mt. Madison ▲
Mt. Jefferson ▲   ▲ Mt. Adams
BRETTON WOODS ●   ▲ Mt. Washington
                  ▲ Mt. Monroe
LISBON ●   ● FRANCONIA

WHITE
MOUNTAIN
NATIONAL
FOREST

Old Man of
the Mountains

Ossipee
Lake

Squam
Lake

Dartmouth College

HANOVER ●

Lake
Winnipesaukee

Winnisquam
Lake ● LACONIA

Saint-Gaudens
National Historic Site ■

● CORNISH

Sunapee
Lake

NEWPORT ●

● NEWBURY

DOVER ●

★ CONCORD

MARLOW ●

PORTSMOUTH ●
Strawbery Banke
RYE ●

ISLES OF
SHOALS

Hampton
Beach

DUBLIN ●
Grand Monadnock ▲   ● PETERBOROUGH   ● MANCHESTER

● DERRY

Robert
Frost's farm

*Atlantic
Ocean*

NASHUA ●

Androscoggin River
Connecticut River
Pemigewasset River
Merrimack River
MERRIMACK VALLEY

THE PEOPLE AND THE LAND

Population: 1,103,200

Area: 9,279 sq. mi.

Population per sq. mi.: 119

Capital: Concord (pop. 31,000)

Largest city: Manchester (pop. 149,900)

Major rivers: Androscoggin, Connecticut, Merrimack

Elevation: Sea level to 6,288 ft. (Mt. Washington)

Leading industries: Tourism, manufacturing (machinery, electronics), agriculture (dairy products, eggs), lumber, mining (sand, gravel)

Bird: Purple finch

Flower: Purple lilac

Tree: White birch

Motto: Live Free or Die

Song: "Old New Hampshire"

Origin of name: Named for the county of Hampshire in England, by Capt. John Mason

Nicknames: Granite State, Mother of Rivers, Switzerland of America, White Mountain State

INFORMATION

New Hampshire Office of Vacation Travel
P.O. Box 856
Concord, NH 03302-0856
Telephone: 603-271-2343

HISTORICAL HIGHLIGHTS

1603 British merchants hire Martin Pring to explore mouth of Piscataqua River.

1614 Capt. John Smith arrives at Isles of Shoals, off coast of New Hampshire.

1623 Groups sent by the Laconia company in London establish the first permanent settlements at present-day Dover and Rye.

1641 New Hampshire becomes part of Massachusetts Bay colony.

1679 As a new royal province, New Hampshire separates from Massachusetts.

1769 Dartmouth College opens at Hanover.

1776 New Hampshire is first colony to declare independence from Great Britain.

1784 The New Hampshire state constitution is adopted.

1788 New Hampshire becomes ninth state by ratifying the U.S. Constitution.

1838 The state's first railroad begins operation.

1853 Franklin Pierce, a New Hampshire native, is inaugurated as 14th president.

1909 Direct primary law is passed.

1944 Representatives of 44 nations attend the International Monetary Conference held at Bretton Woods.

1964 New Hampshire holds the first state lottery in the U.S.

1986 Christa McAuliffe, a Concord teacher and *Challenger* crew member, is killed when space shuttle explodes.

FAMOUS SONS AND DAUGHTERS

Mary Baker Eddy (1821 – 1910). The founder of Christian Science, Eddy became devoted to spiritual healing after a period of personal illness and misfortune. She launched *The Christian Science Monitor* in 1908.

Daniel Chester French (1850 – 1931). French's sculptures depict a number of notable Americans. Best known are the giant marble statue of Abraham Lincoln at the Lincoln Memorial in Washington, D.C., and the Minute Man in Concord, Mass.

Robert Frost (1874 – 1963).

The renowned poet lived on a farm near Derry. Much of his work, including the poem "Stopping by Woods on a Snowy Evening," is set in New England. Frost won four Pulitzer Prizes.

Sarah Josepha Hale (1788 – 1879). Born in Newport, Hale edited the women's magazine *Godey's Lady's Book.* She also wrote the enduring children's verse "Mary Had a Little Lamb."

Franklin Pierce (1804 – 69). The son of a New Hampshire governor, Pierce was elected president in 1852. His term was marked both by economic prosperity and by increasing tension between North and South.

Augustus Saint-Gaudens (1848 – 1907). The eminent sculptor, who created many of America's public monuments, worked in Cornish, where his studio, home, and elegant gardens are preserved as the Saint-Gaudens National Historic Site.

Alan B. Shepard, Jr. (1923 –) In 1961 Shepard became the first American to travel in space. Ten years later, as commander of the *Apollo* 14 lunar landing mission, he walked on the moon.

Daniel Webster (1782 – 1852). Famous for his eloquent oratory, Webster was a brilliant lawyer and statesman. He championed a strong federal government and served as a U.S. senator (1827 – 40) and as secretary of state under Presidents Harrison, Tyler, and Fillmore.

ODDITIES AND SPECIALTIES

Helping to brighten the holidays are the 100,000 or so Christmas trees that are harvested in New Hampshire each year.

High on Mt. Washington, the tallest mountain in the Northeast, grows the delicate dwarf cinquefoil, a yellow flower that exists nowhere else in the world.

An uncommonly literate state, New Hampshire boasted one of the nation's first free public libraries, opened in Peterborough in 1833. About a dozen magazines are published in Peterborough, and nearby Dublin publishes *Yankee* and *The Old Farmer's Almanac.*

With 400 members, the state legislature of New Hampshire is the largest in the nation. It also happens to be the fourth largest deliberative body in the English-speaking world.

PLACES TO VISIT, THINGS TO DO

Franconia Notch State Park (Franconia). Featured here are the Old Man of the Mountains, a gigantic granite "profile," and the Flume, an 800-foot-long chasm that ends in a graceful waterfall.

Hampton Beach This long, lovely beach is a popular summer attraction, with water sports, arcades, fireworks, and nearby campgrounds.

Isles of Shoals These beautiful, windswept islands, clustered nine miles off the New Hampshire mainland, can be reached by steamship.

Lake Winnipesaukee (near Laconia). The state's largest lake (72 square miles), with hundreds of islands large and small, is a recreational mecca.

Mt. Sunapee State Park (near Newbury). Some 2,000 acres of wooded, mountainous parkland overlook the sparkling waters of Lake Sunapee.

Strawbery Banke (Portsmouth). This charming section of Portsmouth features dozens of early American buildings, lovely gardens, and historical exhibits.

Winter sports Skating, ice fishing, and iceboating are popular pastimes on New Hampshire's frozen lakes, while mountains provide prime terrain for skiing, snowmobiling, and tobogganing.

New Jersey

Hidden treasures
off the beaten path

Some visitors, racing along the turnpike between Philadelphia and New York, might agree with Benjamin Franklin, who quipped that New Jersey was like "a barrel tapped at both ends" by these two major cities just across its borders. But, like Franklin, highway speedsters miss the hidden pleasures that are uniquely New Jersey's. The state is filled with secret splendors that are readily apparent to those who pause to explore and savor.

A WELL-PLACED PENINSULA

Perhaps New Jersey's best-kept secret is that it is a peninsula, bounded on the west by the Delaware River and on the east by the Hudson River and the Atlantic Ocean. Throughout its history, this position has made it the crossroads of the East Coast.

As early as colonial times New Jersey's rich farmlands — today among the most productive in the nation — attracted immigrants from Germany, Scandinavia, and the British Isles. During the American Revolution the peninsula's position gave it strategic importance throughout the mid-Atlantic region. George Washington and his army spent more time in New Jersey than in any other colony and fought four major battles there. The Philadelphia – New York corridor has always been the state's area of greatest growth. A canal and a railroad in the mid-1830's and finally the New Jersey Turnpike in 1952 provided ever more efficient transportation along this route. But the wonders of New Jersey lie off this heavily beaten path.

A tugboat moving past the towering cliffs of the Palisades proclaims that commerce is thriving along the lower Hudson River.

Completed in 1834, the 44-mile-long canal connecting the Delaware and Raritan rivers was built across New Jersey's narrow waist to speed shipments between Philadelphia and New York. Today sections of it are preserved as a state park enjoyed by canoeists and hikers.

THE HILLY NORTH

Only 35 miles west of the turnpike is the 7,000-acre Great Swamp National Wildlife Refuge, where pink lady's slippers bloom along the boardwalks, muskrats swim boldly past the observation blinds, and barred owls call "Who cooks for you, who cooks for you all?" at dawn and dusk. Another 50 miles farther north the land opens up to farmland, and to forested hills that the unknowing traveler might mistake for the Catskills or the Berkshires. These are the Kittatinny Mountains, New Jersey's section of the Appalachian chain. The horizon holds sweeping vistas of trees and sky in all directions, and the local ponds are the work of beavers. White-tailed deer are abundant, and coyotes and wild turkeys have become increasingly common as forest management has improved.

THE PINE BARRENS

In the south of the state lies an area unlike any other: the Pine Barrens. One million acres of pine and oak forests, white cedar swamps, cranberry bogs, sand roads, and 17 trillion gallons of some of the cleanest water on earth (in the Cohansey aquifer) have been preserved here since the Pinelands Protection Act of 1979. The most celebrated inhabitant is the Pine Barrens tree frog, a two-inch-long green amphibian with lavender stripes and a voice as loud as a duck's. In addition, more than 850 species of plants have been found here, among them wild blueberries, which were cultivated for the first time by Elizabeth White in Whitesbog in 1916. Ever since, a traditional Pinelands summer has begun with blueberry picking in June and ended with the cranberry harvest in September and October.

The Red Mill at Clinton Historical Museum Village ground both grain and graphite before it was closed in 1920.

White-tailed deer, like other New Jersey residents, enjoy the woodlands.

The dunes at Island Beach State Park glow in the soft light of the setting sun.

THE WORLD SERIES OF BIRDING

When the great flocks of migrating birds arrive in New Jersey each spring, bird watchers from all over the world gather at Cape May Point to take part in one of the eastern seaboard's most unusual tournaments: the World Series of Birding. Sponsored by the New Jersey Audubon Society each May, the competition serves to catalog the species that pass along the Atlantic flyway. Participants organize into teams that vie to spot the greatest number of different species within 24 hours.

Cape May, with its unique mix of ocean, bay shores, saltwater meadows, freshwater creeks, and thick forests, is one of the best places in the country for such a contest: more than 400 of North America's 700 regularly occurring species have been seen here.

Less competitive bird watchers can enjoy the cape's avian spectacle any time of year. Kittiwakes, loons, and sea ducks feed just beyond the breakers from December through March. Northbound migrants begin arriving in February, and by the first week of May, bushes and trees are filled with songbirds. Summer visitors include blue grosbeaks, terns, and even brown pelicans. In the course of just a few weeks each autumn, some 60,000 south-ward-bound hawks pass Cape May Light-house, swirling overhead to test the winds before they head out across the 14 miles of open water at Delaware Bay.

COASTAL TREASURES

New Jersey's 127-mile shoreline on the Atlantic Ocean is best known for the boardwalks of Asbury Park and Wildwood and the casinos of Atlantic City, but here too are hidden places where quiet still rules. Much of the shore is a ribbon of barrier beaches, whose sheltered waters attract a magnificent array of wildlife. Snowy owls occasionally spend the winter at Island Beach State Park, and diamondback terrapins come ashore each summer to lay

their eggs in the sand above the water line. Each spring and fall hundreds of thousands of waterfowl pause on the New Jersey shore during their migration along the Atlantic flyway. In October or November a lone harrier hawk cruising low over the marshes at Brigantine National Wildlife Refuge can send a thousand snow geese swirling and barking into the air.

Cape May, New Jersey's southernmost point, extends into the Atlantic Ocean like a welcoming hand, beckoning migrating birds northward at winter's retreat and also providing a jumping-off point for their autumn migration south. As early as the 1760's the cape also welcomed vacationers. More than 600 preserved Victorian buildings now recall the resort's golden age in the late 1800's.

Today beachcombers walking the sands of Cape May's Sunset Beach can still scoop up handfuls of translucent quartz pebbles, known as Cape May diamonds. For all those who stop to look, New Jersey's beauty is right at hand.

Each spring the flowering plum trees burst into bloom at Washington Crossing State Park. It was here that George Washington landed his troops after a daring crossing of the Delaware River on Christmas night 1776.

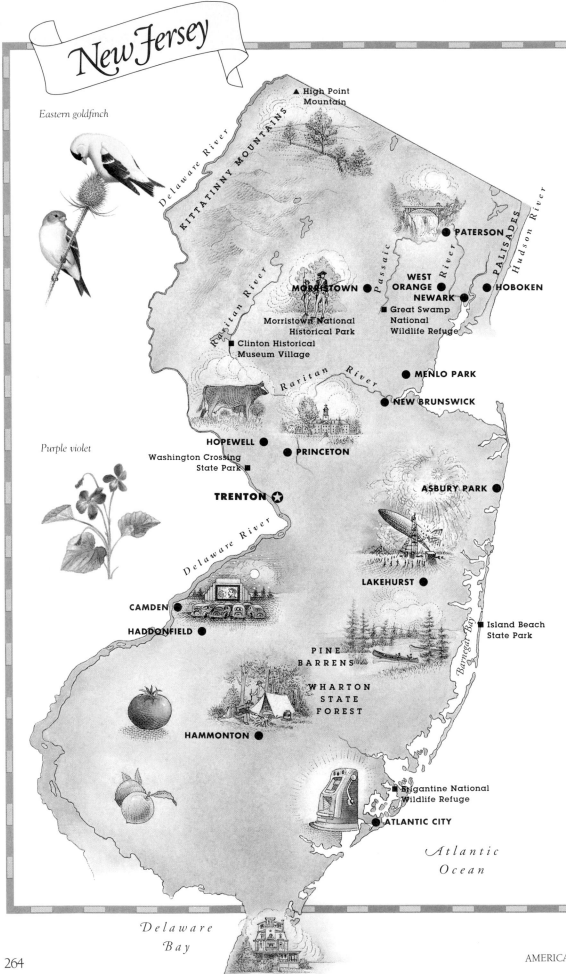

New Jersey

Eastern goldfinch

Purple violet

High Point Mountain

DELAWARE RIVER

KITTATINNY MOUNTAINS

Passaic River

PATERSON

PALISADES

Hudson River

Raritan River

MORRISTOWN

WEST ORANGE

NEWARK

HOBOKEN

■ Great Swamp National Wildlife Refuge

Morristown National Historical Park

■ Clinton Historical Museum Village

Raritan River

MENLO PARK

NEW BRUNSWICK

HOPEWELL

PRINCETON

Washington Crossing State Park

TRENTON ☆

ASBURY PARK

Delaware River

LAKEHURST

CAMDEN

HADDONFIELD

■ Island Beach State Park

Barnegat Bay

PINE BARRENS

WHARTON STATE FOREST

HAMMONTON

■ Brigantine National Wildlife Refuge

ATLANTIC CITY

Atlantic Ocean

Delaware Bay

CAPE MAY

THE PEOPLE AND THE LAND

Population: 7,617,400

Area: 7,787 sq. mi.

Population per sq. mi.: 978

Capital: Trenton (pop. 331,000)

Largest city: Newark (pop. 1,886,200)

Major rivers: Delaware, Hudson, Passaic, Raritan

Elevation: Sea level to 1,803 ft. (High Point Mountain)

Leading industries: Finance, insurance, construction, manufacturing (chemicals, electronics, machinery), agriculture (hay, corn, fruit, dairy)

Bird: Eastern goldfinch

Flower: Purple violet

Tree: Red oak

Song: No official state song

Motto: Liberty and Prosperity

Origin of name: For the Isle of Jersey in the English Channel, of which Sir George Carteret, one of the early proprietors of the colony, had been governor

Nicknames: Camden and Amboy State, Clam State, Garden State, Jersey Blue State, Pathway of the Revolution

INFORMATION

New Jersey Division of Travel and Tourism
20 West State Street, CN-826
Trenton, NJ 08625-0826
Telephone: 609-292-2470

State flag

HISTORICAL HIGHLIGHTS

1660 The Dutch found Bergen, the first permanent settlement.

1664 The Dutch cede New Jersey to England.

1758 New Jersey establishes first Indian reservation in America, a 3,000-acre tract of land in Burlington County.

1776 Led by George Washington, American soldiers cross the Delaware River on Christmas night to defeat Hessian troops deployed by British at Trenton.

1787 New Jersey becomes third state to ratify U.S. Constitution.

1825 John Stevens constructs first successful steam-powered locomotive in the U.S.

1838 Samuel Morse demonstrates his electric telegraph at Morristown.

1879 Thomas Edison invents the incandescent electric light in his Menlo Park laboratory.

1912 Gov. Woodrow Wilson, known for his state reforms, is elected president.

1927 Holland Tunnel, connecting Jersey City and New York, opens to traffic.

1932 The infant son of legendary aviator Charles A. Lindbergh is kidnapped from the family home at Hopewell.

1957 Walt Whitman Bridge is completed, linking Philadelphia with southern New Jersey.

1967 Five days of race rioting in Newark cause 26 deaths.

1978 Casino gambling commences in Atlantic City.

FAMOUS SONS AND DAUGHTERS

Aaron Burr (1756 – 1836). While serving as Thomas Jefferson's vice president, Burr mortally wounded political rival Alexander Hamilton in a duel. His scheme to found a new nation in the Southwest led to his trial for treason. Although he was acquitted, his political career was ruined.

Stephen Crane (1871 – 1900). Famous for his realistic style, Crane is best known for *The Red Badge of Courage,* a novel about a Civil War soldier.

Thomas Edison (1847 – 1931). America's master tinkerer patented over 1,000 inventions, among them the telephone transmitter and the phonograph. His laboratory in West Orange is now a national historic site.

William Carlos Williams (1883 – 1963). A prolific poet and a practicing physician for more than 40 years, Williams used verse to express the emotion of ordinary people's lives.

Woodrow Wilson (1856 – 1924). After serving as president of Princeton University and governor of New Jersey, Wilson was elected president of the U.S. in 1912. At the end of World War I, he was a powerful proponent of the League of Nations, a forerunner of the United Nations.

ODDITIES AND SPECIALTIES

The first dinosaur skeleton discovered in North America — a duck-billed hadrosaur — was found by W. Parker Foulke at Haddonfield in 1858.

Many entertainers have roots in New Jersey, among them Lou Costello, Count Basie, Vivian Blaine, Dorothy Kirsten, Paul Robeson, Frank Sinatra, Bruce Springsteen, and Sarah Vaughan.

The first organized baseball game took place in Hoboken in 1846, with the New York Nine defeating the New York Knickerbockers. Intercollegiate football also began in New Jersey: Rutgers beat Princeton at New Brunswick in 1869.

In the heyday of dirigibles, Lakehurst was a center of world travel. Starting from there the *Graf Zeppelin* completed a round-the-world voyage in 21 days in 1929. Eight years later the *Hindenburg* crashed while landing at Lakehurst, killing 35 people. The tragedy ended the popularity of these airships as "ocean liners of the sky."

The Institute for Advanced Study, a research center in Princeton, has provided a workplace for some of the world's most brilliant minds, including physicists Albert Einstein and J. Robert Oppenheimer and diplomat George F. Kennan.

In 1933 Richard Hollingshead, Jr., opened America's first drive-in movie theater, near Camden.

The boardwalk, saltwater taffy, and Miss America all were invented in Atlantic City. The first Miss America Pageant was held there in 1921.

PLACES TO VISIT, THINGS TO DO

Branch Brook Park (Newark). Some 2,700 Japanese cherry trees burst into bloom here each April, turning this urban park into a horticultural display.

Brigantine National Wildlife Refuge (Oceanville). One of the East Coast's premier sites for observing migrating birds, this wetlands sanctuary can be explored on hiking trails or auto routes.

Great Falls of Paterson (Paterson). Seventy-foot falls plunge spectacularly over basalt cliffs in the Passaic River.

Morristown National Historical Park (Morristown). The area where George Washington's army camped during the bitter winter of 1779 – 80 was designated the nation's first national historical park in 1933. The Ford Mansion, Washington's headquarters, is open to the public, as are replicas of his soldiers' huts in Jockey Hollow.

Wharton State Forest (Hammonton). This is the largest public area in the Pine Barrens, a delightful place for hiking, canoeing, and observing wildlife.

New Mexico

A blend of three cultures in the vibrant Southwest

Before the Pilgrims stepped ashore in Massachusetts, European settlements were already thriving in what is now New Mexico. Spaniards following the Rio Grande north from Mexico had established missions and ranches in the river valley at the end of the 16th century. And in 1610 they founded the town of Santa Fe.

In the early 19th century, American settlers arrived in New Mexico with the completion of the Santa Fe Trail from Missouri — and by 1850 the land that had been part of the Spanish West was a U.S. territory destined to become the 47th state. Despite Americanization, it is the original Spanish culture, blended with that of the Indians who occupied the land long before the Spaniards arrived, that gives New Mexico its special character.

THE EASTERN PLAINS

The state called the Land of Enchantment has changed little on its physical surface since early settlement. The eastern third of the state, part of the Great Plains, is still largely agricultural. From a high plateau in the north, mostly home to cattle ranchers, the land slopes south to the wheat, barley, and cotton fields of the lower Pecos River valley. Herds of sheep share the valley with coyotes, badgers, and fleet-footed, antelopelike pronghorns. Farther south, on land yet to have its thirst quenched by irrigation, kit foxes and jackrabbits scurry through the dry gullies called arroyos.

In the southernmost part of this region is one of the largest known caves in the world,

Pure gypsum, carried down over time by runoff from the San Andres Mountains, creates a sea of undulating dunes at White Sands National Monument.

Juniper branches lie scattered in a meadow in Carson National Forest, the woodland that cradles the Rio Grande in the Sangre de Cristo Mountains.

Jemez Canyon, blessed with hot springs, has been inhabited since the 14th century. Coronado counted seven thriving pueblos there in 1540.

now protected as a national park: Carlsbad Caverns. When the labyrinthine caverns were first discovered, they were considered little more than a source of the fertilizer called guano — nutrient-rich droppings from the millions of bats that occupied the upper cave (as many as 500,000 bats still live there today). It was not until the early 1900's that a few brave souls ventured into the more remote caverns and discovered some of the most astonishing limestone formations ever seen. Today visitors are led through the ancient chambers to view such wonders as the giant stone columns of the Big Room, a 14-acre cavern with a ceiling so high that a 40-story building would fit inside.

INDIAN COUNTRY

Southwest of the eastern plains lies a vast, arid region of stark, sun-blasted mountains and sprawling desert, split down the center by the Rio Grande. The Continental Divide runs through this part of the state, cresting the dry slopes of the Animas Mountains, the Rocky Mountains' last gasp before they melt into Mexico's Sierra Madre.

In a clear turquoise sky, turkey vultures circle high over the harsh landscape. But the muddy waters of the Rio Grande, dammed at Elephant Butte in 1916, now bring life and industry to some isolated pockets of this desert. Huge, irrigated fields of chili peppers are grown around the tiny town of Hatch,

An adobe oven, or horno, *occupies a corner at Taos Pueblo. To the left is a stairway, clearly for use only by the surefooted.*

A spelunker gazes into a pool at Lechuguilla Cave, the most recently discovered portion of the immense Carlsbad Caverns system.

groves of pecan trees shade the desert near Las Cruces, and vegetables are harvested for market in the little truck gardens that spread north from El Paso, Texas, into New Mexico.

Gradually, the desert rises northward to the foothills of the Black Range and the Mogollon Mountains, where great forests of ponderosa pines, Douglas firs, junipers, and blue spruces shelter the elk herds of the Gila Wilderness high country. Atop a lofty mesa stands the ancient pueblo of Acoma, continuously inhabited for perhaps 13 centuries. The pueblo, also known as Sky City, was so difficult to reach before a road was built, and the ascent so steep, that Coronado reported in 1540 that he and his men "repented as we climbed to the top." Nearby, a number of other pueblos are preserved at Gila Cliff Dwellings National Monument.

More Indian land spreads northward from Gallup, the town that, with the exception of reservations, is home to the country's largest population of American Indians. This arid region, the Four Corners, where the borders of New Mexico, Arizona, Utah, and Colorado converge, is a place of wind-twisted buttes, sand-carved mesas, and sage-blanketed deserts. It is also the site of an isolated, 1,500-foot-high volcanic neck with sheer vertical walls. Pioneers named the massive formation Shiprock because its two jagged spires resemble sails; the Navajos called it "the rock with wings" and considered it sacred.

OLD WORLD AND NEW

Sandwiched between the eastern plains and western deserts is the place where New Mexico's essential character resides — the mysteriously lovely Sangre de Cristo Mountains, jutting down from Colorado and named by the Spaniards after the blood-red color of the peaks at sunset. Two famous towns in the shadow of the mountains, Santa Fe and Taos, attract ever-growing numbers of visitors from around the world to sample the region's intriguing blend of Indian, Hispanic, and Anglo-American cultures and a landscape as starkly beautiful as any in the Southwest.

The historic districts of Santa Fe and Taos are also repositories for one of the most un-

Erosion has created a startling landscape at the Bisti Badlands wilderness area in northwestern New Mexico. Geologists call these vertical formations toadstool rocks, hoodoos, or earth pillars.

Most cactus flowers fold their petals in darkness, but the brilliant blooms of the claret cup hedgehog will stay open through the night.

The strange hills and bluffs around Abiquiu were a favorite subject of the painter Georgia O'Keeffe, who lived on a ranch nearby.

ART OF THE PUEBLOS

For centuries, the Pueblo Indian tribes of New Mexico — among them the Santa Clara, Acoma, and San Ildefonso — have used the warm-hued clay of the Southwest to fashion pottery that ranks among the most artistic on earth. Many potters create vessels the traditional way — not with a potter's wheel but by hand, then painting them with a brush made from a short piece of yucca stem. Pigments for paints come from the soil or from plants. Black is obtained by boiling tansy mustard or mesquite bark; red and yellows by powdering ocher dug from the earth.

Much of the distinctive decoration on Pueblo pottery relates directly to the topography and weather of the Southwest. The finely painted lines that form steps symbolize the mountains that rise from the desert. Mesas and canyons are represented with a crenellated pattern, while inverted pyramids stand for the dust devils, or whirlwinds, that blow across the canyon floors. Whirlwinds that move across the plains are sometimes shown as spirals or circles.

Water and cloud symbols are used as a friendly incantation to the deities. A double staircase pattern represents clouds; forked or zigzag lines show lightning; and a straight line placed over shorter, slanted lines symbolizes the rainfall so welcome in this arid land.

---

usual architectural styles on the North American continent: free-form adobe houses, built with the local soil and aglow with soft earth colors. For centuries, Indians mixed sandy clay with stones to make the cementlike adobe material, which they formed into walls, a handful of adobe at a time. The Spaniards strengthened the adobe with straw and molded it into the bricks with which they built their houses, missions, and churches.

Some centuries-old adobe buildings in Santa Fe and Taos seem to be sculpted from the earth on which they stand. In the late 20th century, their timeless design has enjoyed new appreciation, with modern public buildings and private houses in the fashionable Santa Fe style cropping up in other parts of the Southwest and elsewhere.

Taos, a few miles from the Taos pueblo that was built by Indians around 1190, sits on a broad plateau at the foot of Mount Wheeler, the highest peak in New Mexico. Modern Taos traces its reputation as an artist's colony back to a group of New York painters and illustrators who began to move there just before the turn of the century. Since then, painters, sculptors, and writers have made the town their home. No doubt they are attracted by the special quality of the light, the isolation, the mix of cultures, and a terrain so dramatic that at times it seems almost unreal. They would be hard pressed to find a more inspiring setting, even in the magical land that is New Mexico.

A Spanish ruin stands at Pecos National Monument, its adobe bricks slowly melting away.

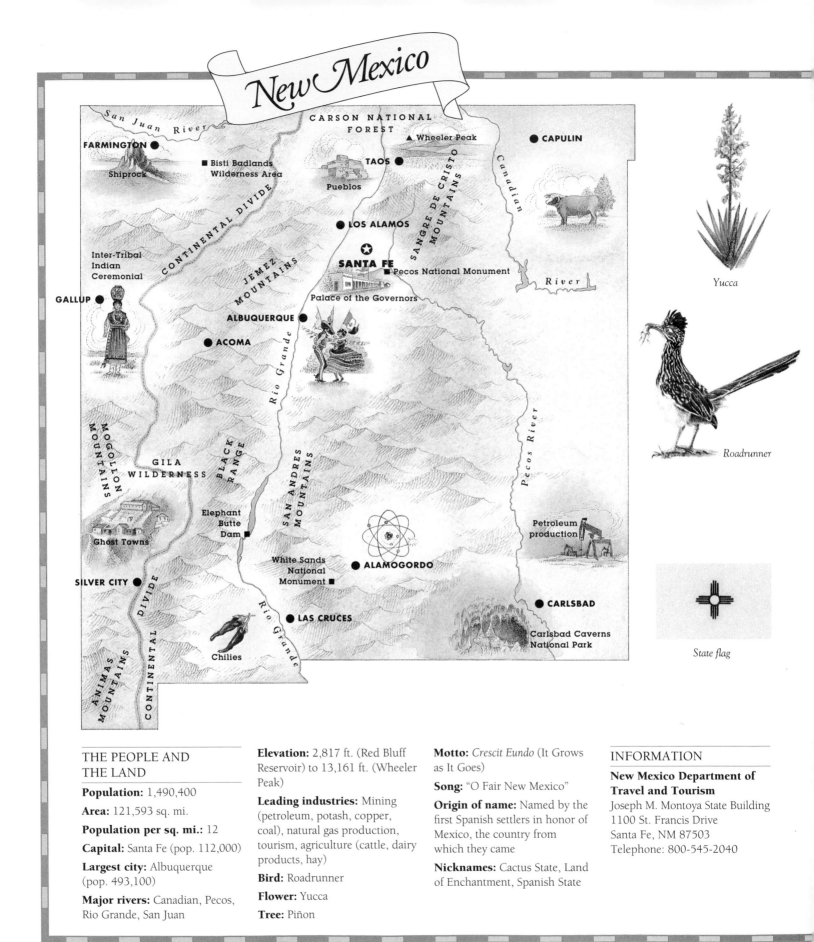

New Mexico

San Juan River

CARSON NATIONAL FOREST

▲ Wheeler Peak

● CAPULIN

● FARMINGTON

■ Bisti Badlands Wilderness Area

Shiprock

● TAOS

Pueblos

CONTINENTAL DIVIDE

SANGRE DE CRISTO MOUNTAINS

Canadian River

● LOS ALAMOS

JEMEZ MOUNTAINS

☆ SANTA FE

■ Pecos National Monument

Inter-Tribal Indian Ceremonial

Palace of the Governors

● GALLUP

● ALBUQUERQUE

Rio Grande

● ACOMA

MOGOLLON MOUNTAINS

GILA WILDERNESS

BLACK RANGE

SAN ANDRES MOUNTAINS

Pecos River

Ghost Towns

Elephant Butte Dam ■

Petroleum production

White Sands National Monument ■

● ALAMOGORDO

● SILVER CITY

CONTINENTAL DIVIDE

● CARLSBAD

ANIMAS MOUNTAINS

Rio Grande

● LAS CRUCES

Chilies

Carlsbad Caverns National Park

Yucca

Roadrunner

State flag

THE PEOPLE AND THE LAND

Population: 1,490,400

Area: 121,593 sq. mi.

Population per sq. mi.: 12

Capital: Santa Fe (pop. 112,000)

Largest city: Albuquerque (pop. 493,100)

Major rivers: Canadian, Pecos, Rio Grande, San Juan

Elevation: 2,817 ft. (Red Bluff Reservoir) to 13,161 ft. (Wheeler Peak)

Leading industries: Mining (petroleum, potash, copper, coal), natural gas production, tourism, agriculture (cattle, dairy products, hay)

Bird: Roadrunner

Flower: Yucca

Tree: Piñon

Motto: *Crescit Eundo* (It Grows as It Goes)

Song: "O Fair New Mexico"

Origin of name: Named by the first Spanish settlers in honor of Mexico, the country from which they came

Nicknames: Cactus State, Land of Enchantment, Spanish State

INFORMATION

New Mexico Department of Travel and Tourism
Joseph M. Montoya State Building
1100 St. Francis Drive
Santa Fe, NM 87503
Telephone: 800-545-2040

HISTORICAL HIGHLIGHTS

1540 Francisco Vásquez de Coronado begins his exploration of New Mexico.

1598 Juan de Oñate establishes first Spanish settlement near present-day Española.

1610 Second Spanish governor, Pedro de Peralta, founds Santa Fe.

1680 Pueblo Indian tribes rebel against Spanish settlers, who flee to Mexico.

1692 Diego de Vargas reconquers province for Spain.

1706 Albuquerque is founded.

1821 With Mexico's independence from Spain, New Mexico comes under Mexican rule. William Becknell blazes Santa Fe Trail from Missouri.

1846 In the Mexican War, U.S. government gains control of New Mexico.

1848 Defeated in Mexican War, Mexico cedes New Mexico and other parts of the West to U.S.

1850 Congress establishes New Mexico as a territory.

1862 In the Civil War, Union soldiers win Battle of Glorieta Pass and force Confederate troops from New Mexico.

1879 Atchison, Topeka, & Santa Fe Railroad links New Mexico with the eastern U.S.

1912 New Mexico enters Union as 47th state.

1916 Mexican renegade Pancho Villa raids town of Columbus.

1945 First atomic bomb is tested in the desert at Trinity Site near Alamogordo.

1970 Congress gives Taos Pueblo Indians title to 48,000 acres in Carson National Forest, including the Blue Lake the Pueblos consider sacred.

1986 Governor proclaims New Mexico a sanctuary for Central American refugees.

FAMOUS SONS AND DAUGHTERS

Billy the Kid (1859 – 81) This notorious outlaw, whose real name was William H. Bonney, grew up in Silver City. Said to wear an eternal smile, the Kid nevertheless committed five known murders.

Kit Carson (1809 – 68). As a teenager, Carson ran away from Kentucky and joined an expedition going to Santa Fe. He gained fame as a trapper, guide, Indian agent, and Union general.

Conrad Hilton (1887 – 1979). Hilton's career started in his family's inn in San Antonio, N.M. He eventually became "king of the innkeepers" with his international hotel chain.

Jean Baptiste Lamy (1814 – 88). The life of this hardworking French-born priest, archbishop of Santa Fe, was the inspiration for Willa Cather's novel *Death Comes for the Archbishop*.

Bill Mauldin (1921 –). Mauldin's award-winning cartoons, focusing on the day-to-day lives of American soldiers in World War II, were internationally acclaimed.

Georgia O'Keeffe (1887 – 1986).

This painter, who lived much of her life on a ranch in Abiquiu and came to be identified with the Southwest, derived inspiration from New Mexico's landscape.

Popé (? – 1688). The leader of the Pueblo Indians masterminded the successful revolt against the Spanish in 1680.

ODDITIES AND SPECIALTIES

One of New Mexico's culinary specialties is the red chili pepper. After the fall harvest, peppers are hung outside houses in decorative strings, called *ristras*, to dry.

New Mexico produces nearly half of the nation's uranium.

Santa Fe is not only the oldest capital city in the U.S.— founded in 1610 — but the highest, at almost 7,000 feet.

The state's many ghost towns attest to the boom-and-bust quality of mining in frontier times. Some of the "ghosts" in these places are legendary — Judge Roy Bean, Butch Cassidy, Lillian Russell.

Los Alamos National Laboratory developed the first atomic and hydrogen bombs. Today the laboratory focuses on nuclear research and development.

PLACES TO VISIT, THINGS TO DO

Bandelier National Monument (Los Alamos). Ancient Indians carved rooms out of canyon walls and built pueblo villages here. The ruins can be seen from a trail along the canyon floor.

Capulin Mountain National Monument (Capulin). Once an active volcano, Capulin is now clothed in dense forest. From its summit, visitors have a sweeping view of five states.

Carlsbad Caverns National Park (27 miles south of Carlsbad). Among the caverns that can be viewed by the public is the Doll's Theater, its ceiling massed with delicate stalactites. Another, the Hall of the Giants, has columns that rise 60 feet.

Chaco Culture National Historical Park (45 miles southeast of Farmington). These ruins, in 15-mile-long Chaco Canyon, include the huge Pueblo Bonita and 10 other major pueblos.

Inter-Tribal Indian Ceremonial (Gallup). This five-day marathon of arts-and-crafts displays, rodeos, and Indian ceremonial dances is held every August. Some 25 tribes from the U.S. take part.

Old Town (Albuquerque).

Albuquerque's original plaza, which dates from 1779, has a number of historic buildings. Among them is the "folk Gothic" Church of San Felipe de Neri.

Palace of the Governors (Santa Fe). The oldest government building in the U.S. was built in 1610. Now a museum, it includes re-creations of reception rooms and offices with period paintings, rugs, and pottery.

New York

A realm of solitude, far from Manhattan

Traveling through the Finger Lakes region of western New York in 1833, the English actress Fanny Kemble found it to be a realm of "beautiful solitudes" that were "blessedly apart from the evil turmoil of the world." Unwittingly, she had described the dual nature of the Empire State, which possesses one of the world's capitals of frenzy and haste, New York City, as well as rural solitudes in endless variety. New York State is very nearly the size of England. And upon it nature has mapped out her own brand of dukedoms and baronies — the Adirondack and Catskill mountains, the Finger Lakes, the valley of the Hudson River — each a world unto itself, with its own mood, myths, and varied charms.

FRONT DOOR TO AMERICA

With its glitter and wealth, its tense human dramas, and its relentless pace, New York City draws all eyes to itself and dismisses the territory north of the Bronx as "upstate," unreachable by subway. To the east, Long Island is the site of two of the city's five boroughs (Brooklyn and Queens), then stretches in 80 miles of fertile farmland and sandy beaches to the Hamptons, the onetime fishing villages that have become chic retreats for the rich.

New York City sees itself as a center, but it has always been a gateway too, the front door to America for immigrants and for commerce. The western boundary of Manhattan, the Hudson River, was and is the start of a corridor to the heartland of the continent. It was named for Henry Hudson, who explored it in 1609.

Forty miles north of New York City, the peaceful Hudson winds through the wooded Hudson highlands. To the right is Bear Mountain Bridge.

The phloxlike blooms of dame's rocket fill the woods with a heady fragrance on spring evenings. The plant, a Eurasian perennial, has become naturalized in the forests around the Finger Lakes.

Two centuries later, in 1825, when the 363-mile-long Erie Canal was opened, the Hudson was linked with the Great Lakes.

From its source in the Adirondacks near beautiful Mount Marcy (the state's highest peak) to its mouth in New York Harbor, the Hudson flows for 315 miles. In some places, stone cliffs rise on both sides. The broad expanse of river moving placidly through looming immensities of granite is one of the greatest of all American landscapes, a dramatic spectacle that inspired the Hudson River school of painters and scores of writers. The bright, hazy light of the river was captured in the canvases of artists Jaspar Cropsey and John Frederick Kensett in the style known as luminism. Washington Irving, author of "Rip Van Winkle" and "The Legend of Sleepy Hollow," wrote his short stories and books in a comfortable cottage by the river; and the painter

LIFE IN THE PARK

Amid the steel and glass towers of New York City there flourishes a surprising oasis of nature — Central Park. Ornate fountains, clipped lawns, and well-kept flower beds to the contrary, some parts of this 843-acre preserve look like untamed countryside or dense woodland, thick with oaks, maples, and black cherries and blooming with wild asters.

Several species of birds and animals occupy the park. Some — warblers, gray squirrels, woodchucks, and bats — have lived there since soon after the park took shape in the mid-19th century. Others, like the cottontail rabbits that hop across the meadows, have taken up residence more recently, establishing a foothold in the park after urban dwellers released them there. Raccoons, too, have been spotted by the lakes in the woods.

The wildlife that most visitors to the park encounter, however, is behind the gates of the Central Park Zoo, a beloved Manhattan institution in operation since 1864. Here polar bears swim behind huge glass walls, face to face with delighted children, before lumbering out of the pool to lounge in the sun. Squawking penguins play tag in the Edge of the Icepack section, while tamarind monkeys swing from vines in the Tropic Zone. In both the zoo and the open spaces of Central Park, wildlife has found a place in the heart of Manhattan.

Jewel of the Finger Lakes region is Watkins Glen, a two-mile gorge at the southern tip of Seneca Lake. A foot trail through the chasm takes visitors past 19 glistening waterfalls spilling into deep pools shaded by hemlock, yew, and mountain maple trees.

Castle Rock, one of the majestic houses built along the Hudson in the 19th century, crowns a hill near West Point. Among the families who lived on estates on the river were the Vanderbilts, Roosevelts, and Goulds.

Barn owls are one of more than 200 species of birds that nest permanently in Adirondack Park. Other feathered inhabitants include loons and great crested flycatchers.

Frederick E. Church built his home and studio on a hill overlooking it.

The U.S. Military Academy at West Point occupies a promontory below which the Hudson makes a sharp S-shaped curve through the high rock walls of a gorge. Because the site has a panoramic view of the river valley, it became an important strategic point in the Revolutionary War. George Washington made his headquarters in nearby Newburgh. To keep British warships from moving upstream during the war, Washington's forces strung a massive iron chain across the river. Each link of the chain weighed 300 pounds.

"FOREVER WILD"

West of the Hudson rise the Catskill Mountains, not a particularly lofty range — the blunted mountaintops reach little more than 4,000 feet — but a place of magical allure. A heavy mantle of needle and broad-leaf forests give the Catskills a striking blue cast from a distance. Up close, the scenery is made all the more spectacular by the countless rocky glens that deeply score the mountainsides.

To the north, the Adirondack Mountains form one of the nation's oldest preserves. In 1892 the state legislature marked off 2.8 million acres on a map with a blue line and declared that the area would remain "forever wild." Since then the boundary, still called the Blue Line, has expanded to encompass almost 6 million acres, making Adirondack Park by far the largest state park in the country and about the size of Vermont.

New York State owns almost half of Adirondack Park. Private owners control the rest, and some of the land has begun to be developed. But an average snowfall of more than 100 inches in winter, the inescapable biting blackfly in summer, and a growing season that rarely exceeds 100 days combine to keep the population low. The 125,000 residents of the park, accustomed to their isolation, think of everything beyond the Blue Line as Outside.

For nearly two centuries, visitors have come to relax by the tranquil blue lakes and exquisite waterfalls of the Adirondacks, as well as to fish, hunt, and hike. The largest lake, Champlain, links the Hudson River to the St. Law-

rence Seaway by way of the Champlain Canal. Like its neighbor, Lake George, it is surrounded by forested mountains and boasts resort hotels that date from the 19th century.

LAKES AND INSPIRATION

New York's other famous lakes — 11 slender ones gouged out by glaciers — lie in the west-central part of the state. Viewed on a map or from the air, the five largest look like the outspread fingers of a huge hand — hence their name, the Finger Lakes. At the western edge of Cayuga Lake (longest of the lakes, at 40

miles), the Taughannock Falls tumble down from 215 feet — one of the longest vertical drops east of the Rocky Mountains.

Vineyards stud the peaceful countryside around the Finger Lakes, which became a major producer of wine in the 19th century. The area has also nurtured eccentrics and visionaries. The "beautiful solitudes" that delighted Fanny Kemble have given inspiration to writers, social reformers, and pioneers of the spirit. Mormonism was born here when Joseph Smith said he discovered golden tablets on a hillside. The woman suffrage move-

Few natural wonders have inspired more awe than Niagara Falls. Honeymoon couples have come to gaze upon the thundering torrent ever since Napoleon's nephew, Jerome Bonaparte, and his bride started the trend in 1803.

TO SAVE THE HUDSON

Early European settlers in the Hudson River valley found that the Indian tribes already living there got along remarkably well with each other — perhaps because they were all sustained by the bountiful river. The pristine Hudson seemed an endless source of fish, supplying more than enough to go around.

By the early 1970's there were scarcely any fish at all in the river. Pollutants generated on its highly industrialized shores had contaminated the water so badly that it seemed beyond reclamation.

But environmentalists refused to let the Hudson die. First, the Federal Pollution Control Act of 1972 outlawed the dumping of untreated sewage in the river. Then, in the private sector, nonprofit organizations sought to make citizens aware of the river's delicate ecology. Today the Hudson is healthy enough to support some 150 species of fish.

Still, efforts continue to reclaim the unsullied river that the Indians once knew. Symbol of those efforts is the *Clearwater* (above), a sloop that plies the waters from New York Harbor to Albany. Supported by an 11,000-member group of well-wishers, the sloop serves as a floating classroom, hosting groups of schoolchildren who participate in environmental programs. The Clearwater organization also sponsors waterfront events up and down the river, as well as the Great Hudson River Revival Festival that is held every June in Valhalla.

ment had its roots in a convention held in 1848 in Seneca Falls. Mark Twain worked on many of his books at a farm outside Elmira. And Amelia Bloomer, wife of the postmaster of Seneca Falls, made it her mission to encourage "rational dress" for Victorian ladies — trousers under a short skirt, a costume that came to be known as bloomers.

North of the Finger Lakes lies Lake Ontario, New York's northern border for 200 miles. Below the lake, in the westernmost part of the state, is the grandest of New York's natural wonders — Niagara Falls, which have provoked amazement ever since 1678 when a group led by the French explorer La Salle came upon them. More than 3,000 feet wide, the "sublime cataract," as a traveler called it in the 1840's, straddles the Canadian border.

The falls remain one of America's greatest spectacles. Thundering away at virtually the opposite end of the state from New York City, they seem to echo the tumult of that metropolis — a natural dynamo in a land that is otherwise serene.

The wild and beautiful Adirondacks, seen above in the vicinity of Elk Lake, were one of the nation's earliest vacation spots. A group of Yale students made the first known tourist excursion here in 1818. By the 1820's, fashionable resorts had sprung up.

HISTORICAL HIGHLIGHTS

1524 Explorer Giovanni da Verrazzano sails into New York Bay.

1609 Henry Hudson travels up Hudson River through area that will become known as New Netherland.

1624 Dutch build Fort Orange at present-day Albany.

1625 Dutch found city of New Amsterdam, now New York.

1626 Peter Minuit, director general of New Netherland, purchases Manhattan Island from Manhattan Indians.

1664 British capture New Amsterdam.

1765 New York City hosts congress to fight British Stamp Act.

1776 A provincial congress approves the Declaration of Independence.

1777 British general John Burgoyne surrenders at Saratoga.

1788 New York ratifies U.S. Constitution, becoming 11th state.

1789 George Washington is inaugurated as first president of the U.S.A. in New York City.

1814 Americans defeat British on Lake Champlain during the War of 1812.

1825 Opening of Erie Canal connects New York City with Great Lakes via Hudson River.

1827 The state abolishes slavery.

1863 Antidraft rioting during Civil War causes 1,000 casualties.

1886 Statue of Liberty is dedicated in New York Harbor.

1901 President William McKinley is assassinated in Buffalo.

1929 Panic hits New York Stock Exchange as market crashes.

1939 "World of Tomorrow" World's Fair opens in Queens.

1946 United Nations selects New York City as site for its headquarters.

1964 The second New York World's Fair begins.

1987 The New York Stock Exchange experiences a record drop in the Dow-Jones average.

FAMOUS SONS AND DAUGHTERS

Grover Cleveland (1837–1908). The former mayor of Buffalo was elected president in 1884, defeated in 1888, and reelected in 1892 — the only president to serve nonconsecutive terms.

Aaron Copland (1900–90). Copland, composing for orchestra, ballet, and film, captured the spirit of the American landscape in his music. Among his works is *Appalachian Spring*.

George Eastman (1854–1932). Eastman introduced the Kodak and built the world's most successful camera company, in Rochester. He eventually became a leading philanthropist.

George Gershwin (1898–1937). One of the best loved of American composers, Gershwin wrote popular songs as well as complex works like *Rhapsody in Blue* and the opera *Porgy and Bess*.

Franklin D. Roosevelt (1882–1945). Taking office in the midst of the Great Depression, the 32nd president instituted New Deal programs to provide relief and recovery. His wife, Eleanor, won worldwide admiration for her humanitarian concerns.

Theodore Roosevelt (1858–1919). Elected vice president in 1900, "Teddy" became president the next year, when McKinley was assassinated. He was awarded the Nobel Peace Prize in 1906 for mediating the end of the Russo-Japanese War.

Jonas Salk (1914–) A physician and researcher, Salk developed the first effective polio vaccine in the 1950's. He continued his work into the 1990's, searching for a cure for AIDS.

ODDITIES AND SPECIALTIES

Abstract expressionism, which emerged in New York in the 1940's, was the first American school of painting to influence the work of artists overseas.

The tuxedo takes its name from Tuxedo Park, where it was introduced during the 1920's by socialites, who wanted something less formal than a waistcoat for small dinners.

Among the New York natives who have become internationally acclaimed authors are Herman Melville, Arthur Miller, Eugene O'Neill, Walt Whitman, Edith Wharton, Henry James, James Baldwin, and J. D. Salinger.

New York City has always been a melting pot. As early as the mid-1600's, at least 18 languages were spoken there.

PLACES TO VISIT, THINGS TO DO

Fire Island National Seashore Sand dunes give this 32-mile-long barrier island, on the southern coast of Long Island, a wild beauty. No cars are allowed.

Fort Ticonderoga (Ticonderoga). Soldiers in period costume parade on the grounds of the restored fort, which was seized from the British in 1775 by Ethan Allen and his Green Mountain Boys.

Franklin D. Roosevelt National Historic Site (Hyde Park). Roosevelt's stately home remains as it was in 1945. The Rose Garden now holds the graves of the president and his wife, Eleanor. Nearby are a library and museum.

Lake Placid This Adirondack village, site of the 1932 and 1980 Winter Olympics, is a center not only for skiing but also for golfing and other summer sports.

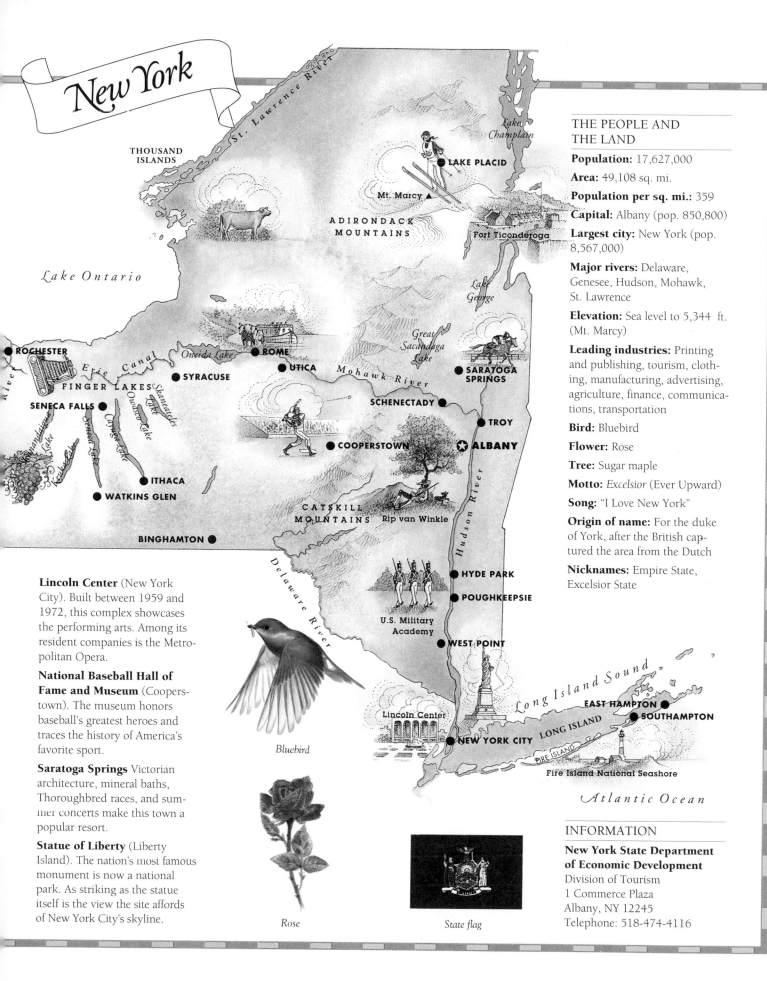

New York

THOUSAND
ISLANDS

St. Lawrence River

Lake Champlain

● **LAKE PLACID**

Mt. Marcy ▲

ADIRONDACK
MOUNTAINS

Fort Ticonderoga

Lake Ontario

Lake George

Great Sacandaga Lake

● **ROCHESTER**

Erie Canal

Oneida Lake   ● **ROME**

FINGER LAKES   ● **SYRACUSE**   ● **UTICA**

Mohawk River

● **SARATOGA SPRINGS**

Skaneateles Lake

Owasco Lake

SENECA FALLS ●

Cayuga Lake

SCHENECTADY

Canandaigua Lake

Seneca Lake

Keuka Lake

● **TROY**

● **COOPERSTOWN**   ☆ **ALBANY**

● **ITHACA**

● **WATKINS GLEN**

CATSKILL
MOUNTAINS   Rip van Winkle

Hudson River

BINGHAMTON ●

Delaware River

● **HYDE PARK**

● **POUGHKEEPSIE**

U.S. Military
Academy

● **WEST POINT**

Long Island Sound

EAST HAMPTON

Lincoln Center   ● **SOUTHAMPTON**

● **NEW YORK CITY**   LONG ISLAND

FIRE ISLAND

Fire Island National Seashore

Atlantic Ocean

Bluebird

Rose

State flag

THE PEOPLE AND THE LAND

Population: 17,627,000

Area: 49,108 sq. mi.

Population per sq. mi.: 359

Capital: Albany (pop. 850,800)

Largest city: New York (pop. 8,567,000)

Major rivers: Delaware, Genesee, Hudson, Mohawk, St. Lawrence

Elevation: Sea level to 5,344 ft. (Mt. Marcy)

Leading industries: Printing and publishing, tourism, clothing, manufacturing, advertising, agriculture, finance, communications, transportation

Bird: Bluebird

Flower: Rose

Tree: Sugar maple

Motto: *Excelsior* (Ever Upward)

Song: "I Love New York"

Origin of name: For the duke of York, after the British captured the area from the Dutch

Nicknames: Empire State, Excelsior State

Lincoln Center (New York City). Built between 1959 and 1972, this complex showcases the performing arts. Among its resident companies is the Metropolitan Opera.

National Baseball Hall of Fame and Museum (Cooperstown). The museum honors baseball's greatest heroes and traces the history of America's favorite sport.

Saratoga Springs Victorian architecture, mineral baths, Thoroughbred races, and summer concerts make this town a popular resort.

Statue of Liberty (Liberty Island). The nation's most famous monument is now a national park. As striking as the statue itself is the view the site affords of New York City's skyline.

INFORMATION

New York State Department of Economic Development
Division of Tourism
1 Commerce Plaza
Albany, NY 12245
Telephone: 518-474-4116

North Carolina

From highlands to Hatteras, a green and unspoiled land

In 1584 two explorers returning to England from the New World told Sir Walter Raleigh about a remarkable land: "the most plentiful, fruitful, and wholesome of all the world." Such superlatives were more apt than these early visitors knew, for this land — known today as North Carolina — claims the loftiest mountain east of the Mississippi (6,684-foot Mount Mitchell), the longest chain of barrier islands (the Outer Banks), the highest sand dune (140-foot Jockey's Ridge), and the greatest natural diversity in the East (in this one state are more kinds of trees than in all of Europe).

North Carolina is also a land of many firsts: the first three attempts to colonize America, the first birth of an English child on American soil, the first American gold rush, the country's first school of forestry, and the first successful airplane flight. And, in 1776, North Carolina was the first colony to instruct its delegates to the Continental Congress to vote for independence from Great Britain.

THE CRUEL AND BEAUTIFUL COAST

Unlike most coastal states, North Carolina was settled from its interior because its coastline offered no suitable ports. Its gleaming strands of barrier islands both tempted and thwarted 16th-century seamen as they tried to navigate the cruel shoals off Cape Hatteras (the "graveyard of the Atlantic") or to steer through tricky inlets into the quiet waters of Albemarle or Currituck sounds.

Two early attempts at colonization, in 1526 and 1585, failed utterly. A third attempt, in

The ancient Blue Ridge Mountains, where blossoming rhododendrons reach their peak in mid-June, roll into the distance like huge swells on an azure sea.

Fog blankets fields near Valle Crucis in the Blue Ridge Mountains. The lower slopes in this area, which have a more temperate climate than is found higher in the mountains, have been used for generations to raise cattle and tobacco.

1587, Raleigh's famous Lost Colony, ended in mystery when its 119 men, women, and children vanished without a trace except for one word — CROATOAN — carved on a tree. Although by 1710 settlers from the Virginia colony had founded such tidewater towns as Bath, Beaufort, and Edenton, the Outer Banks remained sparsely populated until well into the 20th century.

Today these lovely islands are North Carolina's crown jewels. Hang gliders soar over the dunes not far from where the Wright brothers first proved man could fly. Surfers ride the waves near the treacherous shoals that sank so many ships (parts of their wrecked hulls are still visible in the sand). From Bodie Island in the north, through Pea Island National Wildlife Refuge, where thousands of shorebirds and waterfowl converge during migration, the wide protected beaches of Cape Hatteras National Seashore stretch some 70 miles to the picturesque village of Ocracoke. Nearby, the infamous pirate Blackbeard met his death at the hands of the British in 1718.

Inland, across brackish marshes and inlets teeming with fish, crabs, and snowy egrets, lies the tidewater land of swamps, lazy rivers, and Carolina bays. Here are found such botanical rarities as the insect-devouring Venus flytrap, native only to the Carolina lowlands.

To the west of this wide coastal plain rises the Piedmont, a region of gentle slopes and low ridges that has become the most populous and progressive part of the state. Nevertheless, the industrial Piedmont manages to balance its bustling cities with pleasantly rural, rolling landscapes. The renowned Raleigh – Durham – Chapel Hill think tank known as the Research Triangle is located here. And, at the remarkable North Carolina Zoological Park, near Asheboro, elephants, gorillas, ostriches, baboons, and hundreds of other exotic animals roam freely through jungles and grasslands that re-create their natural habitats.

HIGH IN THE MISTY MOUNTAINS

West of the Piedmont are the beautiful North Carolina mountains — Blue Ridge, Great Smokies, Black, Unaka, Bald, and others — their craggy peaks vaulting to 6,000 feet. Lush forests and fields of wildflowers soften their slopes. Ascending from foothills to summit, one may pass through several different zones of climate and vegetation. Cove hardwood forests dominate the lower altitudes. The higher reaches are the domain of the red spruce and Fraser fir, evergreens similar to those found in the boreal forests of Canada. Here such "northern" birds as saw-whet owls, red crossbills, and black-capped chickadees make their home all year round.

The mountain country was settled after 1770 by farmers from Pennsylvania, Virginia, and Maryland who were looking for new land. Many were of Scotch-Irish descent, and decided to move deeper into the rugged terrain that reminded them of their ancestral home. Later the whole Asheville area became a summer retreat for wealthy Charleston and Savannah residents seeking to escape the torpid coastal climate, as well as for the Rockefellers, Fords, Roosevelts, and Vanderbilts. One magnificent monument to this opulent era is George Vanderbilt's colossal Biltmore House,

Spanish moss, draped over the boughs of trees in this coastal bottomland forest, is a familiar sight along the banks of the South River. In colonial times, flat-bottom boats plied the river, carrying goods across the southern coastal plain to Wilmington.

Meadows like this one in Watauga County, near the Tennessee border, once bore the footprints of Daniel Boone, who hunted there during the 1760's.

AMERICA: LAND OF BEAUTY AND SPLENDOR

A few scattered buildings are all that remain of Portsmouth, at one time the largest town on the Outer Banks. Although the inhabitants are long gone, the buildings are maintained by the Cape Lookout park service, and campers seek out the area for its beauty, serenity, and unbroken solitude.

a 250-room mansion set on some 8,000 acres of gardens, reflecting pools, and woodland.

Today North Carolina's mountains, traversed by the splendidly scenic Blue Ridge Parkway and including about half of Great Smoky Mountains National Park, are prime vacationland with luxurious resorts. Yet simple rustic cabins, mountain music, and traditional crafts such as dollmaking, rug weaving, and fiddlemaking are also found throughout the highlands, and the natural beauty of the land remains refreshingly unspoiled.

Despite more than three centuries of habitation, most of North Carolina is still superlatively green. This speaks well for the people who, in writing their constitution, wisely resolved "to preserve as a part of the common heritage of this state its forests, wetlands, estuaries, beaches, historical sites, openlands, and places of beauty."

THE DEADLY CHARMS OF THE VENUS FLYTRAP

On the wet coastal plains of North Carolina, and part of South Carolina as well, grows a fascinating and somewhat bizarre plant that occurs naturally in no other part of the world — the Venus flytrap. Since the sandy, peaty, acid soils of its native habitat are deficient in nutrients, the plant obtains them elsewhere — from insects that it traps in its leaves and devours.

The hinged leaves of the Venus flytrap can open and close like clamshells. When an unsuspecting insect lands on a leaf, it sets off special trigger hairs, and in a split second the leaf snaps shut. The plant's digestive juices then start to work on the hapless victim, extracting the nutrients from its dissolving body. A few days later, the trap reopens, ready to lure another victim.

Each year thousands of Venus flytraps are gathered from wild areas, contributing to the decline of the species. An even greater threat to its survival, however, is man's continuing destruction of its native habitat.

HISTORICAL HIGHLIGHTS

1524 Giovanni da Verrazzano explores the coast.

1585 The first English colony in America is built on Roanoke Island but is abandoned in 1586.

1629 King Charles I of England grants Carolana (Land of Charles) to Sir Robert Heath.

c. 1650 Settlers from Virginia come to Albemarle area.

1663 Charles II grants the Carolina territory to eight lords proprietors (ruling landlords).

1729 North Carolina becomes a royal colony.

1765 Sons of Liberty protest British tax laws.

1774 North Carolina sends delegates to First Continental Congress in Philadelphia.

1776 North Carolina is the first colony to instruct its delegates at the Continental Congress to vote for independence.

1781 British win costly victory at Battle of Guilford Courthouse but withdraw from North Carolina.

1789 North Carolina becomes the 12th state.

1861 The state secedes from the Union, the next to last to do so.

1868 North Carolina is readmitted to the Union.

1933 The state government takes over support of public schools.

1959 The Research Triangle is launched, combining resources of universities in Raleigh, Durham, and Chapel Hill.

1960 In Greensboro four black students remain seated at a restricted lunch counter after they are refused service, leading to a series of sit-in demonstrations throughout the state.

1981 The U.S. government and the University of North Carolina decide on state school-system desegregation guidelines.

FAMOUS SONS AND DAUGHTERS

James B. Duke (1856 – 1925). A superb businessman, Duke transformed a modest family enterprise into the giant American Tobacco Company. He gave money to many charities and endowed Duke University, which bears his name.

Richard J. Gatling (1818 – 1903). An inventor, Gatling is best known for his rapid-fire Gatling gun, once standard equipment in the army and navy.

Billy Graham (1918 –). Through his tours, books, and media appearances, this fiery Southern Baptist minister became one of America's most popular and enduring evangelists.

Dolley Madison (1768 – 1849).

Known for her charm and tact, Madison served as the White House hostess during the presidencies of both Thomas Jefferson, a widower, and her husband James Madison.

Thelonius Monk (1917 – 82). The eccentric pianist and composer, known for his unique style, played a major role in the development of modern jazz.

Edward R. Murrow (1908 – 65). The eminent newscaster covered the London blitz in World War II and later hosted a number of television shows, including *See It Now* and *Person to Person*.

O. Henry (1862 –1910). Born in Greensboro, William Sydney Porter later adopted O. Henry as his pen name. His short stories are known for their ironic, surprise endings.

Joseph B. Rhine (1895 – 1980). The father of psychic research, Rhine headed the parapsychology laboratory at Duke University, where he performed many ground-breaking experiments in extrasensory perception (ESP).

Thomas Wolfe (1900 – 38). Wolfe wrote novels known for their lyricism and emotional intensity. His first, *Look Homeward, Angel*, reflects his childhood at his mother's boarding-house in Asheville.

ODDITIES AND SPECIALTIES

North Carolina is the nation's leading producer of tobacco, textiles, and furniture.

Each year, Spivey's Corner (population 49) holds a National Hollering Contest to honor the form of communication that, before telephones, could be heard far and wide in these parts.

The Cape Hatteras Lighthouse is the tallest brick lighthouse (208 feet) in the country.

The potatoes brought from Roanoke Island and planted on Sir Walter Raleigh's Irish estate produced Ireland's first potato crop.

The nickname Tarheel State dates from the Civil War. When a group of soldiers retreated during a battle, their fellow North Carolinians threatened to put tar (a state product) on their heels so they would "stick better" the next time around.

On December 17, 1903, Orville and Wilbur Wright flew the first powered airplane near Kitty Hawk, at present-day Kill Devil Hills. The Wright brothers chose the Outer Banks area for its constant winds.

PLACES TO VISIT, THINGS TO DO

Biltmore Estate (Asheville). George Vanderbilt's extravagant French Renaissance château, built in the 1890's, has a baronial banquet hall with an arched ceiling some 70 feet high.

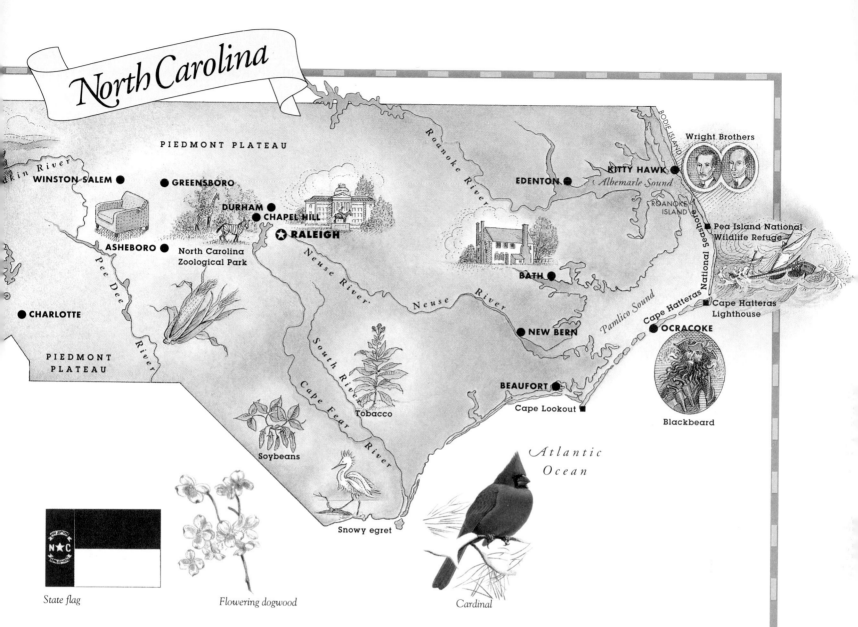

North Carolina

PIEDMONT PLATEAU

Yadkin River

WINSTON-SALEM ●

● **GREENSBORO**

DURHAM ●
● **CHAPEL HILL**

☆ **RALEIGH**

ASHEBORO ●
North Carolina Zoological Park

Pee Dee River

● **CHARLOTTE**

PIEDMONT PLATEAU

Cape Fear River

South River

Neuse River

Tobacco

Soybeans

Snowy egret

Roanoke River

EDENTON ●
Albemarle Sound

KITTY HAWK
Wright Brothers

BODIE ISLAND

ROANOKE ISLAND

BATH ●

Neuse River

NEW BERN ●

Pamlico Sound

Cape Hatteras National Seashore

Pea Island National Wildlife Refuge

■ Cape Hatteras Lighthouse

OCRACOKE ●

BEAUFORT ●
Cape Lookout ●

Blackbeard

Atlantic Ocean

State flag

Flowering dogwood

Cardinal

Cape Hatteras National Seashore (headquarters at Roanoke Island). Encompassing some 30,000 acres of Outer Banks dunes, beaches, and wetlands, this was the first protected seashore in the U.S.

Grandfather Mountain (near Linville). The highest of the Blue Ridge Mountains got its name because it resembles the profile of an old man. Its summit may be reached on foot via a mile-high suspension bridge.

Nantahala National Forest (Asheville). Mountain panoramas, deep gorges, and spectacular waterfalls make these 515,000 acres especially scenic.

New Bern Many well-preserved federal-style and Victorian structures lend a distinctive charm to this colonial port town. Tryon Palace, a Georgian mansion with extensive gardens, was originally built for the royal governor.

Old Salem (Winston-Salem). In this restored Moravian village, costumed interpreters demonstrate what everyday life was like there in colonial days.

Wright Brothers National Memorial (Kill Devil Hills). The memorial includes the brothers' re-created camp and hangar, flight-distance markers, a reproduction of the famous plane, and a stone monument.

THE PEOPLE AND THE LAND

Population: 6,553,000

Area: 52,669 sq. mi.

Population per sq. mi.: 124

Capital: Raleigh (pop. 683,500)

Largest city: Charlotte (pop. 1,112,000)

Major rivers: Cape Fear, Neuse, Pee Dee, Roanoke, Yadkin

Elevation: Sea level to 6,684 ft. (Mt. Mitchell)

Leading industries: Agriculture (tobacco, corn, soybeans), manufacturing (textiles, tobacco products, chemicals, electronics, furniture)

Bird: Cardinal

Flower: Flowering dogwood

Tree: Pine

Motto: *Esse Quam Videri* (To Be Rather Than to Seem)

Song: "The Old North State"

Origin of name: From the Latin Carolus, meaning Charles, in honor of King Charles I

Nicknames: Old North State, Tarheel State, Turpentine State

INFORMATION

North Carolina Travel and Tourism Division
430 North Salisbury Street
Raleigh, NC 27603
Telephone: 800-847-4862

North Dakota

Fields of grain on the windswept plains

North Dakota's best-known landscape may be the mysterious badlands, but lush fields of wheat and sunflowers are far more characteristic of this midwestern outpost. Farming is the mainstay of North Dakota, where cultivated land stretches all the way from the fertile black soil of the Red River valley in the east to the rugged buttes of the west. The state is, in fact, the most rural in the nation, with only four cities — Fargo, Grand Forks, Bismarck, and Minot — having populations of more than 20,000.

Until well into the 19th century, the area was inhabited mainly by Indians. In the 1880's, thousands of immigrants, eager to obtain the land offered by the Homestead Act, arrived in a migration known as the Great Dakota Boom. Norwegians, Germans, and Canadians flocked to the territory and found a level prairie that they soon transformed into a sea of wheat — and became the envy of the nation for their hugely profitable farms.

A COMMON DEPENDENCE ON WHEAT

But the wealth was not easily won. The immigrants found North Dakota winters as bitter as those of their homelands. Efforts by large corporations to monopolize the wheat trade threatened farmers and caused them to band together in one populist movement after another. The settlers' common goal in the face of shared hardship led to an egalitarianism as strict as any on earth. "Hired man or town banker, wheat was the common denominator of this democracy," wrote television commentator Eric Sevareid, a native North Dakotan.

Cut in broad swaths, a field of barley awaits harvest in the valley of the Red River of the North.

The Little Missouri River meanders through Wind Canyon in the South Unit of Theodore Roosevelt National Park, established in 1978.

AMERICA: LAND OF BEAUTY AND SPLENDOR

"Perhaps it was our common dependence upon wheat that made all men essentially equal."

The settlers brought all three of North Dakota's distinct geographic regions into cultivation. The valley of the Red River of the North (so called to distinguish it from the Red River in the south-central United States), a 40-mile-wide strip along the Minnesota border, is blanketed with fields of sugar beets, potatoes, beans, and more sunflowers than even Kansas grows. To the west, the Drift Prairie, named for the deposits of fertile drift — clay, sand, and other earth materials — left behind by glaciers, is now a prime producer of wheat, barley, and oats.

Dotting the gentle hills of the prairie are innumerable small bodies of water called potholes, where flocks of migrating waterfowl nest. Bird watchers gather at Audubon, Long Lake, and other wildlife refuges to observe piping plovers and sharp-tailed grouse. Nature lovers make their way to the prairie's northern edge to fish and hike in the forested Turtle Mountains (average height only 700 feet).

Wheat is also grown in the western portion of the state that lies within the Missouri Plateau. Mineral discoveries here have helped diversify the economy, with lignite mined near Beulah and oil pumped around Williston.

The Missouri Plateau boasts the state's most dramatic scenery: the badlands. Three separate sections of this extraordinary terrain are now a national park named for Theodore Roosevelt, who became enamored of the loneliness and vastness of the landscape when he first saw it as a young man.

The park is a fantastic world of canyons, buttes, and spires that the Little Missouri River, rain, and wind have carved out of the plain. Flowing mud, baked into a bricklike mass by the heat of smoldering lignite — a woody-textured coal that is often ignited by lightning — make some of the hillsides look like the work of an abstract sculptor. Wildflowers cling to slopes scored deeply by erosion. It is a rugged and mysterious place that, unlike the rest of North Dakota, has been changed not by the hand of man but only by the elements.

A red sandstone bluff in western North Dakota overlooks the grassy plains that spread from the banks of the Missouri River. Wild prairie roses bloom in the foreground.

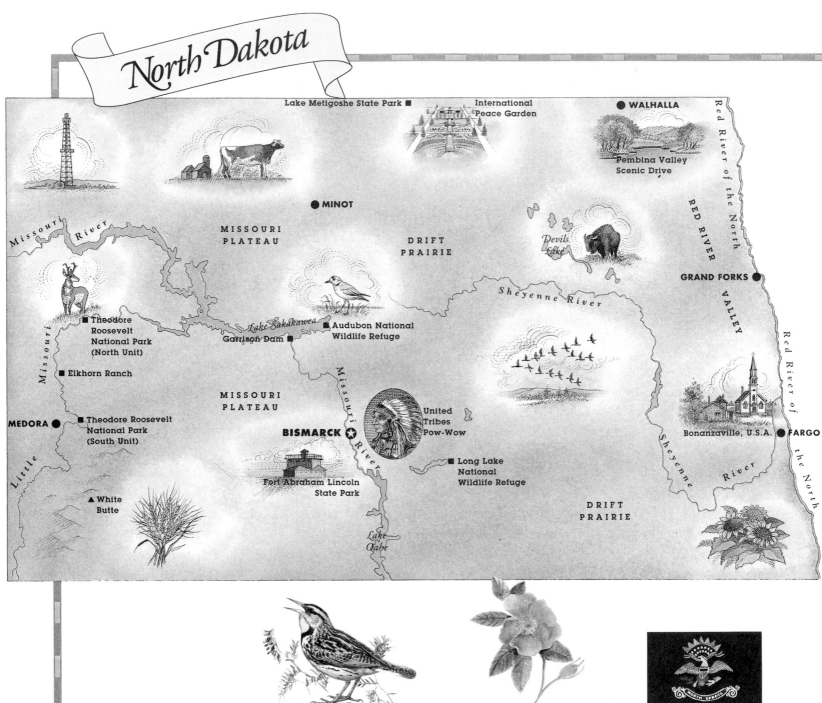

North Dakota

Lake Metigoshe State Park ■

International Peace Garden

● WALHALLA

Pembina Valley Scenic Drive

Red River of the North

● MINOT

MISSOURI PLATEAU

DRIFT PRAIRIE

Devils Lake

RED RIVER

VALLEY

Missouri River

GRAND FORKS ●

Sheyenne River

■ Theodore Roosevelt National Park (North Unit)

Garrison Dam

Lake Sakakawea

■ Audubon National Wildlife Refuge

■ Elkhorn Ranch

MISSOURI PLATEAU

Missouri River

United Tribes Pow-Wow

Red River of the North

MEDORA ●

■ Theodore Roosevelt National Park (South Unit)

BISMARCK ☆

Bonanzaville, U.S.A. ● FARGO

Little

Missouri River

Fort Abraham Lincoln State Park

■ Long Lake National Wildlife Refuge

Sheyenne River

▲ White Butte

Lake Oahe

DRIFT PRAIRIE

Western meadowlark

Wild prairie rose

State flag

THE PEOPLE AND THE LAND

Population: 634,200

Area: 70,702 sq. mi.

Population per sq. mi.: 9

Capital: Bismarck (pop. 85,800)

Largest city: Fargo (pop. 148,400)

Major rivers: Missouri, Red River of the North, Sheyenne

Elevation: 750 ft. (Red River of the North) to 3,506 ft. (White Butte)

Leading industries: Agriculture (wheat, beef cattle, barley, sunflower seeds), mining (oil, lignite), manufacturing (processed foods, farm machinery)

Bird: Western meadowlark

Flower: Wild prairie rose

Tree: American elm

Motto: Liberty and Union, Now and Forever, One and Inseparable

Song: "North Dakota Hymn"

Origin of name: From the Sioux word meaning friend or ally

Nicknames: Flickertail State, Land of the Dakotas, Peace Garden State, Sioux State

INFORMATION

North Dakota Tourism Promotion
604 East Boulevard
Bismarck, ND 58505
Telephone: 701-224-2525

HISTORICAL HIGHLIGHTS

1682 Robert Cavelier, sieur de La Salle, claims region for France.

1738 Pierre La Vérendrye explores area that will become the central part of North Dakota.

1797 Trading post for furs is established at Pembina.

1803 With Louisiana Purchase, U.S. acquires southwestern North Dakota.

1804 Lewis and Clark build Fort Mandan on the Missouri River and spend the winter.

1812 Scottish and Irish colonists establish a settlement at Pembina.

1818 Through an agreement with Britain, U.S. gains remainder of North Dakota.

1861 Congress establishes Dakota Territory.

1863 Land becomes available under the Homestead Act.

1871 Northern Pacific Railroad reaches Fargo.

1883 Bismarck becomes capital of the territory.
University of North Dakota opens at Grand Forks.

1889 North Dakota joins Union as 39th state.

1915 Farmers create Nonpartisan League to fight for state control over wheat trade monopolies.

1929 Seven-year drought begins, bringing dust storms and hardship to farmers.

1947 Theodore Roosevelt National Park is authorized.

1951 Oil is discovered near town of Tioga.

1956 Garrison Dam, on the Missouri River, begins to produce electric power.

1968 Garrison Diversion Project, to increase state's water supply, is begun.

1988 Drought kills much of North Dakota's wheat crop.

FAMOUS SONS AND DAUGHTERS

Louis L'Amour (1908 – 88). One of the best-selling authors of all time, the prolific L'Amour wrote 86 western novels. Many were made into movies.

William Langer (1886 – 1959). As governor and U.S. senator, Langer endeared himself to his constituents — and made a number of political enemies in Washington — with his tactics to help farmers.

Peggy Lee (1920 –). After touring with Benny Goodman's band, Lee recorded a series of hit songs. Though known primarily for her distinctive singing style, she is also a songwriter and an actress.

Eric Sevareid (1912 –). Sevareid, who rose to fame as a news commentator, became interested in journalism while still a child in Velva. Newspaper reporting led to his long career in radio and television.

Vilhjalmur Stefansson

(1879 –1962). Born in Canada and raised in North Dakota, Stefansson was a dedicated explorer who spent more than five years mapping the Arctic. He later wrote a number of books about his experiences.

Lawrence Welk (1903 –). Welk transformed the accordion music played in North Dakota's German communities into the "champagne music" of his dance bands. His television show ran for more than 15 years.

ODDITIES AND SPECIALTIES

President Benjamin Harrison signed the papers admitting North and South Dakota to the Union at the same time, covering the names so that no one would know which was admitted first.

To call North Dakota's weather extreme is to understate the case. During one year, 1936, the temperature ranged all the way from –60° F to 121° F.

Flickertails are ground squirrels that thrive in central North Dakota — hence its nickname, the Flickertail State.

Theodore Roosevelt lived on his North Dakota ranch, Elkhorn, from age 26 to 28. The ranch is now part of the national park that bears his name.

In the early 19th century, Lewis and Clark took note of the abundance of waterfowl in North Dakota. Modern observers still do: more of these birds nest in this state than in any other.

PLACES TO VISIT, THINGS TO DO

Bonanzaville, U.S.A. (West Fargo). Named for North Dakota's profitable 19th-century "bonanza" farms, this period village includes a town hall, a rural church, and a sod house.

Fort Abraham Lincoln State Park (near Mandan). Beauty and history are the dual attractions at this park, which contains a fort and Indian village.

International Peace Garden

(Dunseith). Dedicated in 1932 and situated on the U.S.-Canadian border, this colorful, 2,339-acre garden commemorates the pledge of lasting peace between the two countries.

Lake Metigoshe State Park (near Bottineau). This wooded recreation area lies along the shores of a beautiful lake in the Turtle Mountains.

Pembina Valley Scenic Drive (Walhalla). State Highway 32 offers one of the loveliest forest drives in the state, following the Pembina River through a 30-mile chasm.

Theodore Roosevelt National Park (headquarters at Medora). North Dakota's only national park, set in the harshly beautiful badlands, pays tribute to the 26th president's conservation efforts. Colorfully striped buttes and gorges are home to buffaloes, pronghorns, and prairie dogs.

United Tribes Pow-Wow (Bismarck). Every September, thousands of people come to watch this singing and dancing competition among Sioux, Chippewa, and other Indian tribes. Indian food and crafts are featured.

Ohio

A cherished land between a great lake and a long, winding river

Before 1800, Ohio was a rugged frontier, the gateway to the Northwest Territory and the scene of ferocious battles between white men and Indians. Over the years it evolved into a land of farms, where life centered on the Bible and the plow. Later, smokestacks became as familiar as silos with the growth of sprawling cities such as Cleveland, Columbus, Toledo, and Cincinnati.

Today the character of Ohio is perhaps best reflected in the state's "40 towns" — small cities with populations of 10,000 to 25,000, usually including a Main Street, a brick courthouse, and a town square with a band shell for summer concerts. White Victorian houses, their wide wooden porches furnished with gliders and wicker chairs, line tree-shaded streets named Elm or Maple. This familiar and cherished part of America is often called, affectionately, the Heartland.

ERIE'S SHORES TO AMISH COUNTRY

Bustling cities and tranquil towns predominate across the Ohio landscape, but the state has a generous share of natural wealth — secluded forests, deep caverns, extensive marshlands, and glistening lakes. Most notable of the lakes is Erie, whose shores, stretching from Toledo in the west to Conneaut in the east, form most of Ohio's northern border. Between Toledo, the third-largest port city on the Great Lakes, and Sandusky Bay some 30 miles to the east, the lake's vast marshy shoreline serves as a temporary home for Canada geese, great blue herons, and le-

At Warner's Hollow in northeastern Ohio, gentle Phelps Creek flows through a mile-long gorge, its base carpeted with the lush growth of midsummer.

Autumn hues daub the hemlocks, maples, and tulip trees along sandstone bluffs at Conkles Hollow State Nature Preserve. Located in Hocking Hills State Park, about 40 miles southeast of Columbus, Conkles Hollow is one of 90 state nature preserves scattered throughout Ohio.

AMERICA: LAND OF BEAUTY AND SPLENDOR

gions of other migrating birds. At the end of the long, fingerlike peninsula above Sandusky Bay is Marblehead, where magnified candlelight once beamed from Ohio's oldest lighthouse.

Farther east the shoreline is dominated by greater Cleveland. Moses Cleaveland was a Connecticut Yankee who in 1796 led a band of surveyors to Ohio's Western Reserve — a tract of land "reserved" by King Charles II for settlers from Connecticut. Here they cleared the land and laid out a town much like the ones they left behind in New England.

Ohio's rich farmland drew a group of people for whom farming was not just a livelihood but a way of life. The Amish — Swiss and German followers of the religious leader Jacob Amman, who faced persecution in their homelands — took up residence in Wayne, Holmes, and other counties south of Cleveland. There they have preserved the ways of their ancestors to the present day. Dressed in old-fashioned clothes, the Amish travel by horse and buggy, hitching their reins to parking meters in the towns where they shop. Their country stores stock nonelectrical tools and appliances (such as gas-run refrigerators) for their own use, while visitors come to buy the exceptional Amish cheeses, honeys, and handmade quilts. Such products are never in short supply, for some 60,000 Amish live in Ohio — more than in any other state.

Another devout group to settle near Cleveland was the United Society of Believers in Christ's Second Appearing. Sometimes called Believers, they were commonly known as Shakers because of the bodily quivering and shuddering that took place during their moments of religious fervor. Though the Shakers' adherence to celibacy led to their demise in Ohio by the early 1900's, their community is memorialized at its original site by the elegantly planned town of Shaker Heights.

Some 87,000 farms are found all across Ohio. This one, located south of Cleveland, is run by an Amish family. Since their religion forbids the use of modern machinery, the Amish till their fields as their ancestors did — with horse-drawn plows.

The 8,300 acres of wetlands at the Ottawa National Wildlife Refuge near Toledo offer sanctuary to migrating ducks and geese.

A SERPENT FROM THE DISTANT PAST

In a remote part of southern Ohio near Locust Grove stands an ancient and mysterious earthen monument known as the Great Serpent Mound. About 5 feet high, 20 feet wide, and a quarter mile long, the sinuous mound was named for its snakelike appearance. The tail coils into a spiral and the head has wide open jaws that grasp a giant oval egg.

Exactly when the Great Serpent Mound was built is not known, but archeologists believe it was the work of the Adena people, prehistoric Indians who lived in southern Ohio between 800 B.C. and A.D. 400. Many of the mounds found in Ohio — some towering as high as 60 feet — were used for burial or fortification, but the Great Serpent Mound, it is supposed, played some significant role in Adena religious ceremonies.

In 1887 this remarkable site was almost destroyed, but Frederic Ward Putnam, the Harvard professor who first excavated the mound, raised enough money to save it. In the following year Ohio passed the first law in the country to preserve such archeological wonders for posterity.

BY THE BEAUTIFUL OHIO

Far below Cleveland, in the southeastern part of the state, lie the Appalachian foothills, which contrast dramatically with the rest of Ohio's flat to rolling landscape. This area embraces some of Ohio's most beautiful countryside, and includes gigantic Wayne National Forest, consisting of about 176,000 acres of dense woodland, rocky outcrops, white-water streams, and plunging waterfalls. Much of the wilderness here looks the same today as it did when the first settlers arrived two centuries ago.

The Ohio River, which serves as the state's southeastern border near Marietta, forms the southern border once it swings westward. The "Beautiful Ohio" celebrated in song passes the little river towns of Pomeroy, Gallipolis, Portsmouth, Ripley, and eventually, in Ohio's southwestern corner, the genteel city of Cincinnati. Here barge traffic has long since replaced the stern-wheelers that once chugged up the Mississippi River from New Orleans, but a few of the old-time steamboats still ply the waters along Cincinnati's shores, often within earshot of the roaring crowds assembled at Riverfront Stadium.

Between the Ohio River and Columbus — the state capital, positioned like a bull's-eye in the center of the state — thousands of square miles of rich farmland are interspersed with reminders of Ohio's Indian past. History comes alive in the labyrinthine passages of the Olentangy Indian Caverns, where the Wyandot Indians used to hide from enemy tribes.

In central and southwestern Ohio, the ancient Adena and Hopewell Indians built earthen mounds at hundreds of sites, which they used for fortification, burial, or ceremonial purposes. A number of the monuments have survived to this day. Though very little is known about these people of antiquity, they probably spent their lives fishing, hunting, and gathering wild plants, and no doubt felt a tranquil kinship with the land. For their successors, on farms and in small towns all across Ohio, the tranquillity endures.

In Crane Creek State Park on Lake Erie are two plants named for their wet habitat: swamp rose mallow, with large pink blossoms, and swamp milkweed, with clusters of small, star-shaped blossoms.

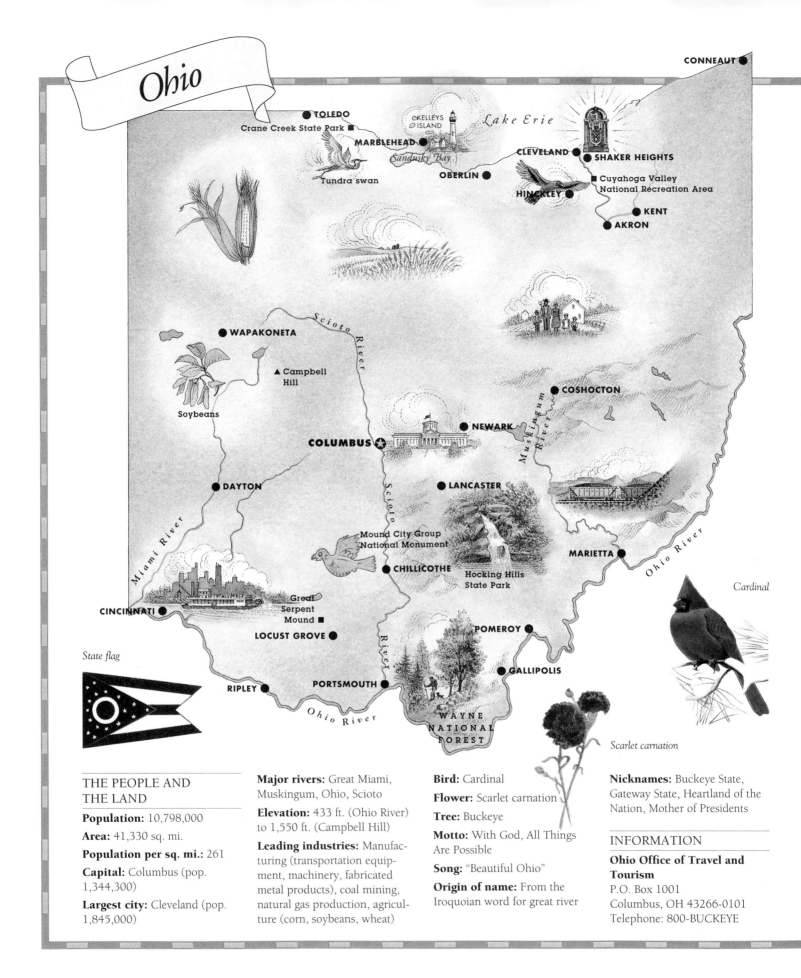

Ohio

CONNEAUT

TOLEDO
Crane Creek State Park
KELLEYS ISLAND
MARBLEHEAD
Lake Erie
Sandusky Bay
Tundra swan
OBERLIN
CLEVELAND
SHAKER HEIGHTS
Cuyahoga Valley
National Recreation Area
HINCKLEY
KENT
AKRON

Soybeans

WAPAKONETA

▲ Campbell Hill

Scioto River

COSHOCTON

Muskingum River

NEWARK

COLUMBUS ✪

DAYTON

LANCASTER

Mound City Group
National Monument

Scioto River

Hocking Hills
State Park

MARIETTA

Ohio River

CINCINNATI

Great
Serpent
Mound

CHILLICOTHE

LOCUST GROVE

Miami River

POMEROY

Ohio River

RIPLEY

PORTSMOUTH

GALLIPOLIS

WAYNE
NATIONAL
FOREST

Ohio River

Cardinal

Scarlet carnation

State flag

THE PEOPLE AND THE LAND

Population: 10,798,000

Area: 41,330 sq. mi.

Population per sq. mi.: 261

Capital: Columbus (pop. 1,344,300)

Largest city: Cleveland (pop. 1,845,000)

Major rivers: Great Miami, Muskingum, Ohio, Scioto

Elevation: 433 ft. (Ohio River) to 1,550 ft. (Campbell Hill)

Leading industries: Manufacturing (transportation equipment, machinery, fabricated metal products), coal mining, natural gas production, agriculture (corn, soybeans, wheat)

Bird: Cardinal

Flower: Scarlet carnation

Tree: Buckeye

Motto: With God, All Things Are Possible

Song: "Beautiful Ohio"

Origin of name: From the Iroquoian word for great river

Nicknames: Buckeye State, Gateway State, Heartland of the Nation, Mother of Presidents

INFORMATION

Ohio Office of Travel and Tourism
P.O. Box 1001
Columbus, OH 43266-0101
Telephone: 800-BUCKEYE

HISTORICAL HIGHLIGHTS

c. 1670 Robert Cavelier, sieur de La Salle, it is believed, crosses land that is now Ohio.

1747 The Ohio Company of Virginia is organized to colonize the Ohio River valley.

1787 The Northwest Territory, including Ohio, is established.

1794 U.S. troops defeat Indians at Battle of Fallen Timbers, opening the way to the West.

1795 With Treaty of Greenville, the Indians lose about two-thirds of their Ohio land.

1803 Ohio becomes 17th state.

1813 Commodore Oliver H. Perry defeats fleet of British warships in Battle of Lake Erie during War of 1812.

1833 Oberlin, the nation's first coeducational college, opens.

1869 Cincinnati Red Stockings become world's first professional baseball team.

1870 In Cleveland the Standard Oil Company is organized by John D. Rockefeller.

1913 – 14 Floods cause over 350 deaths, prompting Conservancy Act for flood control.

1955 Ohio Turnpike opens.

1959 St. Lawrence Seaway connects Lake Erie to Atlantic Ocean.

1970 Four Kent State University students are killed by national guardsmen during a campus protest against the Vietnam War.

1990 A Cincinnati art museum is acquitted of obscenity charges for exhibiting the photographs of Robert Mapplethorpe.

FAMOUS SONS AND DAUGHTERS

Neil Armstrong (1930 –). In 1969 the astronaut, a Wapakoneta native, became the first person to set foot on the moon.

Clarence Darrow (1857 – 1938). An eminent corporate lawyer, Darrow represented Nathan Leopold and Richard Loeb in their murder trial and John Scopes in his trial for teaching evolution in public schools.

Harvey Firestone (1868 – 1938). A farmer's son, this captain of industry founded the Firestone Tire & Rubber Company.

Clark Gable (1901 – 60). Gable's rakish charm made him the King of Hollywood, where he starred in more than 70 films, including *Gone With the Wind*.

John Glenn (1921 –). In 1962 Glenn became the first American to orbit the earth. Later he served as a U.S. senator from Ohio.

Annie Oakley (1860 – 1926).

A sharpshooter from childhood on, Oakley won international acclaim as a performer in Buffalo Bill's Wild West Show.

Edward V. Rickenbacker (1890 – 1973). A World War I flying ace, Rickenbacker later served as the president of Eastern Airlines.

William Tecumseh Sherman (1820 – 1891). The Union general whose Atlanta campaign and "March to the Sea" ended the Civil War was born in the city of Lancaster.

James Thurber (1894 – 1961). Thurber's wistful and ironic humor lent a unique flavor to his cartoons and writings, which occasionally reflected his early life in Columbus.

Wilbur Wright (1867 – 1912) and **Orville Wright** (1871 – 1948). The famous brothers used their Dayton bicycle-repair shop to design flying machines. In 1903 they made the first flight in a powered plane.

ODDITIES AND SPECIALTIES

Seven Ohio natives became U.S. presidents: Ulysses S. Grant, Rutherford B. Hayes, James A. Garfield, Benjamin Harrison, William McKinley, William Howard Taft, and Warren G. Harding. Another president, William Henry Harrison, was an Ohio resident when he took office.

The phrase "First Lady" entered the language when a newspaper reporter used it to refer to Lucy Webb Hayes.

A former Ohio governor, Salmon P. Chase, who served as Lincoln's secretary of the treasury, determined that our paper money would be green.

Martha, the world's last passenger pigeon, died in the Cincinnati Zoo in 1914.

Every year on the third weekend in March, hundreds of buzzards land in Hinckley before migrating north. Residents celebrate the event with a buzzard festival.

In the early 1950's, a Cleveland disc jockey, Alan Freed, coined the term "rock and roll" and the city hosted the first rock concert.

PLACES TO VISIT, THINGS TO DO

Cuyahoga Valley National Recreation Area (Brecksville). This green, graceful valley occupies some 32,000 acres along the Cuyahoga River, which stretches between Cleveland and Akron.

Hocking Hills State Park (near Logan). The popular 1,900-acre park contains a spectacular mixture of woodlands, cliffs, caves, gorges, and waterfalls.

Indian Mounds Among the more notable of these prehistoric sites are the Mound City Group (near Chillicothe), with a wealth of ancient artifacts, and Newark Earthworks (in Newark), where some 50 acres are enclosed by an eight-sided earthen ridge and smaller areas are surrounded by circular walls.

Kelleys Island The Lake Erie resort island is known for its Indian pictographs and the unusual grooves etched in limestone outcrops by glaciers.

Ottawa National Wildlife Refuge (Oak Harbor). These tracts of marshland on Lake Erie provide oases for tundra swans, egrets, ducks, geese, and other migrating birds.

Roscoe Village (Coshocton). A restored community depicting life in the 1800's, the town features an excellent museum and offers a horse-drawn boat ride on the old Ohio and Erie Canal.

Oklahoma

Where the face of America changes

Oklahoma stands where North America changes from shady woodlands to stark desert buttes. In the eastern part of the state, lush, green, wooded hills and valleys, spilling over from Missouri and Arkansas, are so reminiscent of the South that Oklahomans call this area Little Dixie. At the state's center, vast grasslands stretch southward from the great American prairie. Farther west, in the panhandle, stark silhouettes of lonely buttes dominate the flat, dry High Plains terrain.

The weather also can change dramatically here. Cool, dry air from the north colliding with southern breezes gives the state nearly constant winds and violent storms. Within days, streams change from ribbons of sand to gushing torrents. High winds flatten fences and whip up tornadoes. When a stranger asks, "Does the wind blow this way all the time?" a native Oklahoman is likely to reply, "No. Half the time it blows the other way."

A VOLATILE PAST

As if taking a cue from the weather, the state itself has had a volatile past. Oklahoma was home to the Plains Indians when, in 1825, the U.S. government declared the region Indian Territory. During the next half century more than 60 tribes from the East and the northern Plains were forcibly moved to reservations there. Then, under pressure from homesteaders, the government took back reservation lands. At noon on April 22, 1889, the territory was instantly transformed as white settlers raced to claim homesteads in the first of Okla-

In the northwest corner of the panhandle, dark clouds over Black Mesa, Oklahoma's highest point, portend the momentary violence of a gathering storm.

In the Chickasaw National Recreation Area, Rock Creek wends through an ecological transition zone where woodlands meet grasslands. Cardinals of the eastern woods and roadrunners of the arid Southwest are among the birds that can be seen here.

homa's land rushes. By evening whole cities of tents had sprung up on the grassy plains.

When these homesteaders arrived, the Oklahoma tallgrass prairie was a waving sea of green that sometimes towered over their covered wagons. But within 40 years the soil was so overtilled that it was waiting for disaster, and in the 1930's tragedy struck in the form of drought. As vegetation died, the dry soil was blown away by the winds. Oklahoma and much of the southern Great Plains turned into America's Dust Bowl.

After World War II, however, Oklahomans harnessed their abundant system of rivers to

build mammoth water-management projects aimed at preventing disaster in future droughts. Today, with some 1,800 reservoirs and nearly 200,000 farm ponds, the state has a greater ratio of water to land than Minnesota, the Land of Ten Thousand Lakes.

UNEXPECTED LANDSCAPES

To outsiders who think of Oklahoma as flat prairie, its mountains come as a surprise. In the east the Ouachitas and the Ozarks boast idyllic valleys with crystalline streams. To the southwest, part of the Wichita Mountains are included in a large national wildlife refuge.

In the far west, in the panhandle, the landscape is stark and arid. With rainfall less than 16 inches a year, trees are so scarce that early settlers burned buffalo chips for fuel, calling them prairie coal.

Since the 1880's, the oil boom has sped Oklahoma's development, so that today the rocking arms of oil well pumps are familiar sights in fields, on farms, and even on city streets. Amid the incongruities of this rapidly changing landscape, however, the character of Oklahoma somehow remains constant in its rocky eastern hills, waving fields, and the limitless horizons of its western plains.

The granite hills of southwestern Oklahoma in and around Quartz Mountain State Park were once sacred ground for the Kiowa and Comanche Indians. Today sweeping fields of grain are nestled among their craggy outcroppings. Bald eagles frequent the area in winter.

HISTORICAL HIGHLIGHTS

1803 U.S. acquires Oklahoma as part of Louisiana Purchase.

1825 U.S. government reserves Oklahoma as Indian Territory. In the following years it forces the Five Civilized Tribes — Cherokee, Chickasaw, Choctaw, Creek, and Seminole — to relocate there from the southeastern states.

1866 In a treaty with U.S., the Five Civilized Tribes agree to free their slaves and to cede part of Oklahoma for resettlement by other Indian groups.

1872 Railroad extends into Oklahoma. Commercial coal mining begins near McAlester.

1889 Oklahoma's first producing oil well is drilled near Chelsea. Land is opened to white settlers in a series of land rushes.

1890 Congress annexes panhandle to Indian Territory and establishes Oklahoma Territory.

1893 Dawes Commission distributes tribal lands of the Five Civilized Tribes to individual Indians in order to break tribal control of the area.

1907 Oklahoma enters Union as the 46th state.

1930's Economic depression and prolonged drought devastate farmers throughout Oklahoma and other Plains states.

1959 Statewide prohibition of liquor sales is repealed.

1971 The Arkansas-Verdigris waterway connects Muskogee and Tulsa to the Mississippi River, making them thriving inland ports.

1987 State's 29 bank failures are exceeded only by those of Texas.

FAMOUS SONS AND DAUGHTERS

Carl Bert Albert (1908 –). Elected to the House of Representatives in 1946, Albert was instrumental in passing social legislation during the 1960's. He served as speaker of the House from 1971 to 1977.

Ralph Ellison (1914 –). In his acclaimed novel *Invisible Man* Ellison explored the problems of a black man in America.

Woody Guthrie (1912 – 67). An itinerant laborer and folksinger, Guthrie wrote songs about social justice and equality, including "This Land Is Your Land."

Mickey Mantle (1931 –). Mantle hit 536 home runs during his career with the New York Yankees and was elected to the Baseball Hall of Fame in 1974.

Will Rogers (1879 – 1935). Rogers started his stage career doing cowboy rope tricks and quickly won the nation's heart as an entertainer and columnist with dry wit and a down-home perspective.

Maria Tallchief (1925 –). The renowned ballerina, whose father was an Osage Indian, danced primarily with the New York City Ballet.

Jim Thorpe (1888 – 1953). A Sauk and Fox Indian, Thorpe starred in the pentathlon and decathlon at the 1912 Olympics and played both baseball and football professionally.

ODDITIES AND SPECIALTIES

Oklahoma proclaims its Indian heritage on its state seal, where the Five Civilized Tribes are represented, and on its state flag, which shows an Osage warrior's shield and a peace pipe.

Before it was attached to Oklahoma, the panhandle was called Robber's Roost, a no-man's-land where outlaw gangs such as the Daltons hid out.

Oklahoma is identified with cowboys as well as Indians. Many famous cowboy entertainers — among them Gene Autry, William "Hopalong Cassidy" Boyd, and Tom Mix — hail from Oklahoma. The International Professional Rodeo Association has its headquarters in Pauls Valley.

PLACES TO VISIT, THINGS TO DO

Beavers Bend State Park (Broken Bow). Visitors to this 5000-acre woodland park can swim, fish, camp, or view the log sculptures and dioramas at the Forest Heritage Center. Nearby is Talimena Skyline Drive, a scenic auto route through the Winding Stair Mountains.

Cherokee Heritage Center (Tahlequah). The national museum of the Cherokee Indians is here, as well as reconstructions of two Cherokee villages, one from the 1600's and another from the period 1875 – 90.

▲ Black Mesa

Chickasaw National Recreation Area (near Sulphur). Nestled in the Arbuckle foothills, this 10,000-acre park has springs and creeks, wildflowers and wildlife. A large lake invites fishermen and water sports enthusiasts.

Great Salt Plains State Park (near Cherokee). The national wildlife refuge among the salt flats here is a haven for more than 250 species of birds.

Indian City USA (Anadarko). The highlights of this museum are re-created dwellings from a variety of tribes, especially Plains Indians, and demonstrations of Indian dancing.

National Cowboy Hall of Fame and Western Heritage Center (Oklahoma City). Paintings, sculptures, artifacts, a sod homestead, and the Rodeo Hall of Fame celebrate the cowboy and the Old West.

Pioneer Woman Statue and Museum (Ponca City). A handsome bronze statue commemorates the role of pioneer women, and the museum exhibits artifacts from the frontier era.

Woolaroc (Bartlesville). Oilman Frank Phillips's estate is now a 3,500-acre preserve of woods and prairie where buffalo graze.

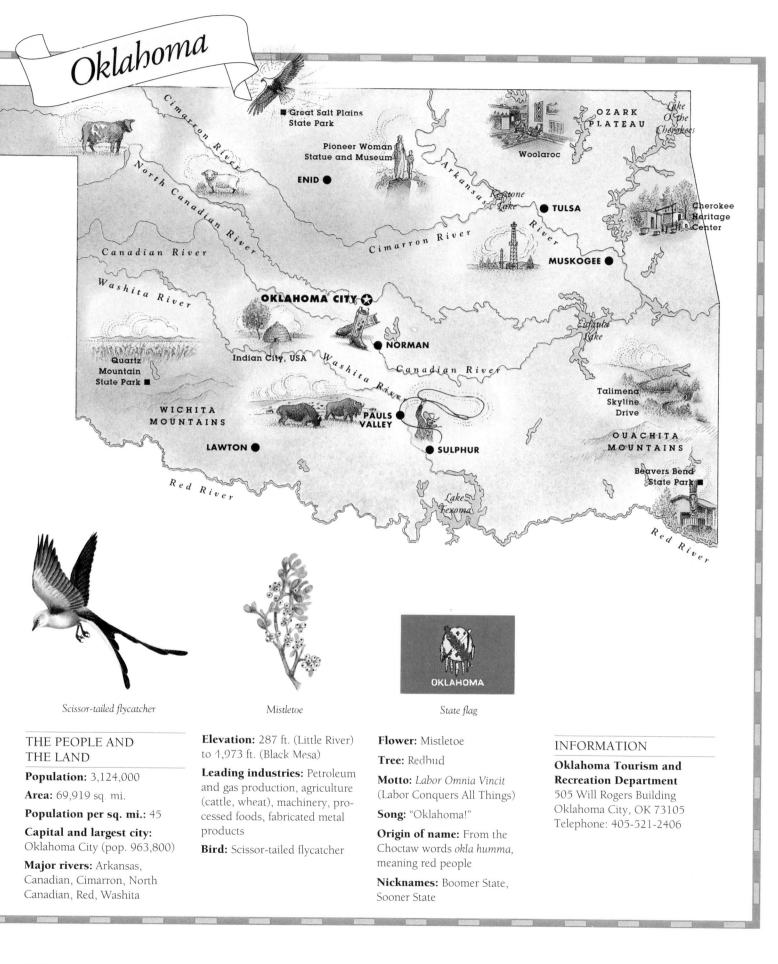

Oklahoma

■ Great Salt Plains State Park

Pioneer Woman Statue and Museum

ENID ●

Cimarron River

North Canadian River

Canadian River

Washita River

OKLAHOMA CITY ☆

Indian City, USA

Quartz Mountain State Park ■

WICHITA MOUNTAINS

LAWTON ●

Red River

Arkansas River

Keystone Lake

TULSA ●

OZARK PLATEAU

Lake O' the Cherokees

Woolaroc

Cherokee Heritage Center

MUSKOGEE ●

Cimarron River

NORMAN ●

Washita River

Canadian River

Eufaula Lake

PAULS VALLEY ●

SULPHUR ●

Talimena Skyline Drive

OUACHITA MOUNTAINS

Lake Texoma

Beavers Bend State Park ■

Red River

Scissor-tailed flycatcher

Mistletoe

OKLAHOMA

State flag

THE PEOPLE AND THE LAND

Population: 3,124,000

Area: 69,919 sq. mi.

Population per sq. mi.: 45

Capital and largest city: Oklahoma City (pop. 963,800)

Major rivers: Arkansas, Canadian, Cimarron, North Canadian, Red, Washita

Elevation: 287 ft. (Little River) to 4,973 ft. (Black Mesa)

Leading industries: Petroleum and gas production, agriculture (cattle, wheat), machinery, processed foods, fabricated metal products

Bird: Scissor-tailed flycatcher

Flower: Mistletoe

Tree: Redbud

Motto: *Labor Omnia Vincit* (Labor Conquers All Things)

Song: "Oklahoma!"

Origin of name: From the Choctaw words *okla humma,* meaning red people

Nicknames: Boomer State, Sooner State

INFORMATION

Oklahoma Tourism and Recreation Department
505 Will Rogers Building
Oklahoma City, OK 73105
Telephone: 405-521-2406

Oregon

Green valleys, thick forests, and a heritage of preservation

For more than 150 years Oregon has sparkled in the American imagination like the pot of gold at the end of the rainbow. It is a land where countless Americans have believed their dreams would come true. During the 19th century, mere rumors of the territory's incredible fertility were enough to induce "Oregon fever." Thousands of land-poor pioneers succumbed and traveled 2,000 miles across the wilds of the American West. Those who survived learned happily that most of the rumors were true. The Willamette Valley was an agricultural heaven. The winters were mild, the rain was gentle, and the soil was among the richest in North America. They also learned that Oregon was one of the West's most diverse territories. Although the Willamette Valley was an agrarian dream, to get there, one had to cross the Snake River gorge, the Blue Mountains, and the trackless high desert east of the looming Cascade Range.

THE GREAT DIVIDE

A series of imposing mountains soaring to heights of more than 11,000 feet, the Cascades in Oregon run the entire length of the state from the Columbia River to the California border. Pacific storms, unable to rise above the range, drop most of their moisture on the coastal lowlands to the west. Plant life grows profusely, creating what Oregonians call their "chlorophyll commonwealth."

Though some residents bridle at the suggestion that they rust in summer instead of tanning, the fact remains that this part of the

Waves sweep the shallow shore at Ecola State Park near Cannon Beach, their whitecaps a counterpoint to the cliff's warm glow at sunset.

The Painted Hills in the John Day Fossil Beds National Monument are formed from layers of volcanic ash, which create the banded appearance.

state can receive as much as 130 inches of rain a year. From November to May, marine storms dampen everything west of the Cascades with a fine drizzle, and fog can seem a permanent fixture along the rocky northern coast. But east of the Cascades, where the mountains block the reach of moist Pacific air, the landscape changes to sagebrush deserts, wind-scored canyons, rugged hills, and patches of open forest.

FORESTS PRESERVED

The image most Americans have of Oregon, however, can be summed up in one word: trees. Nearly half of Oregon's land area is covered by dense forests that make the state America's leading producer of timber. Along the coast, the towering Sitka spruce, a tree that thrives in wet, mild climates, reigns supreme.

Cedar, mountain hemlock, noble fir, and California laurel cover the western Cascades. In the drier eastern regions, ponderosa pine predominates. But Oregon's most valuable and widely planted tree is the Douglas fir, which grows throughout the western part of the state. It is a true giant of the forest, rising from a thick base to more than 200 feet, or about the height of a 10-story building.

Oregon's forests are even more impressive when one considers the effort that has been required to preserve them. By 1920 wanton cutting had decimated the great forests of the Midwest, and the nation increasingly depended on Washington and Oregon for lumber. It seemed that these Pacific woodlands were doomed to be destroyed too, until in the late 1930's forests were finally recognized as renewable but fragile resources that re-

Heavy rain and frequent fog make Oregon's coastal forests dense and eerie. The twisted trees here atop the promontory at Cape Lookout are in part the result of nearly constant winds blowing from the Pacific Ocean.

Lower Proxy Falls in the Three Sisters Wilderness of the central Cascades plunge over a cliff that is the remnant of an ancient lava flow.

AMERICA: LAND OF BEAUTY AND SPLENDOR

Amid the sagebrush and sand dunes in the high desert of Oregon's central plains there is a 9,000-acre ponderosa pine forest that seems mysteriously out of place. The closest forest to it is more than 40 miles away, so the trees here cannot be the result of windblown seeds. And the annual local rainfall of nine inches is nearly five inches less than what is normally required to support ponderosa pines. Why are these trees here? How do they survive?

Lost Forest, as this area northeast of Christmas Valley is called, is a relic from the end of the last ice age, a time when a moister climate than today's allowed pine forests to stretch eastward from the Cascade Range across much of what is now arid plains. The key to Lost Forest's survival lies in the soil. Debris spewed from ancient volcanoes covered the shallow basin in which it stands, creating a thick layer of pumice. This deep, sandy soil holds moisture well and limits evaporation, allowing Lost Forest to endure while forests that once surrounded it were destroyed by drought. Research also suggests that the seeds of the trees at Lost Forest germinate especially quickly, perhaps an adaptation to the dryness.

quired care if they were to be both harvested and preserved. An early champion of this conservationist view was the powerful timber baron Frederick Weyerhaeuser, who established the nation's first tree farms in Washington and Oregon in the early 1940's.

Public sentiment for ecological preservation is strong in Oregon. It was the first state to impose heavy fines for littering, ban the use of nonreturnable beverage bottles, and prohibit the storage of nuclear waste. Protective legislation enacted in 1913 and 1967 has maintained the beauty of the 296-mile Oregon coast much as it was when Spanish explorers first navigated its treacherous waters in the 16th century.

This coastline is famed for its wildness and splendor. Except for a 44-mile stretch of sand dunes, it is a rocky escarpment buffeted by winds blowing relentlessly off the Pacific Ocean. "No calm comes to these shores . . ." wrote naturalist John Muir. "The breakers are ever in bloom and crystal brine is ever in the air."

THE WAY WEST

Although the purchase of the Louisiana Territory from France in 1803 gave Americans visions of westward expansion, President Thomas Jefferson knew that Great Britain and Spain continued to have interest in the Northwest. Therefore, in 1804 Jefferson sent Meriwether Lewis and William Clark off to survey the continent all the way to the Pacific shore. Their expedition significantly strengthened the United States' claim to the area. It was not until 1846, however, that all of the Pacific Northwest below the 49th parallel officially became part of the United States, opening the way for the flood of immigration over the next decades.

Portions of the Oregon Trail — which was one of the pioneers' main routes west — still can be seen alongside Interstate 84 in the northeastern part of the state. But today's motorists, like the wagon drivers of a century and a half ago, usually hurry on to the Willamette Valley. Those who do stop to explore, however, discover a region of alpine mead-

At Smith Rock State Park, east of the Cascades, the Crooked River has carved dramatic cliffs from mounds of once-molten volcanic cinders.

AMERICA: LAND OF BEAUTY AND SPLENDOR

Beautiful, pure, and isolated, Crater Lake was sacred to the Modoc and Klamath Indians, who kept its existence a secret from white explorers for decades.

ows that blossom during spring and summer with brilliant fireweed, scarlet columbine, and mountain iris.

South of the Oregon Trail, the desert badlands offer startling contrasts. In 1843 explorer John C. Frémont and his guide Kit Carson led a government party to survey the region. After crossing a lava-encrusted ridge they climbed to 7,000 feet amid howling winds and snow. Suddenly, they looked down to a lake some 3,000 feet below surrounded by thick grass and trees gently swaying in a balmy breeze. Frémont and Carson's experience is typical of the extraordinary juxtapositions of natural beauty found throughout the state. Thanks in large part to the vigilance of Oregonians, the grandeur of the western mountains, the panorama of the eastern desert, and the fertility of the Willamette Valley survive as some of the nation's most splendid natural treasures.

BEAUTIFUL BUT DEADLY

Anyone who explores the tide pools of the Pacific Northwest is sure to be fascinated by what seem to be brightly colored flowers growing from the rocks below the water. Despite appearances, however, these are not plants but sea anemones, carnivorous animals related to jellyfish.

Although the sea anemone can crawl slowly, it generally attaches itself to rocks, shells, and other submerged objects by means of secretions from its base. Its body has no skeleton, but is merely a tube of thick muscles surrounding a large stomach. Its top is a mass of sticky tentacles encircling its mouth.

As small aquatic animals float within reach, the sea anemone snares and immobilizes them with its stinging tentacles. It then quickly curls the tentacles inward, pushing the prey into its mouth and gullet. The hapless victims are digested whole in its stomach.

When an anemone is stranded out of water at low tide, it curls inward until it looks like a small gelatin blob, a defense mechanism it also uses when attacked by predators, such as starfish. When the water returns, the anemone quickly springs open again, ready to resume its deadly waiting game along the shore.

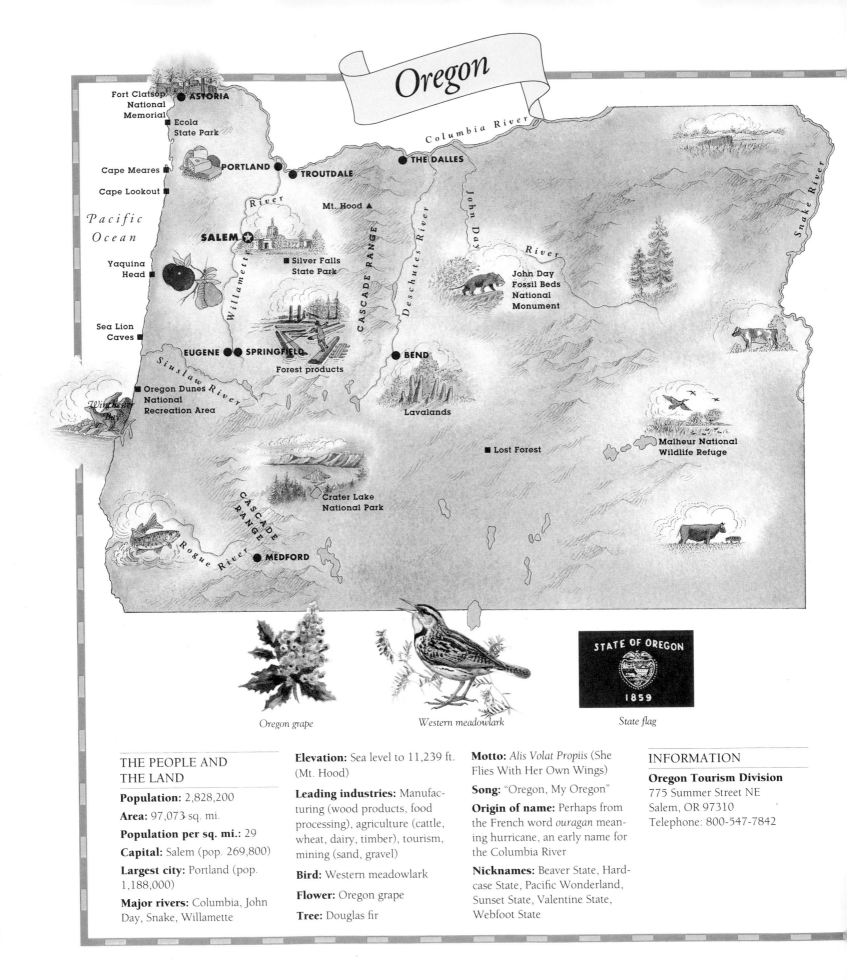

Oregon

Fort Clatsop National Memorial

● **ASTORIA**

■ Ecola State Park

Cape Meares ■

PORTLAND

● **TROUTDALE**

Cape Lookout ■

Pacific Ocean

Columbia River

● **THE DALLES**

Mt. Hood ▲

Willamette River

SALEM ☆

Yaquina Head ■

■ Silver Falls State Park

CASCADE RANGE

Deschutes River

John Day River

John Day Fossil Beds National Monument

Sea Lion Caves ■

EUGENE ● ● **SPRINGFIELD**

Forest products

● **BEND**

Lavalands

Siuslaw River

Snake River

■ Oregon Dunes National Recreation Area

Winchester Bay

■ Lost Forest

Malheur National Wildlife Refuge

CASCADE RANGE

■ Crater Lake National Park

Rogue River

● **MEDFORD**

Oregon grape

Western meadowlark

STATE OF OREGON 1859

State flag

THE PEOPLE AND THE LAND

Population: 2,828,200

Area: 97,073 sq. mi.

Population per sq. mi.: 29

Capital: Salem (pop. 269,800)

Largest city: Portland (pop. 1,188,000)

Major rivers: Columbia, John Day, Snake, Willamette

Elevation: Sea level to 11,239 ft. (Mt. Hood)

Leading industries: Manufacturing (wood products, food processing), agriculture (cattle, wheat, dairy, timber), tourism, mining (sand, gravel)

Bird: Western meadowlark

Flower: Oregon grape

Tree: Douglas fir

Motto: *Alis Volat Propiis* (She Flies With Her Own Wings)

Song: "Oregon, My Oregon"

Origin of name: Perhaps from the French word *ouragan* meaning hurricane, an early name for the Columbia River

Nicknames: Beaver State, Hardcase State, Pacific Wonderland, Sunset State, Valentine State, Webfoot State

INFORMATION

Oregon Tourism Division
775 Summer Street NE
Salem, OR 97310
Telephone: 800-547-7842

HISTORICAL HIGHLIGHTS

1792 Capt. Robert Gray sails into Columbia River and names it after his ship.

1805 Lewis and Clark reach Pacific Ocean and spend the winter at Fort Clatsop.

1811 Fur traders employed by John Jacob Astor found Astoria, first white settlement in region.

1818 Treaty between Great Britain and U.S. allows both countries to occupy area.

1843 Willamette Valley settlers adopt a provisional government. Some 900 people migrate to the region via Oregon Trail.

1848 Congressional act creates Oregon Territory.

1853 Washington Territory is separated from Oregon Territory by act of Congress.

1859 Oregon enters Union as 33rd state.

1868 State's first salmon canning plant opens at Westport.

1883 Northern Pacific Railway connects Portland to the East.

1887 Railroad connects Portland and San Francisco.

1902 Crater Lake National Park is established.

1912 Women get right to vote.

1933 Tillamook Burn forest fire destroys 300,000 acres.

1937 Bonneville Dam hydroelectric project is completed on Columbia River.

1946 Reorganization of public education benefits rural schools.

1960 Oregonians elect their first woman to the U.S. Senate, Maurine Neuberger.

1966 Astoria Bridge spans Columbia River, linking Oregon and Washington.

1971 Oregon adopts nation's first bottle law, banning nonreturnable bottles and cans.

1977 Statewide ban on aerosol sprays established.

1985 Notorious commune Rajneeshpuram closes after its guru pleads guilty to fraud.

FAMOUS SONS AND DAUGHTERS

John McLoughlin (1784 – 1857). As chief agent of the Hudson's Bay Company, McLoughlin expanded fur trade in Oregon and encouraged early settlement.

Wayne Morse (1900 – 74). Dean of the University of Oregon Law School from 1931 to 1944, Morse represented Oregon in the U.S. Senate from 1945 to 1968, serving first as a Republican and then after 1955 as a Democrat. He championed liberal causes.

Linus Pauling (1901 –). A two-time winner of the Nobel Prize, Pauling won the award in chemistry in 1954 and the Peace Prize in 1962 for his work to ban nuclear weapons. His advocacy of vitamin C to prevent colds created much controversy.

John Reed (1887 – 1920). A journalist and political radical, Reed is famous for his eyewitness account of the Russian Revolution in 1917, *Ten Days That Shook the World*.

ODDITIES AND SPECIALTIES

Say "cheese" when you're in Oregon. The coastal towns of Tillamook and Bandon churn out many fine types, including Cheddar, Jack, and Brie.

Volcanic lava-tube caves in central Oregon have been used as sources of ice, refrigerators for meat, summer shelters for livestock, and hiding places for stills during Prohibition.

The nation's densest concentration of waterfalls is in Silver Falls State Park, where 10 can be found along a seven-mile trail.

Fort Stevens, near Astoria, was attacked by a Japanese submarine during World War II. It is the only military site in the contiguous 48 states that has been attacked by a foreign enemy since the War of 1812.

Mt. Hood is one of few places in the contiguous 48 states with year-round skiing.

The Wildlife Safari in Winston is one of the world's foremost cheetah breeding centers.

PLACES TO VISIT, THINGS TO DO

Columbia River Gorge From The Dalles to Troutdale, cliffs and waterfalls line this famous chasm in the Cascade Range. The old Columbia Gorge Highway is especially scenic.

Crater Lake National Park (near Medford). Like a jewel in an ornate setting, this astoundingly clear blue lake, the nation's deepest, lies in the cone of an ancient volcano.

Fishing The coast offers many fishing areas. Try the Siuslaw River for cutthroat trout and salmon, the Rogue River for steelhead, and Winchester Bay for striped bass.

John Day Fossil Beds National Monument (John Day). Fossils up to 45 million years old are preserved here, including those of a cat and a three-toed horse.

Lavalands (near Bend). This section of Deschutes National Forest contains many remnants of volcanic action.

Malheur National Wildlife Refuge (near Burns). More than 275 species of birds have been spotted in the desert and wetlands near Malheur Lake, a stopping place on the Pacific flyway.

Mt. Hood Wilderness This alpine preserve includes the state's highest point. The loop highway here is among the nation's most famous scenic drives.

Oregon Dunes National Recreation Area (headquarters in Reedsport). Shifting dunes, some 200 feet high, stretch from Florence to Coos Bay.

Sea Lion Caves (near Florence). A huge sea cave is the mainland's only known permanent home for wild sea lions.

Washington Park (Portland). From May through November 400 varieties of roses are in bloom here.

Whale watching Seaside bluffs make excellent vantage points. Favorite viewing spots include Cape Meares and Yaquina Head.

Pennsylvania

Gentle vistas in the cradle of independence

Pennsylvania is rock-ribbed. The steely mountain ranges of the Appalachian chain lock the state's midsection in a series of ridges and valleys not unlike a rib cage. But plant life and the hand of man have gradually softened the rough terrain. Few vistas in the eastern United States are more bucolic than the cultivated fields of Pennsylvania Dutch country, and few forests offer a more verdant display than those of the Allegheny Plateau.

THE PEACEFUL EAST

Farmers have tilled the fertile soils of southeast Pennsylvania since the 1600's. As soon as William Penn proclaimed "the foundation of a free colony for all mankind," his Quaker brethren arrived from England and Wales to clear the land for crops. An official policy of religious tolerance then drew Germans, including Amish, Mennonites, and Dunkers. So industrious were these "Pennsylvania Deutsch" that southeastern Pennsylvania became one of colonial America's most important breadbaskets. Today the patchwork of fields in Lancaster County is among the most pleasing sights in the state, with quaint barns and silos — often decorated with hex signs — sitting against a backdrop of wooded hills.

Philadelphia was and is the metropolis of eastern Pennsylvania. Overlooked today by a statue of William Penn high atop City Hall, the city was laid out in 1682 in a grid — a new idea at the time that was later copied in many of the cities built across the West. The orderly "greene Countrie Towne" that Penn

Classic pastoral landscapes can be seen from one end of Pennsylvania to the other. This farm is near the town of Export, just east of Pittsburgh.

A profusion of ironweed and goldenrod blooms in a clearing at Erie National Wildlife Refuge in northwestern Pennsylvania.

AMERICA: LAND OF BEAUTY AND SPLENDOR

founded became America's preeminent city of the 18th century and the birthplace of its independence.

THE HARD WAY WEST

Pennsylvania's Appalachians are not as lofty as most stretches of the range. Still, for centuries they proved to be a formidable barrier. Settlers who crossed the seemingly infinite expanse of crests and troughs named the range the Endless Mountains — a name that still sticks in the northeastern part of the state. Traveling in central Pennsylvania remained difficult well into the 20th century, with roads so steep and winding that trucks usually detoured to longer but safer routes farther north.

If crossing Pennsylvania by land was difficult, it was impossible by water: no east-west river system crosses the state. Nature's oversight was remedied in the 1840's, with the completion of a system of canals and railroads linking Philadelphia and Pittsburgh.

Nonetheless, rivers have been of critical importance to Pennsylvania. The Delaware gave Philadelphia access to the sea; the Lehigh carried coal and iron ore from the Appalachians to the foundries of Bethlehem; the Susquehanna linked Pennsylvania farmlands with Chesapeake Bay. But perhaps the most important water route is at Pittsburgh, where the Allegheny and the Monongahela rivers come together to form the Ohio River, the great migration and trade route to the West.

Pittsburgh was the "Gateway to the West" until the frontier shifted and St. Louis inherited the title. When its role in the migration of pioneers was finished, the city gained greater renown and wealth as the foremost manufacturer of steel. Until the 1970's, factories lined the banks of its three rivers for miles on end.

The gentle meadows and brooks of Lancaster County beckoned the first Pennsylvania Dutch settlers, who turned the countryside into productive farmland.

Pine Creek Gorge, in the north-central part of the state, is called the Grand Canyon of Pennsylvania. The gorge winds through dense woodlands for 50 miles.

A MINGLING OF ELEMENTS

Pittsburgh sits on the Allegheny Plateau, a land of broad ridges and deep valleys north and west of the Allegheny Mountains, an Appalachian subrange. The beautiful hardwood forests, fields, bogs, and streams of the plateau, once the home of the Seneca Indians, now draw hikers, fishermen, and photographers. In autumn, old stands of beech, birch, and maple set the woods aflame with color; in June, mountain laurel bursts forth with delicate pink blossoms.

Also on the plateau, some 70 miles southeast of Pittsburgh, is situated one of the finest man-made works in Pennsylvania — the celebrated house called Fallingwater, which Frank Lloyd Wright designed for the Pittsburgh businessman Edgar J. Kaufmann in 1936. Built of local sandstone and concrete, it perches on a craggy waterfall in a forest setting. When Kaufmann gave the property to a conservation group he said that Wright had created it "as a declaration that in nature man finds his spiritual as well as physical energies." The house is a mingling of elements that express the character of Pennsylvania: an energetic combination of natural and man-made, rugged and refined.

The oldest surviving botanic garden in America is the legacy of our first native-born botanist — John Bartram of Pennsylvania. In 1728, at a farm he purchased on the Schuylkill River in what is now southwestern Philadelphia, Bartram laid out a five-acre plot where he cultivated specimens he collected in the region. He also conducted experiments in cross breeding. Later he made collecting expeditions into New York, west to the Ohio River, and in the South. On a trip to Georgia with his son, Bartram discovered a rare tree with beautiful white flowers resembling camellias. He named it *Franklinia* after his friend Benjamin Franklin.

Although he had only a fourth-grade education, Bartram, born in 1699, learned enough Latin to read the books of the renowned Swedish botanist Linnaeus, and eventually gained recognition as a botanist himself. In 1765 King George III appointed him King's Botanist, and Linnaeus lavished praise on Bartram, calling him "the greatest natural botanist in the world."

During the Revolutionary War British soldiers made camp at the farm, but they treated the famed plantings with respect. Later, Bartram's heirs and the subsequent owners of the property took care to maintain the garden. In 1891 it was acquired by the city of Philadelphia and flourishes today as Bartram's Garden, open for the public to enjoy.

In east-central Pennsylvania, forests of sugar maples turn a brilliant yellow in October. In late winter the trees can be tapped for their sweet sap.

Lake Erie

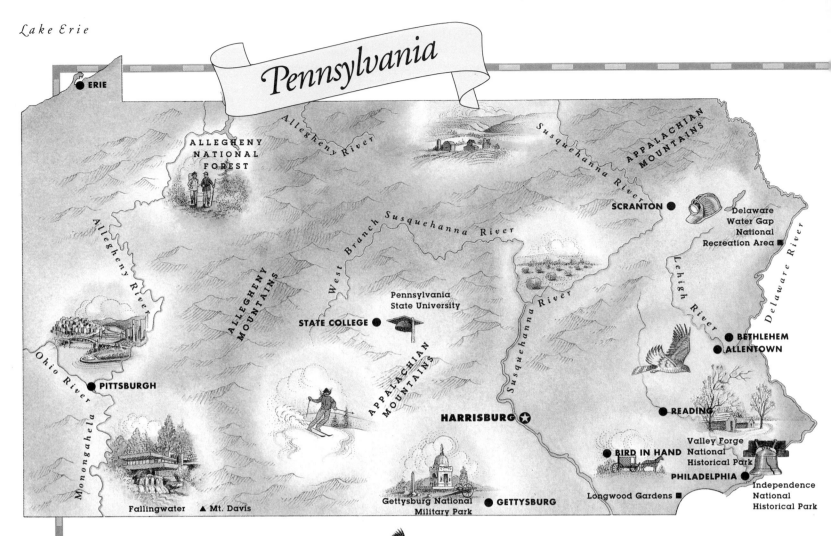

Pennsylvania

ERIE

ALLEGHENY NATIONAL FOREST

Allegheny River

Susquehanna River

APPALACHIAN MOUNTAINS

SCRANTON

Delaware Water Gap National Recreation Area

Allegheny River

West Branch Susquehanna River

ALLEGHENY MOUNTAINS

Lehigh River

Delaware River

Pennsylvania State University

STATE COLLEGE

Susquehanna River

BETHLEHEM

ALLENTOWN

Ohio River

PITTSBURGH

APPALACHIAN MOUNTAINS

READING

HARRISBURG

Monongahela

BIRD IN HAND

Valley Forge National Historical Park

PHILADELPHIA

Fallingwater ▲ Mt. Davis

Gettysburg National Military Park

GETTYSBURG

Longwood Gardens

Independence National Historical Park

State flag

Ruffed grouse

Mountain laurel

THE PEOPLE AND THE LAND

Population: 11,764,000

Area: 45,308 sq. mi.

Population per sq. mi.: 260

Capital: Harrisburg (pop. 52,100)

Largest city: Philadelphia (pop. 4,920,400)

Major rivers: Allegheny, Delaware, Ohio, Susquehanna

Elevation: Sea level (Delaware River) to 3,213 ft. (Mt. Davis)

Leading industries: Manufacturing (machinery, steel, clothing, metal products, processed foods), coal mining, agriculture (dairy products, cattle, corn)

Bird: Ruffed grouse

Flower: Mountain laurel

Tree: Hemlock

Motto: Virtue, Liberty, and Independence

Song: No official song

Origin of name: Latin for "Penn's woods" — honoring the father of the colony's founder, William Penn

Nicknames: Keystone State, Quaker State

INFORMATION

Department of Commerce
Bureau of Travel Marketing
Forum Building, Room 453
Harrisburg, PA 17120
Telephone: 717-787-5453

"Mother and Child" by Mary Cassatt

HISTORICAL HIGHLIGHTS

1609 Henry Hudson sails into Delaware Bay.

1643 Swedes settle on Tinicum Island in Delaware River.

1655 Dutch take possession of Swedish colony.

1664 English troops conquer Dutch territory.

1681 King Charles II grants region to William Penn.

1754 French and Indian War begins in western Pennsylvania.

1776 Declaration of Independence is signed in Philadelphia.

1787 Constitutional Convention meets in Philadelphia. Pennsylvania is the second state to ratify Constitution.

1794 Federal troops squelch the Whiskey Rebellion, a tax protest.

1856 Philadelphia hosts first Republican National Convention.

1859 The nation's first commercial oil well is drilled in Titusville.

1889 Johnstown flood causes more than 2,000 deaths.

1940 First section of the Pennsylvania Turnpike, the nation's first multilane, limited-access highway, opens.

1972 Tropical storm Agnes causes devastating floods, killing more than 50 people.

1979 Accident at Three Mile Island nuclear power plant near Harrisburg threatens major release of radiation.

1982 Steel plants begin to close as foreign competition grows and domestic demand decreases.

FAMOUS SONS AND DAUGHTERS

Marian Anderson (1902 –). The acclaimed contralto sang in Philadelphia church choirs as a child. After gaining fame as a concert artist, in 1955 she became the first black diva to sing with the Metropolitan Opera

Andrew Carnegie (1835 – 1919). The Scottish-born philanthropist, who made a phenomenal fortune through his Pittsburgh steel company, endowed more than 2,800 public libraries in the U.S. and other English-speaking countries.

Mary Cassatt (1845 – 1926). A painter, Cassatt spent most of her life in Paris, where she became the only American artist to exhibit with the French impressionists of the late 19th century.

Stephen Foster (1826 – 64). This self-taught musician composed more than 200 sentimental and minstrel songs, including "My Old Kentucky Home."

Benjamin Franklin (1706 – 90).

Franklin ended his formal education at age 10, yet became one of the most creative men of his time — inventor of bifocals, experimenter in electricity — and a Founding Father of the U.S.

Robert Fulton (1765 – 1815). An inventor, Fulton built America's first commercially successful steamboat, the *Clermont*, which journeyed between New York City and Albany.

George Catlett Marshall (1880 – 1959). As secretary of state, the former army general proposed the Marshall Plan, a U.S.-financed self-help program for European nations that had suffered in World War II. He was awarded the Nobel Peace Prize in 1953.

ODDITIES AND SPECIALTIES

The ice-cream soda was invented in Pennsylvania in 1874.

No one knows for certain when the Liberty Bell, now housed in Philadelphia, was cracked. It may have been an original flaw that worsened with time. In 1846 the crack was patched up long enough to ring the bell for Washington's Birthday. It has not been rung since.

The Kentucky rifle used by men migrating West was actually made in Lancaster, once known as the "arsenal of the colonies" for its gun production.

The list of Pennsylvania's firsts is staggering. It includes the first root beer, circus, pencil with an eraser, zoo, pretzel, cable car, U.S. mint, firefighting company, motion picture show, commercial radio station, lending library, weekly newspaper, savings bank, Little League baseball game, and symphony orchestra.

PLACES TO VISIT, THINGS TO DO

Allegheny National Forest (Warren). Rivers and creeks rush through this vast hardwood forest, noted for the beauty of its foliage in autumn. The 8,000-acre Hickory Creek Wilderness is popular for hiking.

Bird in Hand (Lancaster County). Visitors to this picturesque Pennsylvania Dutch village can mingle with the Amish and see how they live. Restaurants feature apple dumplings, shoofly pie, and other local specialties.

Delaware Water Gap National Recreation Area (Dingmans Falls). The Delaware River formed this gap through the Kittatinny Ridge, creating an area perfect for water sports, hiking, wildlife watching, and scenic drives.

Gettysburg National Military Park (Gettysburg). The site of the Civil War's bloodiest battle and Lincoln's most famous speech is now a 3,500-acre park with 1,300 gravestones.

Independence National Historical Park (Philadelphia). Take a walk through history: Independence Hall, Carpenters' Hall (site of the First Continental Congress), the First and Second Banks of the U.S., and other 18th-century buildings have been preserved here, as has the Liberty Bell.

Longwood Gardens (Kennett Square). Spectacular gardens, fountains, and conservatories make this one of the world's leading horticultural displays. The gardens are open year-round.

Three Rivers Arts Festival (Pittsburgh). At this 17-day extravaganza, held every June, hundreds of artists from around the country exhibit and sell their work. Events include live musical performances, many by big-name stars.

Valley Forge National Historical Park (Valley Forge). One of the great shrines of the American Revolution, this is the site of the stone house that served as Washington's headquarters and of reconstructions of the huts used by his guard during the winter of 1777 – 78.

Rhode Island

A jewellike corner of New England, steeped in history

The smallest state in the country, and proudly so, Rhode Island measures a modest 47 miles from north to south and only 40 miles from east to west. But given the surprising variety of destinations within its borders — emerald forests, eye-soothing farmland, dynamic cities, spectacular seasides — Rhode Island's compact size is a traveler's blessing, for no one place is ever more than a short drive from any other. It is possible to tour historic city streets in the morning, picnic by a lazy country stream in the afternoon, and stroll beside the moonlit surf in the evening.

PROVIDENCE PLANTATIONS

In northwestern Rhode Island, forests of birch and cedar are dotted with shining lakes and ponds. Country roads pass by sprawling dairy and poultry farms, recalling the early years when outlying towns were called plantations and the state was given the official name State of Rhode Island and Providence Plantations.

In the northeastern part of the state, the Blackstone River courses south to Pawtucket. Here Samuel Slater built the first water-powered cotton mill in 1790, ushering in an industrial revolution that drew legions of immigrants to Rhode Island. Slater himself came from England, where cloth manufacturing secrets were so jealously guarded that textile workers were forbidden to leave the country. To get out, Slater disguised himself as a farmer.

South of Slater's restored mill in Pawtucket lies Rhode Island's cosmopolitan capital, Providence. Roger Williams, who left strictly Puri-

Block Island's admirers have called it the Bermuda of the North. One of the island's most prominent landmarks is Southeast Lighthouse, built in 1873.

The harbor at Warren, off Narragansett Bay, was an important center for whaling, oystering, and shipbuilding in the 19th century.

tan Massachusetts in search of religious freedom, founded the city in 1636, and in the next two centuries it became one of the East Coast's busiest ports. Here flourished the infamous triangular trade — West Indies molasses for New England rum for African slaves.

The Providence of today, though a busy urban center, is filled with reminders of the past. Dozens of elegant 18th-century homes, each with a bronze plaque recording the date it was built and the name of its first owner, are found along Benefit Street and the area surrounding Brown University on College Hill.

"THE OCEAN STATE"

Sweeping from the Atlantic Ocean all the way inland to Providence is Rhode Island's most impressive natural treasure — gigantic Narragansett Bay, which endows the tiny state with a staggering, 400-mile coastline (without the bay the coastline would be only 40 miles long). On the bay are some 35 islands, known by such quaint and quirky names as Hog, Hen, Rabbitt, Patience, Hope, and Despair. The largest is named Rhode Island, aptly enough, but to avoid confusion residents use the island's Indian name, Aquidneck.

On the southern end of Aquidneck lies the celebrated resort town of Newport. Its prim colonial churches, brick squares, and weathered wharves recall the Newport of 200 years ago, when it was an active port and a center for shipbuilding. But in the last century Newport has become a symbol of opulence, with luxurious yachts bobbing at anchor and palatial turn-of-the-century mansions. Called "cottages" by their owners, they have housed such astronomically wealthy Americans as the Astors, Morgans, Dukes, and Vanderbilts.

Off the mainland lies another, more solitary island. A tranquil, treeless place of rolling moors and towering bluffs, Block Island is, except for a few vintage Victorian hotels, refreshingly undeveloped. Only seven miles long, the island — like the state of Rhode Island itself — is both compact and beguiling.

From Cliff-Walk, a seaside footpath in Newport, strollers can steal glimpses of sumptuous mansions built from the Gay Nineties to the Roaring Twenties.

This 200-year-old windmill at Prescott Farm in Middletown still grinds corn.

Rhode Island

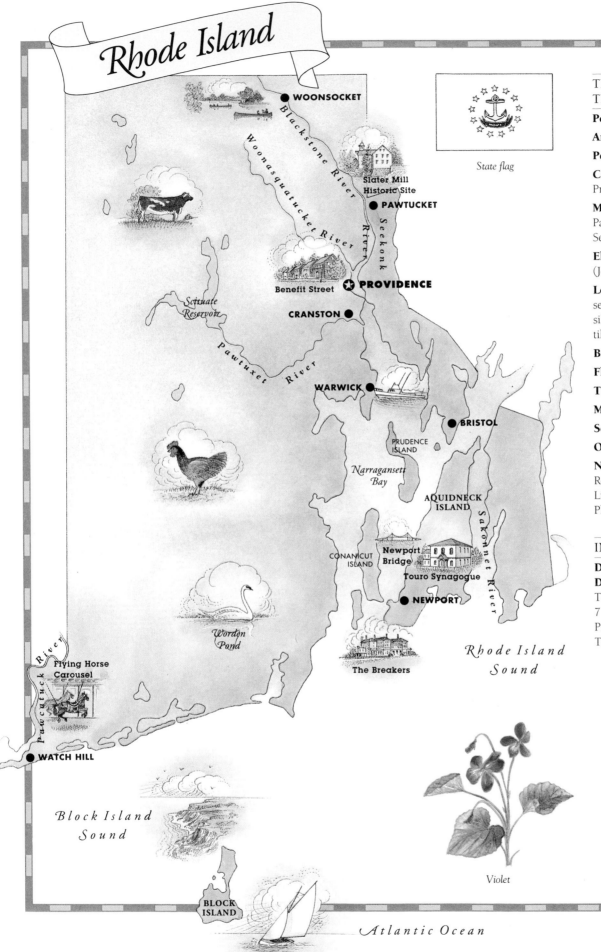

State flag

THE PEOPLE AND THE LAND

Population: 988,600

Area: 1,210 sq. mi.

Population per sq. mi.: 817

Capital and largest city: Providence (pop. 646,800)

Major rivers: Blackstone, Pawcatuck, Pawtuxet, Sakonnet, Seekonk, Woonasquatucket

Elevation: Sea level to 812 ft. (Jerimoth Hill)

Leading industries: Health services, manufacturing (jewelry, silverware, toys, machinery, textiles), ship and boat building

Bird: Rhode Island Red

Flower: Violet

Tree: Red maple

Motto: Hope

Song: "Rhode Island"

Origin of name: Unknown

Nicknames: America's First Resort, Land of Roger Williams, Little Rhody, Ocean State, Plantation State, Smallest State

---

INFORMATION

Department of Economic Development
Tourism Division
7 Jackson Walkway
Providence, RI 02903
Telephone: 401-277-2601

Violet

Rhode Island Red

HISTORICAL HIGHLIGHTS

1524 Giovanni da Verrazzano, sailing on behalf of France, enters Narragansett Bay.

1614 Dutch mariner Adrian Block lands on the island that will bear his name.

1636 Roger Williams founds Providence, the first permanent settlement.

1663 Charles II of England grants Rhode Island a charter.

1772 Colonists protesting trade restrictions burn a British revenue ship, the *Gaspee*.

1774 Rhode Island prohibits importation of slaves.

1776 Rhode Island is the first colony to declare its independence from England.

1790 Rhode Island joins the Union as the 13th state.

1842 Dorr's Rebellion leads to more liberal state constitution.

1938 A devastating hurricane and tidal wave cause more than 250 deaths and about $100 million in property damage.

1969 Newport Bridge links Jamestown and Newport, spanning Narragansett Bay.

1971 The legislature approves a state personal income tax.

1976 Operation Sail sends tall ships to Newport and New York for the Bicentennial.

1980 Voters approve a referendum pledging $87 million to protect Narragansett Bay.

FAMOUS SONS AND DAUGHTERS

George M. Cohan (1878 – 1942). The versatile Broadway entertainer wrote, directed, and produced most of the shows in which he danced, sang, and acted. He wrote such classic songs as "Over There" and "The Yankee Doodle Boy."

Nathanael Greene (1742 – 86). Greene became an important general in the Revolutionary War. A superb strategist, he served as commander in the decisive Carolina campaign.

Anne Hutchinson (1591 – 1643). An outspoken religious leader, Hutchinson helped found present-day Portsmouth, R.I., in 1638 after being banished from the Massachusetts Bay Colony for her dissident views.

Matthew Calbraith Perry (1794 – 1858). In 1854, the distinguished naval officer succeeded in convincing Japan to open its ports to world trade.

Oliver Hazard Perry (1785 – 1819). Like his brother Matthew, Perry had a great naval career. Upon defeating the British in the Battle of Lake Erie, he sent the famous message: "We have met the enemy, and they are ours."

Gilbert Stuart (1755 – 1828). A portrait painter with an elegant style, Stuart is best known for his portraits of George Washington.

Roger Williams (c. 1603 – 83). The founder of Providence and father of Rhode Island, clergyman Williams held strong views on the separation of church and state, which later influenced the framers of the U.S. Constitution.

ODDITIES AND SPECIALTIES

More than 20 percent of the nation's registered historic landmarks are in Rhode Island.

The state capitol's self-supported marble dome is second in size only to that of St. Peter's Basilica in Rome.

Watch Hill claims America's oldest carousel, called the Flying Horse because the horses, hung from chains, swing outward.

Newport's Touro Synagogue, built in 1763, is the country's oldest Jewish house of worship.

Newport is well known for its yachting events, including the Newport-to-Bermuda race and the America's Cup race.

The ledges and sandbars off Block Island have sunk more than 1,000 ships. A long time ago plunderers, hoping to loot cargo, lured vessels toward the rocks by waving lanterns. The wrecks are memorialized by such place-names as Cow Cove, where shipwrecked cows once made their way to shore.

Developed in Little Compton in 1854, the Rhode Island Red was so superior to other chickens both in its egg-laying ability and the quality of its meat that it turned poultry-raising into a major U.S. industry.

The tiny town of Bristol swells to many times its population every Fourth of July, when it hosts the nation's oldest Independence Day parade and celebration, dating back to 1785.

PLACES TO VISIT, THINGS TO DO

Block Island Accessible by ferry, the island is known for its timeless charm, with lovely beaches, cliffs, ponds, and Victorian inns.

Cliff Walk (Newport). Along this three-mile coastal path are a number of opulent mansions, including The Breakers, built by Cornelius Vanderbilt. Several of these palatial homes are open to the public.

Discount shopping Factory outlets, many located in former textile mills, are found in the Blackstone River Valley, where the country's first factory outlet opened in 1954.

Fishing Narragansett Bay teems with striped bass, bluefish, cod, tuna, and a variety of shellfish.

Great Swamp Management Area (next to Worden Pond). In this island-dotted swamp, deer and mute swans live among some 4,000 kinds of plants, including orchids and arctic moss.

Mile of History (Providence). Along Benefit Street are restored 18th- and 19th-century buildings, among them the elegant John Brown House, which contains a magnificent collection of antique furniture.

Slater Mill Historic Site (Pawtucket). Here, on the banks of the powerful Blackstone River, is Samuel Slater's restored cotton mill, along with a museum tracing the development of industrial technology.

South Carolina

*Uplands, lowlands, and a
gracious sense of the past*

South Carolinians like to say that Charleston is the place where the Ashley and Cooper rivers join to form the Atlantic Ocean. The enormous pride embodied in the joke seems oddly incongruous with this quiet Atlantic seaboard state tucked between the mountains of North Carolina and the red clay hills of Georgia. South Carolina's beauty is subtle rather than spectacular, emanating from grassy savannas and shady pinewoods, lonely marshlands and windswept beaches.

PLANTERS AND FARMERS

The English and Barbadian colonists who settled near Charles Town in 1670, and the French Huguenots who arrived a few years later, discovered that the swampy lowlands surrounding them were ideal for rice paddies. Starting with a single bag of Madagascar rice bought from a sea captain in about 1685, the colonists were exporting their own crop by 1690. By 1700 a complex plantation system was established.

Meanwhile, the hilly and forested Piedmont above the lowlands was being settled by arrivals from the northern colonies. Mostly hardscrabble farmers, they resented the airs and influence of the coast-dwelling aristocrats. Conflicts between up-country and low country arose early and persisted even after the state's capital was moved, as a compromise, to Columbia, midway between the two areas. Regional distinctions began to blur only when the cotton craze swept the entire state in the late 1700's. Vast tracts of forest fell to make

With more than 1,000 species of plants, including 250 varieties of azaleas and 900 varieties of camellias, Magnolia Plantation and Gardens near Charleston is in colorful bloom throughout the year.

Stands of gangling palmetto trees proliferate along the boggy shores of South Carolina's many coastal rivers and canals.

way for the new crop. The shot fired on Fort Sumter on April 12, 1861, was aimed at protecting South Carolina's "white gold."

UPLANDS AND LOWLANDS

In the rugged northwestern corner of the state, the Cherokee Foothills Scenic Highway winds close to such impressive sights as craggy Caesar's Head, Table Rock Mountain, and 420-foot Raven Cliff Falls. In boggy Ashmore Tract Heritage Preserve, botanists have found such rare plants as the carnivorous mountain sweet pitcher plant, which grows only in the Carolina highlands. Although the hilly Piedmont region forms the industrial core of the state, the countryside is still pleasantly dotted with lakes, horse farms, golf courses, peach orchards, and fields of soybeans.

To the southeast lies the low country, including the 60-mile sweep of beach known as the Grand Strand; the historic towns of Georgetown, Beaufort, and Charleston; and

the marshy wetlands where Francis Marion, the Swamp Fox, baffled the redcoats during the American Revolution. Here also are the fabled Sea Islands. Hilton Head, with tasteful contemporary homes and 20 golf courses, exudes wealth and leisure. On Daufuskie blacks still preserve the Gullah language and lore of their forebears, early American slaves. On Cape Romain, loggerhead sea turtles crawl up the beaches to lay their eggs.

Charleston, lying in the heart of the coastal lowlands, is a city of infinite charms. Its citizens were alert to its uniqueness so early that in 1929 it became the first city in America to protect its historic district. Today the city has more than 70 buildings predating the American Revolution, 200 built before the War of 1812, and 850 before the Civil War. To walk among these old houses lining the battery along the harbor is to step back into the gracious elegance that rice and cotton created at the mouth of the Ashley and Cooper rivers.

According to an ancient Cherokee legend, flat-topped Table Rock Mountain, above, served as a dining table for a giant chief who sat on a smaller nearby hill called The Stool.

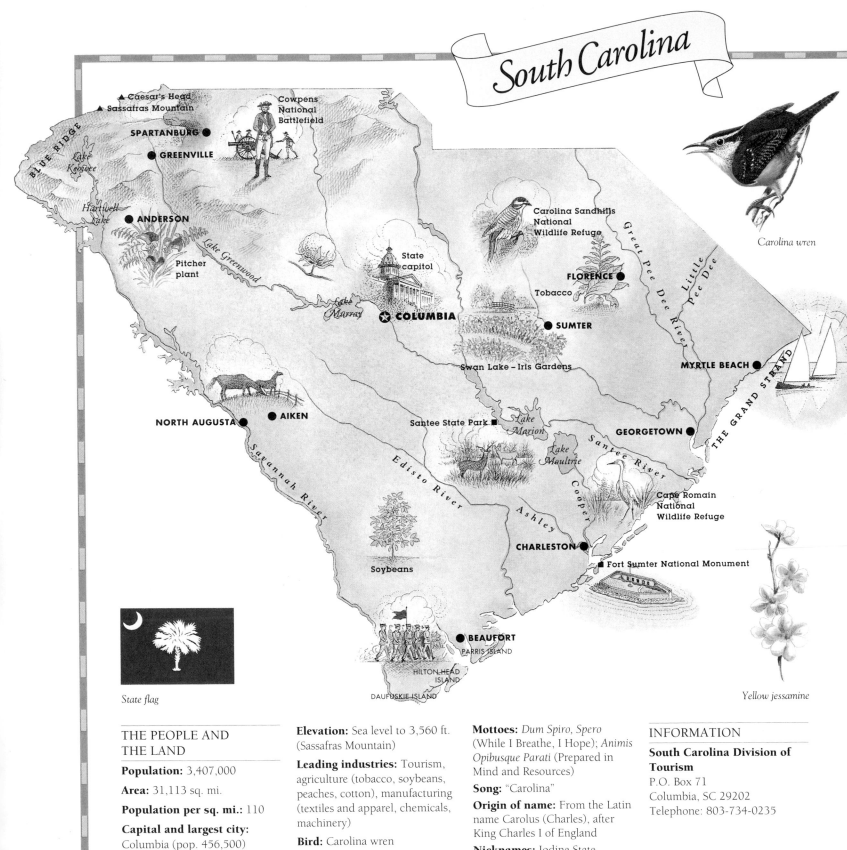

South Carolina

Carolina wren

State flag

Yellow jessamine

▲ Caesar's Head
▲ Sassafras Mountain

SPARTANBURG

Cowpens National Battlefield

GREENVILLE

Blue Ridge

Lake Keowee

Hartwell Lake

ANDERSON

Pitcher plant

Lake Greenwood

Carolina Sandhills National Wildlife Refuge

State capitol

Lake Murray

FLORENCE

Tobacco

Great Pee Dee River

Little Pee Dee

COLUMBIA

SUMTER

Swan Lake – Iris Gardens

MYRTLE BEACH

NORTH AUGUSTA

AIKEN

Santee State Park

Lake Marion

Lake Moultrie

GEORGETOWN

THE GRAND STRAND

Savannah River

Edisto River

Santee River

Cooper

Cape Romain National Wildlife Refuge

Ashley

CHARLESTON

Soybeans

Fort Sumter National Monument

BEAUFORT
PARRIS ISLAND

HILTON HEAD ISLAND

DAUFUSKIE ISLAND

THE PEOPLE AND THE LAND

Population: 3,407,000

Area: 31,113 sq. mi.

Population per sq. mi.: 110

Capital and largest city: Columbia (pop. 456,500)

Major rivers: Ashley, Cooper, Edisto, Great Pee Dee, Little Pee Dee, Santee, Savannah

Elevation: Sea level to 3,560 ft. (Sassafras Mountain)

Leading industries: Tourism, agriculture (tobacco, soybeans, peaches, cotton), manufacturing (textiles and apparel, chemicals, machinery)

Bird: Carolina wren

Flower: Yellow jessamine

Tree: Palmetto

Mottoes: *Dum Spiro, Spero* (While I Breathe, I Hope); *Animis Opibusque Parati* (Prepared in Mind and Resources)

Song: "Carolina"

Origin of name: From the Latin name Carolus (Charles), after King Charles I of England

Nicknames: Iodine State, Keystone of the South Atlantic Seaboard, Palmetto State, Rice State, Swamp State

INFORMATION

South Carolina Division of Tourism
P.O. Box 71
Columbia, SC 29202
Telephone: 803-734-0235

HISTORICAL HIGHLIGHTS

1526 Spanish adventurer Lucas Vásquez de Ayllón establishes a short-lived settlement.

1663 English king Charles II grants region to eight lords proprietors for colonization.

1670 Colonists from England and Barbados settle near present-day Charleston.

1729 After a rebellion against the proprietors, the Carolinas become a British royal province.

1780 – 81 Defeat of loyalist troops at battles of Kings Mountain and Cowpens are turning points in American Revolution.

1788 South Carolina joins Union as eighth state.

1790 State capital is moved from Charleston to Columbia to ease tension between low-country and up-country inhabitants.

1822 Slave uprising suppressed.

1832 State legislature nullifies a federally imposed tariff, leading to a crisis over states' rights.

1860 South Carolina is first state to secede from Union.

1861 Confederate attack on Fort Sumter begins Civil War.

1865 Union troops led by Gen. William Tecumseh Sherman burn Columbia.

1868 South Carolina is readmitted to Union.

1877 Federal troops leave state as Reconstruction ends.

1886 Earthquake rocks Charleston, killing 92 people.

1895 State revises constitution, disenfranchising most blacks by denying them right to vote in Democratic Party primaries.

1921 Boll weevil destroys cotton crop, forcing diversification.

1947 Federal court ruling upholds blacks' right to vote in Democratic Party primaries.

1951 Atomic Energy Commission builds Savannah River Plant near Aiken to refine plutonium.

1964 Desegregation of public schools begins.

1989 Hurricane Hugo devastates coastal area.

FAMOUS SONS AND DAUGHTERS

Bernard Baruch (1870 – 1965). Born in Camden, Baruch made a fortune on Wall Street. Later he served as an adviser to every president from Wilson to Eisenhower.

John C. Calhoun (1782 – 1850).

Secretary of war, U.S. vice president (1825 – 32) and later a powerful U.S. senator, Calhoun was an eloquent and energetic defender of states' rights.

Althea Gibson (1927 –). Gibson was the first black to become an international tennis champion, winning at Wimbledon in 1957 and 1958. After retiring, she became a professional golfer.

Strom Thurmond (1902 –). Governor of South Carolina from 1947 to 1951, Thurmond has been a U.S. senator since 1955. He ran for president in 1948 as a states' rights democrat.

Charles H. Townes (1915 –). Townes's work in maser and laser research earned him a share of the 1964 Nobel Prize in physics.

ODDITIES AND SPECIALTIES

Nearly all the Marine Corps recruits in the eastern U.S. are trained at Parris Island.

The first Reform Jewish congregation in America was established at Charleston in 1824.

The poinsettia gets it name from South Carolinian Joel Poinsett, who discovered the flower in Mexico while serving as U.S. ambassador there.

DuBose Heyward and George Gershwin based their opera *Porgy and Bess* on Heyward's novel *Porgy,* which is set in Charleston.

Among the state's culinary delights is she-crab soup, made with white crabmeat and roe.

Although South Carolina's most famous dance may be the Charleston, its best-loved is the shag. A kind of swing dance step dating back to the 1930's, the shag became the state's official dance in 1984.

PLACES TO VISIT, THINGS TO DO

Aiken Three historic districts preserve the opulent architecture and atmosphere of Aiken in the 1890's, when it was a winter colony for wealthy northerners. This is the heart of South Carolina's horse-breeding country.

Cape Romain National Wildlife Refuge (Awendaw). Stretching over three islands, this 35,000-acre refuge of marshes and beaches attracts wintering waterfowl and shorebirds.

Carolina Sandhills National Wildlife Refuge (McBee). These wooded hills protect a large population of the endangered red-cockaded woodpecker.

Gardens (Charleston area). *Cypress Gardens* offers a unique blend of cypress trees, bright flowers, and lagoons. *Magnolia Plantation and Gardens* features masses of azaleas and camellias, and boat tours through a 125-acre wildlife refuge. *Middleton Place,* an 18th-century plantation, includes what may be the nation's oldest landscaped gardens.

Myrtle Beach Besides swimming and fishing, this seaside resort offers 60 golf courses.

Santee State Park (Santee). With cottages, campsites, and nature trails, this is an ideal base from which to explore Lake Marion and Lake Moultrie. Santee National Wildlife Refuge is a short drive away.

Savannah River Scenic Highway This scenic route wends its way for more than 100 miles along the Savannah River north of Augusta, Georgia.

Swan Lake – Iris Gardens (Sumter). Six of the world's eight species of swans have been gathered here on a 45-acre lake surrounded by a 150-acre garden planted with 25 varieties of irises.

South Dakota

Black Hills, Badlands, and wide open spaces

South Dakota is a land of bewildering variety and breathtaking extremes. Here are limitless expanses of space and very few people, sweeping treeless plains and steep forested mountains, sunny skies and torrential rains, rich farmland and uninhabitable badlands, scorching heat and bone-chilling cold, soothing silence and historic strife.

Writers rhapsodize about South Dakota's vastness. They speak of "the smell of distance," "the pull of horizon," and the "great quietness broken only by the wind." Even so, this giant land — the size of Ohio and Indiana combined — is so thinly populated that cattle outnumber people five to one.

In South Dakota the sun shines brightly and cheerfully almost every day; yet monstrous thunderstorms can appear out of nowhere, hammering the land unmercifully. In summer 100-degree temperatures are not uncommon, but in winter the thermometer plunges well below zero, ushering in ground-splitting frosts and arctic blizzards.

EAST AND WEST OF THE MISSOURI RIVER

Rectangular South Dakota is sliced through the middle by the mighty Missouri River, which makes its way through the state from north to south for some 550 miles. From the air the river looks like a jagged blue scar, shimmering and zigzagging across the land. No longer the much-feared, rampaging Big Muddy of earlier times, the Missouri — thanks to its many modern dams — is now a series of long, sinuous reservoirs. Called the Great Lakes

The otherworldly landscape of Badlands National Park is composed of sedimentary rock that has been eroded by wind, rain, and frost for some 35 million years.

In the Black Hills, purple-pink dame's rockets carpet the ground under cottonwood trees, whose leaves Sioux children once made into toy tepees.

AMERICA: LAND OF BEAUTY AND SPLENDOR

of South Dakota, they have transformed the river into a mecca for fishing and boating.

The river also draws droves of bird watchers. They come to steal glimpses of cormorants, tundra swans, great blue herons, sandhill cranes, red-tailed hawks, and other regional and migrating birds. Plant life thrives near the river too. The surrounding hills and plains bloom with black-eyed Susans, prairie buttercups, and the pasqueflower, South Dakota's purplish, fur-petaled state flower.

George Fitch, a 19th-century humorist, wrote that the Missouri "rearranges geography" and "dabbles in real estate." That was before the age of dams, when erosion and flooding drastically altered both the form and value of the land. Still, the great river does cut the state into two distinct halves. To the east are low hills, small lakes, and endless stretches of fertile cropland — the legacy of glaciers — where wheat, corn, oats, and hogs are raised. Called East River, this half of the state is where 70 percent of South Dakotans live — in Sioux Falls, Watertown, Huron, and Aberdeen, and on the farms in between.

The land west of the river (or West River), untouched by the mammoth glaciers that bulldozed the east, is laced with deep canyons, ragged badlands, cathedrallike mountains, and rolling plains. Buttes rise 600 feet above the green grasslands, their burnt red contours set against the bright blue sky. Here legions of buffalo once grazed, blackening the land as far as the eye could see.

The western half of South Dakota is steeped in frontier history. In the early days, intrepid explorers and fur traders fought the elements, and the 19th century saw frenzied gold rushes and bloody battles with the proud Sioux, who defended their territory against the encroaching white man. Today vast Indian reservations and sprawling cattle ranches share the land.

LANDS BOTH BAD AND BEAUTIFUL

To the southwest are the hauntingly beautiful Badlands. Here, over millions of years, wind, rain, snow, and ice have carved out an eerie, lifeless moonscape of gorges, mesas, ridges, pyramids, knobs, and spires. As the sun moves across the sky, the myriad formations change

Buffalo still roam in Custer State Park, where thunder from the sky sometimes seems to echo the thundering of the great herds that stampeded here a century ago. Sharing the grassy slopes today are deer, elk, antelope, and an occasional coyote.

The yellow-headed blackbird nests in freshwater marshes and nearby fields.

A dusting of snow on granite boulders adds a bracing note to the serenity of Sylvan Lake in the Black Hills. In the 1920's sculptor Gutzon Borglum considered the area as a possible site for the sculptures that now adorn Mount Rushmore.

their hues from pastel pinks and tans to deep reds and browns. At dusk they loom from the earth like phantoms in a land bewitched.

So forbidding was this geological obstacle course, where travel was aggravatingly slow and water dangerously scarce, that the Sioux called it *mako sica* ("bad land"), and wary French trappers dubbed the region *les mauvaises terres à traverser* ("bad lands to travel across"). The name was kept by modern geologists, who view the Badlands as examples of erosion gone berserk.

Skirting the state's western border are the Black Hills, so named by the Sioux because they look dark and somber when viewed from the distant plains. In the 1870's the stampede for gold saw white men by the thousands invade the Black Hills, which the Sioux regarded as the sacred home of the Great Spirit.

The Sioux rose in outrage, ushering in the 15-year-long Indian wars. They ended in 1890 with the death of some 200 Indians, shot by U.S. troops near Wounded Knee Creek.

Today travelers flock to the scenic Black Hills — which are actually mountains towering to heights of up to 7,200 feet — for recreation. The land below contains miles of mazelike caves, and the hills themselves are blanketed with pine and spruce trees and ornamented with spectacular outcrops.

While the hand of nature has sculpted dizzying granite pinnacles atop these impressive mountains, the hand of man has carved gigantic presidential faces into the side of Mount Rushmore. The many-faceted Black Hills, like the rest of South Dakota, make it abundantly clear why the state has been nicknamed the Land of Infinite Variety.

THE FACES AT THE END OF THE TUNNEL

One of the lesser known man-made wonders of the Black Hills is Iron Mountain Road. This spiraling, 17-mile route connects Custer State Park with Mount Rushmore National Memorial — where the faces of George Washington, Thomas Jefferson, Theodore Roosevelt, and Abraham Lincoln are immortalized, on a colossal scale, in stone.

In the early 1930's, Peter Norbeck, a U.S. senator and former South Dakota governor, wanted to build a scenic road from the park across 5,445-foot Iron Mountain to Mount Rushmore. Setting out on horseback to plot the road, Norbeck was struck with a remarkable idea. He envisioned the looping road constructed in such a way that motorists traveling through any one of its short tunnels would see Mount Rushmore in the distance, perfectly framed by the opening at the other end.

Although most engineers dismissed the idea as impossible, one pondered the challenge and confidently told Norbeck: "With enough dynamite, anything is possible." So blast away they did.

For decades now, Iron Mountain Road has gracefully spiraled its way through the natural splendor of the Black Hills. Like a great painting that is enhanced by a carefully chosen frame, magnificent Mount Rushmore, when viewed through any one of the three granite tunnels that so neatly frame it, is an unmistakable masterpiece.

The eerie solitude of Badlands National Park is underscored by a lone juniper tree that has somehow managed to carve out a niche in this hostile environment. The rocky mounds, though they look solid enough, are being eroded at a rate of an inch or more per year.

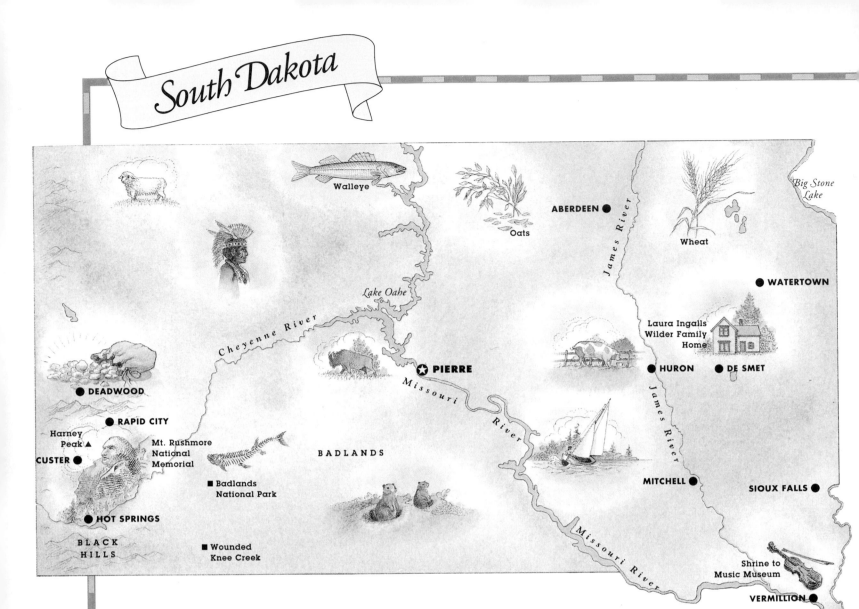

South Dakota

Big Stone Lake

Walleye

Oats

ABERDEEN ●

Wheat

James River

● **WATERTOWN**

Lake Oahe

Cheyenne River

Laura Ingalls Wilder Family Home

⭐ **PIERRE**

Missouri River

● **HURON**   ● **DE SMET**

● **DEADWOOD**

James River

● **RAPID CITY**

Harney Peak ▲

Mt. Rushmore National Memorial

CUSTER ●

BADLANDS

■ Badlands National Park

MITCHELL ●

SIOUX FALLS ●

● **HOT SPRINGS**

BLACK HILLS

■ Wounded Knee Creek

Missouri River

Shrine to Music Museum

VERMILLION ●

THE PEOPLE AND THE LAND

Population: 693,300

Area: 77,116 sq. mi.

Population per sq. mi.: 9

Capital: Pierre (pop. 14,000)

Largest city: Sioux Falls (pop. 128,000)

Major rivers: Cheyenne, James, Missouri

Elevation: 962 ft. (Big Stone Lake) to 7,242 ft. (Harney Peak)

Leading industries: Agriculture (cattle, corn, wheat), gold mining, food processing

Bird: Ring-necked pheasant

Flower: Pasqueflower

Tree: Black Hills spruce

Motto: Under God the People Rule

Song: "Hail, South Dakota"

Origin of name: From the Sioux word for friends or allies

Nicknames: Artesian State, Blizzard State, Coyote State, Land of Infinite Variety, Sunshine State

INFORMATION

South Dakota Department of Tourism
711 East Wells Avenue
Pierre, SD 57501-3369
Telephone: 800-843-1930

State flag

Pasqueflower

Ring-necked pheasant

HISTORICAL HIGHLIGHTS

1743 François and Louis-Joseph La Vérendrye are first white men to explore South Dakota.

1803 U.S. acquires most of Dakota region from the French with the Louisiana Purchase.

1809 St. Louis Fur Company begins trade in the upper Missouri valley.

1831 The *Yellowstone*, the first steamboat on the upper Missouri River, reaches banks of present-day Fort Pierre.

1858 Yankton Sioux cede vast lands to U.S.

1861 Congress establishes the Dakota Territory.

1874 Gold is discovered in the Black Hills.

1877 Sioux are forced to surrender the Black Hills.

1878 A land rush initiates Great Dakota Boom.

1889 South Dakota joins Union as 40th state.

1890 Federal troops kill some 200 Sioux at Wounded Knee Creek, ending the Indian wars.

1927 Gutzon Borglum begins carving Mt. Rushmore National Memorial.

1944 The Flood Control Act authorizes dam construction on Missouri River.

1963 Minuteman intercontinental ballistic missiles are positioned at town of Wall.

1972 Flooding causes more than 200 deaths in Rapid City area.

1973 American Indian Movement members and sympathizers occupy village of Wounded Knee for 71 days.

1980 U.S. Supreme Court orders federal government to pay Sioux tribes more than $205 million to compensate for 1877 forced surrender of Black Hills.

FAMOUS SONS AND DAUGHTERS

Crazy Horse (c.1840 – 77). This Oglala Sioux chief led his people against white encroachment in the Black Hills.

Gall (c.1840 – 94). An ally of Sitting Bull at the Battle of Little Bighorn, this Sioux chief later helped improve relations between his people and whites.

Hallie Flanagan (1890 – 1969). During the 1930's Flanagan headed the Federal Theatre Project of the Works Progress Administration. She staged over 1,000 productions nationwide.

Ernest O. Lawrence (1901 – 58). Lawrence won the 1939 Nobel Prize in physics for his atomic research, including the development of the cyclotron.

George McGovern (1922 –). McGovern represented South Dakota in the U.S. House (1958 – 62) and Senate (1962 – 80). In 1972 he ran for president against Richard Nixon.

Sitting Bull (c.1834 – 90).

Born on the Grand River, Sitting Bull became an esteemed Hunkpapa Sioux chief and medicine man. His refusal to move to a reservation led to the Battle of Little Bighorn, an important victory for the Sioux and the scene of Custer's last stand.

ODDITIES AND SPECIALTIES

Thousands of bushels of corn make up the murals, redone annually, on the Corn Palace in Mitchell. Moorish domes and minarets add to the building's whimsical appearance.

De Smet, known as the Little Town on the Prairie, was the home of Laura Ingalls Wilder in the 1880's. Her children's books tell of life on the Great Plains.

Gold lured such colorful Old West figures as Wild Bill Hickok, Calamity Jane, and Poker Alice to the mining town of Deadwood. In 1876, while holding what has since been called the "deadman's hand" of aces and eights, Hickok was killed by Jack "Crooked Nose" McCall in Deadwood's Saloon No. 10.

The Badlands have yielded a wealth of fossils, including those of rhinoceroses and camels.

Beginning in 1927, sculptor Gutzon Borglum labored for 14 years to create the images of four presidents on Mt. Rushmore. He planned the sculptures to extend to the waists but died before they were completed.

Sculptor Korcazk Ziolkowski worked from 1948 until his death in 1982 to fashion an equestrian image of Crazy Horse out of a 600-foot-high mountain near Mt. Rushmore. Being completed by his family, the work will feature an outstretched arm the length of a football field and a horse's head 22 stories high.

South Dakota has its own state jewelry, Black Hills gold. It combines rose, green, and yellow gold in grapes-and-leaves designs.

PLACES TO VISIT, THINGS TO DO

Badlands National Park (Interior). Etched by erosion, the landscape here is filled with thousands of bizarre and beautiful rock formations.

Custer State Park (Custer). One of the world's largest herds of buffalo roam this park in the forested Black Hills, where Needles Highway winds around giant granite pinnacles.

Jewel Cave National Monument (Custer). The jewels within this labyrinthine cavern are calcite crystals that gleam from its walls and ceiling.

Shrine to Music Museum (Vermillion). On view are more than 3,000 instruments, spanning some five millennia.

Walleye fishing The Missouri River and the many glacial lakes in the eastern half of the state teem with this popular fish.

Wind Cave National Park (Hot Springs). Odd formations called boxwork, frostwork, and popcorn adorn the 53-mile maze of passageways in Wind Cave.

Tennessee

Misty mountains, music, and the Mississippi

Road signs at the Tennessee border once welcomed puzzled visitors to the "Three States of Tennessee," and residents, when asked where they hail from, still specify East, Middle, or West Tennessee. The Tennessee flag shows three stars enclosed within a circle, representing the three Tennessees, and even the state constitution recognizes what it calls "three grand divisions." Stretching from the craggy Appalachian Mountains to the banks of the Mississippi River, Tennessee does, in fact, encompass three distinctly different regions.

THE SPIRIT OF THE MOUNTAINS

The first East Tennesseans settled isolated mountain ridges in the mid-1700's. They labored tirelessly to hew beams for their homes, clear the land for crops, and preserve foods for winter — often entertaining themselves with songs and fiddle music whose roots go back to the British Isles. Their self-sufficiency, passed down from one generation to the next, continues today. According to one Smoky Mountain dweller, "Our land produces everything we need except sugar, soda, coffee, and salt."

The natural beauty of Great Smoky Mountains National Park attracts millions of visitors each year. Late in spring, rhododendron and mountain laurel blossoms adorn the mountainsides with a show of red and pink, and in autumn, a fiery brilliance sweeps south along the undulating peaks. Hovering over the landscape year-round is a bluish haze — created by moisture and oils released by trees — that inspired the names of both the Blue Ridge and the Smoky Mountains.

The golden meadows of Percy Warner Park look decidedly rural but are not far from downtown Nashville.

Atop Chattanooga's Lookout Mountain, a Civil War cannon looms over the Tennessee River.

Cades Cove, in the Great Smoky Mountains, was a thriving farm community in the 1800's.

WALKING HORSES AND TWO-STEP TUNES

In Middle Tennessee the land rises and falls at a gentler pace. The Cumberland River, which meanders through the center of the state, once served as a highway through the wilderness. It brought the first settlers to the site of present-day Nashville on Christmas Day, 1779.

Today the city of Nashville is a cosmopolitan center where universities and financial institutions mingle with the machinery of state government. The city owes its world renown, however, not to the progress on which it

prides itself, but to the earthy sounds of country music. On the six city blocks known as Music Row, stars and would-be stars record their songs, and in clubs throughout the city country musicians showcase their talent while fans tap their feet or dance the two-step. The largest and most venerable of Nashville's music halls is, of course, the Grand Ole Opry, now a part of an amusement park. Situated downtown is Ryman Auditorium, the Grand Ole Opry's former home. For decades, country music was broadcast nationwide from its

battered wooden stage, and the building has since become a virtual shrine.

Just south of Nashville, back roads make their way through rolling bluegrass country, often skirting white-columned, antebellum mansions. Farther south, near Wartrace and Shelbyville, long, low stables and white-fenced pastures mark what is known as Tennessee walking horse country.

In the late 19th century, farmers in the area, who spent long hours on horseback overseeing their crops, prized those mounts that

This lush, hazy scene, showing a country pond south of Nashville, typifies midsummer in Middle Tennessee. Nearby are sprawling tobacco farms and the genteel old town of Franklin.

Tub Mill, near Gatlinburg, is one of the stops on a five-mile nature trail that winds through a dense Smoky Mountain forest in East Tennessee.

GIFT OF THE TREMBLING EARTH

The tremors began in December 1811. For weeks the earth shook, spewing out plumes of sulfurous smoke. Then, on February 7, 1812, a cataclysmic earthquake totally rearranged the northwest corner of Tennessee. The cottonwood and cypress forests along the Mississippi River collapsed like a badly baked cake, falling some 20 feet below their original level. Convulsed by monstrous waves, the Father of Rivers surged backward to fill the new void and formed a vast, shallow lake.

According to local lore, the Chickasaw Indians who lived nearby named the lake Reelfoot after one of their chiefs. Covering about 14,500 acres of sunken forestland, Reelfoot Lake is now a haven for wildlife. More than four dozen kinds of fish swim among the submerged limbs and trunks of trees, and their sheer quantity attracts legions of migrating birds.

Among the fish-loving fowl are a large population of bald eagles, who in turn attract thousands of bird watchers to the lake. Fishermen use specially designed "stump-jumper" boats to maneuver through the shallow water. When the shy eagles dare to come close enough, the anglers toss them fish, sharing with these majestic visitors the bounty of Reelfoot Lake.

---

offered the gentlest ride. With this in mind, they selectively bred animals with smooth gaits. The result was a new breed, the Tennessee walking horse, known for its rhythmic, high-stepping walk.

COTTON AND THE BLUES

In West Tennessee, the land is flat and the soil is rich. The lavishly abundant topsoil extends to a depth of 14 feet, creating prime farmland. From the early 1800's, cotton was the mainstay both of West Tennessee's strong plantation culture and of the emerging city of Memphis, which land speculators laid out on bluffs overlooking the Mississippi. The name Memphis, taken from the ancient Egyptian city on the Nile, was the inspiration of one of the town's founders — future president Andrew Jackson.

While most of West Tennessee remains serenely agricultural, Memphis is one of the South's busiest ports and commercial centers. It is also the city where W. C. Handy gave voice to that unique and influential brand of American music known as the blues. From Beale Street, the blues surged downriver to New Orleans, upriver to St. Louis and Chicago, and thence around the world.

The bittersweet sound of the Memphis blues is a far cry from both the foot-tapping country music of Nashville and the old-time mountain music of the Great Smokies. But these three musical traditions, each with its own distinctive character, reflect the deep-rooted differences in history, culture, and geography that set apart the three states of Tennessee.

A veil of mist hovers over the purple slopes of the Great Smoky Mountains. Geologists believe these peaks, 16 of which soar above 6,000 feet, are the oldest in North America.

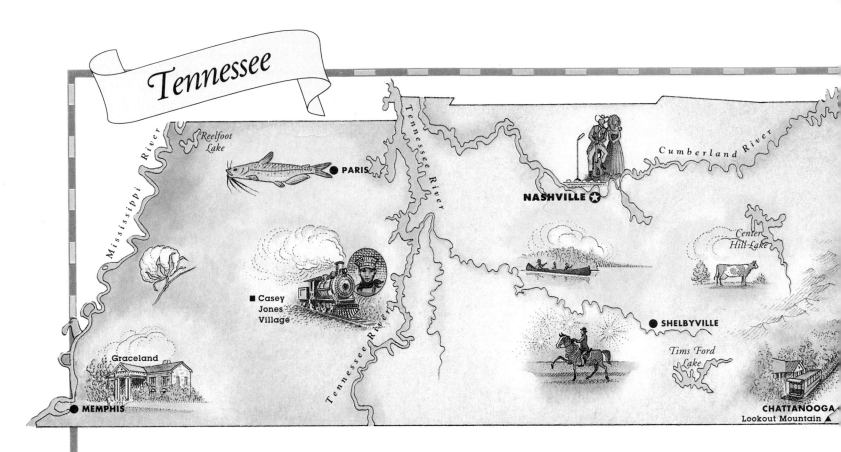

Tennessee

HISTORICAL HIGHLIGHTS

1540 Hernando de Soto leads Spanish party in raid on Indian villages in Tennessee River valley.

1682 La Salle claims region for king of France.

1763 France cedes land east of Mississippi River to Great Britain.

1772 Settlers form a government, calling it Watauga Association.

1784 East Tennessee settlers establish State of Franklin, which lasted only until 1789.

1796 Tennessee enters Union as 16th state.

1818 U.S. buys West Tennessee from the Chickasaw Indians.

1838 The Cherokees are forced out of Tennessee, taking the Trail of Tears to Oklahoma.

1861 Tennessee secedes from Union, the last state to do so.

1866 Tennessee is first state to be readmitted to Union.

1878 Yellow fever epidemic causes death of more than 5,000 Memphis residents.

1925 The famous Monkey Trial, testing the teaching of evolution in schools, is held in Dayton.

1933 Congress creates Tennessee Valley Authority.

1942 The federal government builds atomic energy research plant at Oak Ridge.

1968 Martin Luther King, Jr., is assassinated in Memphis.

1982 Knoxville World Fair opens on May 1.

1985 Tennessee-Tombigbee Waterway links Tennessee River to Gulf of Mexico.

FAMOUS SONS AND DAUGHTERS

James Agee (1909 – 55). Born in Knoxville, the celebrated writer was best known for his book on southern tenant farmers, *Let Us Now Praise Famous Men,* and for the novel *A Death in the Family.* Published after his death, the novel was awarded the 1957 Pulitzer Prize for fiction.

Eddy Arnold (1918 –). The popular singer known as the Tennessee Plowboy gained a wide audience for country music by performing on radio and television. Over the years he has sold some 85 million records.

Davy Crockett (1786 – 1836).

A legendary frontiersman and Indian fighter, Crockett served three terms in the U.S. House of Representatives. He was killed in Texas, defending the Alamo.

Andrew Jackson (1767 – 1845). The son of poor immigrants, Jackson became a lawyer, land-owner, general, and the seventh president of the U.S.

Andrew Johnson (1808 – 75). Johnson became president after Lincoln was assassinated. His treatment of the South, which some thought too lenient, brought about his impeachment, but he was quickly acquitted.

Estes Kefauver (1903 – 63). A Chattanooga lawyer, Kefauver represented Tennessee in both houses of Congress. As a senator he investigated crime, and in 1956 became Adlai Stevenson's presidential running mate.

Grace Moore (1901 – 47). Moore, born in Slabtown, had a beautiful soprano voice that took her from musical comedy to opera to film. She died in a plane crash in Denmark.

James K. Polk (1795 – 1849). Extremely hardworking, the 11th U.S. president accomplished all of his stated goals, including the acquisition of California.

Sequoya (c.1760 – 1843). This highly esteemed Cherokee developed an alphabet and a written language for his tribe. The giant sequoia tree is named for him.

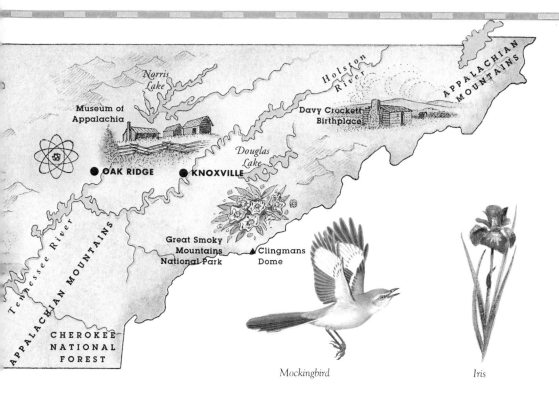

State flag

Mockingbird

Iris

Alvin York (1887 – 1964). "Sergeant York" grew up on a Tennessee farm. A conscientious objector at first, he later became a World War I hero, earning the highest honors for his bravery.

ODDITIES AND SPECIALTIES

The ramp, which grows in the foothills of the Appalachian Mountains, has been called the world's "vilest-smelling, sweetest-tasting" vegetable. The town of Cosby celebrates the onionlike delicacy with an annual festival.

Kenton, in western Tennessee, is home to a rare colony of white squirrels, which are in fact albino gray squirrels.

Paris, Tenn., claims that its annual feast — of over 8,500 pounds of catfish — is the "World's Largest Fish Fry."

Casey Jones, the railroad engineer who inspired the well-known song, was born in Jackson. Seeing that a collision was imminent, Jones remained on his train rather than jump. He saved lives by slowing down the train, which reduced the impact of the crash, though he himself died.

A full-scale replica of the Greek Parthenon can be seen in Nashville, the "Athens of the South." Built in 1897 for the Tennessee Centennial Exhibition, today it houses an art museum.

PLACES TO VISIT, THINGS TO DO

Belle Meade (Nashville). Renowned in the 1800's for the breeding of Thoroughbred horses, this 5,300-acre plantation was one of the Old South's finest.

Cherokee National Forest (headquarters at Cleveland). Some 500 miles of trails, spanning 10 counties, lead hikers through the rugged Appalachians.

Graceland (Memphis). Elvis Presley's estate, open to the public, includes the singer's mansion, memorabilia, and grave.

Grand Ole Opry (Nashville). Begun as a radio show in the 1920's, the Grand Ole Opry became the nation's most venerable showcase for country music. It is now located in Opryland USA.

Great Smoky Mountains National Park (headquarters at Gatlinburg). Evergreen-scented peaks and abundant wildlife attract legions of visitors to this beautiful 520,000-acre park.

Lookout Mountain (Chattanooga). Aptly named, this promontory offers a sweeping view of Moccasin Bend on the Tennessee River. Visitors can take a steep ride to the summit on the Incline Railway.

Museum of Appalachia (Norris). This replica of a pioneer village features some 30 buildings, including a smokehouse, corn mill, church, and loom house.

THE PEOPLE AND THE LAND

Population: 4,877,200

Area: 42,144 sq. mi.

Population per sq. mi.: 116

Capital and largest city: Nashville (pop. 985,100)

Major rivers: Cumberland, Mississippi, Tennessee

Elevation: 182 ft. (Mississippi River) to 6,643 ft. (Clingmans Dome)

Leading industries: Wholesale and retail trade, community and personal services, chemical manufacturing, food products (dairy and produce), machinery

Bird: Mockingbird

Flower: Iris

Tree: Tulip poplar

Motto: Agriculture and Commerce

Song: The state has five official songs, including "The Tennessee Waltz"

Origin of name: From the Cherokee word *tanasi*, referring to a village and a river of the same name

Nicknames: Big Bend State, Mother of Southwestern Statesmen, Volunteer State

INFORMATION

Department of Tourist Development
P.O. Box 23170
Nashville, TN 37202
Telephone: 615-741-2158

Texas

The giant state that was once a nation

Texas encompasses so many regions that it might as well be a country — and it once was. As a sovereign nation after its separation from Mexico in 1836, Texas was unique among territories admitted to the Union. Also unique was the agreement that it negotiated with the United States: a promise that Texas can, if it chooses, form as many as five new states within its borders.

It is unlikely that the Lone Star State will ever break up into smaller units. But if it were to do so, no one who believes in natural boundaries would be surprised. Beyond the Texas of the popular imagination — endless flat plains peopled with cowboys and oilmen — lie dense forests, craggy hills, white sand beaches, silent deserts, and even the southern tip of the Rocky Mountains.

THE SHEER SIZE OF IT

"Big," the Texan's world-famous brag, is no exaggeration. Texas has two time zones and takes up one-twelfth of the contiguous United States. Its coast on the Gulf of Mexico, lined with resorts like those on Galveston and Padre islands, is the third-longest of any state's, after Florida and California.

The sheer size of Texas explains not only its range of landscapes but also its diversity of plant and animal life. The state supports more than 5,000 species of flowering plants and 100 kinds of cacti. It is also home to mountain lions, ocelots, coyotes, prairie dogs, and two of nature's stranger creatures — the horned toad and the armadillo.

In Big Bend National Park, prickly pears and scrub grass glisten in the wake of a rare frost storm. Rising from the mist are the Chisos Mountains.

The leaves of an agave fall into shadow as the rays of the setting sun strike Lost Mine Peak (left) and Casa Grande (far right) in Big Bend National Park.

The human population is varied as well. Some 26 percent of the state's residents are Hispanic in origin, and many cities are virtually bilingual. This long-standing cultural mix goes by the name of Tex-Mex, and bears fruit in everything from the state's fiery-hot cooking to the Spanish-style architecture of the modern suburbs. But Texans are still Texans: the big event in most small towns remains the annual rodeo or quarter horse show, no matter what language the proceedings are conducted in. And an enduring fondness for cowboy boots, wide-brimmed Stetsons, and pickup trucks seems to cross all ethnic lines.

EAST TEXAS, DEEP SOUTH

White settlement in Texas took hold in the fertile valleys of the Brazos and Colorado rivers, with the influx of Stephen F. Austin's Old Three Hundred — Anglo-Americans allowed in by the Mexican government in 1821. Most were farmers, tilling the rich river bottoms and establishing lucrative cotton plantations.

Cotton is still a mainstay of the Texas economy, blanketing much of the flat black land in the eastern half of the state. Interspersed with fields of alfalfa and sweet potatoes, cotton fields stretch right up to the dense Piney Woods along the Louisiana border, an area where the main industry is logging.

With its forests and farmland, East Texas has more in common with the Deep South than it does with the Southwest. Even bayous and bald cypresses are found within the Piney Woods — particularly at Caddo Lake and farther south, in the Big Thicket.

Until this century, the tangle of trees and underbrush in the swamps of the Big Thicket was virtually impenetrable. Three million acres in size before man began to whittle away at it, the thicket is now considerably smaller. But it remains one of the state's environmental treasures — a biological crossroads where eastern forests intertwine with southeastern swamp plants, southwestern desert flora, and subtropical species from Mexico.

Ushering in the Texas spring, a thick carpet of bluebonnets and Indian paintbrushes blooms on a Hill Country slope.

Deer abound in the Piney Woods of East Texas.

A crop duster flies low over an emerald green rice field on the Gulf Coast. Texas ranks as one of the nation's largest rice producers.

THE WEST'S "BARKING SQUIRRELS"

Prairie dogs — actually members of the squirrel family — were given their fanciful name by early explorers, who thought their barks sounded more canine than rodentlike. Scientists later called them *Cynomys*, or "dog mouse," a term that reflects both their voice and appearance.

Prairie dogs inhabit shortgrass prairies in the western half of the continent, including the flat grasslands of the Texas panhandle and the arid grazing lands farther south. Because the creatures are a favorite prey of coyotes, as well as hawks and other raptors, they dig their burrows in areas where the grass is low and they can more easily see their predators approaching. A small mound constructed at the mouth of each tunnel provides an elevated vantage point for the prairie dog's characteristic upright lookout stance.

Prairie dog "towns" throughout the West once held huge populations. The Lewis and Clark expedition in the early 19th century recorded that it had found the animals "in infinite numbers." Like the bison that shared the plains, the prairie dog suffered as the land was fenced and plowed. Cattle ranchers saw them as competing with their livestock for forage, and countless millions of prairie dogs were destroyed.

Still, these little barking squirrels survive today in Texas and points west, especially at preserves like the Muleshoe National Wildlife Refuge, where they remain safe from human interference.

Another distinct region exists in south-central Texas. After the flatness of East Texas, the rough-hewn beauty of this part of the state, called the Hill Country, comes as a surprise. Rocky, juniper-cloaked hills are cut through by clear green rivers. Along the roadsides, deer leap cedar-rail fences and flocks of doves take flight.

Also unexpected is the Hill Country's German character. German immigrants established the town of New Braunfels in 1845 and later moved west to found the hamlets that thrive in the area today. The German heritage of Fredericksburg, Boerne, and other towns is evident in their wurst houses, festivals, and even their buildings. Quaint "Sunday houses" — neat little timber-and-limestone houses built by 19th-century farmers for their weekend visits to town — still stand.

RANCHES AND DESERTS

Beyond the Hill Country, Texas belongs to the arid West. Cedars melt into mesquite, the mesquite into cactus-covered desert. In the north, cotton fields and farms give way to the vast ranches and wheat fields of the panhandle.

Cowboys still work these ranches, some of which are hundreds of thousands of acres in size. Much of the shortgrass prairie is used for grazing cattle or sheep, all the way to the mountains in the far western part of the state.

Southernmost of these mountains are the Chisos, which Spanish explorers considered hopelessly inhospitable. But eventually a few prospectors and other hardy souls moved to what became known as Big Bend Country (after the 80-mile northward bend of the Rio Grande). Today Big Bend National Park encompasses the scenic canyons and deserts of the region.

From this dramatic western landscape to the fertile fields of the east, one common factor has united the huge state — oil. When the first gusher blew in at Spindletop in 1901, the Texas oil boom was born, and today there is not a county without a history of oil exploration.

Oil, cotton, and cattle created Texas and the outsize myths that surround it. Now, with an economy sustained by finance and trade, the state has become more urbanized, more sophisticated. Yet the Texas mystique seems unshakable and still larger than life.

Mariscal Canyon, most isolated of the three major canyons in Big Bend, can be reached on foot only by a 6½-mile hike. Rafting down the Rio Grande makes it more accessible.

Dense growths of palmettos and native irises surround the Ottine Swamp in Palmetto State Park, 60 miles east of San Antonio.

AMERICA: LAND OF BEAUTY AND SPLENDOR

Enchanted Rock, a 70-acre dome of granite near Fredericksburg, is so called because it makes creaking noises as it cools after a day in the sun.

THE TOWN THAT BLEW AWAY

Texas's weather is as extreme as its landscapes. Hurricanes, tornadoes, and floods have wreaked havoc in one town after another. But perhaps the most poignant record of nature's stormy script is the ghost town of Indianola.

Founded in 1844 on the Gulf Coast, Indianola quickly became a major port with links to London and Le Havre. Long before anything approaching the civilized life reached the interior of Texas, the town boasted sophisticated amenities and fine Victorian houses.

Then, in 1866, a hurricane swept in. Damage was great, but the residents repaired the buildings and went on as be-

fore. Nine years later, a worse storm hit. This time, most of the town was destroyed and some 300 people were killed.

The townspeople rebuilt yet again. But a still bigger hurricane blew in on August 19, 1886. This one left virtually nothing behind, and the surviving residents gave up. Most moved inland to escape the winds for good. Thus did Indianola, once home to 6,000 people, completely disappear.

Today nothing remains of the town that seemed destined for preeminence as a port. Visitors find only the disintegrating stones of the courthouse foundation, washed by the tides.

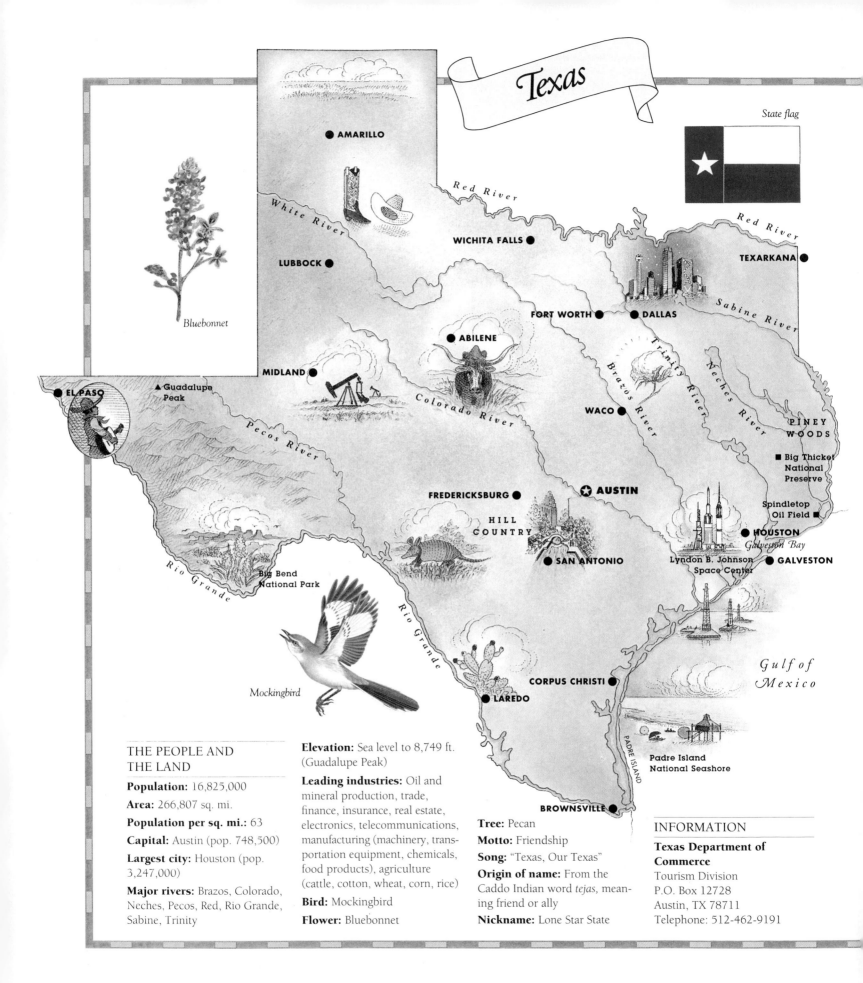

Texas

State flag

Bluebonnet

● AMARILLO

Red River

● WICHITA FALLS

● LUBBOCK

White River

Red River

● TEXARKANA

Sabine River

FORT WORTH ●   ● DALLAS

● ABILENE

Trinity River

Neches River

● MIDLAND

Colorado River

● WACO

Brazos River

PINEY WOODS

● EL PASO

▲ Guadalupe Peak

Pecos River

■ Big Thicket National Preserve

● FREDERICKSBURG

☆ AUSTIN

Spindletop Oil Field ■

HILL COUNTRY

● HOUSTON

Galveston Bay

● SAN ANTONIO

Lyndon B. Johnson Space Center

● GALVESTON

Rio Grande

Big Bend National Park

Mockingbird

Rio Grande

Gulf of Mexico

● CORPUS CHRISTI

● LAREDO

PADRE ISLAND

Padre Island National Seashore

● BROWNSVILLE

THE PEOPLE AND THE LAND

Population: 16,825,000

Area: 266,807 sq. mi.

Population per sq. mi.: 63

Capital: Austin (pop. 748,500)

Largest city: Houston (pop. 3,247,000)

Major rivers: Brazos, Colorado, Neches, Pecos, Red, Rio Grande, Sabine, Trinity

Elevation: Sea level to 8,749 ft. (Guadalupe Peak)

Leading industries: Oil and mineral production, trade, finance, insurance, real estate, electronics, telecommunications, manufacturing (machinery, transportation equipment, chemicals, food products), agriculture (cattle, cotton, wheat, corn, rice)

Bird: Mockingbird

Flower: Bluebonnet

Tree: Pecan

Motto: Friendship

Song: "Texas, Our Texas"

Origin of name: From the Caddo Indian word *tejas,* meaning friend or ally

Nickname: Lone Star State

INFORMATION

Texas Department of Commerce

Tourism Division
P.O. Box 12728
Austin, TX 78711
Telephone: 512-462-9191

HISTORICAL HIGHLIGHTS

1519 Spaniard Alonso Alvarez de Piñeda explores and maps Texas coast.

1528 After being shipwrecked, Cabeza de Vaca and party venture into Texas interior.

1541 Coronado and his party travel into West Texas.

1682 Spanish Franciscans build two missions near present-day city of El Paso.

1685 La Salle builds Fort St. Louis on coast.

1718 Spaniards found San Antonio de Valero mission, later called the Alamo, on San Antonio River.

1821 When Mexico gains independence from Spain, Texas becomes part of Republic of Mexico. Mexico allows Stephen F. Austin to bring Anglo-American settlers to Texas.

1835 Anglo-Americans revolt against Mexico.

1836 Americans are defeated at Battle of the Alamo, which pitted 184 Texans against several thousand Mexicans. Six weeks later, Texans win Battle of San Jacinto and form Republic of Texas.

1845 Texas enters the Union as the 28th state.

1861 Texas joins Confederacy.

1900 Hurricane in Galveston takes 6,000 lives.

1901 Spindletop oil field, near Beaumont, begins production, signaling the birth of the modern petroleum industry.

1947 Ship explosion at Texas City refinery dock kills 500 and injures 4,000.

1963 President John F. Kennedy is assassinated in Dallas. Vice President Lyndon B. Johnson, a former Texas senator, is sworn in as president.

1986 Drop in oil prices sends Texas economy into recession.

FAMOUS SONS AND DAUGHTERS

Stephen F. Austin (1793 – 1836). When Moses Austin died soon after being granted a charter to bring 300 Anglo-American families into Texas, his son Stephen stepped in and carried out the mission. Later he played a significant part in Texas's revolt against Mexico.

Sam Houston (1793 – 1863). This former congressman from Tennessee moved to Texas in 1833. As army commander, he liberated Texas from Mexico at the Battle of San Jacinto and later was elected first president of the new republic.

Howard Hughes (1905 – 76). After inheriting his father's Houston oil well supply business, Hughes became a motion picture producer, aviator, and America's best-known recluse. He was also one of the world's richest men.

Lyndon B. Johnson (1908 – 73). Raised on a Hill Country farm, this earthy, skillful politician rose from state politics to Congress to the presidency. He was the architect of the "Great Society" social programs.

Mary Martin (1914 – 90).

A voice and dance teacher from the town of Weatherford, Martin moved to New York City in the 1930's and later became the celebrated star of *Peter Pan* and other musicals.

Babe Didrickson Zaharias (1914 – 56). An extraordinary all-round athlete, Zaharias won two gold medals in track and field at the 1932 Olympics. Later she became a professional golfer, winning every major tournament before she died of cancer at age 42.

ODDITIES AND SPECIALTIES

Every fall, millions of people flock to State Fair Park in Dallas to attend the country's largest state fair. Greeting them is a talking, 52-foot-tall mechanical cowboy named Big Tex.

Chili, known locally as "a bowl o' red," is Texas's culinary gift to the world. It originated in the hills of south-central Texas in the mid-19th century.

Before oil was considered "black gold," workers drilling a city water well in Corsicana in 1894 were chagrined to find that their efforts yielded petroleum instead of water. But they soon found a way to make use of the state's first major oil strike, sprinkling the sticky fluid on city streets to keep the dust down.

A horned toad was found alive after 31 years in a time capsule at the Eastland County courthouse. Old Rip, now embalmed, is today on constant display in the courthouse foyer.

PLACES TO VISIT, THINGS TO DO

The Alamo (San Antonio).

The most famous battle of the Texas Revolution was fought over this old Spanish mission. The building, surrounded by skyscrapers in the heart of downtown, is open daily for tours.

Big Bend National Park (headquarters at Panther Junction). The Rio Grande has cut colorful canyons through the mountainous desert of West Texas. The area also hosts a wide assortment of plant life, including the giant dagger, a rare variety of yucca.

Guadalupe Mountains National Park (headquarters at Salt Flat). These low-slung mountains, remnants of an ancient ocean reef, contain historic Indian ruins, fossils, forests, canyons, desert, and Guadalupe Peak, the state's highest mountain.

Lyndon B. Johnson Space Center (Houston). The headquarters for NASA's spacecraft projects has extensive exhibits that include films and photos taken from space.

Padre Island National Seashore (headquarters at Corpus Christi). This flat, 80-mile-long barrier island draws shell collectors, snorkelers, and scuba divers, as well as sunbathers, to its sandy white shores.

Utah

Where the earth is sculpted into fantastic forms

Francisco Coronado was Spain's most ambitious conquistador, but even he had to admit defeat when it came to exploring Utah. In 1540 he reported to Mexico that the land north of the Grand Canyon was impenetrable desert unsuited to human habitation. For the next three centuries Utah largely remained a mysterious black hole on the North American continent. Not until 1843 did explorer John C. Frémont systematically survey the country "around which," he wrote, "the vague and superstitious accounts of trappers had thrown a delightful obscurity."

Frémont's reports described a severe and forbidding land filled with "rivers and lakes which have no communication with the sea" and "savage tribes which no traveler has seen or described." Thus forewarned, most American pioneers avoided the mountainous badlands. Those who entered, seeking a shortcut to California, soon wished they had not. Their suffering and misadventures became public lore through the lyrics of one of the West's most popular songs, "Sweet Betsy from Pike":

They came to the desert and salt water lakes,
The ground it was teemin' with varmints
*   and snakes,*
Beset by wild Indians, Comanche and Sioux,
'Tis a glorious tale how they ever got through!

THE FERTILE VALLEY

Brigham Young, president of the Church of Jesus Christ of Latter-day Saints — the Mormons — studied Frémont's reports and noted an intriguing fact. Nestled between the Great

The Anasazi pueblos of Utah overlooked a world of rock and sand. This scene, with the ruins of a granary in the foreground, is in Canyonlands National Park.

In Goosenecks State Park, a January snow brings the terraces of the San Juan River canyon into sharp relief. The river flows in symmetrical bends for six miles to cover a point-to-point distance of one mile.

Salt Lake Desert on the west, the towering Wasatch Range on the east, and the barren Colorado Plateau to the southeast was a large valley uninhabited by Indians. Moreover, the valley appeared to be a veritable oasis. Storms moving east dropped most of their moisture on the western slopes of the Wasatch Range, where mountain streams created fertile alluvial deltas that could produce enough food to support a considerable population.

In 1847 Young urged the Mormons to follow him to the Salt Lake Valley. By the end of

Standing above rippled red dunes is one of the immense monoliths of Monument Valley.

THE WATERPOCKET FOLD

When forces deep within the earth gradually pushed the vast Colorado Plateau upward some 15 million years ago, the elevation was so uniform that the surface of the land stayed relatively undisturbed. Only in a few places did the earth's crust warp. One of them, a 100-mile-long wrinkle called the Waterpocket Fold, today is encompassed by Capitol Reef National Park.

Just as the canyons of the plateau provide geologic records of the region over millions of years, so does the Waterpocket Fold (named for the rain-trapping holes on its surface). The difference between them is that the canyons were etched deep into the earth's surface by rivers; the fold rose from the earth.

Exposed along the face of this giant escarpment is the evidence of ancient shallow seas that retreated and advanced eons before the land was uplifted — deposits of sediment that formed colorful layers of limestone, sandstone, and shale. Interspersed are bands of ash that piled up when prehistoric volcanoes were active.

Long before the Waterpocket Fold was formed, erosion was already at work sculpting soft rock into the famous canyons and extraordinary landforms of the Colorado Plateau — such revealing geological specimens as the Grand Canyon and Bryce Canyon. The fold that rises out of the desert floor, likened by early explorers to an ocean reef, provides still another opportunity for geologists to observe the fascinating record of creation.

the first year more than 4,000 had answered the call, making the soon-to-be-proclaimed State of Deseret (from a word in the *Book of Mormon* that means honeybee) the first functioning theocracy since the early days of the Massachusetts Bay Colony.

A waterfall cascading into a canyon at Zion National Park nurtures an oasis of pines, cottonwoods, and maples.

THE MORMON CRICKET

Locusts, grasshoppers, and crickets inhabit every part of the United States. But in few places are they as unpredictable as in the arid regions west of the Rocky Mountains, where the hot weather and lack of food sometimes prompt them to migrate in great swarms. The early Mormons of Utah found that one variety was capable of inflicting a plague of biblical dimensions.

Certainly in the summer of 1848 it seemed that Brigham Young's infant settlement was the object of God's wrath, when millions of voracious crickets began advancing over the horizon. "We were a thousand miles from supplies, our provisions were giving out and what little we had grow-

ing was being eaten up," pioneer Priddy Meeks recalled in his autobiography.

As if in answer to the settlers' prayers, a flock of sea gulls appeared and began devouring the crickets. Each day the birds returned, until all of the insects were consumed. Wrote one diarist: "It seems the hand of the Lord is in our favor."

Though Utah's farmers use insecticides today to control the occasional invasions of the Mormon cricket, as it is now called, they have not forgotten the plague of the summer of 1848. Just east of Salt Lake City's Assembly Hall is a monument to the sea gulls (left), whose timely intervention is still considered a miracle.

A thin layer of galleta grass covers the South Desert in Capitol Reef National Park. Looming behind are the Henry Mountains.

Balanced Rock (left) is among the hundreds of unusual sandstone formations in Arches National Park. The park has the world's largest concentration of natural arches, some of which are seen here in the background.

Brigham Young's imperial vision ended in 1850 when Congress transformed Deseret into the territory of Utah. But the dismantling of the Mormon government did not diminish the church's position of primacy. Mormons still dominate the state's economy and politics.

Salt Lake City, the capital the Mormons built, is among the most orderly of America's metropolises. It seems immune even to traffic jams — Young laid out streets wide enough to turn a span of oxen.

The city takes its name from the Great Salt Lake, a shallow saline sea whose size has fluctuated dramatically over the centuries. During the Ice Age, when the lake was fed by glaciers, it was so large it covered all of northern Utah west of the Wasatch Range. Today, the silvery lake that remains is surrounded by enormous desert salt flats stippled with cactus and a series of terraces scoured into the mountain slopes by the waves of the once-vast inland sea. Still, the lake is something of a recreation area, with so much buoyancy in its salty, eye-stinging water that swimmers cannot help but stay afloat.

FIVE NATIONAL PARKS

South of the Salt Lake Valley lies the rugged Colorado Plateau, thrust upward some 15 million years ago. Over time, rivers and the elements have carved the soft sandstone of the plateau into remarkably intricate forms, creating some of the most extraordinary landscapes on earth. Not surprisingly, southern Utah is the site of five national parks — besides Alaska and California, the most in any state.

The first chunk of Utah scenery to be protected, in 1909, was Zion National Park, whose focal point is a canyon with sheer walls plunging 2,000 feet. Within a 330-mile drive to the northeast lie four other national parks: Bryce Canyon, a fantasyland of rose-colored pinnacles; Capitol Reef, some of whose formations reminded early American explorers of an ocean reef and the dome of the capitol in Washington, D.C.; Canyonlands, a vast badlands of mesas and gorges; and Arches, named for its natural bridges of red sandstone.

Nearby, Monument Valley has scenery as magnificent as that of the parks — a series of huge red sandstone monoliths rising abruptly from the desert floor. Ever since director John Ford filmed *Stagecoach* in 1938, these hulking, flat-topped giants have been used as a backdrop in dozens of western movies. Today they are among the most familiar icons of the American West.

Intersected by desert washes, swirling streams, and rivers thick with sediment, the Colorado Plateau traditionally has been a place where men go to escape. Outlaws, including Butch Cassidy, hid out in the Capitol Reef area so often that it came to be known as one of the West's many robbers' roosts. Ironically, the mazelike canyons and towering rocks that once prompted a homesteader to describe Utah as a "helluva place to lose a cow" now attract thousands of visitors. On a crowded summer weekend, Utah often seems full to capacity. But with a permanent population of less than 2 million, the Beehive State still has plenty of room to grow.

In late afternoon, the delicate pinnacles of Bryce Canyon seem to glow from within.

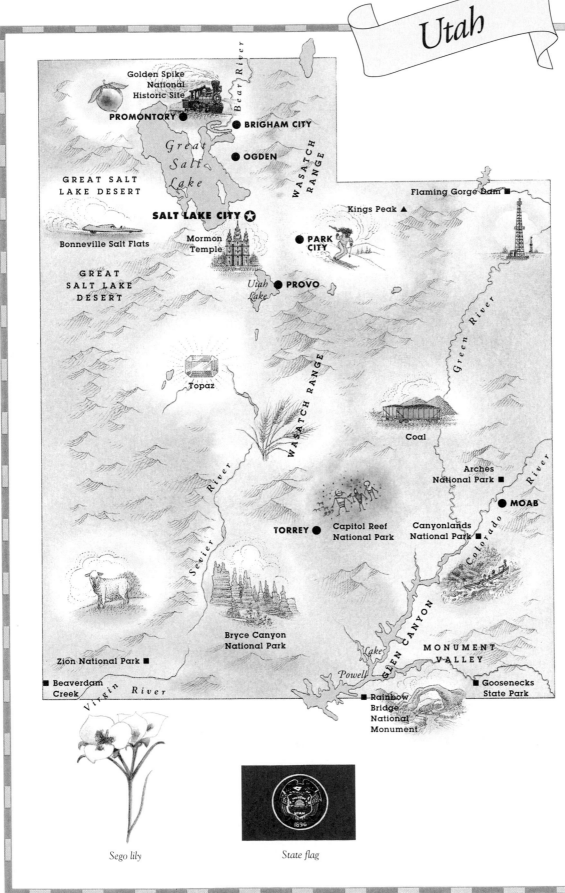

Golden Spike
National
Historic Site

PROMONTORY ●

● **BRIGHAM CITY**

Great Salt Lake

● **OGDEN**

Bear River

GREAT SALT
LAKE DESERT

SALT LAKE CITY ☆

Bonneville Salt Flats

Mormon
Temple

WASATCH RANGE

Flaming Gorge Dam ■

Kings Peak ▲

● **PARK CITY**

GREAT
SALT
LAKE
DESERT

Utah Lake

● **PROVO**

Topaz

WASATCH RANGE

Green River

Coal

Sevier River

Arches
National Park ■

Colorado River

● **MOAB**

TORREY ●

Capitol Reef
National Park

Canyonlands
National Park ■

Bryce Canyon
National Park

Zion National Park ■

■ Beaverdam
Creek

Virgin River

Sevier River

Lake Powell

GLEN CANYON

MONUMENT
VALLEY

■ Rainbow
Bridge
National
Monument

■ Goosenecks
State Park

Sego lily

State flag

Sea gull

THE PEOPLE AND THE LAND

Population: 1,711,000

Area: 84,899 sq. mi.

Population per sq. mi.: 20

Capital and largest city: Salt Lake City (pop. 1,065,000)

Major rivers: Bear, Colorado, Green, Sevier, Virgin

Elevation: 2,000 ft. (Beaverdam Creek) to 13,528 ft. (Kings Peak)

Leading industries: Missile construction, manufacturing (machinery, electronics, transportation equipment), beef cattle, sheep, trade, services, tourism, oil, mining (coal, copper)

Bird: Sea gull

Flower: Sego lily

Tree: Blue spruce

Motto: Industry

Song: "Utah, We Love Thee"

Origin of name: From *eutaw*, the Navajo name for a Shoshoni tribe that lived in the mountains

Nicknames: Beehive State, Land of the Saints, Mormon State, Salt Lake State

INFORMATION

Utah Travel Council
Council Hall
Capitol Hill
Salt Lake City, UT 84114
Telephone: 801-538-1030

HISTORICAL HIGHLIGHTS

1776 Franciscans Francisco Atanasio Dominguez and Silvestre Velez de Escalante explore region.

1826 Jedediah Smith leads trading party across Utah.

1837 Antoine Robidoux builds Utah's first trading post on Green River.

1847 Brigham Young brings Mormon pioneers to the fertile valley east of the Great Salt Lake.

1849 Mormons establish the State of Deseret.

1850 Congress designates Utah a U.S. territory.

1855 Population grows from 10,000 to 60,000 in five years.

1857 Army troops accompany governor sent to Utah to replace Brigham Young.

1869 First transcontinental railroad is completed at Promontory.

1890 Mormon leaders renounce polygamy.

1896 Utah enters Union as the 45th state.

1911 Strawberry Reservoir diverts Colorado River to provide power and irrigation.

1952 Uranium deposits are discovered near Moab.

1964 Flaming Gorge Dam on Green River begins generating electrical power and spurs industrial growth.

1977 In first U.S. execution in 10 years, Gary Gilmore is killed by firing squad in Provo.

1985 Great Salt Lake floods area.

FAMOUS SONS AND DAUGHTERS

Maude Adams (1872 – 1953). One of the most beloved of American actresses, Adams made her first appearance on stage at the age of nine months. Her most famous role was in *Peter Pan*.

John Moses Browning (1855 – 1926). Son of a Mormon gunsmith, this inventor developed the Browning automatic rifle, which became a standard army shoulder weapon from 1918 until the late 1950's.

Philo T. Farnsworth (1906 – 71). Farnsworth invented an electronic camera tube that became known as the image dissector. The dissector was later combined with other technology to create modern television.

George Romney (1907 –). Romney grew up in Utah and held high positions in the Mormon Church. After serving as president of American Motors, he became governor of Michigan and U.S. secretary of housing and urban development under President Richard M. Nixon.

Brigham Young (1801 – 77).

Young rose to leadership of the Mormon Church after founder Joseph Smith's assassination. He established and headed the community in Salt Lake City.

ODDITIES AND SPECIALTIES

In Zion National Park live canyon frogs, whose bleat is often mistaken for that of a sheep's, and tiny Zion snails, found only here.

The Bonneville Salt Flats provide an ideal surface for racing cars — a 12-mile strip of tightly packed salt that is almost like concrete. World speed records have been set here.

When frontier scout Jim Bridger tasted the water of the Great Salt Lake in 1824, he mistook the lake for an ocean. Actually, it has a higher saline content than either the Atlantic or Pacific oceans.

Communities in agriculturally rich Box Elder County celebrate the harvest every year with such festivals as Peach Days and Wheat and Beet Days.

Utah is a rockhound's dream, an endless source of agate, obsidian, and other stones. The world's largest topaz beds lie just west of the Little Sahara Recreation Area.

PLACES TO VISIT, THINGS TO DO

Arches National Park (headquarters at Moab). More than 2,000 sandstone arches stand alongside balanced rocks, pinnacles, and other formations in this unique landscape.

Bryce Canyon National Park (near Panguitch). The vertical, deeply eroded formations of red sandstone here resemble everything from standing crowds of people to cathedrals.

Canyonlands National Park (headquarters at Moab). The Colorado and Green rivers, along with wind and rain, slowly sculpted these chasms, mesas, and the dramatic range of pinnacles known as The Needles.

Capitol Reef National Park (near Torrey). Embracing a long bulge in the earth's crust called the Waterpocket Fold, this park has monolithic cliffs, some with figure drawings that were made by Fremont Indians more than 700 years ago.

Glen Canyon National Recreation Area (south-central Utah). Lake Powell, the nation's second-largest man-made lake, is surrounded by the red sandstone cliffs of Glen Canyon. Among the attractions is Rainbow Bridge, a massive natural arch.

Golden Spike National Historic Site (32 miles west of Brigham City). Every May 10, local citizens celebrate the completion of the transcontinental railroad in 1869 and reenact the driving of the last spike. Period locomotives and other railroad exhibits are on display from May to September.

Park City Ski Area (Park City). This ski resort, Utah's largest, is one of nine within an hour's drive of Salt Lake City. Also near Park City are the resorts of Park West and Deer Valley.

Temple Square (Salt Lake City). This 10-acre center of the Mormon faith includes such architecturally impressive buildings as the six-spired Mormon Temple, imposing Tabernacle, and picturesque Assembly Hall.

Zion National Park (headquarters at Springdale). Waterfalls and hanging gardens adorn Zion Canyon, a 2,500-foot-deep chasm carved by the Virgin River. Lofty cliffs and templelike formations add to the grandeur.

Vermont

*Green mountains, green valleys —
America's northern Eden*

To find solace from the hectic life of cities and suburbs, Americans often head to places where, it is said, "time seems to have stopped," places where vestiges of a slower era still exist. In Vermont, time not only stopped, it went backward. Hills and valleys that were once stripped bare of trees for agriculture turned green again as forests reclaimed abandoned fields and pastures. Moose, salmon, and the peregrine falcon, which were chased from the region decades ago, have started to come back, though the lordly mountain lion may never be seen here again.

NORMAN ROCKWELL'S AMERICA

In the 1800's, farmers gave up on the thin, stony soil and ventured either west or to the state's industrial centers. Fortunately, the handsome, sturdy buildings of Vermont's small towns survived. White church spires, outlined against a green hillside, continue to preside over peaceful town commons, where these days groups of touring bicyclists pause to rest. Both the places and the people of Vermont provided Norman Rockwell with the subjects for some of his most famous works — paintings that virtually define the popular notion of what it was to be an American in a small town in the days when time passed with sweet slowness.

The poet Robert Frost, who lived for a while in South Shaftsbury in the 1920's, said that Vermont is "a state in a natural state." To outsiders it does seem that Vermont has managed to reclaim some stake on a preindustrial Eden. Native Vermonters, however, can be

An early morning mist hovers over East Corinth, in central Vermont. The quiet charm so evident here is shared by villages all across the Vermont landscape.

Beyond the snow-covered pastures of this northern Vermont farm looms regal Mount Mansfield, the highest peak in the state. Five miles long and 4,393 feet high, Mansfield is popular with skiers.

forgiven if they have a somewhat different view. While blessed with fiery autumnal colors, they must cope with frequent fogs. They know that the dazzling white of the ski slopes will eventually yield to the brown misery of mud season and that for every luscious gallon of maple syrup that is produced, someone had to haul many more gallons of sap. Despite all this, Vermonters stay on, a loyal knot of hardy folk who accept with remarkable good humor both the long, sub-zero winters and the relentless cheerfulness of vacationers.

THE WORKINGS OF THE ICE AGE

Vermonters had Ice Age glaciers to thank for the abundance of stones in their soil. Before they could begin plowing in spring, farmers

had to haul out a harvest of rocks heaved up from below by frost. But the glaciers that dumped these annoying lumps into Vermont's lap also carved and smoothed the Green Mountains into a gentle range, grinding down craggy peaks to form a kindly mountainscape — a romantic, rolling panorama without the menacing wildness of New York's Appalachians.

Although the Green Mountains give the state its character, they do not completely dominate its topography. More than half of the state's western border is formed by Lake Champlain, the sixth-largest lake in the country. Beyond its shores lie the Lake Champlain lowlands. Not only is this area the most fertile farmland in the state, it is one of Vermont's most picturesque places. Here one can view

An early-rising angler wades thigh-deep in the still, misty waters of a pond near Manchester. Here fly fishing is so revered it inspired a local fishing tackle manufacturer to offer instruction in the sport and to create the American Museum of Fly Fishing.

the graceful mountains at a distance and Champlain's soothing shade of blue up close.

The northeastern corner of the state is another world entirely. Isolated, with very few roads, this sparsely settled expanse of 2,000 square miles is called the Northeast Kingdom. White and black spruce — trees of the subarctic — flourish in its cold climate. The persistent chill and the region's poor drainage discourage agriculture, but the timber industry provides employment for the few people who make their home here.

WHERE DOGWOODS MEET RED SPRUCE

Vermont is a meeting ground of temperate-zone and arctic plant life. Dogwoods flower in the state's milder areas, while on Camels Hump

THE MORGAN HORSE

In the summer of 1795 a poor Vermont music teacher, Justin Morgan, took possession of an unusual colt named Figure in payment for a debt. Figure was short, heavily muscled, and compact, with a thick neck and broad shoulders and hindquarters. Even though he weighed less than 1,000 pounds at maturity, he soon became well known around his owner's hometown of Randolph, Vermont, for his remarkable combination of strength and speed.

Morgan hired Figure out to a farmer, who reportedly made a bet that the horse could pull a heavy pine log that no other horse had been able to budge. To make the bet more interesting, the farmer allowed three stout men to sit on the log. At the command "Git up!" Figure gave a mighty lunge and hauled the huge log and its passengers to the sawmill.

When it came to racing, Figure easily beat all of the local challengers as well as a Thoroughbred that was brought all the way from Long Island. Farmers and horse breeders came from far and wide, eager to have their mares mated with him.

Figure, who was eventually renamed after his owner, was a genetic rarity. The horse resembled neither his dam nor his sire, and his offspring resembled him and not the mares with which he was bred. From this amazing stallion sprang the Morgan horse, North America's oldest native breed. Figure's descendants are treasured today not only for their strength and speed but also for their gentle disposition.

In autumn, the trees lining virtually every roadside in Vermont explode with colors as brilliant as those in the showiest flower gardens. This route winds through Jacksonville, in southern Vermont, where a white table wine is made from the juice of locally grown apples.

384

The Middlebury River, a favorite of swimmers in summer, is clothed in snow and ice as it journeys down the Green Mountains in winter.

and Mount Mansfield one can find holdouts of alpine tundra left over from the Ice Age. Red spruce trees grow in the colder northern areas and at high elevations. As tough as they are, these trees are sensitive to pollution. It was an analysis of dying red spruce trees on Camels Hump that first demonstrated the effects of acid rain on our forests.

Today the sugar maple is the most common hardwood species in Vermont. It is sap from this tree that gives Vermont its maple syrup, the balm that brings a dollop of cheer to mud season. On the other end of the calendar, it will be the sugar maple that puts on the spectacular show of reds and purples for which the state is famous. Botanists who have studied the secret workings of autumnal beauty have discovered that an accumulation of sugar gives these leaves their vibrant colors. It is sweetness itself that blazes across Vermont in the fall.

Pumpkins shine beneath a moody sky at the Ethan Allen homestead in Burlington.

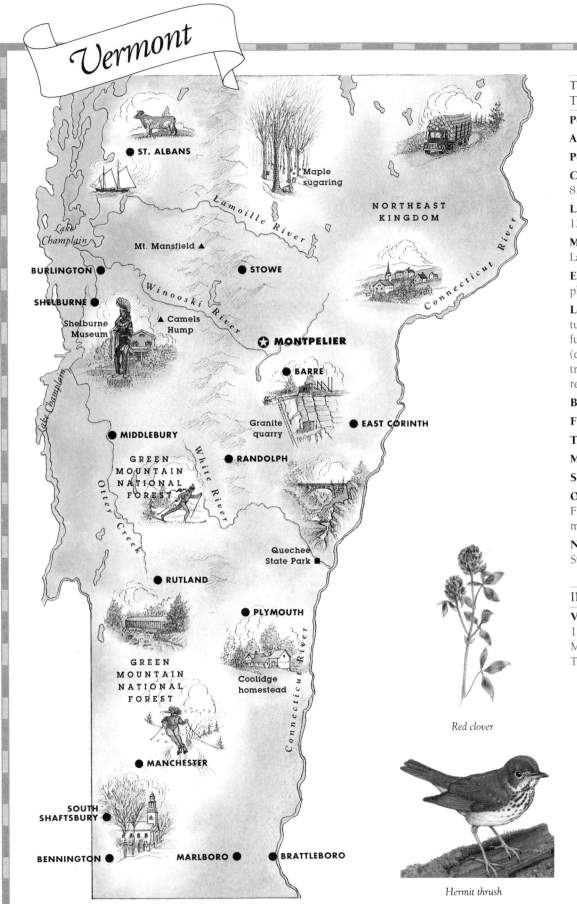

Vermont

ST. ALBANS

Maple sugaring

NORTHEAST KINGDOM

Lamoille River

Lake Champlain

Mt. Mansfield ▲

BURLINGTON

Winooski River

STOWE

SHELBURNE

Shelburne Museum

▲ Camels Hump

☆ **MONTPELIER**

BARRE

Connecticut River

Granite quarry

MIDDLEBURY

White River

EAST CORINTH

GREEN MOUNTAIN NATIONAL FOREST

RANDOLPH

Otter Creek

Lake Champlain

Quechee State Park ■

RUTLAND

PLYMOUTH

Connecticut River

GREEN MOUNTAIN NATIONAL FOREST

Coolidge homestead

MANCHESTER

SOUTH SHAFTSBURY

BENNINGTON   **MARLBORO**   **BRATTLEBORO**

THE PEOPLE AND THE LAND

Population: 560,000

Area: 9,609 sq. mi.

Population per sq. mi.: 58

Capital: Montpelier (pop. 8,200)

Largest city: Burlington (pop. 129,000)

Major rivers: Connecticut, Lamoille, White, Winooski

Elevation: 95 ft. (Lake Champlain) to 4,393 ft. (Mt. Mansfield)

Leading industries: Manufacturing (electronic equipment, furniture), tourism, agriculture (dairy, apples, maple syrup), trade, finance, insurance, real estate

Bird: Hermit thrush

Flower: Red clover

Tree: Sugar maple

Motto: Freedom and Unity

Song: "Hail, Vermont!"

Origin of name: From the French words *vert* and *mont*, meaning green mountain

Nickname: Green Mountain State

INFORMATION

Vermont Travel Division
134 State Street
Montpelier, VT 05602
Telephone: 802-828-3236

Red clover

Hermit thrush

State flag

HISTORICAL HIGHLIGHTS

1609 Samuel de Champlain claims area for France and discovers Lake Champlain

1724 First permanent settlement is built at Fort Dummer (present-day Brattleboro).

1764 New York gains jurisdiction over Vermont.

1770 Green Mountain Boys, led by Ethan Allen, drive New York settlers from Vermont.

1775 Green Mountain Boys help capture Fort Ticonderoga from British forces.

1777 Vermont declares independence from Great Britain and prohibits slavery in its constitution.

1791 Vermont joins Union as 14th state.

1823 Opening of Champlain Canal links Vermont to Hudson River and New York City.

1864 Confederate soldiers raid St. Albans.

1923 Calvin Coolidge accedes to presidency.

1934 Nation's first ski tow is built in Woodstock.

1940 First chair lift makes its ascent on Mt. Mansfield.

1970 Environmental Control Act limits major developments.

1984 State elects its first woman governor, Madeleine M. Kunin.

FAMOUS SONS AND DAUGHTERS

Ethan Allen (1738 – 89). As leader of the Green Mountain Boys, organized to keep New York from taking over Vermont land, Allen had a price put on his head by New York's governor. In 1775, Allen was taken by the British and held captive in Canada for nearly three years.

Chester A. Arthur (1830 – 86). Arthur became president when James Garfield was assassinated in 1881. Though a machine politician, he was known for his honesty and efficiency.

Calvin Coolidge (1872 – 1933). The embodiment of Republican conservatism, "Silent Cal" was elected Warren G. Harding's vice president in 1920. When Harding died in 1923 Coolidge succeeded him in office.

George Dewey (1837 – 1917). Dewey's naval maneuvers in the Battle of Manila Bay in 1898, in which he swiftly defeated the Spanish fleet, made him a hero of the Spanish-American War.

John Dewey (1859 – 1952). A philosopher and psychologist, Dewey is best known for his influence on American education. His principles were the basis for the progressive education movement.

Dorothy Canfield Fisher (1879 – 1958). This writer celebrated Vermont life in novels and other books. But neither her outlook nor her life was provincial. She wrote books on the Montessori method of education and, during World War I, moved to France to do war work.

ODDITIES AND SPECIALTIES

Only three Vermont cities — Bennington, Burlington, and Rutland — have more than 15,000 people. Montpelier is the smallest capital city in the nation.

Starting in the 1850's, Vermonters chose only Republican candidates for Congress, governor, and president. This remarkable consistency was broken in 1958 for Congress, 1962 for governor, and 1964 for president.

The world's largest granite quarry, 350 feet deep and covering 20 acres, is in Barre. Vermont also boasts the country's largest marble-production center, at Proctor. The Lincoln Memorial is made of Vermont marble.

Given Vermont's many dairy farms, it's no surprise that the state produces over 100 million pounds of cheese a year, including its famous Cheddar.

George Washington granted the first U.S. patent to Pittsford resident Samuel Hopkins, who made potash out of wood ashes.

The Morgan horse is Vermont's state animal.

PLACES TO VISIT, THINGS TO DO

Camels Hump State Park and Forest (Huntington Center). Trails lead to the summit of Camels Hump and a sweeping view of Lake Champlain.

Green Mountain National Forest (headquarters at Rutland). Encompassing much of the Green Mountains, this 295,000-acre forest has miles of scenic roads and, for hikers, the 261-mile Long Trail that winds through the length of the state.

Lake Champlain (west Vermont). Several choice areas, including Burton Island and Sand Bar state parks, offer many opportunities for water sports.

Marlboro Music Festival World-famous performing artists play chamber music on the Marlboro College campus every July and August.

Mt. Mansfield State Forest (between Stowe and Jefferson). This forest includes the state's highest peak and Smuggler's Notch, a deep, scenic gorge.

Quechee State Park (White River Junction). The beautiful, mile-long Quechee Gorge is lined with hemlock, wild columbine, violets, and asters.

Shelburne Museum (Shelburne). Preserved here is Electra Webb's collection of Americana, including 37 restored buildings, a covered bridge, an old railroad station, and the paddle wheeler S.S. *Ticonderoga*.

Skiing Vermont's 24 alpine and nearly 50 cross-country ski areas, including the popular Stowe, have some of the best slopes in the Northeast.

Sugarhouses From late February into April, watch the process of turning maple sap to syrup and sample the results.

Virginia

The gracious home of America's forefathers

Virginia's many nicknames — Old Dominion, Mother of Presidents, Mother of States — attest to the state's deep roots in American history. It was in Virginia in 1607 that Jamestown, the first permanent English colony in America, was founded. Eight of America's presidents were born in Virginia, and eight other states, in whole or in part, were carved out of Virginia's original territory. Two great wars ended on Virginia soil — the Revolutionary War at Yorktown and the Civil War at Appomattox.

THE PAST PRESERVED

The flavor of Virginia's past is nowhere more evident than in Colonial Williamsburg. When Williamsburg was the state capital, between 1699 and 1780, it was the busiest city in the colonies, but it fell into a decline after 1780. Not until the 1920's was the town brought back to life. Teams of experts followed a 1781 "Frenchman's Map" and copied minute architectural details supplied by a 1740 copperplate engraving of the city. Today, with block after block of restored and reconstructed buildings, the town is a living time capsule showing life as it was in colonial days.

Williamsburg is set amid the low, sandy plain known as the Tidewater. Roads with names like the "Plantation Route" and "Colonial Parkway" lead to former battlefields, historic towns, and stately plantations along the James River. At the Tidewater's southern limits, the James flows by the naval ships at Norfolk and empties into the Chesapeake Bay.

The solitude and simplicity of rural life in old Virginia are evoked by this log cabin built on the densely wooded shores of the Dan River, near Danville.

Dense forests and lush, rolling fields are beautifully intermingled in much of western Virginia's Shenandoah Valley. One of America's first frontiers, the rich valley was called "the breadbasket of the Confederacy," and today is host to some two million visitors a year.

AMERICA: LAND OF BEAUTY AND SPLENDOR

Just across the bay lies Virginia's Eastern Shore, a section of the long Delmarva Peninsula that the state shares with Delaware and Maryland. It is occupied by salt marshes, truck farms, fishing villages, and windswept dunes. Parallel to the peninsula are the barrier islands of Chincoteague and Assateague, sanctuaries for herons, ospreys, and other wildlife.

A HERITAGE OF STATELY HOMES

Northern Virginia, though close to the hubbub of greater Washington, D.C., is not without its islands of serenity too. Across the Potomac from the nation's capital, Arlington National Cemetery occupies the land once owned by Robert E. Lee. Nearby are the now-tranquil sites of bloody Civil War battles: Chancellorsville, Fredericksburg, and Manassas (or Bull Run). In autumn, the baying of hounds can be heard in the green valleys of hunt country, where red-coated equestrians have chased foxes since George Washington's day.

South of Washington, D.C., lies Mount Vernon, the plantation home of George Washington for some 45 years. An excellent farmer, Washington was also a tireless host who in 1785 alone entertained well over 400 dinner guests at his beloved estate.

In Virginia's midsection a wide, fertile plateau of farms and forests extends from the Tidewater in the east to the Blue Ridge in the west. Interspersed among vineyards, tobacco fields, and peach orchards are thriving cities like Richmond, the lovely capital overlooking the falls of the James River. A French architect, together with America's most esteemed Renaissance man, Thomas Jefferson, created its distinctive capitol building. Jefferson's architectural legacy continues beyond Richmond. In Charlottesville is his celebrated home, Monticello, which he meticulously built and rebuilt over a period of 40 years.

"DAUGHTER OF THE STARS"

To the west of the Blue Ridge Mountains, the beautiful Shenandoah Valley stretches for more than 200 miles from Winchester in the north to Roanoke in the south. Viewed from Skyline

A lone school bus makes its way over the hills of Highland County in a remote part of western Virginia, where sheep outnumber people. Old-fashioned rail fences like the one along this roadside originated in old Virginia.

Elegant cascades adorn the Upper Doyle River Falls in Shenandoah National Park.

THE FLOWERS OF DARKNESS

South of Front Royal, in the Shenandoah Valley, are caves containing lovely and mysterious underground treasures. Called anthodites by geologists, these mineral formations, found on the ceilings of rooms in Skyline Caverns, are popularly known as cave flowers.

The formations grow in fragile clusters made up of thin needles of snow-white calcite up to four inches long. The slender projections radiate in all directions, defying the law of gravity, and the shapes they take suggest delicate blossoms.

Estimated to grow at a rate of only one inch every 7,000 years, the cave flowers are, to say the least, irreplaceable. To reach them, visitors must pass through a double set of doors, which keep bats from entering the chamber and causing dam-

age. If well cared for, the cave flowers will be on view for some time to come — perhaps even seven millennia from now, when they will be an inch longer.

Drive, the valley (whose Indian name means "daughter of the stars") presents a broad, colorful patchwork of vineyards, apple orchards, emerald pastures, and fields of grain.

The valley was carved by an ancient sea,

which left behind spectacular limestone formations, including the famous Natural Bridge and Luray Caverns. In the early 1800's, Grand Caverns was the scene of candlelit dances held in a ballroom-sized "grand hall," and during the Civil War, Stonewall Jackson's troops camped in the caves. No corner of Virginia — not even its darkest subterranean realms — has remained untouched by the pageant of American history.

Oaks tower over neat rows of young corn in a field near Tazewell, in southwestern Virginia.

HISTORICAL HIGHLIGHTS

1607 Jamestown, first permanent English settlement in America, is founded.

1619 House of Burgesses, America's first representative legislature, convenes. Dutch traders bring Africans to sell as indentured servants.

1693 College of William and Mary, named for the king and queen of England, is founded.

1781 Britain's Lord Cornwallis surrenders at Yorktown, ending Revolutionary War.

1788 Virginia enters Union as 10th state.

1789 George Washington becomes first U.S. president.

1831 Nat Turner's rebellion leads to stricter slavery laws.

1861 Virginia secedes from Union. Richmond becomes Confederate capital.

1863 Northwestern Virginia splits off to join Union, forming West Virginia.

1865 General Lee surrenders at Appomattox, ending Civil War.

1902 A new state constitution disenfranchises blacks by instituting a poll tax and a literacy test.

1918 College of William and Mary admits women.

1959 The first school integration in Virginia history takes place.

1964 Chesapeake Bay Bridge – Tunnel links Norfolk/Virginia Beach to Eastern Shore.

1969 A Republican governor is elected, the first since 1869.

1971 A new, more liberal state constitution goes into effect.

1989 L. Douglas Wilder becomes the first elected black governor in U.S. history.

FAMOUS SONS AND DAUGHTERS

Richard E. Byrd (1888 – 1957). A daring and renowned aviator, Byrd, along with Floyd Bennett, was first to fly over the North Pole. He later led several U.S. expeditions to Antarctica.

Patrick Henry (1736 – 99). A brilliant orator, Henry spoke out for liberty at the time of the American Revolution. He also served as governor of the Commonwealth of Virginia.

Robert E. Lee (1807 – 70). General Lee, who led the Confederate armies during the Civil War, not only was idolized in the South but was also greatly respected in the North.

Cyrus H. McCormick (1809 – 84). McCormick succeeded where his father had failed, in inventing the first mechanical reaper, which revolutionized grain harvesting.

Edgar Allan Poe (1809 – 49). A brilliant critic, poet, and fiction writer, Poe is best known for his macabre short stories.

Walter Reed (1851 – 1902). While working in Havana, this U.S. army surgeon demonstrated that yellow fever was transmitted by a mosquito.

Booker T. Washington (1856 – 1915). The eminent black educator founded Tuskegee Institute in Alabama and wrote many books, including *Up From Slavery*, his autobiography.

ODDITIES AND SPECIALTIES

Virginia Beach has managed to combine trash disposal with public beautification. The city covered a 70-foot-high mound of garbage with soil and landscaped it to create a park, called Mt. Trashmore.

Eight U.S. presidents were born in Virginia: George Washington, Thomas Jefferson, James Madison, James Monroe, William Henry Harrison, John Tyler, Zachary Taylor, and Woodrow Wilson.

Loudoun County is the home of fox-hunting and steeplechasing, equestrian sports whose roots go back further in Virginia than in any other state — all the way to the 17th century.

The smell of hickory smoke pervades the town of Smithfield, where a secret curing process produces the distinctive flavor of Smithfield ham.

Chincoteague Island is known both for its salt oysters and its finely crafted duck decoys.

In the mountains of southwestern Virginia, fiddlers and other musicians play in a traditional style, called Old Time, which is similar to bluegrass and can be traced back to Great Britain.

George Washington carved his initials on it. Thomas Jefferson bought it. The Monocan Indians worshipped it. Today Natural Bridge is called one of the seven natural wonders of the world.

Virginia is dubbed the Mother of States because land from its original territory now makes up, wholly or in part, the states of Illinois, Indiana, Kentucky, Michigan, Minnesota, Ohio, West Virginia, and Wisconsin.

PLACES TO VISIT, THINGS TO DO

Luray Caverns (near Luray). This huge cave abounds in colorful formations reflected in clear pools. Visitors are amazed by an organ whose tone-producing pipes are stalactites.

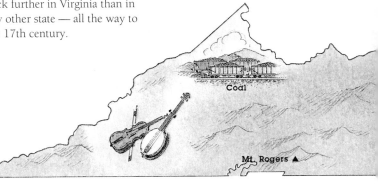

Plantations along the James River Among the many historic plantations in this area are Berkeley, birthplace of President William Henry Harrison, and Carter's Grove, an elegant Georgian mansion.

Shenandoah National Park (Luray). Stretching for some 105 miles through the Blue Ridge Mountains, the park is an untamed wilderness endowed with waterfalls and wildflowers.

Skyline Drive and Blue Ridge Parkway Splendid vistas are commonplace along this drive through Shenandoah National Park, the George Washington and Jefferson national forests, and the Blue Ridge Mountains.

Virginia

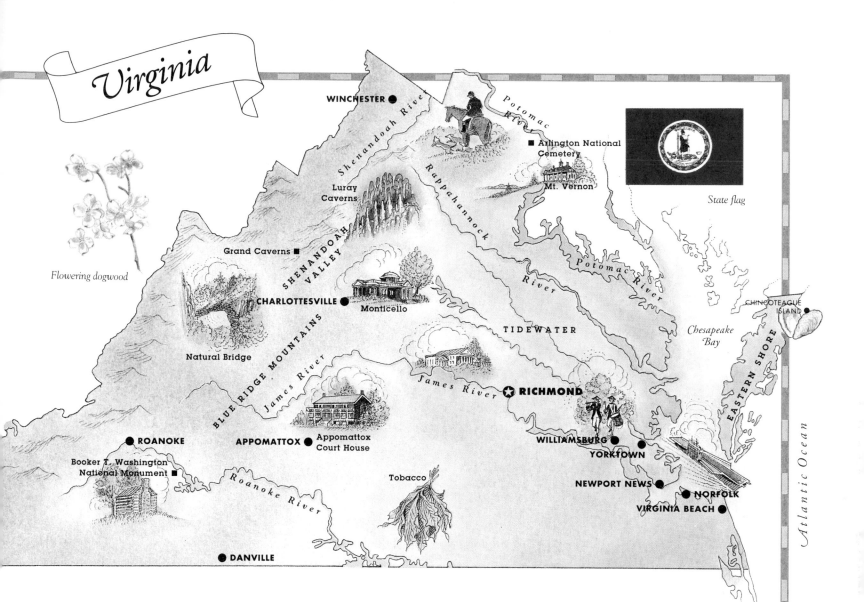

WINCHESTER

Shenandoah River

Potomac Rio

Arlington National Cemetery

Mt. Vernon

State flag

Luray Caverns

Rappahannock River

Grand Caverns

SHENANDOAH VALLEY

Potomac River

Flowering dogwood

CHARLOTTESVILLE

Monticello

CHINCOTEAGUE ISLAND

Natural Bridge

BLUE RIDGE MOUNTAINS

James River

TIDEWATER

Chesapeake Bay

EASTERN SHORE

RICHMOND

James River

ROANOKE

APPOMATTOX

Appomattox Court House

WILLIAMSBURG

YORKTOWN

Booker T. Washington National Monument

Atlantic Ocean

Roanoke River

Tobacco

NEWPORT NEWS

NORFOLK

VIRGINIA BEACH

DANVILLE

Williamsburg Historic District
The first and finest of America's restored towns, Colonial Williamsburg takes visitors back in time, allowing them to experience everyday life in early America.

THE PEOPLE AND THE LAND

Population: 6,128,000

Area: 40,767 sq. mi.

Population per sq. mi.: 150

Capital: Richmond (pop. 844,300)

Largest city: Norfolk – Virginia Beach – Newport News (pop. 1,380,000)

Major rivers: James, Potomac, Rappahannock, Roanoke, Shenandoah, York

Elevation: Sea level to 5,729 ft. (Mt. Rogers)

Leading industries: Government and community services, trade, manufacturing (textiles, transportation equipment, electronics, food processing, chemicals), agriculture (tobacco), coal mining

Bird: Cardinal

Flower: Flowering dogwood

Tree: Flowering dogwood

Motto: *Sic Semper Tyrannis* (Thus Always to Tyrants)

Song: "Carry Me Back to Old Virginia"

Origin of name: For Queen Elizabeth I, "Virgin Queen" of England, by Sir Walter Raleigh

Nicknames: Cavalier State, Mother of Presidents, Mother of States, Mother of Statesmen, Old Dominion

INFORMATION

Virginia Division of Tourism
1021 East Cary Street
Richmond, VA 23219
Telephone: 804-786-4484

Cardinal

Washington

The picture-perfect corner of the Northwest

The classic postcard picture of Washington is a photographer's dream — glistening, snow-white mountains looming over a wilderness of evergreens. But that much-reproduced image presents only one side of this state in the Pacific Northwest. Like neighboring Oregon, Washington is divided by a mighty mountain range into two quite different worlds: lush alpine landscapes to the west; semiarid plains and hills to the east.

The Cascade Range forms this great divide, running from north to south in a broad band of tall peaks, glacial lakes, and thickly wooded valleys. No fewer than three national parks, two of them in Washington and one in Oregon, have been marked out in the most spectacular stretches of the range.

In the north, extending down from the Canadian border, is North Cascades National Park, site of some 750 of the 1,100-odd glaciers found in the lower 48 states. Grinding away for millennia, the glaciers have worked the granite mountains into sharp points. Climbers who meet the challenge of Mount Terror, Mount Triumph, and other park summits are rewarded with a stunning sight — the icebound Cascades receding into the distance like the breaking waves of an ocean, for as far as the eye can see.

THE MOUNTAIN

As the great range moves southward it becomes less rugged, though no less spectacular. Crowning the southern Cascades is the glacier-clad volcano that Washingtonians simply call

A hiker threads through boulders and fallen trees to approach the beach at Cape Flattery, the point of land at the extreme northwest corner of the state.

In April, tulips bloom in the commercial flower fields south and east of Puget Sound. These red specimens grow in Skagit Flats, one of the largest bulb-producing areas in the world.

A month-old cougar kitten explores the world in Okanogan National Forest in northeastern Washington.

the Mountain, known to the rest of the world as Mount Rainier. The immense white cone, centerpiece of the state's second national park, dominates the south-central Washington landscape. It is visible on clear days from more than 100 miles away. Seen from Seattle skyscrapers, the distant Rainier seems to float among the clouds.

Two more volcanoes punctuate the southern Cascades. One is Mount Adams, which geologists think may still be active. The other is Mount St. Helens, the restless giant that achieved the notoriety of a Vesuvius in 1980 when it blasted away 1,200 feet of its summit and devastated the surrounding countryside with ash and debris.

A NEW TERRITORY

The world west of the Cascades is moist and green, a place of huge trees and legendary lumberjacks. It was here that pioneers first settled.

Once part of Oregon Territory, this timberland bore its first real wave of white settlement when "Oregon fever" swept the country in the 1840's. Most pioneers made their way

The rain forests of Olympic National Park sustain vegetation that is among the most luxuriant on the continent. Here a bigleaf maple, its gnarled branches lying prone, is enveloped in club moss and huckleberry fern.

SYMBIOSIS IN THE RAIN FOREST

The vegetation of Olympic National Park is extravagantly lush, with ferns dangling overhead and moss sheathing the massive tree trunks like green velvet. An emerald glow suffuses the air as sunlight filters through the 250-foot-high canopy of spruces, hemlocks, and maples. This is true rain forest — the largest one in the continental United States.

The Hoh River valley, a part of this temperate jungle, is also the place where naturalists first observed a previously unknown symbiotic relationship. In 1980 a biologist discovered that some species of trees in the Hoh valley — particularly bigleaf maples, vine maples, and red alders — had developed an interdependence with the mosses that envelop them. Although club moss and other epiphytic plants use tree trunks and branches as an anchor, they derive their nutrients from the air and rain. The trees, on the other hand, actually feed on their guests, extending small aerial roots into the moss to draw out nutrients.

Since this "canopy rooting" was discovered in the Hoh valley, researchers have observed the phenomenon in temperate and tropical rain forests the world over. Persistent rain in such forests quickly washes minerals and other nutrients down to the water table, out of the reach of roots. The mighty trees have adapted by using their moss covers as a kind of soil.

---

to the bountiful Willamette Valley in present-day Oregon, but some ventured north of the Columbia River and into the fertile, wooded lowlands surrounding Puget Sound. Here they milled hemlocks and Douglas firs from forests that a railroad agent described as "surpassing the woods of all the rest of the globe in the size, quantity and quality of the timber."

In 1852, the northerners, feeling that their interests were being ignored by a territorial legislature dominated by Willamette settlers, petitioned Congress to form a separate territory north and west of the Columbia. Congress granted the petition in 1853, extended the eastern boundary of the new territory to the Rocky Mountains, and named it after the nation's first president.

PUGETOPOLIS

The vast estuary known as Puget Sound is still the center of Washington life today. Linked to the Pacific by the Strait of Juan de Fuca, it fingers into the lowlands in a tangle of islands and inlets. The water teems with salmon and shellfish. South of the dense forests, gently rolling hills are dotted with dairy farms and commercial flower bulb fields. Tulips, irises, and daffodils come into view along the roadsides, surprising the traveler with an unexpected patchwork of brilliant color.

So commercially important is Puget Sound that most of its eastern shore — some 75 miles of it — is an unbroken chain of cities and towns linked to Seattle, the Northwest's major port. Washingtonians refer to this glutted urban strip, with Everett at its northern end and Tacoma at the southern, by one collective name — Pugetopolis.

West of Puget Sound is the box-shaped peninsula that forms a large part of Washington's Pacific coastline. Dominated by a mountainous rain forest that is one of the country's wildest places, much of the peninsula has been set aside as Olympic National Park. The mountains here are even less accessible than those of the northern Cascades. Lying beneath them are a number of primeval valleys that have yet to be explored, even though they are less than 50 miles from Seattle.

THE COLUMBIA PLATEAU

While the splendor of western Washington gave rise to the state's picture-perfect image, the parched land east of the Cascades was less than idyllic. Pioneers on the Columbia Plateau had no bounty of timber and salmon, nor even rain. The same Cascades that trapped moisture from the Pacific in the green forests of the west formed a barrier that kept the clouds from reaching the east.

Because glaciers cover much of Mount Rainier (rear), the mountain remains a pristine white even in midsummer.

At the entrance to the Strait of Juan de Fuca, sea gulls rest on the seaweed-covered rocks of Tatoosh Island.

The Columbia Plateau, once a wasteland, is now a prime producer of wheat. This idyllic scene is in the Palouse Hills, near the town of Colfax.

The first eastern settlers clustered where the relatively moist soil along the Columbia River was suitable for small farms. But those who followed were relegated to the drier reaches of the plains. As if the effort to wrest food from the land were not enough, Indian wars erupted after the territorial governor failed to abide by the terms of a treaty with the Cayuse and other tribes. Skirmishes began in 1855 and did not end until 1858.

Eventually the arid Columbia Plateau bloomed, transformed by irrigation into a self-proclaimed Inland Empire, with Spokane as its designated Queen City. Where once no trees grew, apple orchards and wheat fields now stretch to the endless horizon. It is a sight as beautiful in its own way as the more familiar Washington that lies west of the great mountain divide.

SALMON SPIRITS

Indians of the Pacific Northwest gave due reverence to salmon, for their very lives depended on the fish. Each year salmon migrating to the sea along the Columbia and Snake rivers yielded an estimated 18 million pounds of food to the Coast Salish, Puyallup, and other tribes.

The Coast Salish, who live along Puget Sound and the northern Pacific coast, celebrated this bounty with the First Salmon Ceremony, which they still practice today. The rite has its origins in the belief that salmon and humans are the same in spirit, but that the fish voluntarily sacrifice their lives for the good of mankind. They will come back to life, however, if the first catch is given proper respect.

Once the Salish catch the first fish of the season, they enact an elaborate ritual that, by coincidence, has parallels to the Christian sacrament of communion. Celebrants first pay homage to the fish, and then prepare it for communal tasting. Afterward, they return its intact skeleton to the sea so that the salmon may renew itself and return the next year.

Washington

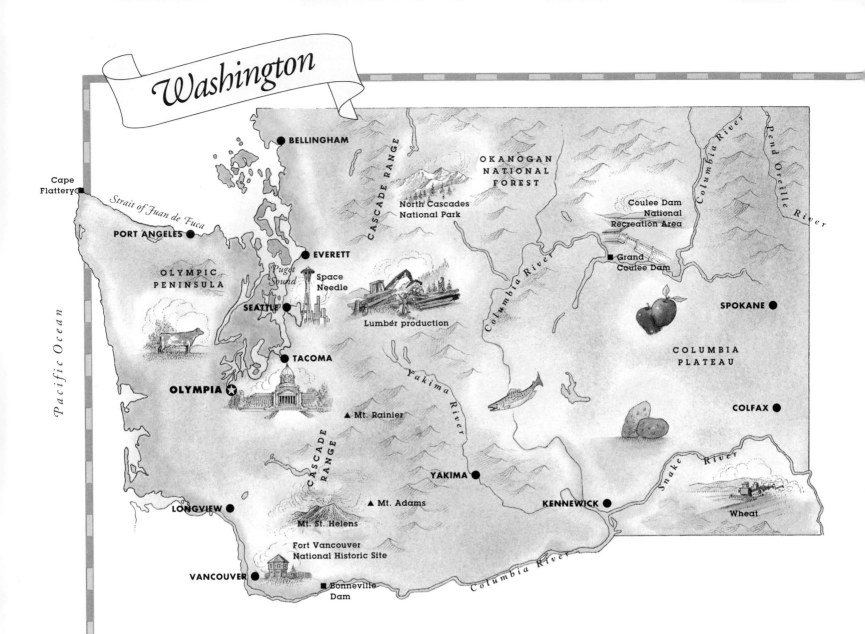

Cape Flattery

Strait of Juan de Fuca

BELLINGHAM

CASCADE RANGE

OKANOGAN NATIONAL FOREST

Columbia River

Pend Oreille River

PORT ANGELES

North Cascades National Park

Coulee Dam National Recreation Area

OLYMPIC PENINSULA

EVERETT

Puget Sound

Space Needle

Grand Coulee Dam

SEATTLE

Lumber production

SPOKANE

Columbia River

Pacific Ocean

TACOMA

COLUMBIA PLATEAU

OLYMPIA ☆

Yakima River

▲ Mt. Rainier

COLFAX

CASCADE RANGE

▲ Mt. Adams

YAKIMA

Snake River

Mt. St. Helens

KENNEWICK

LONGVIEW

Wheat

Fort Vancouver National Historic Site

VANCOUVER

Columbia River

Bonneville Dam

THE PEOPLE AND THE LAND

Population: 4,827,000

Area: 68,139 sq. mi.

Population per sq. mi.: 71

Capital: Olympia (pop. 156,600)

Largest city: Seattle (pop. 1,861,700)

Major rivers: Columbia, Pend Oreille, Snake, Yakima

Elevation: Sea level to 14,410 ft. (Mt. Rainier)

Leading industries: Aerospace, forestry products, food products, primary metals, agriculture (wheat, apples, potatoes, dairy)

Bird: Willow goldfinch

Flower: Coast rhododendron

Tree: Western hemlock

Motto: *Alki* (By and By)

Song: "Washington, My Home"

Origin of name: In honor of George Washington

Nickname: Evergreen State

INFORMATION

Washington State Tourism Division

101 General Administration Building
Olympia, WA 98504-0613
Telephone: 206-753-5600

State flag

Willow goldfinch

Coast rhododendron

HISTORICAL HIGHLIGHTS

1775 Spanish explorers Bruno Heceta and Juan Francisco de La Bodega y Quadra land on Washington coast.

1792 American Robert Gray discovers Columbia River. Britisher George Vancouver explores Puget Sound.

1805 Lewis and Clark follow Snake and Columbia rivers to Pacific Ocean.

1810 British-Canadian fur company builds post near present-day Spokane.

1818 U.S. and Great Britain agree to joint occupation of Oregon Territory, including Washington.

1825 Hudson's Bay Company, a fur trading agency, establishes Fort Vancouver.

1846 U.S. and Great Britain put Canadian-Washington boundary at 49th parallel.

1853 Congress creates Washington Territory.

1855 Indian wars break out.

1881 Northern Pacific Railroad reaches Spokane.

1889 Washington joins Union as 42nd state.

1909 Seattle hosts Alaska-Yukon-Pacific Exposition.

1917 Lake Washington Ship Canal is completed, giving Seattle a freshwater, nontidal harbor.

1937 Bonneville Dam, first hydroelectric project on the Columbia River, is completed.

1942 Grand Coulee Dam, one of world's largest producers of hydroelectric power, opens.

1962 Seattle draws 9.6 million visitors to the Century 21 Exposition, a world's fair.

1964 U.S. and Canada approve cooperative plan for major hydroelectric and river control projects on the Columbia River and its tributaries.

1974 Spokane hosts a world's fair, Expo '74.

1980 Mt. St. Helens erupts, causing more than 60 deaths and extensive damage.

FAMOUS SONS AND DAUGHTERS

Bing Crosby (1904 – 77).

The definitive crooner was a star both on radio and in films. Among his movies were *Going My Way* and, with Bob Hope, the famous "road" comedies, including *The Road to Morocco* and *The Road to Zanzibar*.

Mary McCarthy (1912 – 89). McCarthy excelled as a literary critic, short story writer, and novelist. One of her most successful novels was *The Group*, noted for its biting wit.

Seattle (1786? – 1866). This respected chief of the Duwamish, Suquamish, and other Puget Sound tribes befriended white settlers in the region and signed a peace treaty with them in 1855.

James Whittaker (1931 –). In 1963, Whittaker, member of a U.S. expedition, became the first American to reach the top of Mt. Everest. Accompanied by a Nepalese guide, he scaled the mountain from the south.

ODDITIES AND SPECIALTIES

Among the features of the Columbia Plateau are coulees, dry canyons formed thousands of years ago when glaciers blocked off tributaries of the Columbia River. Best known is Grand Coulee, site of the famous dam.

The first American commercial jet was made in Washington.

When residents of Seattle say "The mountain's out," they mean that it's a nice day. In other words, it is clear enough to see Mt. Rainier in the distance.

Washington's coastal Indians were once proficient whalers, using ocean-going cedar canoes.

Seattle's Skid Road was a street of greased logs, over which lumbermen skidded logs to the mills. After the Klondike gold rush, the street became a hangout for derelicts — the original "skid row."

Chinook and sockeye salmon are two of the delicacies that are exported from Washington around the world.

The Yakima Valley is the leading producer of apples in the U.S.

PLACES TO VISIT, THINGS TO DO

Coulee Dam National Recreation Area Northeast of Grand Coulee Dam, this area boasts lakes and rivers — including the huge Franklin D. Roosevelt Lake — and an abundance of plant and animal life.

Mt. Rainier National Park (headquarters at Longmire). Flower-filled meadows and dense forest surround Washington's highest mountain. Numerous hiking trails include one to the spectacular ice caves of Paradise Glacier.

North Cascades National Park (headquarters at Sedro Woolley). The jagged peaks of the great Cascade Range loom above a vast wilderness, which encompasses dozens of tumbling waterfalls, alpine lakes, and wooded valleys.

Olympic National Park (headquarters at Port Angeles). Untamed ocean beaches, lush vegetation, and snowcapped peaks are the drawing cards in this Olympic Peninsula park.

Seafair (Seattle). Held for three weeks in July and August, this annual fair is a celebration of the various cultural heritages of the Pacific Northwest. Ethnic food, crafts, and entertainment are the featured attractions.

Seattle Center Focal point of this park is Seattle's most famous landmark, the Space Needle, built for the 1962 Century 21 Exposition. A monorail connects the park with downtown.

West Virginia

High in the mountains, deep forests and a love of home

Take me home, country roads" — so go the lyrics to a song about West Virginia popularized by John Denver. There is something about this state — the most mountainous east of the Mississippi River — that taps the American longing for home, summoning up the taste of hot buttered biscuits, the whine of a lonesome fiddle, and the creak of a rocking chair out on the front porch.

West Virginia is mountain country. The Blue Ridge cuts across the state's eastern neck, while the Allegheny Plateau dominates the interior. Looking west from the tiny hamlets near the Virginia border, you can see ridge after ridge rising toward a line of distant summits silhouetted against the sky.

The first settlers who trickled into the area in the early 1700's from Pennsylvania and the Atlantic coast put down roots in valleys carved out by rampaging rivers. There they cleared pastures for their cows and found hunting grounds in the virgin forests that swathed the surrounding hillsides. After they broke away from Virginia in 1861 at the start of the Civil War, their state became the first and only one to be formed through secession.

NATURE'S PAGEANT

Now, as in the past, nature is the state's main event. Springtime is always awash in ethereal clouds of pink crabapple and white hawthorn. Black-eyed Susans, daisies, and goldenrod dot the roadsides during the halcyon days of summer. A circus pageant of color transforms the mountains with the turning leaves of autumn.

Despite its rugged appearance, 63-foot-high Blackwater Falls near the northern edge of Monongahela National Forest is accessible year-round via an easy path.

And in winter, the highlands fall under the white grip of snow, as much as 100 inches of it annually along the Alleghenies.

Eastern West Virginia is a place so high and wild that in some of its most sequestered corners, like Cranberry Glades and the Dolly Sods Wilderness Area, the heath barrens and waist-deep bogs seem almost subarctic. The mountains are blanketed in awe-inspiring forests — spruce, hemlock, oak, and hickory — where black bears, gray and red foxes, and wildcats lurk in the dense shade. A stand of 300-year-old virgin red spruce at Gaudineer Knob is a stately vestige of the primeval woodlands the pioneers encountered.

To the west, the state is speckled with small farms and quiet hamlets tilting down the western slopes of the Alleghenies toward the Ohio River. The presence of pure silica sand made glassmaking a major industry throughout the northwestern part of the state, while hulking steel mills mushroomed around the northern panhandle city of Wheeling.

South of Charleston is coal country, where miners descend into a dark and chilly subterranean world to hack out more than 40 percent of all the bituminous coal the United States produces. Here also is one of America's wildest waterways, the New River, a playground for white-water rafters. Contrary to its name, the New may be the second-oldest river in the world, dating from the Cenozoic era 65 million years ago, when it began carving a gorge now 700 to 1,300 feet deep.

Periodically in recent decades, West Virginians have seen their progeny move away with fluxes in the coal and lumber markets. But their culture has endured in the whirling colors of handmade quilts, bittersweet folk tunes, the breathless glee of a clog dance, and the graceful curves of an Appalachian basket. Residents view their state with wry good humor. As one old-timer quipped, "It's right spread out, and it's might rough; but it's a damned good state for the shape it's in." Above all, it is a place that speaks to a yearning for peace and independence, dual needs that are perfectly satisfied by the picture of a winding country road leading home in the mountains of West Virginia.

Sunrise is peaceful along the Cranberry River high on the Allegheny Plateau. A favorite haunt of backpackers, the Cranberry wilderness also attracts fishermen, who enjoy its many trout streams.

Shy but playful, a young foal snuggles against its mother, as fresh and full of promise as the surrounding springtime pasture.

The restored pioneer farm at Twin Falls State Park recalls the settlers whose commitment reshaped a wilderness into a place they made their home.

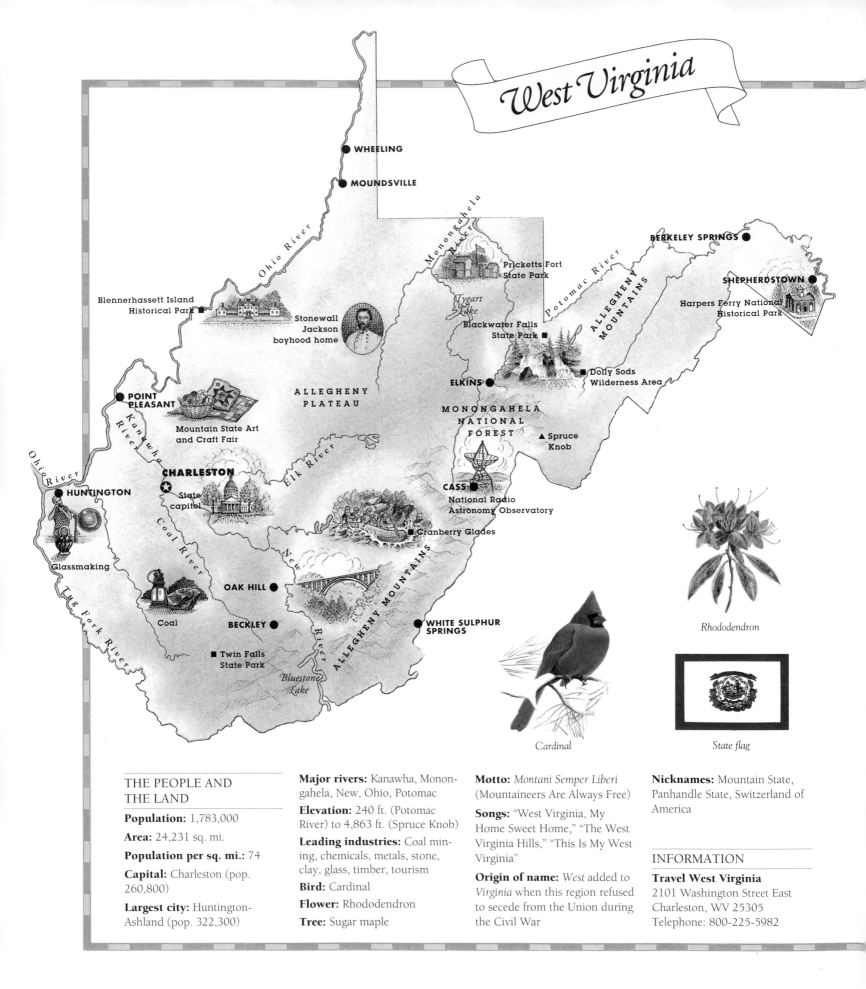

West Virginia

WHEELING

MOUNDSVILLE

Ohio River

Monongahela River

BERKELEY SPRINGS

Potomac River

Pricketts Fort
State Park

SHEPHERDSTOWN

Blennerhassett Island
Historical Park

Stonewall
Jackson
boyhood home

Tygart Lake

Blackwater Falls
State Park

Harpers Ferry National
Historical Park

ALLEGHENY
MOUNTAINS

Dolly Sods
Wilderness Area

ELKINS

POINT
PLEASANT

ALLEGHENY
PLATEAU

MONONGAHELA
NATIONAL
FOREST

▲ Spruce
Knob

Mountain State Art
and Craft Fair

Kanawha River

Elk River

CASS
National Radio
Astronomy Observatory

Ohio River

CHARLESTON
★ State
capitol

HUNTINGTON

Coal River

Cranberry Glades

Glassmaking

New River

Tug Fork River

Coal

OAK HILL

ALLEGHENY MOUNTAINS

BECKLEY

WHITE SULPHUR
SPRINGS

■ Twin Falls
State Park

*Bluestone
Lake*

Rhododendron

Cardinal

State flag

THE PEOPLE AND
THE LAND

Population: 1,783,000

Area: 24,231 sq. mi.

Population per sq. mi.: 74

Capital: Charleston (pop. 260,800)

Largest city: Huntington-Ashland (pop. 322,300)

Major rivers: Kanawha, Monongahela, New, Ohio, Potomac

Elevation: 240 ft. (Potomac River) to 4,863 ft. (Spruce Knob)

Leading industries: Coal mining, chemicals, metals, stone, clay, glass, timber, tourism

Bird: Cardinal

Flower: Rhododendron

Tree: Sugar maple

Motto: *Montani Semper Liberi* (Mountaineers Are Always Free)

Songs: "West Virginia, My Home Sweet Home," "The West Virginia Hills," "This Is My West Virginia"

Origin of name: *West* added to *Virginia* when this region refused to secede from the Union during the Civil War

Nicknames: Mountain State, Panhandle State, Switzerland of America

INFORMATION

Travel West Virginia
2101 Washington Street East
Charleston, WV 25305
Telephone: 800-225-5982

HISTORICAL HIGHLIGHTS

1727 Germans from Pennsylvania settle the area near present-day Shepherdstown.

1742 Coal is discovered along Coal River streambed.

1774 Settlers defeat Indians at Battle of Point Pleasant, called by some the first battle of American Revolution.

1776 Western Virginia residents petition Continental Congress for right to separate from Virginia.

1806 Militia sent to arrest planter Harman Blennerhassett and former Vice President Aaron Burr, accused of treason against U.S. government.

1859 After raiding federal arsenal at Harpers Ferry, abolitionist John Brown is captured, tried, and hanged.

1861 Western Virginia refuses to secede from Union, creating a split with Virginia.

1863 West Virginia joins Union as 35th state.

1907 Explosion at Monongah coal mine kills 361 miners.

1921 Unionizing coal miners fight state police in Battle of Blair Mountain.

1943 Discovery of huge salt deposits in Ohio River Valley attracts chemical companies.

1960 John F. Kennedy defeats Hubert H. Humphrey in presidential primary election, a key victory in his quest for Democratic nomination.

1968 Explosions at Farmingham mines kill 78 people, causing Congress to enact new mine safety laws.

1977 West Virginia Democrat Robert C. Byrd is elected majority leader of the U.S. Senate.

1987 State unemployment rate drops below 10 percent, showing economic recovery.

FAMOUS SONS AND DAUGHTERS

Pearl S. Buck (1892 – 1973).

Winner of the Nobel Prize in literature in 1938, Buck spent her youth in China with her missionary parents and set many of her novels there, including her masterpiece, *The Good Earth*.

Martin Robinson Delany (1812 – 85). A Union Army physician, Delany was the first black to attain the rank of major. He fought against slavery and led a movement that urged American blacks to return to Africa.

Thomas J. ("Stonewall") Jackson (1824 – 63). A daring Confederate general, Jackson was nicknamed for the tenacity of his troops at Bull Run. He was shot accidentally by his own men at the Battle of Chancellorsville and later died from the wounds.

Walter Reuther (1907 – 70). President of the United Automobile Workers, Reuther helped merge the Congress of Industrial Organizations and the American Federation of Labor in 1955, forming the nation's most powerful labor organization.

Charles E. ("Chuck") Yeager (1923 –). At age 24, Yeager became the first person to fly faster than the speed of sound. He went on to become one of the nation's most renowned test pilots.

ODDITIES AND SPECIALTIES

James Rumsey launched a steamboat at Shepherdstown in 1787, two decades before Robert Fulton launched his steam-powered craft in New York.

Family reunions became popular in West Virginia between 1930 and 1950. The Lilly reunion — descendants and kin of colonist Robert Lilly — drew as many as 75,000 people.

Coal underlies nearly half of West Virginia, which boasts about 500 working mines. The resort of White Sulphur Springs has a building made from coal.

Glassblowing and manufacturing are highly developed arts in West Virginia. In addition to fine glassware, nearly all the glass marbles manufactured in the U.S. are made in West Virginia.

PLACES TO VISIT, THINGS TO DO

Berkeley Springs Local Indians enjoyed the warm springs here even before George Washington and his family frequented them in colonial times. A state park provides public access today.

Blackwater Falls State Park (near Davis). Amid evergreens and boulders, the Blackwater River plunges 63 feet, creating a spectacular waterfall.

Cass Scenic Railroad State Park (Cass). Ride a steam train up Bald Knob in this restored turn-of-the-century logging town.

Exhibition Coal Mine (Beckley). Coal cars carry visitors nearly 1,500 feet underground to view one of West Virginia's major industries in operation.

Fishing Bluestone and Tygart lakes are favorite spots for bass, catfish, trout, and crappie.

Grave Creek Mound State Park (Moundsville). Sixty-nine feet high, the burial mound is among the largest built by the prehistoric Adena Indians.

Monongahela National Forest (headquarters at Elkins). Spanning 10 counties, this vast Allegheny Mountain preserve contains hiking trails, trout streams, caves, white-water rivers, and five wilderness areas.

Mountain State Art and Craft Fair (Ripley). One of the nation's largest expositions of country arts and crafts is held annually the week of July 4.

National Radio Astronomy Observatory (Green Bank). View the radio telescopes astronomers use to explore the limits of the universe.

New River Gorge National River (headquarters at Oak Hill). Fifty miles of the New River have been set aside so that boaters may enjoy its beautiful canyon.

Pricketts Fort State Park (Fairmont). A reconstructed fort and 16 cabins recall life on the frontier in the 1770's.

Wisconsin

Rolling pastureland and cool north woods

On the map of America the fist of Wisconsin delivers an uppercut to Lake Superior while its thumb pokes out, like a hitchhiker's, into Lake Michigan. That hand is a beautiful appendage, clothed in cool north woods and rolling green pastureland and studded with diamond-blue glacial lakes. The quiet Mississippi, which delineates much of Wisconsin's western border, is edged with dramatic limestone and sandstone bluffs. Other rivers twine through the deep forests, sometimes driven to frothy rage by melting snow.

A MOVE TO CONSERVE

From the beginning, this luxuriant, river-scored land possessed a seemingly inexhaustible inventory of natural abundance — fur-bearing animals, towering white pines, whitefish and lake trout by the millions, and loamy soil for farming. Within a century of white settlement, however, the cornucopia no longer overflowed. By the 1870's wheat farmers had depleted the soil of southern Wisconsin. Ten years later the Milwaukee River had become so defiled with raw sewage that fish could not live in it. And by the turn of the century, most of Wisconsin's virgin white pines had been cut to the ground.

Precisely because its splendid landscapes were being marred by the hand of man, Wisconsin took an early lead in the incipient American conservation movement. The state fostered some of the crusade's most farsighted and charismatic leaders. William Dempster Hoard used his newspaper, *Hoard's Dairyman*, to convince farmers to stop growing wheat

Dairy farms, here awash in October fog, occupy the rolling land near the hamlet of Cassville in the southwest corner of Wisconsin.

Rock-strewn streams are among the sights along the Ice Age National Scenic Trail, which marks the farthest advance of the last glacier that pushed into Wisconsin. The glacier, the Wisconsinan, covered much of the state up until about 10,000 years ago.

and to take up dairying instead. By doing so, they not only rescued the soil but also secured Wisconsin's economic future as the nation's prime producer of milk, butter, and cheese. Another man, a Scottish immigrant named John Muir, spent his boyhood on a farm in the hills of south-central Wisconsin before going on to become an esteemed naturalist and the founder of the Sierra Club.

One of the earliest environmental victories in America was the fight to save the 32,000-acre Horicon Marsh. Horicon and the other wetlands in Wisconsin were first seen only as an impediment to agriculture, and many tracts were drained in an effort to extend farmland. But in the 1920's Wisconsin conservationists banded together to restore the marsh to its natural state and sought federal and state protection for the land. Situated only 50 miles northwest of Milwaukee, Horicon is now one of the largest freshwater cattail marshes in the United States. It teems with wildlife — otters,

herons, migrating Canada geese, and the imperiled redheaded duck.

Beyond the wetlands, the splendor of Wisconsin is apparent on the shores of the Great Lakes. Door Peninsula, Wisconsin's hitchhiking thumb, is strung with rocky coves and fishing villages reminiscent of the New England coastline. Just off the tip of the peninsula is Washington Island, a craggy outpost that offers sweeping views of Lake Michigan from its majestic limestone cliffs.

At the far north of the state, offshore from the little Victorian lakeport of Bayfield, is a cluster of 22 islands called the Apostles. Standing in Lake Superior like sculpted brownstone platforms, these islands support dense forests of white pine, birch, spruce, and cedar. All but one are now protected as Apostle Islands National Lakeshore. On these wild fragments of land a visitor can enjoy the untouched beauty that residents of Wisconsin have fought for so long to preserve.

Cana Island hugs the shoreline of Door Peninsula, the 80-mile-long limestone promontory that juts into Lake Michigan. The quaint towns and Victorian inns of the region lure weekenders from Wisconsin's larger cities.

Cardinals nest in the white pines of Chequamegon National Forest.

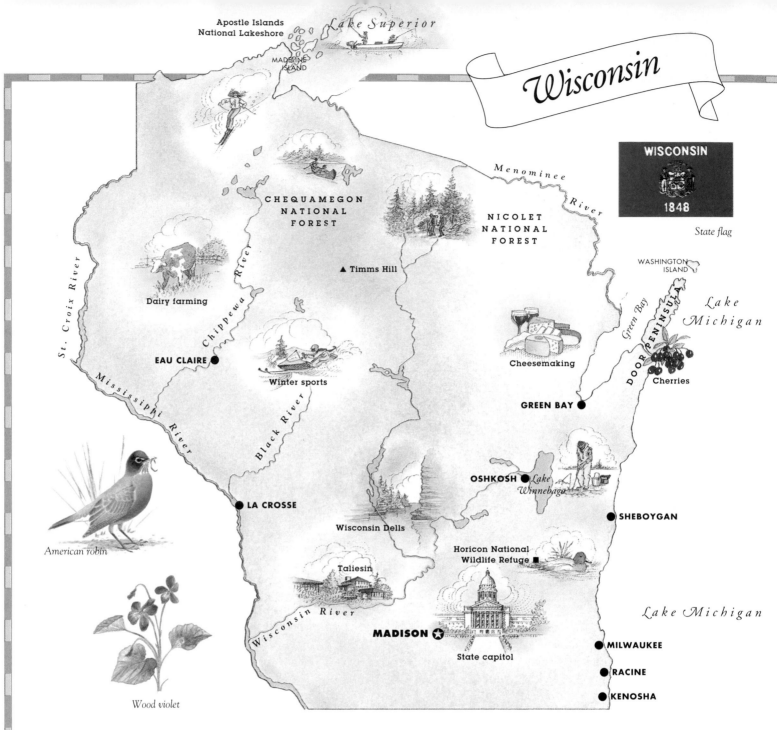

Wisconsin

Apostle Islands
National Lakeshore

Lake Superior

MADELINE
ISLAND

Menominee River

CHEQUAMEGON
NATIONAL
FOREST

NICOLET
NATIONAL
FOREST

▲ Timms Hill

WASHINGTON
ISLAND

Dairy farming

Cheesemaking

Cherries

Lake Michigan

EAU CLAIRE ●

Winter sports

GREEN BAY ●

OSHKOSH ● *Lake Winnebago*

LA CROSSE ●

SHEBOYGAN ●

Wisconsin Dells

Horicon National
Wildlife Refuge ■

American robin

Taliesin

Lake Michigan

Wisconsin River

MADISON ✪

State capitol

MILWAUKEE ●

RACINE ●

Wood violet

KENOSHA ●

WISCONSIN 1848

State flag

St. Croix River

Mississippi River

Chippewa River

Black River

Green Bay

DOOR PENINSULA

THE PEOPLE AND THE LAND

Population: 4,869,600

Area: 56,153 sq. mi.

Population per sq. mi.: 87

Capital: Madison (pop. 352,800)

Largest city: Milwaukee (pop. 1,398,000)

Major rivers: Black, Chippewa, Menominee, Mississippi, St. Croix, Wisconsin

Elevation: 581 ft. (Lake Michigan) to 1,952 ft. (Timms Hill)

Leading industries: Manufacturing (machinery, food products, paper products, fabricated metals), trade, finance, insurance, real estate, transportation, communications, agriculture (dairy, cattle)

Bird: American robin

Flower: Wood violet

Tree: Sugar maple

Motto: Forward

Song: "On, Wisconsin!"

Origin of name: From the Chippewa word, spelled *Ouisconsin* by early explorers, meaning gathering of the waters

Nicknames: America's Dairyland, Badger State

INFORMATION

Wisconsin Department of Development
Division of Tourism
Box 7606
Madison, WI 53702
Telephone: 608-266-2161

HISTORICAL HIGHLIGHTS

1634 French explorer Jean Nicolet lands on Green Bay shore.

c. 1670 Jesuit priests build mission at De Pere.

1673 Louis Jolliet and Fr. Jacques Marquette discover upper Mississippi River.

1701 First permanent settlement is started at Green Bay.

1763 France cedes area to England after French-Indian War.

1783 Wisconsin ceded to U.S. as part of Northwest Territory.

1836 Congress creates Wisconsin Territory.

1848 Wisconsin joins Union as 30th state.

1853 Railway links Milwaukee and Madison.

1854 Republican Party founded in the town of Ripon.

1871 Six-county forest fire kills more than 1,000 people.

1872 William D. Hoard founds state Dairymen's Association.

1901 Progressive era of social reform begins as Robert M. La Follette, Sr., becomes governor.

1911 State legislature sets up teachers' pensions.

1924 La Follette runs unsuccessfully as a Progressive party candidate for U.S. presidency.

1932 Wisconsin passes country's first state unemployment-compensation act.

1959 St. Lawrence Seaway opens, linking Great Lakes with Atlantic Ocean.

1971 State universities are consolidated, forming University of Wisconsin system.

1981 After 133 years, Joseph Schlitz Brewing Company closes its Milwaukee brewery.

1988 When Chrysler Corporation closes Kenosha plant, 5,500 workers lose jobs.

FAMOUS SONS AND DAUGHTERS

Zona Gale (1874 – 1938). This novelist was known for her realistic portrayal of the people of the Midwest. After she adapted her best-known book, *Miss Lulu Bett*, for the stage, she won a Pulitzer Prize for drama.

Harry Houdini (1874 – 1926).

The world's most famous escape artist astounded audiences in America and Europe by escaping from handcuffs, leg-irons, jail cells, and even locked trunks submerged in water. He also worked to expose fraudulent spiritualists.

Robert Marion La Follette (1855 – 1925). As Wisconsin governor (1901 – 06) and U.S. senator (1906 – 25), this progressive Republican was the force behind a number of social reforms, working for what would eventually become the nation's first minimum wage and worker's compensation laws.

Alfred Lunt (1892 – 1977). Lunt and his wife, Lynn Fontanne, were one of the most celebrated acting teams on the American stage, known especially for their performances in sophisticated modern comedies on Broadway.

Spencer Tracy (1900 – 67). This beloved actor starred in more than 60 films, winning Oscars as Best Actor for two of them: *Captains Courageous* (1937) and *Boys' Town* (1938).

Frank Lloyd Wright (1869 – 1959). A towering figure of American architecture, Wright sought to merge his buildings with their settings. A prime example of such organic architecture is Taliesin, Wright's Wisconsin home, which is now an architectural school.

ODDITIES AND SPECIALTIES

Wisconsin, with almost 37,000 dairy farms, banned the sale of margarine until the 1960's.

The nickname of Badger State dates from the 1820's, when miners dug holes in the hillsides to use as winter homes, just as badgers do. Those who fled the severe cold were called suckers, after a fish that migrates south in winter.

When it comes to winter sports, residents of snowy Wisconsin have gone beyond mere skiing. Games played on ice include bowling, volleyball, and broomball, a variation of hockey.

The Belle of Wisconsin was the largest cheese ever made — a 40,060-pound Cheddar. It was said that the yellow monster could top more than a million crackers or provide more than 300,000 grilled cheese sandwiches. After touring the country in its Cheesemobile, the Belle was sliced and sold in 1989.

PLACES TO VISIT, THINGS TO DO

Chequamegon National Forest (headquarters at Park Falls). More than 400 lakes spangle the three separate sections of this vast forest in northern Wisconsin. The rivers are excellent for canoeing, while the Ice Age Trail is popular with hikers.

House on the Rock (near Dodgeville). This unique house, perched atop a column of rock, is the centerpiece of a series of unusual exhibitions, including the world's largest carousel.

Nicolet National Forest (headquarters at Rhinelander). Located in the northern lake district are swamp forests and woodlands, with a deer trail, a natural arch, and plenty of fishing streams.

Summerfest (Milwaukee).

Billed as the World's Greatest Music Festival, this lakefront event is held for 11 days every summer, starting the last Thursday in June. Jazz, blues, country, big band, and rock performers occupy 11 stages.

Wisconsin Dells (south-central Wisconsin). The Wisconsin River carved this beautiful gorge through sandstone, creating cliffs and unusual rock formations.

Wyoming

In the fabled West,
a wealth of natural wonders

In the towering mountain ranges and sweeping grazing lands of Wyoming live fewer people than in any other state. Even Cheyenne, the largest city, has only 75,000 inhabitants. One can wander for weeks through the rugged Tetons without seeing a sign of another person — and when ranch houses are found in the wide open spaces, they often are more than 100 miles apart.

THE ISOLATED FRONTIER

If the place names of this sparsely populated state — Bighorn, Yellowstone, Medicine Bow, and Wind River among them — sound as if they belong in a western novel, it may be because the pioneers wanted to make the isolated region seem as romantic as possible. Settlers were desperately needed to populate the territory so that it could apply for statehood. To encourage women to migrate, the territorial legislature in 1869 guaranteed them equal rights to vote and hold office — a radical reform no other democratic government was even willing to consider at the time.

Many of the settlers who did show up kept right on going once they discovered that the euphonious Wind River Range was bounded by wastelands like Red Desert, Alkali Flat, and Bad Lands Hills. Certainly Wyoming did not impress Daniel Webster. All it would bring to the Union, he warned, was "savages, wild beasts, shifting sands, whirlwinds of dust, cactus and prairie dogs."

What Webster did not know was that Wyoming was also the site of natural wonders that one day would bring the world to its doorstep.

Over time, the mineral deposits left by the waters of Mammoth Hot Springs have created eerie terraces.

Even rugged Yellowstone National Park has its pastoral side. Here pronghorns graze in a meadow at the foot of green mountains.

THE GLORIES OF YELLOWSTONE

Chief among those wonders is the Yellowstone River region, a surreal quadrant of steam-vented land in the northwest corner of the state. John Colter, a private on leave from the Lewis and Clark expedition, was the first white man to see it, in 1807. Yellowstone's mysterious geysers, hot springs, petrified forests, and waterfalls stirred the imagination of all who heard of them. Before long, tale-spinning trappers like Jim Bridger were describing a sulfurous land where a man could catch a fish in a stream, then toss it over his shoulder to cook in a boiling pool.

Preserved for posterity in 1872 as the world's first national park, Yellowstone has lost none of its supernatural aura. Because hot molten rock, or magma, which is usually 10 to 30 miles below the surface, is only one to three miles below the earth's crust here, the region has more geysers, hot springs, mud pots, and volcanic steam vents than are found in all the rest of the world. Attractions such as Old Faithful draw more than 2.5 million visitors to the park each year.

For wildlife lovers, to enter Yellowstone National Park is to step back in time 200 years, to an era when moose and mule deer, bighorn sheep, and bison were kept in rough equilibrium by the dispassionate forces of nature. Some people consider the entire state of Wyoming to be a giant game preserve of sorts. Nearly half of the state's land, in fact, is controlled in some manner by the federal government. Wyoming's two national parks, along with vast forests and wilderness areas, make it one of the few remaining states that still have plenty of room for threatened species such as the majestic grizzly bear, the peregrine falcon, the trumpeter swan, and the black-footed ferret.

His world changed to ice by a February storm, an elk forages for food in the Lamar Valley south of Yellowstone.

Elderberries are plentiful in Medicine Bow National Forest.

ON THE TIMBERLINE

At elevations above 10,000 feet, Wyoming's mountains become desolate, icy realms of wind-scoured rock debris and boulders. Only lichens and sedges grow there, clinging precariously to rocky crevices and ledges.

But on the timberline just below, where the climate can barely support trees, the topmost firs, pines, and spruces have adapted to the inhospitable environment. Windblown ice particles inhibit the growth of their needles and branches on the windward side, so that the trees take on the look of wizened, asymmetrical topiary. Some appear normal at the base of the trunk, which is protected during the winter by drifting snow, but branches higher up are invariably twisted and worn smooth by abrasive arctic blasts.

The trees that are able to tolerate this severe climate grow very slowly. The whitebark pine, for example, takes from 250 to 300 years to reach maturity. Often the winter snows are so heavy that the pine's weighted branches touch the ground and gradually take root. These crooked trees become part of Wyoming's glorious scenery for a few weeks each summer, when the eagles soar above them and the tiny flowers of white phlox and delicate blue forget-me-nots burst into bloom on the slopes.

Bordering Yellowstone on the south is Wyoming's second national park, Grand Teton, where the Teton Range rises abruptly from a green valley named Jackson Hole. Seven lakes shimmer at the foot of the peaks. Jackson Lake, by far the largest, is an established recreation area. But perhaps the most beautiful is Lake Solitude, which mirrors Grand Teton, the tallest mountain in the range. Its name notwithstanding, Lake Solitude attracts so many hikers that the Park Service has banned camping there since the 1970's.

THE CATTLEMAN'S COMMONWEALTH

Although the outside world thinks of Wyoming in terms of Yellowstone and the Tetons, the majority of the state's population lives on the High Plains. This arid grazing country extends from the Colorado border up to the pine-clad Bighorn Mountains, whose tallest peaks soar to 13,000 feet.

By the time Wyoming entered the Union it had come to be called the Cattleman's Commonwealth, dominated by ranchers who grazed their huge herds on public lands. But

The Wind River Range forms an imposing backdrop for the trees and shallow rivers of Shoshone National Forest. Seen here is the group of peaks known as the Cirque of the Towers.

The Tetons, a 40-mile-long segment of the Rocky Mountains, reflect in the Snake River at Schwabacher Landing. From afar, the mountains change from shades of gray to purple, depending on the light. Grand Teton is at right.

HUNTING GROUND OF THE WEST

Wyoming Territory teemed with so much game in the 19th century that it became one of the continent's prime hunting grounds. Fur trappers sought out the region's millions of beavers, whose misfortune it was to have barbed fur that pressed easily into felt. Settlers moving west dined heartily on bison, and wild game disappeared for miles on both sides of the Oregon Trail.

Professional hunters, eager for buffalo hides to ship back east, flooded into the territory. The most efficient of them boasted that they could pick off as many as 100 animals on a good day. And gentlemen sportsmen traveled from afar to reap their share: one Sir St. George Gore, visiting from England, massacred an estimated 2,000 buffaloes and 100 bears, plus 1,600 elk and deer on a three-year hunting trip that began in 1854.

Wyoming's animals finally received protection in the 1870s, when the territorial assembly outlawed the sale of wild meat during the spring and summer months, the time when larger mammals give birth. The territory was also the first to establish penalties for hunting game birds out of season.

Today the only real threats to Wyoming's wildlife come from competition for grazing land and encroaching development. But federal game preserves and judicious range management ensure that the wilderness areas essential for the survival of elk, moose, buffalo, deer, beaver, and other species will remain as they are.

---

this affluent domain had its problems. Cattlemen resented the encroachment of homesteaders, who sometimes acquired herds of their own by appropriating the mavericks (unbranded calves) of the larger ranches. When the ranchers accused the newcomers of rustling, anger erupted on both sides. It boiled over in 1892, when a vigilante group of ranchers invaded suspected rustler territory and killed two men — an incident known as the Johnson County War.

Today ranching continues to be one of Wyoming's leading industries. Cattlemen no longer contend with rustlers, but blizzards, hail, and winds that reach a velocity of 60 miles per hour remain problems.

West of the plains the forested slopes of the Rocky Mountains begin. Five national forests, including Shoshone and Bridger-Teton, lie entirely inside Wyoming, and five others are partially within its borders. Lodgepole pines cover a large part of the woodlands, but spruces, Douglas firs, and aspens also are common.

This green and wildly beautiful part of the state holds on to its aura of seclusion, despite the campers that flock here to Yellowstone and the tourists that stroll the boardwalks of pioneer towns in the shadow of the towering Tetons. In the splendid isolation of Wyoming one can sense the real West, the fabled West that remains an everlasting part of the American dream.

Steam wafts from geyser vents along the Firehole River in Yellowstone National Park.

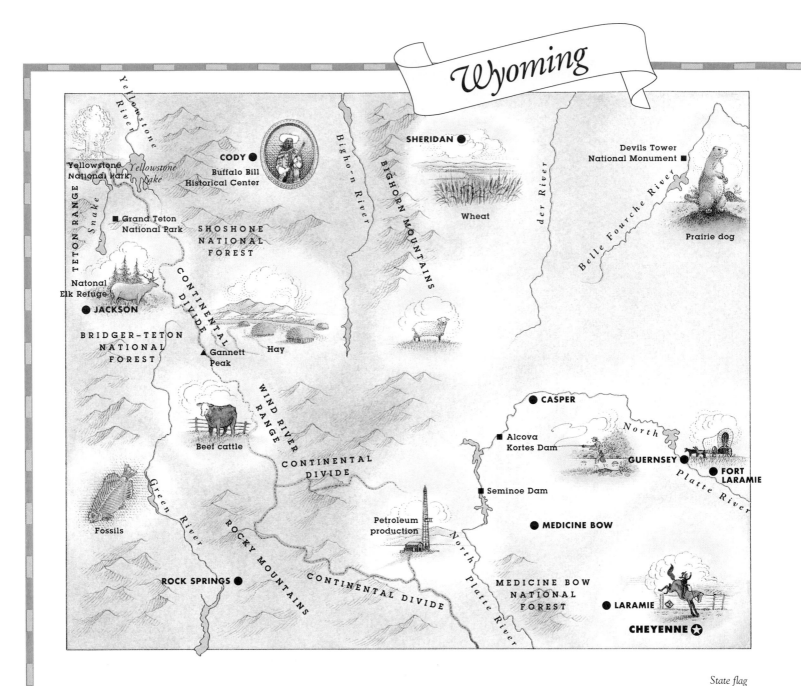

Wyoming

Yellowstone River

Yellowstone National Park

Yellowstone Lake

CODY ●
Buffalo Bill Historical Center

TETON RANGE

Snake

■ Grand Teton National Park

SHOSHONE NATIONAL FOREST

CONTINENTAL DIVIDE

Natonal Elk Refuge

● JACKSON

BRIDGER–TETON NATIONAL FOREST

▲ Gannett Peak

Hay

WIND RIVER RANGE

Beef cattle

CONTINENTAL DIVIDE

Green River

Fossils

ROCKY MOUNTAINS

CONTINENTAL DIVIDE

ROCK SPRINGS ●

Bighorn River

BIGHORN MOUNTAINS

SHERIDAN ●

der River

Wheat

Devils Tower National Monument ■

Belle Fourche River

Prairie dog

● CASPER

North

■ Alcova Kortes Dam

GUERNSEY ●

● FORT LARAMIE

Platte River

■ Seminoe Dam

Petroleum production

North Platte River

● MEDICINE BOW

MEDICINE BOW NATIONAL FOREST

● LARAMIE

CHEYENNE ✪

THE PEOPLE AND THE LAND

Population: 449,900

Area: 97,809 sq. mi.

Population per sq. mi.: 5

Capital and largest city: Cheyenne (pop. 75,200)

Major rivers: Bighorn, Green, North Platte, Powder, Snake, Wind, Yellowstone

Elevation: 3,100 ft. (Belle Fourche River) to 13,804 ft. (Gannett Peak)

Leading industries: Oil and natural gas production, mining (coal, uranium, trona, gravel), tourism, agriculture (cattle, sheep, wheat, hay)

Bird: Meadowlark

Flower: Indian paintbrush

Tree: Cottonwood

Motto: Equal Rights

Song: "Wyoming"

Origin of name: A Delaware Indian word meaning on the great plains

Nicknames: Big Wyoming State, Cowboy State, Equality State

INFORMATION

Division of Tourism
I-25 at College Drive
Cheyenne, WY 82002
Telephone: 307-777-7777

State flag

Meadowlark

Indian paintbrush

HISTORICAL HIGHLIGHTS

1807 John Colter, a trapper and guide, explores the Yellowstone River region.

1812 Robert Stuart discovers South Pass, a route across the Rocky Mountains.

1833 Oil is found near Wind River mountains.

1834 Robert Campbell and William Sublette build the trading post that becomes Fort Laramie, the region's first permanent white settlement.

1867 Union Pacific Railroad enters Wyoming.

1868 Congress creates Wyoming Territory.

1883 Dallas Field is site of Wyoming's first oil well.

1890 Wyoming joins Union as the 44th state.

1892 Cattlemen fight homesteaders in Johnson County War, over issue of cattle rustling.

1910 Shoshone Dam, later renamed Buffalo Bill Dam, is completed in northern Wyoming, providing water for irrigation.

1938 Alcova Kortes and Seminoe dams are completed on North Platte River.

1951 Uranium is discovered in Powder River area.

1960 First intercontinental ballistic missile base is established near Cheyenne.

1965 Minuteman missile installation near Cheyenne is completed.

1974 Jim Bridger Power Plant, in Rock Springs, begins operating.

1986 Nation's first operational MX intercontinental ballistic missiles installed at Warren Air Force Base near Cheyenne.

1988 One million acres of Yellowstone National Park burn in the region's worst forest fire in more than 200 years.

FAMOUS SONS AND DAUGHTERS

Thurman Wesley Arnold (1891 – 1969). As Franklin D. Roosevelt's assistant attorney general, Arnold earned his reputation as a trustbuster by filing over 200 suits against monopolies.

Jim Bridger (1804 – 81).

This colorful fur trapper and guide came to be known as King of the Mountain Men. In 1843 he established Fort Bridger, a trading post for pioneers headed west on the Oregon Trail.

Jackson Pollock (1912 – 56). Influenced by surrealists and modern Spanish and Mexican artists, Pollock developed a style called "action painting," in which he dripped and splattered uneven lines of paint onto large canvases. By the 1950's he was recognized as a leading abstract expressionist.

Nellie Tayloe Ross (1876 – 1977). Ross became the nation's first female governor when she succeeded her husband as governor of Wyoming in 1925. She later scored another first for women when Franklin D. Roosevelt appointed her director of the U.S. Mint in 1933.

Willis Van Devanter (1859 – 1941). After serving as chief justice of Wyoming's Supreme Court, Van Devanter became assistant U.S. attorney general and a federal circuit judge. As a U.S. Supreme Court justice, he was known for his frequent opposition to New Deal legislation.

ODDITIES AND SPECIALTIES

On a summer's night, Wyoming residents may head outside to enjoy a milk can dinner. To make this local specialty they layer potatoes, sausages, and vegetables inside a milk can, add a little water for steam, and set the can over an open fire.

In one sense, Wyoming has the oldest house in the world — a private home, near the town of Rock River, built largely of dinosaur bones.

So many pioneer wagons followed the Oregon Trail through Wyoming that their wheels left permanent ruts — still visible today — in the soft limestone rocks south of Guernsey.

Cheyenne is home to the world's only museum devoted to first edition postage stamps — the National First Day Cover Museum.

Wyomingites are so proud of their cowboy heritage that their license plates depict a rider on a bucking horse.

PLACES TO VISIT, THINGS TO DO

Buffalo Bill Historical Center (Cody). This museum for Old West aficionados includes Frederic Remington paintings, Indian artifacts, Winchester firearms, and a huge collection of Buffalo Bill Cody memorabilia.

Devils Tower National Monument (northeast Wyoming). The remnant of a volcano, this fluted rock column rises 865 feet above its forested base, which itself is over 400 feet high.

Frontier Days (Cheyenne). This July festival, complete with parades, barbecues, and country entertainers, bills its rodeo as "The Daddy of 'em All."

Grand Teton National Park (headquarters at Moose). The Teton Range ascends abruptly from the valley called Jackson Hole. In addition to its stunning scenery, the park's big draw is its abundant wildlife.

Medicine Bow National Forest (headquarters at Laramie). The beauty of the Snowy Range dominates this forest, whose lakes and streams offer some of the best trout fishing in the world.

Register Cliff (near Guernsey). History buffs can read the names and messages that westward-traveling pioneers carved into this soft sandstone bluff, which served as a camping site in the 1800's.

Yellowstone National Park (headquarters at Mammoth Hot Springs). The first national park, Yellowstone is a fantasyland of bubbling mud volcanoes, hot springs, rushing rivers, colorful canyons, plunging waterfalls, and more than 250 geysers, including Old Faithful.

INDEX

CREDITS

1 Gene Ahrens. **2-3** ©1984 Bill Weems. **4-5** Willard Clay. **6-7** Thomas D. Mangelsen/Images of Nature. **10-11** John Marshall. **12-13** David Muench. **14 & 15** Ed Malles. **17** *left* Photograph courtesy of the Country Music Foundation, Inc.; *right* Helen Kittinger/Photo Options. **18-19** Tom Bean. **20** Ed Cooper. **21** *top* Jeff Gnass; *bottom* John Shaw/Tom Stack & Associates. **22** *top left* George S. Stroud; *bottom* Tom Bean. **22-23** Jeff Gnass. **24** Carr Clifton. **25** Tom Bean. **26** *left* The Bettmann Archive; *right* Lael Morgan. **28-29** John Gerlach/DRK Photo. **30-31** Tom Bean. **31** *top* Jeff Gnass, *bottom* Tom Bean/DRK Photo. **32** Willard Clay. **33** *top* David Muench; *bottom* Matt Bradley. **34** *top* Kenneth W. Fink/Bruce Coleman Inc.; *bottom* David Muench. **35** David Muench/H. Armstrong Roberts. **36** *right* Jen & Des Bartlett/Bruce Coleman Inc. **37** *left* Library of Congress; *right* Bob Clemenz. **38-39** Matt Bradley. **40 & 41** Matt Bradley. **42** Garry D. McMichael/Photo Researchers, Inc. **43** J.H. Robinson/Photo Researchers, Inc. **45** *left* Breck Kent/Earth Scenes; *middle* UPI/Bettmann; *right* Chuck O'Rear/West Light. **46-47** Larry Ulrich. **48** Carr Clifton. **49** *top* Larry Ulrich; *bottom* Carr Clifton. **50** *top* Pat O'Hara; *bottom* Carr Clifton. **51** Pat O'Hara. **52** Harald Sund/The Image Bank. **53** *top* Reproduced by permission of The Huntington Library, San Marino, California; *bottom* David Muench. **54** Tim Thompson. **55** *top left* Ralph Clevenger/West Light; *top right* Larry Ulrich; *bottom* Tim Thompson. **57** *left* The Bettmann Archive; *right* Suzanne J. Engelmann/SuperStock International. **58-59** David Muench. **60** *left* David Muench. **60-61** Jerry Jacka. **62** *top* Carr Clifton; *bottom* David Muench. **63** *top* David Muench; *bottom* Carr Clifton. **64** *top* David Muench; *bottom* Steve Mulligan. **65** Tom Till. **66 & 67** David Muench. **69** *left* Culver Pictures; *upper right* Thomas Kitchin/Tom Stack & Associates; *bottom right* SuperStock International. **70-71** Ira Block/The Image Bank. **72** William Hubbell. **73** Steve Dunwell/The Image Bank. **74** *top* Ken Laffal/Mark MacLaren Inc.; *bottom* New York State Office of Parks, Recreation and Historic Preservation/Olana State Historic Site. **74-75** Steve Dunwell. **77** *top* Culver Pictures; *bottom left* Jessica Anne Ehlers/Bruce Coleman Inc.; *bottom right* Paul Rocheleau. **78-79** Mike Biggs. **80** David Muench. **81** *top* Mike Biggs; *bottom* Kevin Fleming. **82** *right* Delaware Art Museum. **83** *left* Courtesy of the Historical Society of Delaware; *right* Everett C. Johnson. **84-85** C.C. Lockwood. **86** Matt Bradley. **87** *top* Doug Perrine/DRK Photo; *bottom* Matt Bradley. **88** *top* David Muench; *bottom* Bruce Hands/Comstock. **89** James Valentine. **90** *top* James Valentine; *bottom* John Netherton. **91** *left* Steven C. Kaufman; *right* Matt Bradley. **92** *center* Historical Pictures Service, Chicago; *bottom left* Photri; *bottom right* John Netherton. **94-95** James Valentine. **96-97** David Muench. **97** *top right* James Valentine; *bottom right* Pat Canova. **98** *top* Gene Ahrens/Bruce Coleman Inc.; *bottom* Jack Alterman. **99** Gene Ahrens/H. Armstrong Roberts. **101** *left* Flip Schulke/Black Star; *middle* Paul G. Beswick/Courtesy Callaway Gardens; *right* Ed Cooper. **102-103** Douglas Peebles. **104** *top* David Muench; *bottom* Robert J. Western. **105** Richard A. Cooke III. **106** *top* Douglas Peebles; *bottom* Camerique/H. Armstrong Roberts. **107** Larry Ulrich. **108** *top* Larry Ulrich; *bottom* Jeff Gnass. **108-109** Jeff Gnass. **110** *top* Lewis Trusty/Animals Animals; *bottom* David Muench. **111** Jeff Gnass. **112** *left* Historical Pictures Service, Chicago; *bottom* FPG International. **113** *bottom left* Darrell Jones/The Stock Market. **114-115** John Marshall. **116** John Marshall. **117** *top* John Marshall; *bottom* David Boehlke. **118** *left* George Wuerthner. **118-119** David R. Stoecklein. **121** *top left* Reproduced by permission of The Huntington Library, San Marino, California; *top right* Ed Cooper; *bottom* Fritz Prenzel/Animals Animals. **122-123** Gary Irving. **124-125** Gene Ahrens. **125** *top right* Terry Donnelly: TSW-Click/Chicago; *bottom right* Gary Irving. **126** *top* Hedrich Blessing; *bottom* Appel Color Photography. **127** Willard Clay. **129** *left* Historical Pictures Service, Chicago; *top* The Bettmann Archive; *right* Photograph ©1990, The Art Institute of Chicago. All Rights Reserved. **130-131** Tom Till. **132 & 133** Darryl Jones. **134** Darryl Jones. **135** *top left* Michael Medford; *top right* Darryl Jones; *bottom* Lee Casebere/Indiana Division of Nature Preserves. **137** *left* The Bettmann Archive; *middle* Photri; *right* Spring Mill State Park. **138-139** Robert Frerck/Odyssey Productions, Chicago. **140** *top left* Grant Heilman/Grant Heilman Photography, Inc.; *bottom left* David Cavagnaro. **140-141** David Cavagnaro. **142** *top* Appel Color Photography; *bottom* M. Dunlap/Living History Farms. **143** Tom Till. **145** *left* Thomas Hovland/Grant Heilman Photography, Inc.; *middle* Culver Pictures; *right* Charles Schneider/FPG International. **146-147** Daniel Dancer. **148-149** Cotton Coulson/Woodfin Camp & Associates. **149** *top right* Daniel Dancer; *bottom right* Jim Brandenburg. **150** Tom Till. **151** *top* David C. Fritts/Animals Animals; *bottom* Terry Evans. **153** *left* New York Public Library, Picture Collection; *middle* UPI/Bettmann; *right* Stephen J. Krasemann/DRK Photo. **154-155** William Strode/Woodfin Camp & Associates. **156** James Archambeault. **157** David Muench. **158** *top* Fred Kaplan/Focus On Sports Inc.; *lower left* Culver Pictures; *bottom right* Lewis Portnoy/Spectra-Action, Inc. **160-161** C.C. Lockwood. **162-163** C.C. Lockwood. **163** *right* Ronny Paille. **164** *top left* David Muench; *bottom left* D. Donne Bryant Stock Photography Agency. **164-165** David Muench. **167** *left* The Bettmann Archive; *right* Philip Gould; *bottom* D. Donne Bryant Stock Photography Agency. **168-169** Gene Ahrens. **170** Glenn Van Nimwegen. **171** *top* J.L. Stage/The Image Bank; *bottom* Carr Clifton. **172** Don Gray: f/Stop Pictures Inc.; **173** *top* John Eastcott/Yva Momatiuk/DRK Photo; *bottom* Linda Bartlett/Photo Researchers, Inc. **175** *left* National Gallery of Art, Washington, D.C.; *top right* Stan Tess/The Stock Market; *bottom right* S.D. Halperin/Earth Scenes. **176-177** Middleton Evans. **178-179** Kevin Fleming. **179** *top* David Muench; *bottom* Middleton Evans. **180** *left* Maryland Historical Society; *right* Middleton Evans; *bottom* AP/Wide World Photos. **182-183** Dan McCoy/Rainbow. **184-185** ©1991 James Trafidlo. **185** *right* George Wuerthner. **186** David Muench. **187** *top* Tom Leigh/Rainbow; *bottom* The Granger Collection, New York. **188** Paul Rocheleau. **189** *top* David Binder/Stock Boston; *bottom* Michael Melford/The Image Bank. **191** *left* Plimoth Plantation; *middle* Culver Pictures; *right* Frank Siteman/The Marilyn Gartman Agency. **192-193** Ed Cooper. **194** Ken Dequaine. **195** *top* David Muench; *bottom* Rod Planck/Photo Researchers, Inc. **196** Ken Dequaine. **197** *top* John & Ann Mahan; *bottom* Daniel J. Cox. **199** *left* Culver Pictures; *top* Traverse City Record-Eagle; *right* Veldheer Tulip Gardens, Inc. **200-201** Craig Blacklock/Blacklock Nature Photography. **202** *top left* Craig Blacklock/Blacklock Nature Photography; *bottom left* Les Blacklock/Blacklock Nature Photography. **202-203** Richard Hamilton Smith. **204** Daniel J. Cox. **205** *left* Steve Schneider; *right* Daniel J. Cox. **207** *left* The Bettmann Archive; *middle* Peabody Museum/Harvard University, Photography by Hillel Burger; *right* Mitch Kezar. **208-209** Gene Ahrens. **210** *top left* Ken Murphy; *bottom left* Connie Toops. **210-211** Balthazar Korab Ltd. **212** Mitchel L. Osborne. **213** *top* David Muench; *bottom* Cecil Rimes. **215** *left* The Bettmann Archive; *bottom right* SuperStock International. **216-217** Grant Heilman/Grant Heilman Photography, Inc. **218-219** Charles Gurche. **219** *top right* Grant Heilman/Grant Heilman Photography, Inc.; *bottom right* Charles Gurche. **220** Charles Gurche. **221** *top* Culver Pictures; *bottom* Charles Gurche. **223** *left* The Bettmann Archive; *middle* Missouri Historical Society; *right* ©Rick Warner/Journalism Services. **224-225** Alan & Sandy Carey. **226-227** George Wuerthner. **227** *top right* Larry Ulrich; *bottom right* Michael S. Sample. **228** David Muench. **229** *left* Amon Carter Museum; *right* Jeff Gnass. **230-231** Larry Ulrich. **231** *top right* Larry Burton; *bottom right* Carr Clifton. **233** *left* Photofest; *middle* The Bettmann Archive; *right* Elaine Swanson. **234-235** ©1991 R. Bruhn. **236 & 237** Glenn Van Nimwegen. **238-239** Tom Bean. **239** *top right* Terry Evans; *bottom right* David Muench. **240** *left* Culver Pictures; *right* Father Flanagan's Boys' Home. **242-243** Tom Till. **244-245** William Carr/Mountain Stock. **245** *right* David Muench. **246** Willard Clay. **247** *top* David Muench; *bottom* Santi Visalli/The Image Bank. **249** *left* Culver Pictures; *middle* Stephen Green-Armytage/The Stock Market; *right* Mark E. Gibson/The Stock Market. **250-251** Clyde H. Smith: f/Stop Pictures Inc. **252-253** Craig Blouin. **253** *top right* David Brownell; *bottom right* David Muench. **254** Craig Blouin. **255** *left* Comstock; *right* Gene Ahrens. **257** *left* Library of Congress; *middle* John M. Burnley/Bruce Coleman Inc.; *right* Fred Sieb. **258-259** Scott Barrow, Inc. **260** Scott Barrow, Inc. **261** *top* Gene Ahrens; *bottom* Len Rue Jr. **262** *top* Gene Ahrens; *bottom* M.P. Kahl/Bruce Coleman Inc. **262-263** Scott Barrow, Inc. **265** *left* The Bettmann Archive; *right* UPI/Bettmann; *bottom* Culver Pictures. **266-267** Jim Bones. **268** Willard Clay. **269** *top* Ed Cooper; *bottom* Mark E. Gibson. **270** Michael Nichols/Magnum. **271** *top* Tom Bean; *bottom* Jim Bones. **272** Jim Bones. **273** *top* Eduardo Fuss Photography; *bottom* Willard Clay. **275** *left* Malcolm Varon; *middle* Tom Bean; *right* Ray Garduño. **276-277** Carr Clifton. **278** Carr Clifton. **279** *left* Susan Desser; *right* Carr Clifton. **280** *top* Scott Barrow, Inc.; *bottom* Tom Brakefield. **281** Henryk T. Kaiser. **282** *left* Scott Barrow, Inc.; **282-283** Albert Gates. **284** *left* The Bettmann Archive; *middle* SEF/Art Resource, N.Y.; *right* Thomas Zimmerman/FPG International. **286-287** David Muench. **288** William Bake/Picturesque. **289** David Muench. **290** William Bake/Picturesque. **291** *top* Aerial Photography Services; *bottom* Jeff Lepore. **292** *both* Culver Pictures. **294-295** Grant Heilman/Grant Heilman Photography, Inc. **296** Glenn Van Nimwegan. **297** David Muench. **299** *left* Culver Pictures; *middle* Erwin and Peggy Bauer/Bruce Coleman Inc.; *right* Sheldon Green. **300-301** Ian J. Adams. **302** Jerry Sieve. **303** Ian J. Adams/Dembinsky Photo Associates. **304** Jerry Sieve. **305** *left* Richard A. Cooke III; *right* Ian J. Adams. **307** *left & top* The Bettmann Archive; *right* Roscoe Village Foundation. **308-309** David Fitzgerald. **310** *left* David Muench. **310-311** David Fitzgerald. **312** *left* The Bettmann Archive; *middle* Culver Pictures; *right* Fred W. Marvel/Oklahoma Tourism Photo. **314-315** Bob & Suzanne Clemenz. **316** Larry Ulrich. **317** Ray Atkeson/American Landscapes. **318** George Wuerthner. **319** Bureau of Land Management. **320** Larry Ulrich. **321** *top* Willard Clay; *bottom* J. Carmichael, Jr./The Image Bank. **323** *left* Hope Harris Collection/Photography by James McInnis; *top* Oregon Historical Society; *right* F. Stuart Westmoreland. **324-325** Stephen Simpson/View Finder Stock Photography. **326** Ian J. Adams. **327** Larry Lefever/Grant Heilman Photography, Inc. **328** Blair Seitz. **329** *left* Lefever/Grushow/Grant Heilman Photography, Inc.; *right* Jeff Gnass. **330** *right* Giraudon/Art Resource, N.Y. **331** *left* The Bettmann Archive; *right* Culver Pictures. **332-333** Anthony Botelho. **334** David Witbeck. **335** *top* David Witbeck; *bottom* Robert D. Hagan. **337** *left* Rhode Island Tourism Division; *top* Nicholas DeVore/Photographers Aspen; *right* Courtesy of the Rhode Island Historical Society/Photography by John Miller Documents. **338-339** George Schwartz/Ric Ergenbright Photography. **340** Tom Blagden, Jr. **341** David Muench. **343** *left* The National Portrait Gallery, Smithsonian Institution; *middle* Rick Sebak; *right* Tom Blagden, Jr. **344-345** Alex S. MacLean/Landslides. **346** Laurance B. Aiuppy/Aiuppy Photographs. **347** *top* Glenn Van Nimwegan; *bottom* John Gerlach/Dembinsky Photo Associates. **348** Laurance B. Aiuppy/Aiuppy Photographs. **349** *left* Allen Russell/ProFiles West; *right* Dick Scott/Dembinsky Photo Associates. **351** *left* The Bettmann Archive; *middle* Al Michaud/FPG International; *right* The Shrine to Music Museum, University of South Dakota at Vermillion. **352-353** Bob Schatz. **354** *top left* David Muench; *bottom left* Willard Clay. **354-355** John Netherton. **356** Adam Jones. **357** *top* Johnny Johnson/Animals Animals; *bottom* Carr Clifton. **358** Culver Pictures. **359** John Netherton. **360-361** David Muench. **362** Jeff Gnass. **363** *top* David Muench; *bottom* Wyman Meinzer. **364** *top* Walter Frerck/Odyssey Productions, Chicago; *bottom* Tom Brakefield. **365** Walter Frerck/Odyssey Productions, Chicago. **366** Laurence Parent. **367** *top* David Muench; *bottom* Archives Division, Texas State Library. **369** *left* NBC/Globe Photos; *middle* State Fair of Texas; *right* Richard & Mary Magruder/The Image Bank. **370-371** Tom Till. **372-373** Tom Till. **373** *top right* Ric Ergenbright Photography; *bottom right* Mike Andrews/Earth Scenes. **374** Larry Ulrich. **375** *top* Lee Foster/Bruce Coleman Inc.; *bottom* Jeff Gnass. **376** David Muench. **377** Larry Ulrich. **379** *left* The Granger Collection, New York; *middle* Brown Brothers; *right* George Lepp/Comstock. **380-381** Gary Irving. **382-383** Fred M. Dole: f/Stop Pictures Inc. **383** *top right* David Brownell; *bottom* Courtesy of Vermont Historical Society/Photography by Lizzari Photographic. **384** Gene Ahrens. **385** *top* Gene Ahrens; *bottom* Kindra Clineff/The Picture Cube. **387** *left* Mt. Mansfield Company, Inc.; *top* The Bettmann Archive; *right* Clemens Kalischer/Image Photos. **388-389** Steve Solum. **390** Rudi Von Briel. **391** Everett C. Johnson. **392** *top left* Ian J. Adams; *bottom left* Skyline Cavern. **392-393** Charles Gurche. **394** Art Resource, N.Y. **395** Virginia Division of Tourism. **396-397** David Muench/The Image Bank. **398** *top left* Charles Gurche; *bottom left* Thomas Kitchin/Tom Stack & Associates. **398-399** Ray Atkeson/American Landscapes. **400** David Cavagnaro/Peter Arnold, Inc. **401** Jeff Gnass. **402** Tim Thompson. **403** *top* Gene Ahrens; *bottom* Jeff Foott/Bruce Coleman Inc. **405** *top left* Roger Werth/Woodfin Camp & Associates; *bottom left* Culver Pictures; *right* Tom Algire. **406-407** Carr Clifton. **408** *top* David Muench; *bottom* Marc Rosenthal. **409** Arnout Hyde, Jr. **411** *left* UPI/Bettmann; *middle* Peggy Powell/West Virginia Division of Tourism and Parks; *right* Larry Belcher. **412-413** Richard Hamilton Smith. **414** Tom Algire/Tom Stack & Associates. **415** *both* Richard Hamilton Smith. **417** *left* UPI/Bettmann; *bottom* Wisconsin Milk Marketing Board; *right* Summerfest –"The Big Gig" Milwaukee, Wisconsin/Photography by James McInnis. **418-419** Steve Mulligan. **420** Barbara Von Hoffmann/Tom Stack & Associates. **421** *top* Bob & Clara Calhoun/Bruce Coleman Inc.; *bottom* Irwin & Peggy Bauer/Bruce Coleman Inc. **422** *left* W.H. Hodge/Peter Arnold, Inc. **422-423** Carr Clifton. **424** Jeff Gnass. **425** *top* Photoworld/FPG International; *bottom* Carr Clifton. **427** *top left* The Bettmann Archive; *bottom left* ©1991 Pollock-Krasner Foundation/ARS, N.Y.; *right* Jeff Gnass.

Every effort has been made to contact the holder of the copyright for each picture. In several cases these have been untraceable, for which we offer our apologies.

TAKE ME HOME, COUNTRY ROADS
By Bill Danoff, Taffy Nivert
& John Denver. Copyright©1971
Cherry Lane Music Publishing
Company, Inc.

Excerpt from "Prairie" in *CORNHUSKERS* by Carl Sandburg. Copyright 1918 by Holt, Rinehart and Winston, Inc., and renewed 1946 by Carl Sandburg, reprinted by permission of Harcourt Brace Jovanovich, Inc.

Reader's Digest Fund for the Blind is publisher of the Large-Type Edition of *Reader's Digest*. For subscription information about this magazine, please contact Reader's Digest Fund for the Blind, Inc., Dept 250, Pleasantville, N.Y. 10570.

Library of Congress Cataloging in Publication Data

America, land of beauty and splendor.
p. cm.
At head of title : Reader's digest.
Includes bibliographical references and index.
ISBN 0-89577-404-6
1. United States — Description and travel — 1981 – 2. United States — Description and travel — 1981 – — Views. I. Title: Reader's digest.
E169. 04.A518 1992
973 — dc20 91-27098